TOXIC VIBES ANTIDOTE
3 BOOKS IN 1

HOW TO DEAL WITH DIFFICULT PEOPLE, SET HEALTHY BOUNDARIES, AND STOP TOXIC PATTERNS

CHASE HILL

CONTENTS

TOXIC MINDS

HEALTHY BOUNDARIES

STOP BEING TOXIC

TOXIC MINDS

HOW TO DEAL WITH DIFFICULT PEOPLE, DISARM NARCISSISTS, AND HANDLE NEGATIVE PERSONALITIES

INTRODUCTION

A few years ago, I found myself in a situation that should have been simple. A friend—let's call him "Kyle"—needed a place to crash for a few days. You've heard this story before: someone's apartment plans fall through, their life gets a little chaotic, and before you know it, your couch becomes their new home.

You'd think it would be easy to tell someone like Kyle to leave, but it wasn't a hostile takeover. Kyle had mastered the art of the low-maintenance guest. He was so good at it that I started to feel guilty. He'd contribute just enough—a dish cleaned here, a grocery run there—that kicking him out felt like evicting someone for being too tidy.

But somewhere along the way, I realized my life was orbiting around his. My couch? His now. TV? Kyle's pick. Even my alone time had to be penciled in between his needs. I had slowly turned into a side character in my own apartment.

Why didn't I say anything? Because I had convinced myself that I was being a good guy. If I spoke up, it would mean confronting the fact that this friendship was less a mutual support system and more like a free Airbnb booking with no checkout date.

I told myself it was just Kyle being Kyle, but really, it was me avoiding conflict. I kept saying, "It's fine," even when it wasn't.

Now, that's the trick with toxicity, right? It doesn't always show up with flashing lights and sirens. It sometimes wears a friendly face, holds a shopping bag full of your favorite snacks, and leaves you too confused to ask, "Why is this draining me?"

But before I continue the saga of my freeloading friend, let me tell you about Jenny.

Jenny didn't notice what was happening until it was too late, and her entire life had been turned upside down. At first, her partner just seemed overly invested in her time. Sweet, right? But then, like an overnight guest who quietly extended their stay, his behavior started to escalate. Plans with friends started getting canceled not because Jenny wanted to, but because her partner "just couldn't handle it" if she left the house. And so, the gradual isolation began.

Jenny thought she was doing the right thing by reassuring him. She didn't want to rock the boat—who does? But by the time she realized how much control he'd taken, she felt completely adrift. Her world had shrunk to revolve around his moods, his needs, and his crises. She had gone from "partner" to "emotional concierge"—responsible for maintaining the fragile balance of his happiness at the expense of her own.

Sophie's story was different. Her toxic encounter wasn't in her personal life—it was at work. She was in the minority at work, so she tolerated more than she should have, fearing that if she spoke up, it might cost her job. Her toxic coworker didn't flip out on day one; it started with "harmless jokes" and slowly escalated into outright racist and sexist comments. Each time Sophie tried to stand up for herself, she was dismissed as "too sensitive." Like Jenny, Sophie found herself stuck in a toxic dynamic that made her second-guess every response.

Like me and Kyle, as well as Jenny and her partner, Sophie had to reckon with a hard truth: toxic people don't often come charging into our lives with obvious malice. They come in quietly, take root, and make us feel like *we're* the ones overreacting for wanting to regain control.

It's the knock-on effect that so many of us have to cope with. It's as if we are being walked all over, but there's nothing we can do about it. You may have noticed this yourself when you try to explain how their actions hurt you, but the conversation takes a turn, and it ends up being your fault. This leaves you feeling powerless, desperate for change that seems impossible to achieve.

It's the isolation that can hurt just as much. Being stripped of your power wrecks your self-esteem, and you naturally lose the strength to enjoy the aspects of life you once loved. As much as you want to talk to someone about the toxicity in your relationship, saying the words out loud can make you feel foolish.

The common thread here isn't that we're all victims of some grand, malicious conspiracy. It's that most of us, at one point or another, have been *too nice*, too accommodating, too willing to put our needs last in the name of avoiding conflict. Whether it's Kyle's indefinite stay on my couch, Jenny's gradual isolation by her partner, or Sophie's daily dose of workplace microaggressions, toxic situations have a way of convincing us that we're stuck.

The truth is, we're not. We've just been tricked into thinking that asking for what we need—space, respect, boundaries—is somehow selfish. But trust me, it's not selfish to want your couch back.

It seems obvious what you need to do, but it's never that simple. You often hear the question, "Why do you keep them in your life?" but you can't find an answer. Deep down, you hope they will change, but there's a constant fear that this will never happen. After so long, you've accepted that this is just how your life is—or worse, that this is what you deserve.

I never wanted to use the word "toxic" to describe some of the people in my life. It sounded too harsh, even cruel. I pushed through my teenage years into adulthood and found myself making excuses for the behavior of others: they were going through a rough time or had suffered in the past. But I believed it wasn't their fault, and I just needed to be more understanding and helpful.

Does this sound familiar? Before you know it, you have lost who you really are. You have changed in order to make the lives of others better, but in the process, you have lost a massive part of yourself. Even to the point where you look in the mirror and can't identify with the reflection.

Unfortunately, toxic people seem to pop up everywhere—at work, in the supermarket, online, and even in our families. When you hear the word "toxic," you might assume that a toxic relationship is one that is physically abusive, and this lack of understanding can lead to normalizing what is happening in your relationship and preventing the crucial change you need.

In reality, toxicity comes with its own spectrum. While physical abuse is no doubt high up on that spectrum, emotional abuse can't be ignored. This could be direct insults, silent treatment, threats, or manipulation techniques.

If you are constantly confused by a person's behavior, you don't feel comfortable around them, or you feel bad about yourself when you are around them, you are experiencing the more subtle signs of toxicity.

A toxic person is anyone whose behavior negatively impacts you or your life. They contribute to your stress levels but won't take responsibility for this, and it's highly unlikely you will get an apology from them.

A little bit of drama in your life is okay, but when these people turn everything into a song and dance, it's just draining. Even minor cases of toxicity, like not having your needs met, can spiral into long-term issues for you. Despite what you have been told, you are worthy of kind and loving relationships.

Most people see the problems in their relationships and assume it's the other person who needs to change. On the surface, they aren't wrong, but it's probable that toxic people don't see themselves as the problem and are, therefore, unlikely to make efforts to improve. This means that the change is down to you.

To do this, we have to start at the very beginning. This involves looking at ourselves and the paths we took to get to where we are today. **We all have toxic traits that we can bring to a relationship**, just like we all have a past that can hinder the way we view things. Even passivity—letting things slide—can be toxic.

It's this self-reflection and self-discovery that lay the foundation for your strength and confidence. With these two qualities, we can dive into the understanding of manipulation, emotional abuse, narcissism, and sociopathy.

Each step of the way, we will cover in-depth techniques to overcome the toxic behaviors you are experiencing so that you can heal and lead a full life where you are in control.

I had to learn the hard way that I had too many toxic people in my life. Growing up, toxic relationships were the norm, so it made sense that most of mine were, too. I became a pushover at work, saying yes to everyone, hoping for an easier time—but it only made things worse.

My breaking point came when I stopped taking care of myself: drinking too much, not exercising, and gaining weight. I hit rock bottom. The only way out was to change. I educated myself, spent a decade studying human psychology, and put strategies into practice. I am a firm believer that knowledge is power, and I created this book with the hope that sharing what I have learned will empower you.

Before we begin this journey, there's one thing you should bear in mind. Everyone has their own story to tell, and because of this, nobody, regardless of their personal or professional experience, has the right to tell you what to do.

Whether you choose to remain in a relationship, romantic or not, is a decision only you can make, and it's one you have control over. The guidance you are about to embark on can help you make that decision.

While change is never easy, it's far more achievable when you know you have someone in your corner supporting you all the way, someone who has been through that transformation and discovered what meaningful relationships really feel like.

With just one step at a time, you can do the same. You can break free from toxic behaviors and connect with people on a deeper level. You can experience the joy of trust, balance, honest communication, and knowing exactly where you stand in a relationship. Ready to take the first step?

CHAPTER 1: DIFFICULTY: THE ONLY CONSISTENCY

> *The only thing more exhausting than being with a toxic person is pretending they're not toxic.*
>
> — *GERMANY KENT*

Toxic people are everywhere, like Wi-Fi signals—constantly present, often invisible, and occasionally disrupting your entire day. We've all come across the emotional saboteurs, the ones who remind you they "just want what's best for you" while setting your self-esteem on fire with the gentlest of matches. Being around these people isn't just bad for your health; it's like binge-eating an entire pizza—terrible for your long-term emotional digestion, but it's hard to resist in the moment.

At the other extreme are toxic individuals who can be abusive or manipulative in more harmful ways. For example, think of a controlling partner or a bully at work—people who use fear or intimidation to get what they want. These individuals create an environment of fear and anxiety. And let's not forget the toxic people shaping the broader world. From corrupt politicians to criminal masterminds, they remind us that toxicity isn't confined to our personal lives. It's everywhere—on the news, in the office, even in the grocery store line, making it difficult to avoid its influence.

So, what causes people to be toxic? Some believe it's in their nature, while others point to neurological and behavioral complexities, along with the influence of the environment. Before we fall into the trap of labeling people as good or evil, it's important to understand more about human psychology. This isn't to excuse their behavior, but understanding what makes them tick might just help you figure out why *you keep* getting stuck listening to their life story for the 437th time.

The Tangled Web of Human Psychology

We know that the brain is an impressive organ. We often only refer to it when talking about our intelligence, yet we know it's responsible for controlling every organ and system in our bodies. The human brain has approximately 100 billion neurons and around 0.15 quadrillion connections between them (Choi, 2016). These connections are vital for the exchange of chemicals. These chemicals are known as neurotransmitters, and 100 different ones have been identified. To put it into perspective, it's like imagining the world's busiest traffic and multiplying it by a billion!

Some neurotransmitters are more well-known, like serotonin and oxytocin, often called the "happy chemicals" or "happy hormones." Dopamine, another important chemical, affects our sleep, mood, and impulses and serves as our "reward" system. Gamma-aminobutyric acid (GABA) helps improve mood and reduce anxiety.

When these chemicals are out of balance, they can lead to unhealthy emotions or mental disorders. For example, studies have shown that serotonin deficiencies can lead to increased violent or impulsive behaviors (Society for Neuroscience, 2007). Chemical imbalances can be influenced by what we consume—not just drugs or alcohol, but also the food we eat. For instance, cocaine causes a buildup of dopamine, and junk food can have a similar, though milder, effect. The pleasure we get from a favorite slice of pizza activates the brain's reward system, producing more dopamine.

Despite their nicknames, no single chemical is responsible for feelings like love, hate, or anger. Many chemicals work together, adjusting our mood depending on the situation. When you face danger, for example, your brain produces chemicals that give you adrenaline to help you react quickly. While we can't directly control these processes, medications like antidepressants can help manage mood by altering brain chemistry.

Neurochemicals are just one factor in human behavior. Individual personalities also play a big role. A study from the University of Carlos III de Madrid examined 541 volunteers in social dilemmas and found that 90% fit into one of four personality types: optimistic, pessimistic, trusting, and envious. Interestingly, envy was the most common type, and this "green-eyed monster" can lead people to act in ways that range from difficult to toxic.

Behavior is another factor in human psychology and the way we interact with others. Our behavior is made up of three components: our actions, cognition, and emotions. For example, the weekend is here and you remember that you have to do the shopping (cognition), so you write the list and do the shopping (action), and finally, you feel somewhat stressed and exhausted (the emotions). This is obviously a very simplified example.

All of us are born with neurochemicals and a personality type, but the behavior is learned. We are products of our environment. We learn a lot of our behavior from our parents, which affects how we act in different situations and treat others. Furthermore, our actual physical environment can influence our behavior and motivations. Noisy environments can cause stress, dark rooms bring about a heavy or depressing feeling. Human interaction is improved in environments that feel safe and secure.

So, really, there are a plethora of reasons why people in your life can be difficult. It could just be that they are simply nasty and enjoy seeing you suffer, or there might be underlying conditions behind their behavior.

The Puzzle of Human Emotions

How is it possible that two people can be watching the same movie, yet one finds it hilarious while the other is mildly amused?

Emergency responders face danger every day, while others are too scared to drive a car or fly in a plane. When you look at neurochemicals, personality, behavior, and environments, you start to see how people interpret situations and other people's emotions in different ways. Let's take a deeper look at some examples.

One of the best examples on a global scale is how people reacted to COVID-19. This threat to our health caused a wide range of emotions and actions. Some people went into panic mode, stocking up on toilet paper and disinfectants. Others thought it was all just a conspiracy theory, while many fell somewhere in between.

How people handle stress varies. Some people thrive on it, leaving things to the last minute to feel that rush of achievement. Others find that if they have an overwhelming amount to do, they become even more stressed at the idea of what they have to do before they even start. Then there are those who give up right away, knowing they will never get it all done.

How we view the task ahead dictates how we handle the stress. And it's not only about the things we have to do. We can react differently to financial stress, the stress of arguments in a relationship, or the stress from work.

It's great to see people who take major life changes in their stride. Moving to a new house should be exciting since you are starting a new chapter in your life. Some people make it look so easy, with everything packed and labeled like a military operation. Others are emotionally drained, feeling sad about leaving their home behind.

We can see the same when people have babies and become new parents. Some moms seem to take it all in their stride like it's second nature. On the other hand, due to the chemical and hormonal changes, other women suffer from postpartum depression. Parenting, in general, can be a highly emotional experience, and each person finds their own way to face the challenges. Many parents seek help and advice from others, while others prefer to handle their problems and emotions internally.

It's interesting to see how different people deal with anger directed at them. Do you respond with anger, or are you the type of person who can stay calm? Some people simply laugh, while others become emotional and cry.

When someone we love passes away, we can work through our stages of grief, but it's also common for people to get stuck in a particular stage, unable to overcome the fury or depression. You may have experienced a loss so great that you turned to addiction of some kind, whether drinking, eating, or exercising—anything to fill the void left by the loss.

The experiences we go through as a child, teenagers, and young adults will also affect our emotions and how we interpret things. In fact, the brain isn't fully developed until the age of 25 (Sapolsky, 2018). Think back to everything that has happened in your life before reaching this age, or if you haven't turned 25 yet, at least up until now. Growing up with parents who are unkind and unloving shows their children what to expect from future relationships. Teenagers who witness their parents' divorce often feel that marriage is unpredictable and unstable (Risch, Jodl, Eccles, 2004).

Narcissistic personality disorder also develops before the brain has fully matured. While its cause could be genetic and/or neurobiological, the environment can play a role.

Parenting styles impact children's experiences. Excessive admiration can lead to an inflated ego and a sense of self-importance. On the contrary, children who have been overly criticized may feel like they fall short of perfection. The narcissist might appear to be full of confidence with a superior attitude, but it is often just a cover for extremely low self-esteem.

What Does All This Mean?

It means we can't be too quick to judge people or label them evil or toxic. Personality types and personality disorders all have root causes. We don't just wake up one day and become a people pleaser, self-absorbed, or sociopathic. It's important to decide if the difficult people in your life are making an effort to improve, just like you are now. They might have accepted the fact that they have a problem, sought professional help, and openly communicated with you to overcome their issues. These individuals can still be difficult and hurt you, but they are trying.

Then there are the people in your life who haven't yet recognized their problem. It's going to be harder with them, but not impossible. When you are well on your way to a better life, you will have the tools and knowledge to show them how their life can improve. You will also have a small handful of people who actually enjoy being the way they are. They will never change because they don't believe it's in their best interest. These individuals will be the most challenging people to deal with, but that's not to say that you have to tolerate their behavior. Instead, navigate life around them despite their presence in your life.

One of our first tasks is to start seeing people for who they really are rather than who we want them to be. We tend to create a set of expectations and beliefs about the people in our lives and this often leads us to know only half of who they really are. This is made worse by our previous experiences.

For example, if you were cheated on in the past, it's tough not to start each new relationship with the assumption that this person may do the same. We must set aside our biases and look at each person for who they really are, without ignoring or excusing them for their words and actions. Making changes in our own lives is what will lead to the best outcomes, not wasting effort trying to change those who don't want to.

Next, imagine life without difficulties. It sounds strange, but it would be a little boring. We need challenges and setbacks in our lives because it's these experiences that allow us to learn and grow. I'm not suggesting we should actively go out of our way to find trouble, but going through tough times can teach us valuable lessons. The person who has lost their job and struggled financially can now appreciate the value of money. The person who has loved and experienced heartbreak now knows more about themselves, their boundaries, and what they don't want in a relationship. Anyone who has had to live with an abusive parent or partner has become stronger as a result.

The Roots of Toxicity: Where It All Begins

Knowing that people aren't born with toxic traits leads to the question, "Where does it come from?" Much like human psychology, it's complex. Not even professionals agree on the answer, and there are no conclusive studies that identify a single source of toxicity. One of the major debates is whether toxic traits come from nature or nurture.

Beginning with nurture, some experts believe it's the environment that contributes to toxic behaviors. Toxic people, especially narcissists, will come across as extremely confident, but this is often a mask for very low self-esteem. They may have suffered from past trauma or grown up in families that exhibit toxic behaviors. Children learn so much from their parents or caregivers, so if they see a particular behavior as normal, they are likely to adopt the same behavior.

Stressful households can also create an environment for toxicity. Imagine a parent who is under severe financial stress, and this converts to anger taken out on the children. They are then full of regret and apologies, only to fly off the handle at their next stressor. This lack of consistency in expressing emotions can lead children to do the same. Similarly, if children grow up without their needs being met, physical or emotional, it could cause problems with understanding needs in adulthood, not being able to recognize or meet their own or others.

At the other end of the scale, there are overprotective and overvaluing parents. These parents may coddle their children, making them feel more special than others. Of course, parents want their children to feel important, but studies have shown taking this to the extreme can lead to adults with grandiose narcissistic traits (van Schie et al., 2020).

Pampering and allowing children to believe they are entitled has its consequences, even if it's unintentional.

While it's possible to learn toxic behaviors from parents, it's also possible to inherit them, which is the natural side of the debate.

Some of the most negative qualities in toxic people are known as The Dark Triad. These traits include:

1.Narcissism: Egoism, grandiosity, and lack of empathy.

2.Machiavellianism: Exploitation and manipulation, disregard of morality, toxic self-interest, and deception.

3.Psychopathy: Lack of remorse, callousness, lack of impulse control, and antisocial behavior (disregarding social norms).(Cikanavicius, 2018)

Research conducted on twins and families revealed that these three traits are partially genetic (Schermer and Jones, 2020). To add to this dilemma, there is the risk of parents passing on these traits through genes and nurture and poor examples of their own behavior.

This doesn't take into consideration mental health conditions, which can also be both genetic or environmental. Personality disorders, especially the Cluster B types, are closely associated with toxic behaviors (Casabiana, 2021). These personality disorders are characterized by dramatics, emotional issues, and erratic behaviors. Examples include narcissistic personality disorder, antisocial personality disorder, borderline personality disorder, and histrionic personality disorder (the need to be the center of attention all the time).

Other mental health conditions such as bipolar disorder, post-traumatic stress disorder (PTSD), anxiety disorders, and depression can all explain a person's toxic traits. Nevertheless, while it can explain a person's traits, it doesn't excuse or justify them, and it's not your responsibility to try and "fix" them. They need to make the decision to seek help before anything else.

Mental health conditions aren't behind all toxic behaviors. Some people may have a lack of emotional intelligence, the ability to recognize and manage their own emotions, as well as recognize the emotions of others.

Their words and actions can cause you a lot of pain, but they don't have the necessary skills to see this.

Other people may be overly negative without having any real reason, which can drain you of your energy and can even affect your outlook on life, putting a damper on things that would otherwise be enjoyable. And, of course, there are some people who are just plain mean because it makes them feel good in the moment. Regardless of their motives, intentions, or lack thereof, you still need to put a stop to it.

The Benefits of Overcoming Toxicity

It can be hard to imagine the positive side of your toxic relationships, but there is a lot to learn. Your gut instincts have been telling you something is wrong for a while now and with good reason. The lesson here is to trust your instincts, and this is helped by being aware of the red flags in a relationship. After the chapters on narcissism, sociopath, and emotional abuse, you will know exactly what you are dealing with early on in new relationships, and you can put a stop to such behaviors sooner. Even if you choose to stay in your current relationship, you still may meet new people who are capable of bringing new waves of toxicity into your life.

For your well-being and the health of your relationships, overcoming toxicity enables you to take care of your needs and stand up for yourself with boundaries. The lessons you learn teach you not to settle because you deserve more.

In the long run, your healing allows for personal growth. Imagine how the toxic people in your life are holding you back right now. It could be the coworker who takes all the credit and advances ahead of you or the partner stopping you from reaching your goals. Each step you take adds to the snowball effect of increased strength and confidence. This doesn't mean complete independence and doing everything alone unless that's what you want. Healthy relationships allow for individual growth at the same time as growing together.

Finally, without change from you, toxic behaviors won't disappear but could get worse. Most relationships start with emotional and physical intimacy, as this is how a toxic person gains power. From there, the emotional abuse starts, with small moments of manipulation that can be twisted into signs of love until the psychological effects become so powerful that a person feels worthless. Once the emotional abuse becomes normalized, the risk of physical abuse can increase. There is nothing beneficial about being at the hands of an abuser. Positivity lies in freeing yourself from it.

To put a positive perspective on toxic people: Everyone we meet has a purpose or a lesson to teach us. Instead of disregarding these experiences, we should embrace them. Learning how to deal with them and not letting their actions affect you as painfully as they have in the past will help you create healthy boundaries, which is the key to happiness.

Putting Chapter 1 into Practice

Take some time to assess the toxic people in your life. How well do you know them, and what are their past experiences? Is there any specific reason or event that could have caused their behavior? Instead of focusing on how they negatively influence your actions, see what positive lessons you can take from these difficult relationships.

CHAPTER 2: SOMETIMES, WE'RE THE PROBLEM

> *Knowing your own darkness is the best method for dealing with the darknesses of other people.*
>
> — *CARL JUNG*

In the last chapter, we explored why others can be difficult. But let's be honest—assuming that everything is always someone else's fault is a bit naive.

Managing difficult people in your life will be tough if you can't take a step back and acknowledge that you might also play a role. This isn't necessarily good or bad—it just is, and no one is perfect. We all have little quirks, habits, and (yes) toxic tendencies that sometimes add fuel to the fire.

Let's face it—if you think you're immune to being a little toxic, that's probably your first red flag. We've all been guilty of it. Maybe you interrupted someone mid-sentence because your story was *obviously* more interesting. Or maybe you "forgot" to return a phone call to a friend in crisis because you were... watching a three-hour Netflix special on the making of potato chips. We've all been there. Welcome to the toxic club, where nobody really wants to be, but hey, at least the membership is universal.

Now, let's talk about how we see the world—because perception plays a big role in how we interact with others.

How Perception Impacts Our Relationships and Interactions

Imagine a spicy chicken curry with three different people about to eat it. It's the same curry—the same smell, color, texture, and taste—but each person has a unique experience. One person may find it too spicy, another thinks the chicken is dry, and the third thinks the color is off-putting. The same thing can be said about our perception of reality. Fifty people can attend the same party, but everyone will have a different experience of the same reality.

How we view each experience depends on our expectations, our past experiences, and even the mood we are in at the time. Studies support this differing view of reality. When two football teams played a game, the fans were asked to write down all the fouls committed. It was the supporters of the winning team who thought there were twice as many fouls as what their team had actually committed (Hastorf & Cantril, 1954). Since this study, others have gone on to show the same results: that people aren't objective and can see things in vastly different ways.

The best example of this today can often be seen in the home regarding equality. At some point, most of us have argued about the housework and who is doing their fair share. Despite all the facts, the couple doesn't seem to agree on the fair share.

Good People, Toxic Traits

If you recall our definition of toxicity, it's any type of behavior that causes harm to others. Bearing this in mind, it's practically impossible to go through life without committing a single toxic act. As a teen, you might recall when you were filled with rage and told your parents that you hated them. Even if you didn't feel this way, those words were still hurtful to them. Perhaps you said something to a partner or argued with a neighbor that you now regret. None of these would make you a toxic person.

Let's take a look at a couple of specific examples. David is a perfectionist, and he never saw this as a bad thing. In fact, at work, his team consistently achieved some of the best results and highest productivity. He attributed this to his high expectations for both himself and his team. It wasn't until his partner pointed out that his standards were too high that he felt the need for self-reflection. Only then did David realize that, while his team produced excellent results, they were also highly stressed and often felt like they were walking on eggshells around him.

Emma has three children, an array of pets, and a full-time job. There was always something to do, and to her, the concept of self-care felt toxic. She mistakenly believed it was synonymous with selfishness. On the contrary, Emma's lack of self-care led to toxic behaviors like snapping at her family when she couldn't handle the stress.

David expected too much, but he also celebrated his team's victories. Emma struggled to manage her stress, but at the end of the day, she always made time for stories and bedtime cuddles. Their behaviors were incidents, not the norm, and that's the difference between good yet imperfect people and toxic people. By actively working on their personal development, they can improve their behavior.

Nevertheless, these moments of toxicity can fuel an already toxic relationship. David could encounter a lazy, uncommitted person in the workplace. Without knowing how to effectively motivate them, conflict is soon to arise. Emma's partner might lack empathy, and without the ability to understand Emma's point of view, he may even resort to gaslighting, leaving Emma feeling like she's the problem.

Accountability is crucial. Self-awareness is fundamental. Just as you may not recognize the extent of toxic behaviors in a relationship, you may not be aware of the impact of some of your behaviors. As you work through this chapter, don't feel guilty because a lack of awareness isn't the same as burying your head in the sand and blaming others. However, to be in a better position to survive the toxic people in your life, you need to make sure you are working on your own flaws too—and we all have them!

Toxic, or Just Having a Bad Day? A Self-Assessment

We must examine ourselves and decide which behaviors and habits we can improve. You can look at Chapter 1 and see if anything rings a bell. Everything that applies to the toxic people in your life can also be applied to you. Below is a self-assessment questionnaire that will help you gain insight into potential negative traits of your personality.

1. Do you prefer speaking to listening?

2. Do you enjoy drama in your life?

3. Do you struggle to see other people's points of view?

4. Do you find it easy to tell lies?

5. Do you enjoy gossip?

6. Do you spend a lot of time thinking about the past?

7. When problems arise, do you blame yourself or others?

8. Is it easy for you to apologize when you are wrong?

9. Do you hold grudges, or can you let things go?

10. Is it okay to make fun of others to get a laugh from the crowd?

11. Do you make things personal, especially in arguments?

12. Do you downplay other peoples' achievements?

13. Do you take more than you give?

14. Can you be too critical of others?

15. Have you noticed that people tend to avoid you or disappear from your life without a particular reason?

16. Are you passive-aggressive, or do you use emotional manipulation like the silent treatment?

People generally aren't toxic or nontoxic. There are varying degrees depending on the situation. You aren't looking for a yes or no answer to whether you are toxic. It might be that you enjoy drama and gossip, but you are also capable of apologizing and forgiving others and moving on from the past. This points to a person who can have toxic moments but is generally kind and liked. The problem is that the tendency to gossip can seriously impact the happiness of others, and they might perceive you as toxic because of this behavior.

The Power of Acceptance

Acceptance can be an incredibly powerful tool for both past and present scenarios. Your past has shaped the person you are today. Maybe it was a rough childhood, you dropped out of college, or you started a business that didn't take off.

All of these actions have been significant in your life, but many of us still hold tight to these moments. But how is this helping you right now? Is it healthy for you to keep replaying the negative moments in your life?

For years, I held on to the relationship my parents had. I looked at my own relationship and compared the issues, made excuses, and blamed my past for the problems I was having. What I should have done was simply accept that it was what it was. Of course, it isn't as easy as it sounds, but it's your choice to accept what has happened to you so far and move on from it.

In the present, the constant trickle of changes and unpredictable events can leave our minds in the midst of a storm, debating the right decisions to make, why these things always happen to you, and how you will survive. Or you can decide to accept the challenges that get thrown at you. Learning to accept is like an incredible thunderstorm. Before the storm, the air is thick and heavy. The moment of acceptance is like the rain, washing away all the negativity. Eventually, you are left with a clear sky, making it easier to see the right path forward.

Be careful not to fall to the other extreme. As Dylan Woon explains in his "Power of Acceptance" TED Talk, acceptance isn't about a state of doing nothing. If someone steals your car, you don't accept it and start the search for a new one. You do, however, report it to the police and accept that this is the situation you are in at the moment.

You also need to take everything from an accepted situation and learn from it. Back to the car example: you have reported it, which is all you can do in this situation, and you have learned the valuable lesson of choosing your parking area better, perhaps even paying for secure parking rather than leaving it in the street. Reliving the situation and playing the what-if game will only mentally drain you, as you don't have the power to change it.

Once you are able to do this with other areas of your past, you will soon see your perspective change, and future events that would otherwise have thrown you back into a storm can now be handled with a positive outlook.

As I said, this isn't easy. Over time, we have subconsciously trained our brains to maintain a firm grip on negative experiences rather than accepting them. It's become a habit, and we know how tough it is to break a habit. After a certain amount of repeated behavior, actions move from the decision part of our brain (the prefrontal cortex) to the habit area of our brain (the basal ganglia).

For example, when we are learning to drive, our prefrontal cortex is highly active, but after some time, the actions become second nature. Driving is no longer a learning experience that requires decision-making but instead a habit.

For the most part, this makes life effortless as we don't need to concentrate on some of our daily tasks. But it doesn't help us with our bad habits, such as being unable to accept what has happened. We have to learn how to break this habit loop.

To break habits, we must recognize what we want to do differently. In this case, we have to admit when we are too attached to an event. If you have regrets from your past—let's say you didn't make a career change when you had the opportunity and now you hate your job—you have to spot the stress and negativity you feel when you start thinking about what you should have done. Immediately start thinking about what you have learned from it. You are now aware that when opportunities arise, you should carefully weigh the pros and cons before making a final decision.

What Can You Do About Your Toxic Behavior?

By this point, you have taken a closer look at yourself and can now see what parts of your personality or behavior are either toxic or perhaps fueling the behavior of the toxic people in your life. While you shouldn't blame others for what has happened in your life, you also shouldn't beat yourself up for it either—this goes back to acceptance. What has happened has happened, and now it's time to move forward.

Below are some steps to help you turn any negative aspects into positivity and kindness:

- **Take** what you've learned about yourself **and see** if others can add to your new understanding. It's not always easy to spot our own faults, so constructive feedback from people you love and trust can give you a more complete picture.

- **Don't get defensive when receiving feedback**. Avoid blaming others or making excuses, as that's not the point of the exercise. Instead, take note of what they're telling you so you can work on incorporating those changes.

- **Broaden your relationships.** This may sound unusual, but consider whether your friends share similar age, race, religion, or background. While there's nothing wrong with that, expanding your circle to include people from different backgrounds can teach you more about handling unfamiliar topics. You might meet people with first-hand experience dealing with issues like narcissism or building trust.

- **Make necessary apologies.** If your introspection and feedback reveal actions that deserve an apology, now is the time. It doesn't need to be over-the-top, but your apology should be sincere. Think of it as a fresh start.

Begin to address your negative behaviors one by one. When making changes, it is always best to make small changes that will last rather than too many in one go that won't last. For example, if you used to downplay your partner's achievements, you could surprise them with a celebratory dinner. Or if you have a habit of speaking too much or interrupting, you could use a timer, retraining your brain to become a better communicator.

Shedding the Victim Complex

Before we begin, I want to clarify something important. The word "victim" can evoke strong thoughts and emotions in today's society. By definition, a victim is someone who has been hurt, killed, or has suffered because of someone's actions or beliefs (Collins, n.d.). However, many people who have experienced physical or emotional abuse don't like being labeled as victims, which is completely understandable. This section is definitely not about minimizing what has happened to you, and no form of abuse is ever your fault.

The victim complex or victim mentality is when a person thinks they are constantly the victim of other people's actions and that nothing is their fault, despite evidence to the contrary. What's more, they may even have the attitude that the world is just against them and take everything that happens personally.

Like toxic traits, moments of self-pity are normal, but when feelings of hopelessness and pessimism become perpetual, they can impact all areas of life. Unfortunately, those who have suffered from past trauma are more susceptible to the victim complex because of their negative outlook on life. Regardless of past experiences, it's hard to see past the negativity, and this can lead to the unintentional need to seek validation from others. Consider if any of the following sounds familiar.

- You blame others for what has happened in your life.
- The glass tends to be half empty.
- When someone tries to offer you advice, you discount it.

- When someone tries to offer you advice, you feel attacked.
- It's hard to make changes in your life.
- You feel powerless against the problems in your life.
- You hold grudges and find it hard to forgive.
- You see the world as unfair.
- You keep scores in relationships.

Another thing that has to be clarified is the genuine victim complex because of past experiences and those who use the victim mentality as a form of manipulation. Toxic people can cleverly use this mentality of "Poor me" to gain sympathy and attention while avoiding all accountability.

To overcome the victim complex, taking responsibility for your own life is necessary. It requires processing your past experiences, and even getting professional help. This will help you put the past behind you and recognize that the circumstances you have had to deal with so far don't determine where you are going. One great way to start taking control of your own life is to start saying no to the things you don't want to do or don't agree with. This is the first step to being accountable for your actions and not blaming others.

The victim complex may stem from unhealthy coping mechanisms. To help get past this, now is the time to start practicing self-care and prioritizing your physical and mental well-being for healthier coping techniques. Doing so gives you the opportunity to take control of your life and reduce those feelings of helplessness. Self-love can help you see you are worthy of more and have the power to make this happen.

For many, this will seem like an odd chapter for a book aimed at helping you deal with others who are toxic. It's more likely that you aren't toxic and that there are just a few things that you can tweak to make your interactions more fruitful and less confrontational. The key takeaway from this chapter is that nobody is perfect and perspective can help you not just now but also in future relationships. You can only hold yourself accountable for your own behavior—the actions of others are their own responsibility.

Putting Chapter 2 into Practice

Spend some time thinking about potential toxic behavior you may have shown in the last few weeks. Try to put yourself in other people's shoes, even those who have toxic traits. Notice if any particular triggers cause your behavior.

Commit to a week of self-reflection, especially when it comes to conflicts. Consider using a journal to further gain perspective and the role you may play in them. Decide on healthy coping strategies to prevent the behaviors you don't like. After a week, reflect again on the positive changes you have made and continue working on them.

CHAPTER 3: CHANGE STARTS WITH YOU

> *If you accept the expectations of others, especially the negative ones, then you never will change the outcome.*
>
> — *MICHAEL JORDAN*

There's nothing more empowering than realizing you have the ability to turn a bad situation around. At the same time, the cliché says to "take a long, hard look in the mirror," which can feel almost impossible when toxic people have drained your self-esteem. Instead of feeling empowered, you might only focus on your flaws and feel even worse about yourself.

The point is that if you can get past the words and actions of others, you will be able to look in the mirror and see your true worth. At first glance, you might notice a few extra wrinkles or a stray gray hair, but if you go beyond that and take a moment to really look at your reflection, you'll start to see kind eyes that hold wisdom and kindness to offer—in the right way and to the right people.

Let's go back to those wrinkles we see in the mirror, and if there aren't wrinkles, there could be bags, blemishes, or other signs of a life filled with struggles. The first time I tried this, I made every excuse possible. The bags under my eyes were due to the stress my relationships were causing me. My bad skin was because of exhaustion, which was also due to the stress caused by my relationships. And you can guess why a double chin had appeared! Well, I didn't have the energy to exercise because of the same issues.

What is actually worse than blaming others for your problems is that you are handing over immense amounts of power. If a person has so much control over your life and can cause such negative effects, then they have too much power. It all starts with finding your own power—not a false power, not one driven by your ego or the need to control, but true power.

What Is True Power and Where Does It Come From?

True power is a cocktail of ingredients, including love, the ability to know who you truly are, and the acceptance that we have spoken about before. It's about building your own life in a way that doesn't force things on others, but at the same time, it doesn't mean allowing people to walk all over you. By setting the right boundaries that don't harm you or others, you get to experience an amazing power from within.

For some, it takes a near-death experience to appreciate the power they have, while others start to find it while on a spiritual or religious path. For the rest of us, it starts by learning who we really are. We have already begun this step by looking at our potential flaws and negative behaviors, but there is more to it than that. If you have been surrounded by toxic people for too long, you may have lost touch with yourself.

Take a moment to think about your positive qualities: your big heart and the love you have to give. What things do you like doing? Do you have any hobbies, or have they been forgotten? The same can be said about your goals. What motivates you, and what do you want to achieve in the next week, month, six months, or year? Once you have answered those questions, you can follow some simple steps to finding your true power.

Enjoy the silence. Have you ever noticed that there is constantly some form of noise or distraction in our lives? Your mobile phone is tempting you, the TV is blaring, or someone is always talking to you. It can be draining. Learn to step away from these distractions and appreciate the calming effect of silence.

Start small—turn your phone on Do Not Disturb for an hour, let your email notifications pile up, and accept the discomfort. It's not the end of the world if you don't respond to a meme in the group chat within 30 seconds.

One trick I've found useful is turning ordinary, mindless tasks into intentional, quiet moments. Whether it's brewing your morning coffee or taking a stroll around the block, put your phone away and just let your mind wander. You won't believe how much quieter everything becomes when you stop multitasking.

Follow a routine. A routine is an excellent way to establish control over your life. It also allows you to structure your day to be efficient and save time. While every routine should allow for some flexibility, organizing your daily tasks into a routine allows you to focus on the more challenging aspects of each day.

Spend more time with those who make you feel positive. We will discuss this further later, but first, you need to create more free time by saying no to those who create negativity. Surrounding yourself with positive energy gives you strength.

Take care of your body. You don't have to go on a super strict diet or head to the gym every day. Regular exercise, such as walking, swimming, or even activities like yoga, is perfect for the body and the mind. Getting more exercise will help you sleep better, and when you combine this with a balanced diet, your energy will increase.

Create a happy home. Again, in terms of your relationships, we will look at this more later on, but there are other ways to make a happy home. It always helps if your home is tidy and, of course, comfortable. When you get home at the end of the day, you need a safe haven where you can relax.

Meditate. Meditation is an extremely valuable tool to connect with your inner power. Not everybody finds it easy to meditate, at least not in the beginning. It helps you focus, calm the mind, and reduce stress and anxiety. You will find that this **guided meditation** video for inner strength and power will help.

Scan the QR code above to open the meditation.

All of these steps will guide you toward discovering yourself and your true power. Only once you appreciate the power within you can you effectively apply the rest of the advice in this book. So, how do we go from finding our power to experiencing freedom?

Turning Your Power into Freedom

While not blaming society, I've come to realize that in our society, it's not easy to express our true feelings. People ask how we are, and we respond with "fine," "good," and "okay," even though we aren't. If we discuss our problems, we're considered a negative bore, and if we talk about our successes, we are simply showing off.

Even when we find our power, there's still a weight burdening us. We have to realize that the only way to get rid of this weight and allow the power to work its magic is by speaking our truth.

There's no need for you to continue suffering in silence. The traumas we experience are too much to struggle with alone. By sharing these experiences, you help yourself and others. Imagine living with an abusive partner. You meet up with a friend who has recently lost their job and their home, and you tell them everything is fine.

Alternatively, imagine if you told your story and opened up about the pain you have experienced. The chances are that other people will also feel more confident about telling their stories and releasing their own burdens. We have seen this on a global scale with movements such as Black Lives Matter or Me Too.

By speaking the truth about our situations, we understand that we aren't alone and that there is a strong community of people who are going through similar experiences. This is empowering for all involved.

Confiding in just one person will enable you to create a much deeper relationship with that person — a genuine friendship built on honesty instead of what we think we should say. What's more, speaking the truth opens the door to new perspectives you hadn't thought of. Your friend might have words of wisdom regarding your abusive relationship, and they will also be able to highlight your positive qualities and, most importantly, remind you of your self-worth.

It's not always easy to open up and share your feelings, especially when you fear being laughed at, told to get over it, or having your experiences belittled. Not everyone has someone in their life to whom they feel comfortable talking. In this case, therapy can be a great solution. Even then, I know that the idea of speaking to a complete stranger can be more terrifying than talking to a friend.

If you're not quite ready to share your truths with the world, at least try keeping a journal. This will be an effective way to start opening up and lessening your burden while you continue to find your inner strength.

Remember that there is a difference between sharing our difficulties and traumas and just complaining all the time. Whether it's your journal or your friend, speaking the truth is about freeing yourself from what prevents you from becoming stronger.

Complaining about the weather, the traffic, and your partner at every opportunity isn't productive. If you start venting, your friend might join in, and then both of you will end up feeling drained. To ensure that both of you walk away feeling lighter, relieved, and more connected, it's better to focus on the more significant, deeper troubles you are going through or have gone through.

Recognizing How Your Choices and Beliefs Limit Who You Are

The choices we made in the past have led us to where we are today, and that's fine because we've accepted it. However, the choices you make from now on will impact every aspect of your life. Each choice we make comes from our thoughts. As we've seen, our views on reality will impact our decisions, but we can't forget about the thoughts and beliefs we create about ourselves. Let's look at two examples:

1. Life is hard. You are stressed, tired, and generally not enjoying yourself. There's a lot of bickering and arguing within your relationships, and you know that a vacation is going to break the cycle and give you a chance to press reset. After a week of rest, you notice that life is definitely better, but it only takes a week, maybe two, for things to start slipping back to how they were.

2. You separated from your partner a while ago and have just started socializing again. At a party, ten people compliment you, but one person makes a comment that offends you. Rather than let your confidence shine for once, you obsess about the one negative comment.

Both of these scenarios go back to the same issue: your thoughts. Although you are making an effort to change your situation, you are caught up in changing your environment or circumstances rather than getting to the bottom of the issue, which is your thoughts about life. You can change your environment by taking a vacation, but it only temporarily changes your thoughts. You have done well by leaving a toxic partner, but until you see yourself in a new light, your mind will still be trapped in that relationship.

Your thoughts are at the root of everything. When you think badly about yourself, your self-esteem decreases. You speak quietly and look down at the ground. You don't have the confidence to make the right decisions, so your choices may not always be right.

On the other hand, when you are able to think about yourself in a good way, your body language reflects this. It becomes easier to see past the gray, which means that alternative paths light up. These alternatives enable you to see problems from different angles and make better choices.

The trick is to take our focus away from what we perceive as the problem and recognize that the real issue is our perception of the problem. You may feel ugly, but the problem isn't that you are ugly—the problem is that you think you are ugly.

When we can change our thoughts on a situation, the solution becomes easier. The solution, in this case, isn't that you need to lose weight, change your hairstyle, and buy new clothes. The solution is to change the way you think about yourself.

Self-Limiting Beliefs Tear You Down

A self-limiting belief is any thought we hold onto about ourselves or the world around us that holds us back from achieving all we want to. It's every time you tell yourself that you can't do something or that you don't deserve something. Perhaps it's those times when you convince yourself you're too old, too tired, or not smart enough. Instead of deciding you need to make changes to achieve your goals, you avoid the potential source of pain as a way of protecting yourself from it.

These types of thought patterns often stem from childhood and get reinforced as the years pass. They can be incredibly debilitating because, at the same time as preventing your growth, they are assumptions you have made rather than facts. For example, you may feel powerless in your current situation, but the truth is, you just don't have the right skills yet, which you have the power to change.

Self-limiting beliefs can lead to a self-fulling prophecy. If you tell yourself enough times that you are powerless, you stop standing up for yourself. If you believe your thoughts and opinions aren't worthy of being heard, you stop expressing yourself.

The longer you spend not standing up for yourself or not speaking up, the more you reinforce the self-limiting belief. If you are wondering just how powerful these thoughts can be, anywhere from 85 to 95 percent of what we do on a daily basis is based on our subconscious (Barberio, n.d.).

Sadly, holding onto these self-limiting thoughts is quite toxic. They can intensify the idea that you don't have a right to your dreams and goals, professional or personal. It's even likely that you won't begin the healing process because you feel you aren't worthy of a happy life full of positive relationships.

Everyone deserves the right to be able to heal and move on. Without falling back into the victim complex, our pasts can be filled with emotional pain, whether that's from the loss of a loved one, ended relationships, job loss, illness, or abuse.

Healing is the process of working through these experiences, unraveling the emotions attached to them, and accepting them. It stops these experiences from intensifying and having even more of an impact on your relationships.

As harsh as it might sound, choosing not to heal is choosing the victim mentality. Though it might be painful, what's on the other side is illuminating, refreshing, positive, and empowering, and no limiting belief should get in the way of this.

And for the toxic people in your life? Yes, they also deserve the opportunity to heal. They have suffered their turbulent pasts and hold on to this, perhaps more than we know. They might not be ready to heal; they may even be in complete denial about their need to heal, but they still deserve to lead a happy and fulfilling life.

Remember that their past doesn't condone their behavior, and it's not up to you to heal them. You can lead a horse to water, but you can't make it drink. Instead, focus on setting the right example and work on your own self-limiting beliefs and healing.

How to Crush Limiting Beliefs and Take the Wheel

We need to take all of our limiting beliefs and first appreciate that the only thing they are doing is holding us back. They are not a method of self-protection. I often hear things like, "Yes, but if I don't start a new relationship, then I won't get hurt again." It sounds like you are trying to protect yourself, but in reality, you are limiting your chances of finding a loving partner.

Your homework for Chapter 3 is to take some time to understand why you tolerate certain behaviors, how to stop putting up with them, and finally, how to overcome your limiting beliefs. We'll achieve this through the following steps:

1.Determine why you tolerate certain behaviors

Why do we often let others take advantage of us without speaking up? Or if your family insists you do things you don't want to, why is it easier to get angry and walk away rather than establish a firm boundary?

We often tolerate these types of actions because we may have been subjected to control, criticism, excessive praise, neglect, or a combination throughout our childhood.

As children, we developed coping methods for these treatments, such as withdrawing, becoming passive and subdued, or becoming angry. We carry these coping methods with us into adulthood.

If you lived with a parent who insisted you did everything their way, you may have tried to fight it as a child and realized your efforts were fruitless. When you find yourself in a controlling adult relationship, you continue with the same behavior you learned as a child. So ask yourself, what behaviors do you tolerate, and where does this come from?

2. Determine the source of your limiting beliefs

Just like you tolerate behavior you don't like, your limiting beliefs also have their origins. Perhaps you were told by a teacher that you would "never get anywhere in life with that attitude," or even something seemingly innocent like, "You need to find yourself a husband/wife."

These kinds of comments can make us believe we can only reach our full potential when we are married.

3. Reset your beliefs

Whatever you were told in the past does not reflect your life today. Remember that when you listen to what toxic people tell you, you are handing over your power. Your attitude can be the key to what will drive you forward. You don't need to get married to be complete. It's the complete opposite; you need to be complete before starting any new relationship.

4. Find role models who align with your positive beliefs

To reinforce your new belief, find people who can back up your new thoughts. For example, if you believe that getting married is not necessary for feeling complete, seek out people who live their lives how they want to while still maintaining healthy relationships. Similarly, if you think you're ugly, spend time with those who compliment you and accept their kind words.

5. Imagine the worst-case scenario

Imagining the worst-case scenario isn't the same as living it. Just because you have pictured it doesn't make it destiny. What it does is prepare you for every possibility.

If you're debating a career change, the worst that could happen is that you absolutely hate it. If that's the case, you need to be prepared to search for another job.

On the other hand, to avoid focusing too much on the negative could also involve meeting new people, networking, learning, or advancing up the career ladder. When you consider the worst-case scenario, you'll see that at the end of the day, you'll survive it!

6. Test your new beliefs

Go out with friends and see how many people actually call you ugly. Instead of constantly feeling like you're missing out on something, be confident in being single. Pursue that new job! Did the worst-case scenario happen? In the unlikely event that it did, you're still standing. If the outcome is positive, it's a validation of your new belief. Proving our old beliefs wrong enables us to break free from our outdated perspectives and leads to growth.

7. Go back to the behaviors you tolerate and make small changes.

Now that you have reset your beliefs about yourself, you'll have a new sense of confidence. You'll start to feel like you're worthy of respect and appreciation.

If you go out of your way to cook a nice dinner to make your partner feel loved and special but don't get a kiss or even a thank you, either tell them that their actions have hurt you or stop making the dinners! If you become angry, learn how to calm down. If you prefer to stay silent instead of causing conflict, learn how to communicate effectively. We'll cover this in more detail later on.

I felt completely weighed down by my parents' toxic behavior. Nothing I could do would ever make them happy or proud or elicit any type of reaction. I spent years trying everything to get them to notice me. I told myself over and over again that I was the problem and that I couldn't do anything right for them.

When I finally understood that the problem wasn't me, but that I was trying to change myself to make them happy, I realized I needed to change myself to make myself happy. That was when I broke free from not just one toxic relationship but, soon after, all the negative relationships I found myself in.

It can be challenging to look at yourself in such an honest way and prioritize your beliefs and thoughts ahead of those around you. It's even more difficult to have faith in them. But you can do it. Before moving on, enjoy this time of self-discovery because, ultimately, it's all about you!

Putting Chapter 3 into Practice

Take a piece of paper and draw a circle in the middle. Inside the circle, write down all the things specific to your life and within your control. Outside the circle, write down all the things that are out of your control. Keep this piece of paper in a visible place as a constant reminder of where you should focus your efforts.

CHAPTER 4: SOCIOPATHY 101: UNDERSTANDING SOCIOPATHS

> *A sociopath will do anything to win. Anything.*
>
> — *DENZEL WASHINGTON*

Before we take a closer look at sociopathic causes and behaviors, I want to clear up the common misconception between a sociopath and a psychopath. TV and movies throw the terms around quite interchangeably, and clinically, they are somewhat similar.

Sociopaths and psychopaths both have antisocial personality disorder (ASPD). We also hear these words to describe extreme behaviors such as serial killings and mass murder.

While this is possible, many of them are just as likely to be a wolf in sheep's clothing, appearing like any other human being.

Sociopath vs. Psychopath: Spot the Difference

A sociopath is someone who clearly shows that they don't care about the feelings of others. It is extremely difficult for them to form emotional attachments, meaning that work and life at home can be difficult to maintain. Sociopaths are impulsive in their negative behavior, especially when it comes to their temper. That being said, they can recognize their bad behavior but will always have some justification for it.

Psychopaths, on the other hand, are capable of pretending to show that they care—the keyword is pretending. Psychopaths can't form real emotional attachments, so their relationships won't be meaningful or genuine. It's possible for psychopaths to love, but it will be on their own terms. Being in a relationship with a psychopath can be particularly hard because they are cold-hearted and won't recognize the struggles and pain of others. It's common for psychopaths to use a "normal" life to cover up illicit activities.

It's also worth mentioning that both sociopathic and psychopathic behaviors have a spectrum. It's possible for psychopaths to feel emotional pain and want to be loved, but it's their own behavior that makes this difficult (Martens, 2020). Violence is also possible for both, but it's just as likely that they are violent toward themselves as to others.

We include an understanding of both because if you notice either of the tendencies, understanding the differences will enable you to choose the best ways to deal with these toxic people. Always bear in mind that many people have not been diagnosed, so they are unaware of their own disorder.

What Lies Behind a Sociopath

The diagnosis is crucial here. We can't go around saying that everyone who has angry outbursts is a sociopath. Narcissism is a personality disorder that takes selfishness and self-obsession to an extreme, but that doesn't mean they are a sociopath. While you may have suspicions about a sociopathic personality, only professionals can correctly diagnose it.

One dictionary definition of a sociopath is someone "who is completely unable or unwilling to behave in a way that is acceptable to society" (Cambridge Dictionary, 2021). This is rather general, as what is acceptable to society changes rapidly. More specifically, sociopaths lack empathy and will not consider the rights or feelings of others.

Manipulation is their go-to technique, but what can hurt the most is that they will show no guilt for the pain they cause. If you smack your head on a barrier, there will be no empathy, so they won't be able to recognize the pain you feel. If a sociopath pushes your head into a barrier, they won't feel guilty about it.

Now, if you look at all of your relationships, it may seem that many people in your life are now sociopaths. I call this "Doctor Google Syndrome." We get the feeling that we know the diagnosis because of one or two symptoms. When we research this, every internet symptom suddenly relates to our situation.

Keep in mind that we are all capable of detaching ourselves from painful situations, which can lead us to appear sociopathic. When going through a divorce, you can either be left devastated or choose to dust yourself off and continue with life. Hearing about a school shooting will leave most feeling awful for the families involved. However, someone who is anti-guns might make a comment about irresponsible gun laws, which can come across as insensitive and unempathetic. Ultimately, these reactions stem from our personal perspectives and beliefs about the world.

If you notice some of these typical characteristics and behaviors in your relationships, it's best to take the safest and most effective actions so that you can start living your life freely.

Here are some of the red flags that could point to a sociopath in your life (WebMD, 2020):

- A complete lack of empathy
- Impulsive behavior
- Using threats or aggressive behavior to control people
- Using charm or intelligence to manipulate people
- Telling lies for personal gain

- Not learning from their past mistakes
- Struggling to form meaningful relationships
- Violence, stealing, and other crimes
- A lack of responsibility when it comes to their job or responsibilities
- Turning to drugs or alcohol

You also need to remember that sociopaths are exceptionally good at masking their disorder in the real world. A colleague who manipulates others can seem like they are highly career-driven. Those with a demanding job can use this as an excuse for their lack of meaningful relationships. Sociopaths either don't care about the damage their actions cause, or they are unable to recognize it.

For this reason, sociopathy is often undiagnosed and left untreated.

How Does Someone Become a Sociopath?

The classic debate between all psychologists is "nature versus nurture." When we look at the nature of sociopaths, we refer to the genetic and biological factors. Nurture, however, is the environmental influence that leads to certain disorders, both psychological and behavioral.

The nurture debate dates back to 1690 when philosopher and physician John Locke believed that almost all human behavioral traits develop from environmental influences. He coined the term "tabula rasa" or "blank slate" in human developmental psychology. This theory is based on the idea that all babies are born with a blank slate and no built-in mental content.

In the early 20th century, John B. Watson took theories from Freud and developed the origins of behavioral psychology. He went on to be known as the father of purist behaviorism. Watson believed that psychologists should focus on behavior that is observed rather than that of the inner mind.

Watson's most famous quote highlights his idea that cultural influence dominated any heredity contribution:

"Give me a dozen healthy infants, well-formed, and my own specified world to bring them up in, and I'll guarantee to take anyone at random and train him to become any type of specialist I might select—doctor, lawyer, artist, merchant-chief, and yes, even beggar-man and thief, regardless of his talents, penchants, tendencies, abilities, vocations, and race of his ancestors" (Watson, 1930).

Another of the most consequential psychologists of the 20th century agreed with Watson. In a television interview, B.F. Skinner stated, "Give me a child and I can shape him into anything" (Skinner, 1972).

The significance of these works is that all favor nurture over nature. This implies that sociopathy, as with other antisocial personality disorders, is a result of how children are brought up. Maltreatment and abuse are clear examples.

Children who suffer from abusive parents are more inclined to grow up to become aggressive, unempathetic, or struggle to form meaningful relationships.

When looking at nurture, we can also include trauma as a cause of sociopathy. Due to antisocial personality disorders going undiagnosed, studies are difficult. This is why most research has been carried out on those who have committed crimes or violence. After extensive brain mapping, scientists have been able to show a link between trauma to the brain and criminal activity. This is known as acquired sociopathy.

The first case was that of Charles Whitman, a former marine sniper who killed 16 people in one day in 1966. His autopsy revealed a brain tumor. Without being biased, some would argue that Whitman's history as a marine sniper could have been a psychosocial stressor and the cause of his violence rather than the brain tumor.

The first published study came from the University of Glasgow. The report included 239 eligible killers and found that 21.34% of them had had or were suspected of having a head injury (Alley, 2013).

One infamous serial killer in Dr. Clare Allely's report was Fred West, who, along with his wife, killed at least 12 people. West was involved in a motorbike accident at the age of 17, which left him unconscious for two days.

Two years later, he was pushed down the stairs by a woman he was trying to abuse, causing a further head injury.

This is certainly not to say that every person who displays sociopathic tendencies is going to go on to be a serial killer! But this is another factor of nurture, whether from childhood abuse or physical trauma, which can lead to sociopathic behaviors in adult life.

Naturally, there are always two sides to every argument. Some believe that nature is a cause of antisocial personality disorders.

Due to the structure of the brain, some people are simply born this way. When using EEGs and MRIs, scientists are able to see the role of the enzyme MAOA, which regulates the emotions in the amygdala and hippocampus. It causes low levels of impulse control in people with antisocial personality disorders (Journal of Forensic Research, 2014).

Aside from an imbalance in chemicals such as dopamine and serotonin, sociopaths may have an abnormal superior temporal gyrus—the scientific term for the area of the brain responsible for the perception of emotions, comprehension of language, and social cognition. So, those in favor of the nature debate will say that a sociopath has structural damage to the brain that has been present since birth.

Interestingly, while many use the terms sociopath and psychopath interchangeably, experts today now believe that the difference between the two is in how they start getting the symptoms. Both are antisocial personalities, but it is now believed that the behavior of a sociopath is created (nurture) and a psychopath is born with their behaviors (nature).

None of this is supposed to scare you. We have looked at the causes of sociopathic behavior in an attempt to better understand the toxic people in our lives, much like we did in the first chapter. Learning the root causes of people's behavior enables us to see things from their point of view. However, as I have also said and must reiterate, understanding is not the same as excusing or tolerating.

How to Spot a Sociopath Before They Run the Show

After reading the previous section, you might feel that the toxic people in your life are not sociopaths or psychopaths because they aren't running around committing crimes and plotting mass murders. These are extreme examples, and as mentioned, those with antisocial personality disorders (ASPD) are excellent at hiding the behaviors that they don't want you to see.

Because of this ability to mask behaviors, it's more likely you know someone with ASPD. The prevalence of psychopathy varies from study to study. In general, 1% of the population has psychopathic traits, so you only need to know 100 people!

According to the *Diagnostic and Statistical Manual of Mental Disorders*, 2013, the prevalence of sociopathy is 4% of the population, or one in 26 people you know would show sociopathic traits.

As we have already mentioned the red flags to help you spot a sociopath, we will now look at specific examples of how people with ASPD may do things.

1. Turn up the charm

There are people in the world who are naturally charming, and it's normal for us to be drawn to these personalities. But their charm is consistent, no matter who their audience is. People with ASPD are able to adapt their charm, so if they're interacting with an introvert, they may dial back their charm, while they might increase their charm when talking to an extrovert.

2. Change your opinion of others

If you meet a new person and at first you like them but then notice characteristics that go against who you are, it's your choice not to like them. If you like someone, but then someone with ASPD starts to gossip or fill your head with poisonous ideas about the other person to make you change your mind, you are witnessing the initial signs of ASPD.

3. Be disloyal

Just as quickly as they convince you not to like someone, they could be this other person's best friend the next day. The lack of empathy and connections with others makes it very easy for them to switch sides in an argument, especially for their own gain.

4. Play the guilt game

Both sociopaths and psychopaths are able to make you feel as if you are to blame for everything. You might try to have a calm conversation about a concern, and all of a sudden, you are the dramatic one; they can't do anything right, and you are constantly complaining. Regardless of how you handle a situation, they will make you feel as if they are the victim. They will also use this as an excuse for not getting along with others because the other person is at fault.

5. Act as though they are above the rules

Despite being highly intelligent and understanding of rules from a game to social interactions, these rules won't apply to them. They have a genuine belief that the same rules you live by don't apply to them. This is certainly the case when it comes to financial gain.

6. Be your most trusted confidant

To manipulate your emotions so they can get what they want, they first have to get you to open up to them. Once they have gained your trust and you start sharing your feelings, they will then have ammunition to use against you. Remember that ASPD is largely about not showing interest in other people's emotions, so question why this person is so keen to help you.

7. Weave a confusing web of lies

People with ASPD will change their stories depending on their audience and their goals. Eventually, so many story changes turn into a complex web of lies that not even they can keep up with. If you spot a lie and present this to them, they will turn the tables. You might feel that you are the paranoid one, and they will have the skills to cause you to doubt yourself.

8. Have a hot and cold personality

On the one hand, they will be very good at controlling their personality. On the other hand, the lack of impulse control and angry outbursts can lead people with ASPD to appear rather Jekyll and Hyde-like.

9. Show no remorse

We all make mistakes at some point, some of which are larger than others. Most people can work through what they have done, appreciate that they are at fault, and feel remorseful. The next natural step is to apologize. ASPD causes them to have no sense of their wrongdoing, or they just don't care. As a result, they won't feel remorseful.

10. Sweep you off your feet

Those first few dates are crucial for laying the foundations of a potential relationship. Some signs are a little too good to be true. The charm is obviously going to attract you to a person, but then watch out for inappropriate attention, such as intense eye contact, showering you with gifts, and any form of physical or verbal attention that you are not comfortable with. You are three times more likely to meet a man with ASPD (National Library of Medicine, 2013), but that is not to say that women aren't just as capable of making you feel like you are instant soulmates.

Sociopaths in Real-Life Scenarios

Christine was excited about the possibility of working for an advertising agency, but the company owner refused to negotiate on the salary. A few months later, the company reached out to Christine again to see if she was still interested. She met with the company owner, who told her he was angry about the negotiations but agreed. At the time, Christine hadn't seen this anger as a red flag.

It was the lies that opened Christine's eyes. Her boss had asked her to lie to clients about her qualifications and the size of their company. The final straw came when the owner of the company had an aggressive outburst toward a highly qualified staff member and then proceeded to fire her for no legal reason. Christine's boss was cold, harsh, deceitful, and impulsive (Day, 2020).

Tom was Charlotte's second husband, but it wasn't until a few years had passed that she became worried about some of his traits. It started with completely reckless spending habits. Then the lies came, and disturbingly, he seemed to find pleasure in other people's suffering.

After some years of unemployment, Tom got a new job that required him to spend a lot of time away, which served as a cover for his cheating. Upon getting caught, Tom asks for forgiveness and even sheds a tear. Naturally, things didn't change, and one day, the other woman phoned Charlotte, revealing that Tom had told her that he was divorced and accused Charlotte of cheating. In response, Charlotte changed the locks, infuriating Tom, and filed for divorce, but he still owes her $12,000 and shows no remorse (Lovefraud Reader, 2023).

Patric knew she was different as early as kindergarten when she noticed she didn't have the same emotions as other children. There was no compassion when a classmate fell and hurt themself or guilt when she lied. As she got older, she turned to crime to fill the sense of nothingness she felt. She described it as claustrophobic, and the more she tried to ignore what was happening, the worse it got. Patric gained a better understanding of sociopathy, but that wasn't enough to find romantic feelings for her husband or an overwhelming love for her children when they were born (Main, 2024).

Every person's story is unique and valid. And you don't need to have experienced financial hardship or have a mother incapable of showing you any emotions to put a stop to sociopathic behavior.

Putting Chapter 4 into Practice

Use the following checklist to identify and track the sociopathic behaviors of others.

- They know right from wrong but don't care

- They are enchanting just to get close to you, but then things change
- They are dishonest and deceitful
- The worst of them comes out when they don't feel they have control over you
- Easily angered
- Will do whatever it takes for personal gain
- Lack of guilt, remorse, and empathy
- Irresponsible or impulsive behavior
- Disregarding social norms and breaking the law

CHAPTER 5: FIGHTING THE SOCIOPATH

> *Letting go doesn't mean that you don't care about someone anymore. It's just realizing that the only person you really have control over is yourself.*
>
> — *DEBORAH REBER*

You can't just switch off your emotions. Your history may not have been all bad, and those fond memories still pull on the heartstrings. What's more, there is a tricky thing called the sunk-cost fallacy, where people stay in unhealthy relationships because of the time and effort they have invested in the relationship. Regardless of your thoughts on the future of your relationship, now has to be the time to protect yourself, which is well within your control.

Self-Protection and Dealing with a Sociopath

First and foremost, if you have a sociopath or psychopath in your life who has a tendency to become violent or you fear for your safety in any way, please get help! Don't tell yourself it's a one-off or they didn't mean it. I know how incredibly hard it is to call the authorities on someone you love but consider looking at it from a different point of view. What if you don't report them, and they take their anger out on someone else?

You are going to feel responsible. What if this isn't the first time, and the next time, they end up putting you in the hospital or worse?If you don't feel comfortable contacting the police, reach out to a friend or relative who can help you.

You should also have a plan in place for when a person does turn violent. A good plan is to have a bag prepared with your essential documents, an extra phone, and a copy of your car key. You can also set up a separate bank account—even if it only has a couple of hundred dollars in it, you know you have enough to leave immediately if needed.

If you don't know anyone to stay with, there is no shame in contacting a shelter for victims of abuse. Your plan will have to be more structured and detailed if children are involved. Whenever possible, leave when the other person is not at home!

Of course, not every situation is going to lead to violence. Here's how to handle a sociopath (and protect yourself in the process):

1. Don't try to fix them

A sociopath may not even be aware of their own behavior and are rarely willing to get the required help. Unfortunately, only qualified psychotherapists can provide specific treatment, so you can't fix them. Trying may only make the situation worse.

2. Avoid disclosing personal information

Because of their need to manipulate, it's always best not to share too much with a sociopath. For example, you shouldn't discuss your salary with an ASPD partner because they can try to use this against you when it comes to paying for things. You should also avoid talking about your other relationships and the details of your work.

3. Trust your instincts

It's perfectly normal to question your instincts if you've had your confidence knocked. Try not to focus on the past and listen to what your gut is telling you now. More often than not, we can sense a lie or manipulation. Have faith in this and try to take a step back instead of reacting and getting wrapped up in their reality.

Never take their words as truth if you feel otherwise; instead, question everything.

4. Set your boundaries and say no

Your boundaries are crucial for your safety and mental and physical well-being. Your boundaries express what you are comfortable with and what you aren't.

For example, you might be happy moving in with someone but don't want to combine your finances. Even when someone insists, you have to remain firm on your no.

This will help to protect you from manipulation.

5. Find the give and take

While there will be some rigid boundaries that are not to be crossed, there are other situations where you might be able to find a solution that doesn't cross your boundary but also stops the sociopath from becoming angry or violent. As with the example before, you might agree on a joint account but still keep your separate accounts.

6. Walk away when necessary

In some cases, it takes all our effort not to get upset or angry. As you are only responsible for your own words and actions, sometimes the best thing you can do is put some space between you and the other person. People with ASPD want to see a reaction, so they keep pushing. Walk away, take some time to process how you are feeling, calm down, and when you are ready, you can go back to the situation.

7. Spend time on other relationships

Make the most of the positive relationships in your life. These could be friends, family, work colleagues, or even someone you just say hi to at the supermarket. You will be able to find strength in your other relationships that will help you when dealing with sociopaths.

8. It's what they do, not what they say

Think about Randall Terry's quote, "Fool me once, shame on you. Fool me twice, shame on me." We have all heard the words, "I will change/I have changed/I'm a different person now." This might be true, but words are easy to say, especially for a sociopath. You will only know if they mean it when you start to see a change in their actions.

9. Talk to a professional

Just because you don't have ASPD, it doesn't mean you aren't under immense pressure. Some people are more comfortable talking to a stranger than to a friend, and a professional counselor will be able to help you understand what you are experiencing and offer guidance.

10. Know when it is best to end the relationship

Ending a relationship or cutting ties with a family member is never going to be easy. It's a personal decision that only you can make. You shouldn't feel guilty about this decision, and you have to be careful not to let them use their manipulative techniques to get you to stay. It's best to cut off all communication with a sociopath when you end a relationship. This means blocking calls and messages and deleting social media profiles. Cutting all contact reduces the chance of them being able to change your mind.

Getting Ahead of Sociopathic Manipulation

Once you start implementing the above points, you'll be able to create some emotional distance between yourself and the relationship. With this space, you can disarm their manipulative behaviors with some relatively simple strategies. Detaching yourself from conversations is also helpful. Avoid allowing yourself to be the subject of the conversation and only say what is absolutely necessary. Stop yourself from using any fluff or filler words like "Um" and "Well," as this could signal to the sociopath in your conversation that you are nervous. Small talk is great for conversation topics because it protects you from deep and meaningful conversations that can then be used against you.

If conversations do get personal, keep your answers short and simple. The other person is expecting you to show your vulnerability, so when this doesn't happen, they can be thrown off their guard. As a sociopath's emotions are limited, it can be hard for them to talk about how they feel, so simple questions to keep in your arsenal are "How are you feeling?" and "How do you feel about...?"

Once you gain a little confidence while communicating with a sociopath, you might be tempted to fight fire with fire. Instead of just allowing them to criticize you, you point out their flaws. I would be very cautious about this for two reasons. Firstly, you would be sinking down to their level, and you are better than that. Secondly, it's more likely that this person just doesn't care about what you think. You may even irritate or anger them. It's best to preserve this energy and use it for techniques that have a greater impact.

Removing a Sociopath from Your Life

You have done well to decide to break away from the sociopathic person in your life, and you have taken that all-important first step. As with any "breakup," it's hard to remain strong and not start thinking about what you might be missing, whether the person has changed, or if you just made a huge mistake.

Your instincts have told you this was the right choice, and we know that sociopaths seldom change. It's far more effective to focus on a brighter future than dwell on a dark past.

Here are some tips and tricks to help you move past this type of toxic relationship:

• Do not contact them! We can't stress this enough. We may be tempted to send a reminder about the AC filters or a happy birthday message. Doing so gives power to the other person; they will see a small crack and work their way back in.

• Don't search for them online, drive past their home, or ask mutual friends about them. Most of the time, we just want to know they are doing okay because that's the nice thing to do. Nevertheless, you are only torturing yourself. You might start to reminisce about the good times and forget or minimize the main reason you left in the first place.

• Lean on friends during tough times. Nobody likes being reminded of the horrible times in a relationship, but if you are finding it particularly hard to stay strong, use your friends to help you through these moments. A good friend won't tell you what you already know, but they'll remind you of why you ended the relationship in the first place.

• Know your triggers. A trigger is anything that can lead you into the same patterns or behaviors as before. Personally, my triggers are birthdays, holidays, and anniversaries. Knowing that these are grim times, I can prepare myself in advance so that I'm better able to resist slipping back.

• Take extra care of yourself. Self-care and patience are two essential factors for recovering your power. Acknowledging that recovery takes time will prevent you from being hard on yourself when things don't bounce back to normal as fast as you had hoped. During this time, you can exercise, focus on your diet, explore new hobbies, make new friends, and relax.

Managing the Emotional Pain of Ending Your Relationship

In some cases, recovering from the emotional pain caused by a sociopath requires self-care, self-compassion, and finding your inner strength to move forward. That doesn't mean to say it's a walk in the park. As you read through the chapters, you will embark on ways to help the gradual process of healing from emotional pain. Here, we will focus specifically on what happens when you struggle to break the bond you have with a sociopath because, as mentioned at the beginning of the chapter, you can't just switch your feelings off.

A trauma bond is a bond that stops people from leaving an abusive relationship, and a lot of this is because of intermittent reinforcement or the cycle of trauma bonding. Stages include:

1. Love bombing

2. Gaining trust

3. Criticism

4. Manipulation

5. Resignation

6. Distress

7. Repetition (Psychology Today, n.d.)

This isn't a weakness on your behalf. It's human nature to form bonds, and it's not something you can or should stop doing. You bonded with the wrong person because you felt genuine love for them. This means you can't blame yourself for the bond you created. Not only is your brain programmed to be loyal to your abuser, but the cycle of trauma reinforces this bond. Unfortunately, you might be stuck in the cycle of trauma bonds from past relationships, and unless you break it, you may find yourself in similar situations in the future.

An effective way to stop blaming yourself is with the defense mechanism called reality training (Darcy, 2023). Write a list of everything this person did. While a journal can be used to process emotions, this list should remain factual and avoid any form of justification for the actions mentioned. Next, take your list and imagine yourself from the perspective of another person, someone who is kind and empathetic, perhaps even the future version of yourself who has successfully broken free from this cycle. This person wouldn't dream of blaming you when reading the list.

Though one part of your healing should be strictly for facts, your emotions can't be ignored. Abuse from a sociopath can cause dumbing of emotions or emotional dysregulation, the rollercoaster of intense emotions. Take several pauses in your day to consider how you are really feeling. Don't allow yourself to say that you are okay when you know you aren't. Also, don't allow yourself to feel guilty for emotions like joy and anticipation. Take this reflection to the next level. If you are sad, ask yourself what the source of this sadness is. If you are frustrated, question the source of this frustration. It's going to hurt, but it's the antiseptic for a wound—it's necessary for healing!

Imagine this moment is your tabula rasa—your blank slate. The hardest part is over, and with the strategies in this chapter, you'll be well on your way to self-empowerment. You'll grow in both strength and confidence and most importantly, you'll be aware of sociopaths and avoid making the same mistakes again. This is refreshing in itself!

There is one area of sociopathy that I have not discussed, and that is narcissistic behavior. This is intentional, as I wanted to focus more on narcissistic behavior in the next chapter.

Putting Chapter 5 into Practice

Picture your life a year from now. How would you love to imagine it, with or without the sociopath in your life? Perhaps you have decided to end the relationship, and you can visualize yourself well on the road to recovery. Or maybe you have broken the cycle of trauma bonding, and you are in a healthier relationship. Visualize this future in detail and often!

Exercise: The "Will This Matter?" Test

Think of the latest drama with the sociopath. Now, ask yourself: Will this matter in a year? If the answer's "no," let it go. Repeat as needed.

CHAPTER 6: NARCISSISM 101: UNDERSTANDING NARCISSISTS

> *A narcissist will always have an excuse for their behavior, and it's never their fault.*
>
> — *MELANIE TONIA EVANS*

One of the biggest traits of a sociopath is narcissism. It can also be one of the most shocking and painful things that we have to deal with when it comes to toxic people. With antisocial personality disorders, the emotional path is very much up and down.

But here's where it gets tricky: not all narcissists are sociopaths, and vice versa. Although narcissism can be part of a personality disorder, it's not sufficient to make a diagnosis. So, while sociopaths may have some narcissistic traits, not all narcissists are antisocial.

Now, living with a narcissist? That's like trying to win a game you didn't know you were playing—only you're constantly reminded that you'll never be as good as them (or as interesting, or as deserving of that last slice of pizza). Sure, we all have days when our self-esteem needs a little pep talk, but living with someone whose sole purpose seems to be undermining your existence? That's a whole new level of psychological whiplash.

The best solution is to recognize the characteristics of a narcissist and steer clear of them before any type of meaningful relationship is formed.

But if you're already entangled with one, there's hope. You just have to figure out how to handle situations *before* they devolve into the emotional equivalent of a reality TV meltdown.

What Is a Narcissist?

Talking to a friend recently, I noticed that the word "narcissist" is often greatly misunderstood. He was sharing about the pain of his breakup and the distance from his children that he was now facing. His ex had called him a narcissist. I was taken aback because all I could see was a broken man trying to do what was best for his children and even his ex, who is the complete opposite of a narcissist.

This led me to a thought-provoking *Los Angeles Times* article from 2011. Today, we completely overuse and misuse the term narcissist. It's like the go-to insult people use, perhaps because it makes them feel more powerful.

Throughout the 90s, we started to see more emphasis on making yourself happy, putting yourself first, and following your goals. And this truly is a good thing. But the downside is that anyone showing more ambition than the social norm or those with self-esteem were then labeled narcissistic.

While it might be a healthy reminder to keep things in perspective and not to trample over others to achieve our goals, in my friend's case, calling someone a narcissist was a hurtful thing to say. Throwing a word around without understanding its true meaning creates a much deeper problem, and now the word "narcissist" has lost its impact.

To put it another way. Think about your definition of the word "classic." We think of classic groups like the Beatles, Queen, and Abba. Classics are defined by the lengthy period of time that they remain of excellent quality. As soon as the word became slang for "awesome" or "cool," it took away some of the true meaning of classic. The same thing has happened with the word "narcissist."

The origin of the word "narcissism" comes from Greek mythology—Narcissus fell in love with his own reflection in a pool of water. It means chasing the satisfaction of your egoistic admiration (Wikipedia). Today's definition hasn't changed, but it has been expanded on. Narcissistic personality disorder (NPD) is a condition where one sees themselves as having more importance than others—they expect special treatment and for others to see them as better. There is also a lack of empathy, a longing for perfection, and a desire for the best of everything. It may seem that a narcissist has all the confidence in the world, but this is often just a front.

With frail self-esteem, any type of criticism will add to the difficulties you have when dealing with them. Despite appearances, narcissists feel incredibly upset when they don't receive the attention that they feel they deserve. Because of the lack of empathy, they are unable to see how certain things affect you and so can't fathom why they aren't getting their attention. What's more, if they see others receiving praise or attention, they can become envious, leading to anger and even depression.

Although you might not see this side of them, narcissists can feel a lot of insecurity and shame. This, toppled with anger issues, impatience, and frustration, is going to make relationships at home and work problematic.

Like sociopaths, narcissists can't see that they are in the wrong. This makes treatment very difficult as they won't actively seek help—they are above this! Narcissistic personality disorder requires treatment from a psychotherapist.

What Causes Narcissistic Personality Disorder?

The exact cause of NPD, like many personality disorders, still doesn't have a definite cause, and again, can go back to the nature vs. nurture debate. That being said, it is more likely to be a combination of the two factors.

If we look at nature first, studies have suggested that genetics plays a role in NPD. Heritability is a metric used to measure the likelihood of genetic influence on a person rather than environmental influences. There is a moderate to high chance of NPD being heritable ("A Twin Study of Personality Disorders," 2000).

When it comes to the structure of the brain, a smaller hippocampus and amygdala have been linked to antisocial behavior seen in narcissists. This is because of the malfunctions in the way people interpret the information received from their senses. Unlike what we have seen before, NPD hasn't been linked to brain trauma. Instead, the trauma is more likely to be a result of childhood environmental trauma.

Parenting styles are often attributed to NPD, and this isn't limited to parents but to all primary caregivers. NPD can be caused by either extreme parenting style.

A parent can completely withdraw attention, causing emotional detachment. Overindulging or being too permissive or even too strict may also impact the behavior of children in their adult years. Other environmental contributions could be abuse (verbal, physical, and/or sexual) and unrealistic expectations.

More recently, cultural influences have also been shown to add to the likelihood or severity of narcissism. NPD is more prevalent in modern societies compared with those that are more traditional ("Modernity and Narcissistic Personality Disorders," 2014).

Be careful of trying to diagnose people who are under 18 years old with NPD. This is because it is extremely complicated to diagnose a personality disorder when a personality is still developing. Those with teenagers may nod their heads while reading some of the symptoms and start to look toward themselves for blame.

Many teenagers will go through phases that can include narcissistic traits, but this is only a part of their development. If you are concerned about your child, you can still seek professional advice.

Are There Different Types of Narcissism?

Narcissism has its own spectrum, meaning there can be different types and degrees. Bear in mind that there is no official number of types. Some are popular among professionals, and others have been researched. For an overview of narcissistic behavior, we will look into the most common types of narcissists.

1. A healthy narcissist

Everyone has a little bit of narcissism in them. It's good to celebrate our wins and to feel proud of the things we do well. It's also healthy to recognize that you deserve respect and happiness. For an official NPD diagnosis, people need to show a minimum of 55% of the most common traits.

2. The overt narcissist

Many would call this the classic narcissist, the person who is self-obsessed, lacks empathy and believes they are superior to those around them.

They are loud and need to be the center of attention. They have little to no respect for boundaries and will try to gradually break down any boundaries you set.

3. The covert narcissist

A covert narcissist is the opposite of an overt narcissist. This type is also known as vulnerable narcissism due to extreme sensitivity.

They live for praise and take criticism very badly. In addition to being envious of others, they will also claim that their problems and sadness are far greater than those of others.

4. The malignant narcissist

These people are just nasty and can be aggressive or sadistic. They enjoy watching others suffer and are masters of manipulation to witness this pain. The malignant narcissist is tough to deal with because of their intelligence, which is directed into manipulation.

5. The psychopathic narcissist

Though not as common, psychopathic narcissists are aggressive and violent and show no remorse for their actions. Typically, serial killers and mass murderers are psychopathic narcissists.

6. The somatic narcissist

The physical body is of extreme importance to a somatic narcissist. They might have to be the best looking or the fittest, so they focus on their weight and appearance. While this doesn't sound too bad, they will put their needs above all others to achieve their idea of physical perfection.

7. The cerebral narcissist

Cerebral narcissists are intelligent, but that is not what defines them. They feel that their intelligence makes them superior to others and will go out of their way to make others feel stupid. Regardless of whether you are right or not, you will never win a debate with them and will probably just end up doubting your own intellect.

8. The bullying narcissist

The name gives you a clear idea of what a bullying narcissist is. They have to win by any means. They socially mock others, put them down, and generally make people feel bad about themselves. A "normal" bully does this to climb the social ladder, while a bullying narcissist has personal motivations.

9. The sexual narcissist

Sexual narcissists may also show traits of somatic and cerebral narcissism, but this is on top of their self-admiration of their sexual abilities. They need to hear how good they are in bed and are obsessed with their performance. Most of their manipulation is related to sex, and it's not uncommon for them to be unfaithful, time and time again.

10. The love bombing narcissist

Love bombing alone may feel amazing in the beginning. The bombardment of affection, kind words, and unexpected gifts in the early days of a relationship may even seem normal. However, narcissistic love bombing is a manipulative technique used to hook a person into a committed relationship before they become aware that they are being played.

11. The celebrity narcissist

This is also known as acquired situational narcissism (ASN) and is related to the acquisition of wealth or fame. Due to so much attention, some people can start to believe they are more important than they are.

Identifying the Narcissist in Your Life

Now that we have clearly defined what a narcissist is and the different types, you probably have a good idea of whether or not you're dealing with one. Still, there are a few other signs worth being aware of:

- Your initial interactions were amazing, but things quickly turned sour.
- They dominate conversations both in topic and the amount of speaking.
- They fish for compliments to feed their self-worth.
- You never feel like your emotions are heard or cared about.
- They don't have any long-term friendships.
- They are gaslighting you, causing you to doubt everything.
- You never get an apology or see any attempts to compromise.
- If you try to break away, they will panic and then become angry.
- You are constantly being controlled by them.
- They don't take responsibility for their actions.
- Everything is either good or bad.
- They project their negativity onto you—if you don't support them, you are pessimistic, etc.
- Their lack of empathy makes it hard for them to work with others or as part of a team.

One word of advice is not to start imagining things that aren't really there, although it's a habit many of us have. If your partner forgets to pay one bill, it might just be an irresponsible moment. This isn't enough to include on your list. The signs have to be something that is regularly seen. We all have moments in our lives when some of these signs have rung true for us too. You may find that numerous issues are relevant. But if some aren't, there is no need to go searching for problems that aren't there.

The Myths Surrounding Narcissism

Because the media has warped the idea of what narcissism is, it's only natural that there are various misconceptions. A dominant myth is that narcissism is caused by bad mothering. We have covered this one because although parenting styles can contribute to personality traits and disorders, there are other influencing factors.

Another myth is that narcissists are aggressive. The problem with believing this myth is that you may assume that the person in your life isn't a narcissist because they aren't aggressive, and you end up overlooking other behaviors. Aggression is not part of the defining criteria of NPD, but it's true that the more aggressive the person is, the more severe the NPD (Lancer, 2023).

Finally, not all narcissists are aware of their behavior because they have been living in this distorted version of reality, which is pretty much all they are used to. Everything they experience, from their thoughts to their emotions, is normal for them. Pointing out their mistakes or highlighting that they might have a problem is fruitless unless they are ready to make a change. You might be inclined to try and explain your feelings to them, hoping that they will change, but it's unlikely that they will change without self-motivation to do so, even if they do listen.

Narcissists in Real-Life Situations

Martin worked in sales, and although he didn't have an official title, he had been on the team the longest. That was enough for him to see himself as above the rest. During a team meeting, the leader highlighted a mistake that Martin had made. This caused Martin to explode and accuse the leader of personally attacking him when it most certainly wasn't part of his responsibility.

As Martin continued to ramble on, he proceeded to take credit for work that other team members had done, and whenever someone went to correct him, he silenced them with a hand in their face.

After the meeting, Martin took the time to chat with each team member, reinforcing what he had done and complaining about other team members.

Jessica loved cooking and experimenting with new recipes, and her husband initially thought this was a great quality in her. As time passed, Jessica noticed comments like, "Oh, but you make such a great curry" and "What I need after a day like I've had is your curry."

These comments made Jessica feel special until she realized her husband was now controlling everything she ate. Then it moved on to the clothes she wore and the people she spent time with.

When she tried to talk to him about this, he would gaslight her with, "You just can't remember that we had X for dinner last week" or "Are you serious? We went out with Y last month; you made the plans." Neither of these was true, but the way he said it made Jessica doubt herself.

Jenny and Katlin had been friends since junior school, but Katlin had never felt that their friendship was balanced. When it was the two of them, Jenny was full of kindness and affection. Jenny felt lucky to have a friend who was always there to offer advice. The older they got, the more the imbalance was felt.

Around other friends, Katlin was the butt of all Jenny's jokes, and she felt less and less significant. Advice started to only benefit Jenny, like when she told Katlin to stop dating a guy because she could do better, only for Jenny to start dating him. Even then, Jenny was "just doing Katlin a favor." Jenny didn't just have her confidence shattered—she felt like she was less worthy as a human being.

People trying to deal with a narcissist invest a lot of time and energy into a relationship, hoping that the narcissist will change, so much so that it's only themselves that ends up changing. It's time to redirect that energy toward making positive changes in your own life.

Putting Chapter 6 into Practice

I know you're eager to see changes quickly, but now that you have a more complete understanding of the different types of narcissism and the behaviors they display (intentional or not), take some time to observe the narcissist in your life. You will probably notice many "Ahh, that makes sense now" moments, and more importantly, you will feel reassured that the issues in your relationship aren't all your fault.

Exercise: The "Reality Check" List

Each time the narcissist in your life makes a comment that leaves you questioning yourself—whether they're subtly undermining, guilt-tripping, or bragging—jot it down in a "Reality Check" list. Next to each comment, write a brief "reality check" of your own.

Example:

Their Comment: "You're too sensitive; I was just joking."

Reality Check: "My feelings are valid, and a joke shouldn't make me feel small."

This exercise helps you challenge their narrative and remind yourself of what's real. Over time, your "Reality Check" list will become a tool to steady yourself, keeping their influence in perspective.

CHAPTER 7: OVERCOMING THE NARCISSIST

> *You will never get the truth out of a narcissist. The closest you will ever come is a story that either makes them the victim or the hero, but never the villain.*
>
> — *SHANNON L. ALDER*

Picture this: You've just spent an hour listening to a narcissist talk about themselves. Now you're wondering if you even exist anymore. Welcome to toxic person fatigue. Let's get you back to normal.

Here is the mistake I made so many times, not just with one narcissist but with all of them.

Each time I made a commitment to changing my own life, I was only 99% on board. There was always that 1% that kept telling me they would change, which held me back.

That's the reason why Alder's quote was so inspiring for me. I appreciated the straightforwardness, villain or hero. Removing that option for change made it easier for me to get past that niggling tiny percentage that was stopping me from being my priority!

What Can You Do If There Is a Narcissist in Your Life?

We are going to assume that there are certain narcissistic people in your life you can't break free from. We are also going to assume that they don't recognize that they have a problem, so professional help is not going to be an option. The first crucial step when dealing with these people is to focus on your boundaries.

The reason we took the time to observe the narcissist and their behavior is so that you are fully aware of what you are being subjected to. At the same time, you now understand that underneath that grandiosity, there is a very fragile ego. While this still isn't an excuse for their behavior, the knowledge you have now is the foundation for defending yourself.

Much like dealing with a sociopath, you must be emotionally strong to handle a narcissist. Self-care is one way to start gaining your strength, and we will go into more detail on this later on. Another strategy is to start surrounding yourself with a strong support system, whether that's friends, family, or even support groups. These trustworthy people will help you stay grounded and remind you of your reality. Don't forget that narcissists will attempt to isolate you from anyone who disrupts the control they have over you, and they will even go to the extent of influencing the people in your support system. This is where online support can be especially useful as not only do the people in these groups have similar experiences, but they also can't be influenced.

Before you start making any changes, check in with your expectations of your relationship. We are now working on the theory that the narcissist isn't going to change.

Another expectation to manage is the emotional connection to expect. Because of their limited emotional connections, you may find that your relationship will never have the same depth as you would like. Only you can decide if this is something you want or not. To gain inner strength, expect nothing from them and focus on your happiness.

Why Are Boundaries So Important When Dealing with Narcissistic People?

Conversations about how things make you feel are going to fall on deaf ears and just waste your energy. Boundaries remove the need for emotional explanations. They are your rules that everyone must follow, and if they don't, there will be consequences.

To create your boundaries, imagine drawing a large circle around you. Think about all of the situations that you are having difficulties with.

Take one situation and decide how close you can get to the line and still feel comfortable. What is the one thing that takes you over the line?

For example, your partner criticizes you in public. You might be okay with this in front of good friends and family, but absolutely not in large social situations or with your work colleagues.

You might also feel that you won't tolerate any form of criticism in front of others. Nobody can create boundaries for you; it's a personal thing.

We know full well that a narcissist is going to push your boundaries, regardless of how well you express them. This means it's essential for you to have consequences when they do cross a boundary.

Using the same example, you might choose to walk away from the situation as soon as they criticize you. Whatever you decide, you have to be 100% confident that you are going to follow through with it.

Communicating your boundary should be short and simple: "I will no longer tolerate you criticizing me in front of others. The next time it happens, I will leave." And full stop!

Don't feel you have to justify your boundary. The best thing is to change the subject so they don't have a chance to manipulate you.

Once you start putting your boundaries and consequences into action, you will notice that certain cycles are broken, and this is a great starting place. You will start to notice your confidence improving as you know you can do this.

Here are some other tips for dealing with a narcissist.

Try not to get caught up in their emotional games.

You'll now be wise to the games they are trying to play and recognize when you're being manipulated. Unfortunately, your reaction will provide more ammunition, and the best thing you can do is take a big step back. The next time you think that the narcissist in your life has only said something to get a reaction from you, just say "Okay." This way, they won't have anything to turn back on you.

Choose your battles wisely.

If the situation calls for it, just say "Okay." However, if you feel that their behavior crosses a line or a boundary, you should speak up for yourself. It's always better to do this calmly. You mustn't let them see your pain. Whatever they say, do not feel blame, shame, or guilt. You know that you can admit when you have made a mistake and apologize. Don't allow people to project their feelings onto you and make you doubt yourself. You are only responsible for your own emotions and your actions.

Lower other expectations.

Even after so much hurt, there's likely a part of you that is still hopeful that they will understand one day. It's time to lower these expectations as a way of self-protection. Stop expecting them to empathize with your situation and stop waiting for that meaningful conversation.

Avoid bringing up the past.

As you have learned about acceptance, this should be easier. What happened in the past should stay there. In the past, you weren't educated on how to deal with a narcissist, so there is little point in bringing up what happened months or years ago. Now that you are more informed, it's best to focus your efforts on the present.

Get the help you need.

If you feel you are going through things you can't cope with, reach out. Your support network is crucial for moving forward in a healthy and positive way. You may have friends or a close family member you can talk with, or you may prefer a therapist. Don't feel you have to suffer alone. As we have seen, personality disorders are far more common than we think, and there is now help available.

What Happens When You Have Tried Everything?

Regardless of gender, ending any relationship is going to be hard. Even though their love for you wasn't real, your love for them certainly was. Even when at rock bottom, there is a small part of your mind and your heart that believes things could be different. The other fear that we may have is not wanting to risk throwing away what we know, just to have the same thing happen again.

It may seem like we are only talking about romantic partnerships, but this applies to all relationships. You can't replace your parents, but you can find fulfilling relationships that will fill you with love and allow you to love.

The first step to breaking free from narcissists is to be absolutely sure you're ready to make the step. One common mistake is the "break up-make up" pattern, which is also seen in non-romantic relationships. You think you have made a decision, then you go back and break away again. Normally, this only prolongs the suffering, and with a narcissist, it definitely will because they won't change. Being absolutely sure of your decision will prevent you from going back.

Next, you need to think of the logistics. If it's a partner, plan out living arrangements and other practicalities. If it's a friend, figure out if you'll be seeing them around mutual friends or if you can avoid them entirely.

What family events will you have to attend together, if any? Is there a way that you can completely distance yourself from your narcissistic coworker? Whenever possible, it's best to make a clean break. If this isn't an option, the contact must be limited to only what is necessary.

Create a fresh list of goals and things you want to achieve. Some ideas include:

- Start a new hobby
- Read a particular book
- Declutter your belongings
- Experience new social events
- Learn a new skill
- Study a course online
- Get more exercise
- Travel
- Get a new haircut/wardrobe
- Advance in your career

This list will help you stay focused and act as a reminder of why you broke away from the person in the first place. It should be filled with all the things you have wanted to do but couldn't.

Prepare what you want to say. Being prepared will help you to feel confident. You don't need a long speech. Let them know that you feel the relationship is no longer healthy and you are going to move on. You do not have to explain your decision. Remember, the more you talk, the more ammunition you give them.

Allow yourself some time to grieve the end of your relationship. It's a process that needs to be worked through in the right way. Don't expect yourself to wake up the next day and feel that life is all better. At the same time, it's important not to get stuck in this period, which is why you should keep your list handy and start ticking off some of your new goals.

Now that you are free from the narcissist, you can start reconnecting with those people with whom you haven't been able to spend time. Ironically, if the narcissist is a parent, this newfound freedom might even allow you to rekindle an old romance. Think about friends from school or college you haven't seen and reach out to them. These people, as well as your current relationships, will act as your support network, particularly while you're building up your strength and getting back on your feet.

An exercise that really helped me was to write a list of all the negative things about my narcissistic people. It was quite extensive, but I made sure I got it all out of my mind and onto paper. I then made every effort to remove reminders of them: photos, gifts, etc. I took a bag, put everything into it, and finally added the list and threw it all away. This provided a great sense of closure.

Focus on the positive things in your life. It will take a while to retrain your brain as you have lived in a swamp of negativity for so long. If you take the time to really look, you'll discover that there are many good things in life. If you're having trouble seeing the good, you might need some therapy—just to give you a little boost in the right direction.

How to Avoid Narcissists in the Future

Through no fault of our own, it's easy to fall for the same behavior that we have been used to. For this reason, you need to give yourself time before jumping into new relationships, regardless of the type. Make sure you give yourself enough time to discover who you really are and what you want from life and your relationships. Dr. Ramani, a licensed clinical psychologist, calls this a deep dive. Look back at what has happened, take what you can from the relationships, and use them to learn more about yourself so you know not to let the same thing happen again.

Dr. Ramani also explains how we store trauma in our bodies. The mind will slowly let go, but there is a very good reason why we should have faith in our gut reactions and the hairs that stand up when we sense something is wrong. There will come a time when you meet new friends, colleagues, and partners. It's wrong to put up your defenses and assume they will treat you in the same way. You aren't being fair or giving them a proper chance. Start each new relationship as a blank slate, but if you feel like you've been down this road before, get out. You want to nip it in the bud early on to protect yourself from the same painful experiences that you've worked so hard to break away from.

So far, we have looked at two of the most toxic types of people. That is not to say that there aren't many other personality types and behaviors we shouldn't have to put up with in our lives. In the next chapter, we'll discuss other types of toxic people who manage to turn our lives upside down.

Putting Chapter 7 into Practice

This is an easy one! Without overthinking, what is the one realistic thing you have always wanted to achieve in your life or the one thing you gave up and wish you hadn't given up because of a toxic relationship? Create a plan to make it happen.

Exercise: The "Empathy Budget"

Think of your empathy like a budget. Each day, decide how much empathy you're willing to spend on the narcissist, and be conscious of when you've hit your limit.

Example:

> "Today, I'm giving them exactly 10% of my energy. No more."

By setting an empathy limit, you'll start noticing how much energy you save for yourself—and you may just realize that the narcissist has been over-budget for years.

Exercise: "Self-Check Phrase"

Pick a go-to phrase you can silently repeat whenever they try to get under your skin. Something like, "This is about them, not me," or "Not my circus, not my monkey." Think of it as your mental shield, a reminder that their behavior isn't your responsibility.

CHAPTER 8: AT TIMES, IT'S NEITHER

> *Stop telling the people who do so little for you control so much of your mind, feelings, and emotions.*
>
> — *WILL SMITH*

Fortunately, not everyone has a narcissist or sociopath starring in their life story. But that doesn't mean they're off the hook for dealing with toxic behavior.

So far, we have examined extremely toxic people. Unfortunately, there are so many other ways a person can be toxic, so much so that we may fall into the trap of trying to mold our lives around them. Just because someone isn't physically abusing you doesn't mean their behavior gets a free pass!

What exactly does it mean to be toxic? Here's the uncomfortable truth: we all have our moments—you, me, your overly critical neighbor.

But there's a difference between having a toxic moment and being a fully certified toxic person. Knowing where to draw the line is important, so let's get into it.

What Constitutes Toxic Behavior

First things first: the person in your life may not actually be toxic—it could just be their behavior. On the flip side, some people have such a consistently negative impact on your well-being that they might as well come with a "toxic" warning label.

Toxic behavior isn't just anything that rubs you the wrong way or leaves you feeling upset. It's the repeated words, actions, or patterns that chip away at your well-being, stir up unnecessary conflict, and somehow leave you questioning your own sanity. With that definition, it's easy to see how anyone can display toxic behavior from time to time.

Take me, for example. Just last week, I caused a friend a ridiculous amount of stress. I hurt their feelings, totally unintentionally, and yes—I apologized, we moved on, and all was forgiven. But in that moment? I was the problem. I was the one causing the pain. That's toxic behavior, plain and simple. Intentional or not, it happens.

The major difference is that I was able to recognize my actions and make amends, which is what most adults are able to do. Those who display more severe toxic behavior will rarely apologize. Going forward, we'll refer to them as toxic people rather than people with toxic behavior. I don't want you to start feeling guilty and worried because you've upset people—you're not a toxic person!

Toxic people can be manipulators, and their behavior will often confuse you because of a lack of consistency. One minute they'll be happy, the next they may be crying out for attention because their life is so terrible. Not only do you feel uncomfortable around these people, but you also don't feel good about yourself when you are around them.

Toxic people live for drama, and if no drama can be found, they will create it. Overstepping boundaries is just one of the ways they create drama.

Substance abuse can be a problem for toxic people. It doesn't mean that every person who takes drugs or drinks is toxic. But when their behavior starts to negatively impact your life, it also becomes your problem.

Unlike narcissists and sociopaths, toxicity isn't classed as a mental disorder or a personality disorder. That isn't to say that the toxic person doesn't have underlying mental health problems that cause their behavior.

What Is the Difference Between a Bad Day and Toxic Behavior?

To understand the fine line between a bad day and toxic behavior, let's explore some real-life examples and break down when ordinary ups and downs cross into toxicity.

Jane, like many of us, had her share of ups and downs. Health problems, unfortunately, brought her relationship to an end. But she was a fighter, managing to secure both a pay raise and a promotion at work. Whenever she felt low, her friend was there—accompanying her to doctor's appointments, even helping to box up her ex-boyfriend's things and clear him out of her life, literally and figuratively.

But when Jane got that promotion and invited her friend out to celebrate, the calls and messages went unanswered. When she finally did get hold of her, the response was a flat, "Isn't that just great," in a tone that was anything but. Two seconds later, her friend had already moved on, gossiping about someone else.

The next time Jane invited her friend to dinner, eager to talk about a new guy she'd met, the response was a sarcastic, "So soon?" followed by a quick decline. Jane didn't feel like she could say anything—after all, this was the same friend who'd been there when she needed her most.

When we share good news with a friend and they aren't quick to share our joy, it's possible they're dealing with their own problems and are genuinely distracted. Jane's friend, however, crossed the line by downplaying every happy moment Jane had. While she didn't completely ignore Jane's reasons to celebrate, her responses were consistently toxic. Sarcasm is like salt; the right amount makes a dish, but too much and it's ruined. This behavior became toxic as soon as Jane's friend only seemed to benefit from the relationship during times of crisis. A healthy friendship is one where you're there for each other—through the good and the bad.

Let's consider the relationship between Carmen and Mike, who both have full-time jobs. Carmen's job involves a lot of emotional labor, while Mike's is more hands-on and physical. They also juggle responsibilities at home, including caring for their toddler.

After a long day, Carmen often finds herself exhausted, managing her job and household duties. When Mike comes home, he tends to unwind by playing video games or watching TV instead of helping out. One evening, after a particularly challenging day with a sick child, Carmen reached her breaking point. She raised her voice, expressing frustration that Mike wasn't contributing more to their shared responsibilities.

Once things calmed down, Carmen apologized and explained that she needed him to be more engaged. Instead of accepting her apology, Mike dismissed her feelings, saying things like, "You always blow things out of proportion," or "If you managed your time better, you wouldn't be so stressed." He made it seem like Carmen was the problem rather than acknowledging that their workload and responsibilities were unbalanced.

From the outside, it's clear that this dynamic is toxic. However, it can be harder to see when you're in such a relationship like that. Carmen had a tough day and expressed her anger—something we all do from time to time.

In contrast, Mike consistently prioritized his needs over those of their family. He avoided taking responsibility for household duties and judged Carmen's feelings instead of supporting her. This created an imbalance in their relationship.

Both partners should feel valued and supported. Carmen doesn't owe Mike the burden of his hobbies on top of her existing responsibilities. Healthy relationships require both partners to share the load and acknowledge each other's feelings. When one partner repeatedly dismisses the other's needs, it leads to toxicity.

James' sister is a complete control freak. Everything in her life is structured and ordered the way she likes it. There are lists for lists, routines can't be broken, and rules must be obeyed. When she comes to James' apartment, she will move a chair to a slight angle because it looks better. She will bring an air freshener because it smells nicer and rearranges the books by height order. And she is right about everything.

If you try to disagree or show her a different point of view, she will treat you as if you were a child with no experience in the matter. She makes plans for family events, and no one can say no or even make a suggestion. James often finds himself in a position where he has to choose the lesser of two evils just to make sure his sister remains calm, and his parents aren't dragged into discussions.

What James' sister does in her own home is up to her. In all fairness, we all have our little quirks that we either can't change or don't want to. I confess, I also like my books in order of height! Her behavior becomes toxic when she tries to control James' life.

He might be happy to accept that she comes to his place and treats it the same way as her own home, which could be the limit of his boundary. But she crosses the line when James is not allowed to have thoughts, feelings, and opinions of his own. This is a human right that we all should have.

Hannah has a colleague who is generally easy to work with. They collaborate well together, and while they are friendly, there's still a degree of professionalism. Hannah's colleague, Jake, likes to be the center of attention and often has a story to entertain the office.

One day, Hannah noticed that Jake had previously claimed to have lived in Melbourne, but now he was saying he had lived in Sydney for a year. When Hannah questioned him, he said, "Yes, that was before," and she thought nothing more of it. Over time, she noticed a pattern developing, and more and more lies were being told. At first, they were harmless white lies, and the only real damage caused was the inability to trust him.

But then, the lies started creeping into work-related things. He would lie about a report being finished or tell the boss that he had asked Hannah to do something when he hadn't. When he lied to a client, and subsequently, the company lost the client, the whole team suffered.

Trust is a crucial part of any relationship. Without it, we have no foundation to build on. If a colleague is telling lies about their personal life, the professional relationship may not suffer. As soon as Jake started telling lies to and about colleagues, his behavior went from supportable to toxic. This is because his actions created negativity not only for Hannah but also for the others who have to work with him. As well as Hannah not being able to trust him, his lies planted seeds of doubt about who can be trusted in the office.

The main point here is that when you look at these situations and nod your head in agreement, it's rather obvious that the behavior is toxic, possibly even the people. So why is it so hard to spot toxic behavior in our own lives? Simply put, it's because love is blind—even to toxic behavior.

Dealing with Other Elements of Toxicity

Though the prevalence of personality disorders isn't common, 6% globally (Cleveland Clinic, n.d.), there are other sources of toxicity. Psychopaths lack empathy and remorse and are also experts at manipulation. Borderline personality disorder (BPD) is a condition that causes extreme mood swings, impulsive behavior, and low self-esteem. If a person with BPD feels love from a partner, the partner is the hero. If the person doesn't feel love, they are the villain. The ups and downs can be highly toxic for a person living with someone who has BPD.

These emotional extremes are similar to the highs and lows experienced by someone with bipolar disorder, a mental health condition, not a personality disorder. These people can go through everything from emotional highs (known as hypomania) and depression. Toxic behaviors can include impulsivity, lack of empathy, and infidelity.

It might sound extreme, but sarcasm can also be toxic. While the occasional witty, smart comment can add humor to a conversation, there are limits.

Sarcasm needs to be used in the right way for it to be funny, and for someone on the receiving end, it can be hurtful. While on the subject of humor, if you notice someone has the habit of turning everything into a joke, this too can be toxic.

It's great to be able to find the funny in things, but there are certain situations where this is inappropriate, especially if the use of humor opens old emotional wounds.

Another trait that can be good in moderation is competitiveness. It has the potential to motivate and drive people to push themselves, but not everything should be approached as a competition. Competitiveness can be incredibly subtle, but when someone isn't happy with your achievements, it's often a sign that their competitiveness is unhealthy.

Here is one final incredibly subtle toxic behavior you might be guilty of — the need to fix everyone and everything. The desire to help others leads to a strong determination to rescue or fix people.

There is no doubt that wanting to help people is an admirable trait, but when taken too far, it's easy to feel that other people's lives have become our responsibility. Subtle toxic behaviors aren't just about what others do to us but also what we do to ourselves.

Over the years, I have noticed that some people will use the words "toxic" and "abusive" interchangeably, and while there are overlaps, there are also a couple of differences, and most of them come down to control.

An abuser will always need to be in control in all areas of their relationship, from sex to finances. They will also want to manage aspects of the other person's life, like who they see and what they can do.

Abusers use bullying tactics, and each move or decision is well-calculated. Abusive behavior doesn't change, whereas, with the right tools and knowledge, toxic behavior can.

What Can You Do When Love Is Causing Blindness to Toxicity?

For those closest to us—our long-term partners, best friends, parents, and siblings—it isn't always so easy. In many cases, we have had these people in our lives for so long that we accept that this is who they are. In other cases, our love is so blind that we don't even see it.

One of the biggest problems with toxic behavior in those closest to us is that it can appear gradually and subtly. Take your family, for example. While growing up, you may not recognize how much your parents' toxic behavior impacted you until you reach adulthood. Your sibling probably used to be your best friend, but as you both start to mold your own lives, they may have been caught up in a circle of toxic people, and it does rub off. Bit by bit, you begin to notice changes in them, and it has a greater impact on your relationship.

When you're with friends, you might start noticing little things that bug you, things you wish could change. It's not until you are in a seriously bad situation together that you realize just how toxic they can be. For example, when your car breaks down in the middle of nowhere, instead of helping, they make things worse by complaining or bailing.

Let's take a look at three specific relationships and how you can spot the most subtle signs of toxic behavior. Remember that some points may apply to all of your closest relationships.

How to spot subtle toxic behavior from your family:

- You are constantly walking on eggshells around them
- There are many arguments, and they make these arguments personal
- They don't accept your sexual preferences
- They don't accept your choice of partner
- They don't respect your opinions or beliefs
- They tell you how to raise your children
- You feel you do things only for their approval

- Your family frequently disappoints you
- They are violent toward you
- They are controlling, expecting you to do what the rest of the family is doing

Ways to know if your friends are toxic:

- They constantly cancel plans or don't show up
- You start to dread social occasions with them
- They bring up your biggest insecurity right after they compliment you
- You are sad, upset, and stressed after social occasions with them
- They drink too much and become aggressive or insult you
- They make you feel guilty for doing what you want to do
- They gossip about you
- You feel like you need a nap after every conversation with them, even though you just had three cups of coffee
- They post negative things about you on social media
- You are never thanked for the things you do for them
- You feel like you are being bullied
- They don't respect your personal space

When love stops you from seeing your partner's toxic behavior:

- You can't communicate without arguing, being bitter, or sarcastic
- There is a lack of support
- You start to feel jealousy and resentment
- Your partner makes important financial decisions without talking to you first
- You have lost other important relationships for fear of upsetting your partner

- You have stopped taking care of yourself, both your mental and physical health
- You don't have time for your hobbies
- In your mind, you keep telling yourself it's a phase and things will change
- You find yourself telling lies so that you don't have to spend more time with them
- They ridicule you in front of friends and family
- There is no balance or equality, a shared understanding of who does what

What is highly dangerous about subtle toxic behavior is that it is contagious. Toxic people often lie, but then you find yourself telling lies to avoid confrontation. How many times have you seen online bullying be retaliated with more bullying?

Even with subtle toxic behavior, you can only take responsibility for your own actions and emotions. And as harsh as it sounds, you have to learn how to stop putting yourself in situations where those closest to you can keep causing pain.

Change Is Possible

After taking off the blinkers and seeing things for how they really are, you are now ready to start taking some small steps to see the necessary changes.

We like to start with the smaller steps because this way, you gain confidence and knowing you can do it makes it easier to tackle harder situations.

1. Don't bring up the past

It's not as simple as "forgive and forget" because the pain people cause stays with us. If your partner is unfaithful, you can't just put it in the past and trust again. When we talk about putting things in the past, it's about not bringing past actions into present conversations. It won't be productive and is more likely to cause tension in the conversation. It's important to focus on the present and the changes you want to see.

2. Get to the bottom of their issues

They might not even be aware of their toxic behavior or the extent to which it is damaging the relationship. Their behavior will stem from some root cause. Make it clear that you do not excuse the way they treat you, but being understanding and helping them work through their issues can reduce the toxicity and strengthen the relationship.

Of course, if they are unwilling to accept the problems, you will struggle to see the changes you need.

3. Focus on accountability rather than blaming

People find it hard to admit they made a mistake or have done something wrong. We sometimes mistake being accountable for admitting to our failings and weaknesses. It's easier to highlight the faults of others and blame them. Even though you're working to prevent the other person's toxic behavior, taking your fair share of the blame for those bad days that turn into toxic acts is good practice. It's a little bit like you're showing them that it's okay to be accountable and how to say sorry when necessary.

Nevertheless, never apologize for things that aren't your fault, and don't allow yourself to be manipulated into saying sorry.

4. Say no to toxic behavior

I know you might feel hesitant to confront the situation, but now is the best time to put a stop to being treated like a doormat. You don't deserve to be treated with anything less than love and respect. When people treat you in a way that causes you to suffer, call them out on this behavior and tell them that it isn't right. Choose the best time to do this. You should make sure you are emotionally calm, and if you're worried about the other person's reaction, do it in a public place or with people around you that you can trust.

5. Set boundaries

Boundaries are essential when dealing with all toxic people. It's another way of letting people know that there are certain things that you will not tolerate—no matter what.

When you have decided on your boundaries, you need to make sure that they are clearly communicated. Because toxic people often try to cross boundaries, you'll have to keep repeating yourself and showing that you are serious by following through with the consequences when your boundaries are crossed. As soon as you don't reinforce a boundary, the toxic person will find a way to revert to old habits.

6. Take care of yourself

If you feel like you have been putting yourself in second place, now is also the time to change this. Others will continue to disregard your needs and place their own ahead of yours until you remind them that your well-being is equally important. Look after yourself by taking time to do the things you want to do, whether that's exercise, a trip to the movies, or going to a particular restaurant. Don't wait for your loved one to agree to come with you. There's something incredibly empowering about doing these things alone—it's not the same as being lonely!

7. Allow some time to see the changes

As long as both of you are actively working to improve, the right changes will come about, but it won't be overnight. You are working to change behavior that is well-established, possibly over the years. It's like learning to drive on the right-hand side of the road, and then all of a sudden, you have to drive on the left. Each day gets easier, but there might be some minor setbacks along the way. Remember that you have to see the changes and not just hear that they will happen.

8. Decide on the level of contact you are happy with

Generally speaking, you can decide on one of three levels of contact. First, you can remove yourself from situations when the person shows toxic behavior. For example, if your best friend becomes toxic after drinking too much, you can refuse to go out with them. Second, you can decide that minimal contact is best. This means you would only see family members at group occasions, weddings, funerals, etc. Third, you can go with no contact at all. This is obviously going to be the most difficult due to how close the relationship is. If minimal contact is still upsetting you too much, you might want to set a period of time with no contact. This could be a month, a few months, or even a year. During this time, you can analyze if your life is better or worse without them in it. It's then up to you to decide if you want to reconnect and whether the person has made any significant changes during the no-contact period.

Real-World Examples of How These Strategies Can Be Successful

To put these strategies into practice, let's take the same examples we saw with Jane, Carmen, James, and Hannah and see how things could have turned out if they had known how to handle toxic behavior.

Jane and the drama-seeking friend

People looking for drama often do so because they are seeking a distraction from their own reality. Our own problems are usually so difficult to resolve that we may feel helpless. But when we see other people in turmoil, it's easier to see the solution. Drama seekers often do so because they can't find solutions to their own problems. Being there during other people's drama keeps them busy, and they feel like they are involved in a solution.

Here, the loved one is only there when you're going through problems. You need to take time to put your problems to one side (temporarily) so that you can try to help this person resolve what is upsetting them. Considering the prevalence of toxicity, they may be trying to deal with their own toxic people.

Jane's best option would have been to shift the focus onto her friend and allow the friend to open up about what is bothering them. Even the toxic words that came out as sarcasm could have been because of her friend's personal problems.

This is what is known as extending an olive branch. You are providing an opportunity for the loved one to explain their behavior, which might be the chance for them to realize that they are in the wrong.

If they don't open up about what is bothering them or they tell you that there is nothing wrong, you need to let them know that their actions and words have hurt you and that in the future, you expect to enjoy both the highs and the lows with your friend.

Carmen and the needy partner

Although getting angry wasn't the best solution, it is not the root of the problem. Carmen and Mike have communication issues, and it's become so bad that Mike has become toxic and Carmen is slowly picking up more toxic behavior.

To break the cycle, Mike and Carmen need to have an open conversation. It's best to do this when neither is tired, and there is someone to take care of their toddler so that they aren't distracted.

The conversation should focus on "I" sentences instead of "You." Sentences that start with "I" focus the attention on your feelings. Sentences that start with "You" can sound like blame. Look at the difference between "I feel hurt when you don't do your share" compared with "You hurt me when you don't do your share."

The conversation should also include a plan for running the home on a more equal basis. Carmen also needs to dedicate some time to herself so that Mike can't accuse her of being jealous. Finally, Carmen will have to be patient, and they should celebrate their wins together.

James and the controlling sister

One of the most common causes of controlling behavior is anxiety disorder. We know the feeling of a crazy world where nothing seems to be in our control—it's stressful, but for some, it becomes too much, and they find peace in controlling everything they can. James can try to be more understanding of her feelings and perhaps encourage her to get professional help for her problems.

If his sister refuses, he will have to set firm boundaries and let his sister know what will happen if she crosses the line. James will also need to decide on an appropriate level of contact so that he protects himself if his sister can't change.

Hannah and the lying colleague

There are many reasons why people lie. It might be to avoid embarrassment, to protect someone else from getting hurt, or to feel better about themselves. As we mentioned before, there is a fine line between the odd white lie about your experiences and a full-blown lie. The minute that Hannah's colleague crossed that line, Hannah should have called him out on it so that he was aware that the workspace does not tolerate lies.

Another very important thing, particularly in a workplace, is to document everything. Every message, email, and lie should be kept in a file. It might sound dramatic, but HR should have a copy of the file if there is any risk to your position or career. Encouraging other colleagues to do the same is a good idea so that one bad apple doesn't spoil the whole basket.

They Don't Deserve Endless Chances Though

Relationships and our experiences are subjective. What one person might see as toxic could be very different from the next person, and only two people ever really know what goes on in a relationship. Other people's advice can be welcoming, but only you can make the final decision as to whether or not there is a future.

I will, however, urge you to strongly consider ending any relationship where you feel your life is in danger (and this applies to your children too) or, at the very least, to get some professional help, whether that's from law enforcement or other support networks.

Here are a few signs that might indicate that you have tried and given them enough chances.

- They continue to put you down
- They pressure you to do things you don't want to
- They are still attempting to manipulate you
- You don't feel supported
- They don't celebrate your successes
- Their negativity drains you
- They don't respect your feelings
- There is no give-and-take
- They continue to lie
- They still always have to be right

Bear in mind that all of your logical side will be telling you that you should leave, and your emotional side is starting to get on board, yet there is still something holding you back. It's perfectly normal to fear ending a toxic relationship, but know that you are, even if you can't see it right now, much stronger than you imagine.

The range of toxicity levels is huge. Toxic behavior can be minor little things that really get to you, or they can be major ones that are now starting to take over your life. Nobody's situation will be exactly the same, and each of us has our own personality. For this reason, there isn't a one-fix solution for toxic behavior.

This chapter has provided some of the most effective solutions to help overcome such issues with those closest to you. Once again, I have purposely not discussed manipulation. All toxic behavior comes from manipulation. We will dedicate the next chapter to the prevalence of manipulation in today's world and take a deep dive into the dark psychology behind it.

Putting Chapter 8 into Practice

Again, this is a moment for observation before taking steps. Just because you don't have a sociopath or a narcissist in your life doesn't mean you aren't suffering. Step outside the home and consider all of your relationships. Look for subtle things that may have dragged you down in the past but blamed yourself for and take a moment for self-reflection in case of subtle toxic behaviors of your own. When you know what you are dealing with, you will be prepared to take action.

CHAPTER 9: THE REAL PROBLEM: MANIPULATION

> *Until you realize how easy it is for your mind to be manipulated, you remain the puppet of someone else's game.*
>
> — *EVITA OCHEL*

Years ago, I felt like such an idiot, and time and time again, I thought, "Man, I have been played again." I was completely unable to see when I was being manipulated, and I definitely couldn't see it coming.

Toxic behavior and manipulation are best friends walking down the street together. They bounce off each other, fuel each other, and creep up on you without you being aware. It's perfectly normal for us not to notice when we are being manipulated, mainly because nobody wants to think that our friends and family are capable of such techniques.

What Is Manipulation?

"Manipulation is the act of controlling someone or something to your own advantage, often unfairly or dishonestly" (Cambridge Dictionary,

2021). When we talk about controlling people, it could be their emotions, perceptions, behavior, and/or relationships.

Remember how we mentioned our habit of saying we're fine or okay when people ask how we are? This is also a form of manipulation because we are controlling how people perceive us. Instead of seeing us as sad, angry, or depressed, they see us as okay. Most of us do this, so there is no need to start worrying that you are a chronic manipulator. This is a common reaction that is not designed to try and gain personally but to prevent others from becoming concerned.

Some examples of manipulation include:

- Lying or withholding information
- Threatening or implying threats
- Isolating people from their loved ones
- Passive aggression
- Verbal abuse
- Intellectual bullying
- Gaslighting
- Using sex to get what they want
- Creating an imbalance of power
- Negative surprises to catch you off guard
- The silent treatment
- Playing the victim

The reasons behind people's manipulative behavior can be unconscious, but it can also reach the other extreme and be completely malicious and intentional.

Victims can be left exhausted both physically and mentally as they try to please these people. They might begin to suffer from anxiety or depression. Not only may they start lying about their emotions, but they might also start to find it incredibly hard to develop trusting relationships.

The manipulator may also have their own mental health issues that are causing this toxic behavior. Narcissists and sociopaths frequently use manipulation and are fully aware of their behavior.

People who have been diagnosed with borderline personality may manipulate others in order to have their needs met. But there doesn't have to be a mental health diagnosis to engage in manipulative tactics. It can also be because a person is scared or anxious and needs to control all of their surroundings.

Why Is Manipulation So Toxic?

There are plenty of examples in the world where manipulation is considered perfectly normal, so much so that we don't even consider being manipulated.

Marketing and advertising use manipulative techniques to convince us to choose particular products or services. This might sound like a trivial example but imagine the cleaning product or toothpaste that you always use—and for good reason. But an ad catches your attention and you decide to try the new product. The cleaning product could be useless or the toothpaste disgusting. But the company managed to change your purchasing behavior for its own gain.

If you look at this example in a non-marketing context, the theory is the same. You make a decision based on your knowledge and your gut.

Despite knowing it's the right choice, somebody can use psychology to change your mind. As what they want goes against your original instincts, it's often not in your best interest and, therefore, harms you.

Manipulation in relationships can become so toxic that the result is a breakdown in that relationship. Let's take a look at an example.

Meet Emily and Tom. They've been dating for about nine months. The honeymoon phase? Still going strong.

He's charming, attentive, and always knows how to make her laugh. They've even got that cute couple banter that makes their friends roll their eyes. Everything's going great—or so Emily thinks.

One evening, Emily mentioned that she had been invited to a big networking event for work. She's excited, maybe even a little nervous, and shares the news with Tom.

His reaction? *"Oh, so you're really going to leave me alone all night?"*

Although he says it with a smile, there's something about his tone that feels a little off. She brushes it aside, convinced he's just being playful. After all, he's been nothing but supportive, right?

Fast-forward a few weeks, and the same pattern emerges. Emily makes plans for happy hour with her coworkers—*"Wow, you must really need a break from me,"* Tom jokes, a half-smile on his face. Emily laughs it off again.

But soon, it's happening with every plan she makes. Dinner with friends becomes a guilt trip. A family weekend turns into a passive-aggressive sigh-fest. Tom's not *forbidding* her from going out—he's just *gently* making her feel like a bad girlfriend for wanting any life outside of their relationship.

There was no particular red flag for Emily because it crept up on her slowly. Tom used the pretense of love and affection to subtly control her life, and before she knew it, Emily mistook his need for control as genuine care.

This kind of manipulation isn't gender-specific—both men and women are capable of manipulating their friends, partners, and even colleagues in ways that are hard to spot until it's too late.

What Do Manipulators Have in Common?

Although people manipulate in various ways, manipulators have a certain number of techniques and traits in common. Understanding these will help you to recognize the signs earlier and be better prepared.

1. They can't just ask for what they need

I prefer to be straightforward when I need help from a friend, and I've been working on being more emotionally aware so that I can respect their response. People who manipulate will never ask for help directly because it means giving up their control. Instead, they use psychological tactics to control others and say things like, "I've just been so overwhelmed lately, and no one seems to care how hard things are for me." They play the victim to get you to offer help without having to ask for it.

2. They are expert gaslighters

Gaslighting is one of the most painful forms of manipulation because you start to question your own reality and sanity. If you ask your partner to do the shopping and they don't, they might turn around and say that you never asked them. Manipulators will use subtle phrases like, "Are you sure you're feeling alright?" to "You're just being crazy," both of which will make you question what has really happened.

3. They project their emotions

Projection is when you displace your own feelings onto another person. In most cases, it's a defense mechanism, but manipulators use it to shift the blame for their own negative emotions. Examples could be an angry manipulator accusing their victim of always being angry or a cheating partner who starts to suspect their partner is also cheating.

4. They make generalizations

Generalizations can hurt because the manipulator doesn't take the time or effort to understand what you are truly saying. Imagine if Dad had a problematic day at work and explains the details to Mom. When the kids ask what's wrong with Dad, Mom says, "He's in a mood again." This is a general statement that makes Dad look bad in front of the kids when, in reality, he has a lot on his plate.

5. They have an inappropriate, nasty sense of humor

Really, it's a little bit like bullying, but if you feel like you're always at the end of a joke and these jokes hurt your feelings, you're dealing with a manipulator. In front of the others, they are just being funny, engaging in a bit of innocent humor. However, they are fully aware that their joke causes you pain, and they might even rub salt in the wound by telling you that you are too sensitive.

6. They divide and conquer

Manipulators have no problems being extra friendly to a person and then talking down about them to others. This technique is used to control how others see you. It's particularly dangerous in groups of friends or with colleagues. Manipulators will also tell you what others are saying about you, often lying or exaggerating.

7. They don't stay on topic

As soon as it looks like a manipulator will have to own their emotions or actions, they'll change the subject. This is sometimes harder to spot because it seems so innocent but they are doing it to avoid accountability.

8. They will always be dissatisfied with you

No matter if you do everything they require or reach the necessary goals, they will move the goalposts and expect more. You will find that you are constantly trying to prove yourself to them and never meeting expectations.

After reading these descriptions, you might suddenly become aware that you are being manipulated and, from personal experience, feel angry at yourself. Don't be. These people have been practicing these techniques for years—it's second nature to them. What matters now is that you're wise to their behavior.

Spotting Manipulative Phrases

If you find it challenging to identify manipulative behavior, which is perfectly natural at first, there are some phrases that are commonly used.

- "I never said that."
- "You shouldn't feel like that."

- "You shouldn't think like that."
- "You're being dramatic."
- "You're overreacting."
- "You made me do it."
- "I said sorry. What else do you want from me?"
- "You're being sensitive."
- "You're being paranoid."
- "I was only joking."
- "You're imagining things."
- "Everyone thinks I'm right."

Let's put a few of these phrases into context. When someone denies saying something, it's possible that they never said what you think they said.Before accusing someone of manipulating you, make sure you are 100% sure they didn't say or do what you think they did. If there's any doubt that you may have misunderstood or if the message wasn't clear, ask for clarification.If you know that they are manipulating you, you'll be able to find strategies to handle this in the next chapter.

The Dark Psychology of Manipulation

Dark psychology focuses on the science of manipulation and control, a subject that psychologists and even criminologists use to understand problems arising from manipulation. The Dark Triad is a set of three harmful and toxic personality profiles: narcissism, psychopathy, and Machiavellianism (Paulhus & Williams, 2002). Although we've touched on The Dark Triad previously, it needs more attention in terms of manipulation. To elaborate, the Dark Triad is:

***Narcissism*:** the inflated ego, a lack of empathy, a superior sense of self

***Psychopathy*:** charming and kind, but selfish and devoid of remorse

***Machiavellianism*:** using manipulation to exploit others with no sense of morals

The Dark Triad sounds so severe that you would assume it's a type of manipulation that is less common, but it is quite the contrary. Here are some ways people use Dark Triad traits in everyday situations:

- **Love flooding or sucking up:** giving gifts, compliments, and affection before asking someone for something.
- **Telling lies:** telling partial truths, exaggerations, or just flat-out lies.
- **Withholding love and affection:** a lack of interest in the person to withholding physical contact, hugs, kisses, and sex.
- **Restricting choices:** offering two or more choices but none of them is the choice the person actually wants to make.
- **Reverse psychology:** Telling someone not to do something to encourage them to want to do it, or vice versa.
- **Using semantics:** Many words have more than one meaning depending on the context; a person can use one definition, and while the understanding is clear, the manipulator will purposely use the other meaning.

Dark psychology and the Dark Triad are quite common. Some people do not make any effort to avoid such behavior but actually teach it, for example, in some sales and marketing companies. This is the extent to which some will go to ensure their goals and needs are met above all else.

Am I Being Manipulated? Can I Avoid It?

Perhaps you have your suspicions, but you can't definitely say yes or no just yet. Being sure of yourself is the first step in understanding the principles of manipulation so that you can identify it when it occurs before it's too late.

Ask yourself the questions below. Try to be firm with yourself and only answer with yes or no. If we answer on a scale or include "maybes," we open the door to excuses for their behavior.

1. Is the situation your responsibility?

2. Will you feel good about making your decision?

3. Are you doing it to avoid feeling emotionally overwhelmed?

4. Are you scared to say no?

5. Are there any strings attached?

6. Would the other person do the same for you if the situation were reversed?

7. Is your gut telling you this is right?

You shouldn't feel obliged to do anything you don't want to do, and we all have the right to say no. If you feel something isn't in your best interest, you have to put the brakes on straight away. Boundaries and saying no are the best ways to avoid manipulation, but these aren't skills that come naturally to everyone. For this reason, we'll take a deeper look at enhancing these essential skills a little later on.

One very simple way to avoid being manipulated is to share your intentions. The more people know how you feel, what you're doing, and what your goals are, the harder it is for manipulators to control how others view you. You should also make sure that everything is documented and that you share this with others too. A manipulator in the office can't deny their responsibilities when you have sent an email telling everyone the steps you are about to take toward the office goal.

On a similar note, expand your support group. The more knowledgeable people you have in your support group, the harder it becomes for a manipulator to isolate you. What's more, with an extended group of kind, positive people around you, you can discuss and share ideas and opinions freely. This is a great strategy for increasing your perspectives and finding faith in your gut instincts.

Finally, be strong, confident, and firm. Tell the manipulator that you're aware of what they're trying to achieve and you won't tolerate it. Keep it factual rather than emotional because it's harder to deny things when there is evidence to support it. Manipulators aren't used to being called out on their behavior, so confrontation is likely, but their reaction is not your responsibility. Remember to keep your goals in mind and be proud of yourself for doing something many would just ignore.

How to Avoid Manipulating Others

In the effort to be completely accountable, it's only fair to reflect on our own behaviors and ensure that we are also not unintentionally manipulating others. Again, this isn't a sign that you are a toxic person. Manipulation can be a learned behavior, so if you grew up in a home where manipulation was common, you may not even realize you're doing it. For example, deflecting blame in an argument, needing to know where people are all the time, and expecting others to know how you feel without communicating are all forms of manipulation, albeit more subtle.

In some cases, manipulative behaviors stem from a need to be in control, and when you aren't in control, you start to feel anxious. A need for control often comes from low self-esteem, which is a great place to start. You deserve to have time to explore your hobbies and passions and discover what you excel at. Once you identify your strengths, you can begin to tame the inner critic and talk to yourself with more kindness and compassion.

For your anxiety, engage in mindfulness and meditation. Find things that bring you peace, whether curling up with a good book or spending time in nature. If you notice that your anxiety stems from perfectionism, it's essential that you let go of the idea that everything has to be perfect. There are just too many things in life beyond your control, and attempting to can only lead to more anxiety. An awesome affirmation for this is, "It's not perfect, but it's better."

Finally, learn how to listen to other people's thoughts and feelings. You may think you're paying attention, but ask yourself if you're formulating a response in your head or if you're genuinely listening to the complete message.

Effective communication is about both parties feeling understood, and this has to go both ways. Just as you wouldn't want people assuming they know how you feel, don't assume you know what they're going through.

Conflict is a given, but respecting the other person, their right to finish expressing themselves, and the right to their own beliefs and opinions can help you see things from their perspective rather than relying on learned behaviors.

Avoiding the manipulator and their tactics is one thing. Knowing you are ahead of the game and have protected yourself is empowering.

If the manipulator has made their way into your life and you aren't sure how to cope with them, we can still put a stop to it and even come out better on the other side. Our next chapter focuses on what to do when you can't avoid a manipulative person.

Putting Chapter 9 into Practice

It's possible you are still doubting whether someone is manipulating you or not. This is the time to pay attention to how a person's words make you feel.

If someone tells you they were just joking, do you feel a sense of relief, or do you feel like you have been made a fool of? Do you feel like the requests you receive are fair, or does a request cause you to feel frustrated?

Pay close attention to these feelings because they aren't signs of being overly sensitive; they are your emotions alerting you that something isn't right.

Exercise: The "Flip the Script" Test

Here's a quick gut check for when someone's request or "joke" leaves you squirming: Flip it around. Imagine you said or asked the same thing of them. How would they react? Would they laugh it off or comply easily? Or would they suddenly get defensive?

Example:

• "If I told them, 'I was only joking' after a critical comment, would they laugh or feel hurt?"

• "If I asked them to cancel plans to help me, would they even consider it?"

This little exercise is a quick way to see if they're playing fair or just playing you. Often, manipulators have one set of rules for you and a different set for themselves. If their behavior only goes one way, that's your sign.

CHAPTER 10: BEATING MANIPULATION

Now that we understand just how common manipulation is, it's clear that we can't avoid it entirely.

Preventing yourself from being subjected to these tactics would involve cutting yourself off from many people in your life, never meeting new people, and, of course, turning off all social media, news, ads, etc. Not only is this unhealthy, but you are also missing out on so many potentially wonderful experiences and relationships.

The fact is, it's okay to have manipulative people in your life as long as you know how to handle them and don't end up being controlled and dictated by them.

That doesn't mean carrying on as if nothing happened. Learning the essential skills to spot and stop manipulation is how you will take back the power over your own life and start to enjoy yourself more.

This chapter offers seven powerful tactics to show your manipulator that their behavior will not be tolerated.

But before that, let's just make sure we haven't missed any manipulative signs.

Recognizing Long-Term Manipulation

In the previous chapter, we spent a considerable amount of time reviewing how to spot manipulation before it occurs. You probably also have a good sense of when people you can't avoid are trying to manipulate you. Manipulation can be covert or overt, so either very subtle or completely self-directed. It's the act of using psychology to control others into feeling or acting in ways that go against their true self.

When we have been around a person for a long time, manipulation often blends in with other toxic behaviors, and it's not so easy to detect. Whether intentional or not, manipulators might rely on the most subtle of ways to slowly break you down. These are the most difficult to spot, especially when it involves those closest to you.

Aside from what we discussed in the previous chapter, a red flag should be waved if you notice that a person always encourages you to speak first. Although it may seem like they're just being polite, they might actually be trying to establish a baseline for your thoughts. They may even follow up with some questions, which again, seems considerate, but their intention may be for you to open up so they can find your weaknesses and then cultivate their own plan.

You should also be wary of people who always decide on the meeting place, regardless of the activity. You might want dinner here, they want it there; you want to shop at X, but they want Y; you suggest hanging out at your house, but they insist it has to be theirs. We are tempted to go along with these plans so as not to rock the boat, but they are trying to draw you out of your comfort zone and force you into locations where they have control.

There are also forms of passive-aggressive behavior that shouldn't be tolerated. One of the classics is playing dumb. This can be with any range of activities, from not knowing how to work the washing machine to not understanding your tax returns or being unable to figure out a new piece of technology. By playing dumb, the person manipulates you to do it for them because it's easier and quicker if you do it rather than explain things.

The guilt trip is another form of passive-aggressive behavior. This can appear playful at times—the bottom lip pout, a smile, and saying, "If you loved me, you would do it." A harsher form of guilt trip is to accuse others of being selfish or not caring in order to fulfill their demands.

Finally, we go back to intellectual bullying. Bombardments of facts and statistics create a sense that they know more than you do. They will then give you very little time to make a decision. Both of these tactics are because they want their own agenda to be followed instead of allowing you time to look at things from alternative points of view. This doesn't have to be only in the workplace. Friends or family can throw information at you when planning events—highlighting reasons why their plan is superior and then saying a decision has to be made immediately so that the booking can be made.

If you feel like you're acting or speaking in ways that go against who you really are or if you feel constantly drained or confused by a particular person, you will want to begin working on the following techniques to start seeing impressive changes.

7 Powerful Tactics to Overcome Manipulation

1. Know and stand up for your fundamental human rights

There are 30 basic human rights according to the Universal Declaration of Human Rights (United Nations, 1948). Some that are subject to manipulation are the right to equality in marriage, the right to own things, the freedom of thought and religion, and the freedom of opinion and expression. You also have the right to privacy.

The very first human right is that all human beings are free and equal. Nobody deserves more or less than the next person. Nobody is superior, despite how they feel or how society paints them. That being said, as we are all free to have our own opinions, the manipulator has the right to feel superior, but it's not right for them to make others feel inferior.

Article 30 states that human rights can't be taken away, which is the key to our understanding. No matter what others try to do, you have rights.

2. Keep your distance as best you can

Just because you spend eight hours a day with a colleague, live with your significant other, or are close to your family, it doesn't mean you have to feel obligated to constantly be by their side. Put some distance between you and the person and only spend the necessary time with them. Taking this step can help you gain confidence, strength, and control during the time apart, which will help you handle them in those moments you can't avoid.

3. Stop blaming yourself

There are two main categories of things we blame ourselves for: things we shouldn't feel guilty about and things that should be left in the past.

You shouldn't blame yourself for your emotions or your needs. They are what they are.

If you feel tired, happy, sad, or fed up, just own it and remember that people don't have the right to judge you. They also don't have the right to make you feel bad because you need a night in to recuperate or want a night out to have fun.

It's common for us to blame ourselves when we can't do something right or if we aren't good at something. Humans aren't supposed to be perfect. Instead of blaming yourself for what you can't do, focus on what you do well, and don't feel guilty for being proud of this.

If you have been hurt by someone you trusted, or there has been an end to a relationship, these things aren't going to change. It is crucial that we learn from our past but don't allow ourselves to keep reliving it (huffpost.com).

I know all of this is easier said than done, particularly if someone in your life constantly reminds you of what they consider to be failings. Following steps 1 and 2 will help you stop manipulators from seeing this self-blame as a weakness they can use.

4. Turn the focus back on the manipulator

Whether the manipulator is aware of their behavior or not, turning the focus back on them will allow them to see their wrongdoings or shock them into realizing you are onto their behavior. To do this, you need to ask them probing questions:

- Does this seem fair to you?
- Is what you're asking of me reasonable?
- Do I have a say in the matter?
- Are you asking me or telling me?
- What am I going to get out of this?
- Are you honestly expecting me to (restate their request)?
- Have you taken my time into consideration?
- Have you taken my opinion into consideration?

The sad fact is that a manipulator won't care about the responses to these questions because their only concern is achieving their goals. Fairness, your opinion and time, or what you will get out of it wouldn't cross their mind. On the other hand, if someone is genuinely interested in your well-being, they will take a moment to answer the questions honestly.

5. Set and establish firm consequences

Most of us have boundaries, even if we aren't fully aware that this is what they are. Our boundaries are our individual set of rules that we live by. This code of conduct comes from our values and beliefs as well as past experiences that we don't want to happen again. People's boundaries are very personal, but most of us would agree that committing a crime is a line we wouldn't cross, along with discrimination, bullying, cheating, and invading personal space. If you aren't 100% clear on what your boundaries are, you must define them now before you try to set them. Take a moment to think about past situations that have hurt you. At what point did it become too much? A peck on the cheek is one thing, but lingering there might have made you feel uncomfortable, so you're clear that this is a boundary for you.

In most personal and professional relationships, people will understand your boundaries and respect them. For a manipulator, there is no such thing as boundaries, and they will happily violate them if their needs are met.

When a person insists on crossing a line and making you feel uncomfortable, their behavior becomes toxic. To show the seriousness of boundary violations, you have to have consequences ready. For example, if a colleague is overstepping the line with physical contact, you need to tell them that if it happens again, you will report them to HR. If a family member or partner gets angry, verbally or physically abusive, let them know that you will walk away from the situation and the relationship if necessary. When friends are constantly late or don't show up, inform them that you won't make plans with them in the future.

Consequences are incredibly valuable, but only if you enforce them. For example, if your partner is yelling at you and you don't walk away, the manipulator will learn that they can continue with their negative behavior and that your boundaries don't mean anything. Only set a consequence if you know you can follow through with it.

To get better at setting boundaries and their consequences, practice what you want to say beforehand to be more confident and articulate.

6. Learn to say NO—and practice it regularly

Saying no is tough for many different reasons. The most common is that we don't want to let people down or are afraid of the other person's reaction. Another less discussed reason is that we don't like the idea that we can't do everything that is required of us. Not being able to juggle work, family life, and a social life can make us feel as if we are failing at something. Despite all of this, saying no is crucial for our mental and physical well-being, putting our needs first and reinforcing those boundaries. It's important to remember that saying no isn't a bad thing at all, but it does take practice and determination. There are a few handy tips to bear in mind when saying no:

• Decide whether you want to say yes or no—if you aren't sure, ask for more time.

• Be kind in your no, not just with the words but also with your tone and body language.

• Thank the person for considering you.

• Offer an alternative that suits you both.

• Be prepared to have to say a firmer no.

Let's expand on this with an example. Samantha's family wants her to bring her children on vacation for two weeks during the summer. Her parents have applied a bit of a guilt trip, saying that they never get to spend time with the grandkids, and who knows how much longer they'll be around! Here are two ways that Samantha could reply:

1. "Thanks for the offer. It would be a lovely trip, but I can't commit as we have plans already. We could do a week, though."

2. "No, I'm sorry. That's not going to work for me."

You can see that the first sentence is the softer way of saying no without actually having to use the word. The second sentence is firmer but still not rude or aggressive. We sometimes need to start with the kinder words and use firmer words if the person pushes back.

These are effective steps for saying no to the average person, but they might not be sufficient for the manipulators in our lives. It's rarely a good idea to explain to a manipulator why you are saying no because they will use your words against you and try to change your schedule so that you have no excuse to say no. Here are some straight-to-the-point phrases you can use to reject a demand from a manipulator.

-Thank you, but no.

-My timetable won't allow for that.

-It's not going to work for me.

-No, I can't.

-I'm too busy today, but I'm free tomorrow.

-I'm not comfortable with that.

-I have a rule not to...

-No!

-I have said no, and I meant it.

There's a chance that the person you are saying no to will get angry or create a scene. This is on them and not you. You have said no in a firm but fair way, and you don't need to justify this answer or feel guilty about it. If the person's reaction is too much for you to handle, let them know you are leaving and will talk about it again once they have calmed down.

7. Confront the bully for what they are—in the right way

Nobody wants to feel like they're being pushed around or walked all over. You can only take so much before a very unexpected and out-of-character outburst occurs. While it might feel good to get it all off your chest, when dealing with a manipulator, it's more likely that it will backfire, suggesting that you are out of control or even crazy. This is why you have to make sure that you are confronting your bully in the right way: safely, calmly, and intelligently. For this to take place, there has to be enough time to have a conversation.

Both parties need to be in the right frame of mind, and most of all, it needs to be calm. It's better to wait if you don't feel like you can control your emotions at the time. If you fear for your safety in any way, make sure that there are people around you in case things turn aggressive or violent. Your safety isn't worth sacrificing just to confront a bully, so choose the time wisely.

Not everyone is out to manipulate you, but life will become more pleasant when you can identify the behavior and master how to handle it. Those who care about you will take on board what you are saying. The changes won't occur overnight as you are changing habits that have been in place for a long time, but you will start to see the efforts bear fruit. Don't forget that a little bit of patience from your end will also go a long way. If you don't see the results you want, it's time to break away from the manipulator so that you can begin new relationships that are balanced with mutual respect.

Putting Chapter 10 into Practice

Confidence is essential when communicating with a manipulator, and I'm not a fan of pretending to be confident when you're not, as a manipulator can see through it. Instead, practice what you want to say in advance. There are plenty of example phrases you can use, but you don't need to use them all at once. Your phrase should be short and concise. The more you talk, the more chances the manipulator has to convince you that you're wrong.

Exercise: The "Pause, Then Respond" Rule

When a manipulator tries to catch you off guard, pause for two seconds before saying anything. Use this time to think, *"Do I need to respond?"* or *"What's the simplest answer?"*

Example:

- Instead of explaining, say, "I'll think about it and let you know."
- Swap "sorry" for, "Thanks for letting me know."
- Or go with a simple, "Interesting point."

That pause keeps you in control. Manipulators crave quick reactions, so slowing down throws them off their game.

CHAPTER 11: COMMUNICATION ≠ POWERLESSNESS

> *Respond intelligently even to unintelligent treatment.*
>
> — *LAO TZU*

We are now aware that there will always be toxic people in our lives. Despite eliminating them as much as possible, new relationships might be started, and it won't be possible to avoid them completely.

You may start a new job you absolutely love—except for that one colleague. You may have a loved one who goes through a traumatic experience and starts to show toxic behavior. Learning how to speak to these people is your best tool for not only survival but also empowerment.

I, like many others, have gone through many different types of relationships that were completely unhealthy. One of two things tends to happen.

The unhealthy relationship drags on for much longer than it should, or it ends, often in a messy way. In both situations, there has been a significant breakdown in communication and the crucial conversations haven't taken place.

Why Communicate?

Talking about how we feel is incredibly hard, and it often seems easier to hold it all in, even remain angry at someone instead of telling them you have been hurt. The problem is that all the words that should be said weigh you down. We are reluctant to have these conversations because of fear or dread of reactions. Perhaps, deep down, we know the relationship is over, but discussing the problems will only confirm this. That alone can prevent us from communicating.

The irony is that speaking with difficult or toxic people can relieve many of the problems and make way for a healthier relationship. Because we tend to live in our own heads and don't rarely stop to consider how we are feeling, talking about them helps you to organize your mind and better describe emotions accurately. Once you rip the initial Band-Aid off and show your vulnerability, talking about how you feel can lead the way to deeper and more meaningful conversations for both of you. It's possible that the person you are dealing with is not toxic like we have seen. It could be that they are lacking in emotional awareness and genuinely don't understand the pain they cause you. In this case, opening up can be incredibly beneficial.

On the other hand, if it doesn't solve issues, you can end the relationship in a more respectful way without it dragging on unnecessarily. This necessary conversation can bring you closure. Closure is about understanding and accepting the end of a relationship. It could mean getting answers to your questions, understanding why things happened, and learning from your situation.

Many people struggle to move forward without closure. You may feel you want the abusive person to take some responsibility for what they have done, even an admission of guilt or an apology. This is where things get tricky, depending on the level of toxicity of the other person. You might get your closure, but toxic people will rarely hold themselves accountable.

Either way, learning how to speak to these types of people will take a great weight off your shoulders, free you from their toxic behavior, and enable you to regain your power. this is how you find closure without waiting for anything from the other person. By trusting your instincts and knowing what type of person you are dealing with, you can determine how much of yourself you are willing to reveal. That being said, if you know the person is toxic, your communication may need a different approach.

7 Tips for Communicating with a Toxic Person

1. Stay cold, show no emotion

We have discussed this in the context of dealing with manipulators and sociopaths, but it applies to all toxic people. While it sounds harsh, particularly if you enjoy being warm toward others, remember that you don't have to be cold with everyone, just with those who are difficult.

The problem is that regardless of their possible mental health issues, difficult people will use any hint of their emotions to manage and control the conversation. If you were to raise your voice even slightly, they could come back at you by saying you always get angry. If you defend yourself, you're considered defensive, and if you cry, you're labeled as too emotional.

You can be honest about your purpose for the conversation, and while facts are important, remain borderline cold.

2. Do not negotiate

The phrase "We do not negotiate with terrorists" has been used in everything from government policy to films and as a popular catchphrase for good reason! It's certainly a phrase that should be constantly playing in your mind. Imagine that this person is a terrorist, making unrealistic, dangerous demands and expecting you to succumb.

Let's face it: for a very long time, probably even years, you have been negotiating with toxic people, and it hasn't led you to a good place. During your conversations with difficult people, there is no gray area, no maybes, and no middle ground. There is black or white, yes or no, depending on your needs and what your instincts are telling you. Again, it sounds harsh and complicated, but you aren't crossing the line into being nasty—you are remaining firm.

3. Stand your ground, but don't be defensive

When our character or behavior is criticized, a natural response might be to become defensive. We feel the need to justify our actions or blame others for the problem. The most dangerous response is to stop listening to what they are saying, as it will cause a breakdown in communication.

Toxic people will go to any lengths to find your defensive button. They will bring up arguments or mistakes you made way back in the past, and they will highlight a weakness that they know will hurt you the most. They do all of this to get an emotional reaction from you.

You should always stand up for yourself and not let others drag up off-topic issues just to see you suffer. At the same time, make sure you are emotionally in control and also stay on topic. Assertively tell the person that you will not be disrespected.

4. Acknowledge that it'll never actually be your turn

It's not going to be your turn to be the one who makes logical sense, to speak without interruption, and to be right. You can keep fighting, or you can choose to accept this because it's the childish game they like to play.

You have the power to rise above this! If you think you will overpower them by beating them at their own game, you are only going to sink to their level. Keep your head held high and stay firm in your expression and values, as this is how they won't be able to drain your power.

5. Keep it short and sweet

Perhaps not short and sweet, as we are still aiming for the firm, non-emotional version of you.

Short and simple —definitely.

The longer you talk, the more likely you start speaking fluff and those emotions will get involved. More often than not, when you keep it short and simple, the conversation is also a lot less dramatic.

Know what point you want to make. Your part should include the problem and the solution. Don't worry if you come across as blunt. Blunt is not the same as rude or bad-mannered. This approach allows for things to be over faster.

6. Protect your Achilles' heel

We all have our weaknesses—not your quick temper or tendency to be overprotective of your kids. Your Achilles' heel here is that one vulnerability that hurts like a stab in the back. My ex would say, "You're mentally not right," and although it doesn't sound like a big deal, she knew it was a concern of mine, and she used it to throw me off balance in any argument.

Going forward and keeping your emotions out of conversations with difficult people will help you protect your weaknesses because they won't be able to see them. For those comfortable attacking your weak spots, prepare yourself in advance. You know that they will mention it, so have some breathing techniques or a happy place to go to in your mind instead of letting them get to you. It also helps to keep your goals in mind and remember why you are having the conversation in the first place.

7. Do it for yourself and not to win

We can all admit to having moments when there is an overwhelming urge to win an argument, even if you don't even know what winning looks like.

The truth is, nobody ever really wins an argument. As soon as either party sees it as something that can be won or lost, you have lost. Another good one is, "You may have won the battle, but you haven't won the war." The point of these conversations is to improve the relationship, not to win.

Conversations with difficult people are necessary for personal growth, a better life, more balance in a relationship, and many other more crucial reasons than scoring a point. Remember that you are doing this for yourself, and this should be your primary concern.

Exact Phrases to Use When Talking with Toxic People

Much of what we have looked at up to this point has been about mental preparation. It's now time to look at specific phrases you can use in your conversations with difficult people. My advice is never to use a phrase if it doesn't feel right for you. At the end of the day, these are all great ideas, but it will be up to you to decide which phrases are best to use in the conversation you are having at that time.

Rebeca Zung, attorney and author, created an excellent video about different types of phrases you can use with toxic people. Her YouTube video **"Phrases to Disarm a Narcissist"** will really help to inspire the right words for each situation. Let's look at some examples:

We know that difficult people are going to say things to get a rise. There is no truth behind these words, and the mental preparation we have worked on allows us to recognize them as empty and meaningless. To keep the situation calm, it's sometimes necessary to agree with difficult people. Since they will be looking for a reaction, these phrases will stop them in their tracks.

- I agree with you
- Okay, if that's how you feel
- You are right

You can only use these types of responses for things that don't matter to you. If somebody attacks your beliefs, religion, or values, then you shouldn't just agree. As much as you want to continue the conversation until they see your point of view, it's not going to happen.

So, it's best to end the conversation sooner rather than later:

- I don't agree, but we both have a right to our opinions
- We will have to agree to disagree

• Your opinion will feel right to you

Some situations will require "I" sentences, as you want the listener to pay attention to how you feel rather than how they make you feel. Other times, "we" is effective.

This way, you aren't blaming them but taking responsibility for your part in the situation:

• We need to improve our communication

• We have both made mistakes

• We can work on this together

You might also want to flatter their ego because, at the end of the day, this is what they require in a relationship. Getting them to weigh in and offer their opinion shows that you value what they have to say. This can also highlight just how ridiculous their idea or behavior is.

Still, don't use these phrases if you don't agree with the plan being put forward:

• What's your opinion on this?

• Do you think this is a good plan?

• How about if we try it this way?

Toxic people have low self-esteem, and there will be times when the best solution is to recognize this and try to help them boost their self-esteem. Rather than letting them feel ignored, show them that you are listening and that what they say matters to you.

• I hear what you are saying

• I understand where you are coming from

• I respect that (and repeat the comment)

Adapt these phrases for your particular situation or the person you are dealing with. Don't forget to practice saying them aloud so that they sound natural and not forced.

Preparing Your Thick Skin for the Harsh Words They Will Use

It amazes me that in English, as well as most other languages, there are more negative words than positive. There are seven basic emotions that are recognized in most cultures: joy, fear, anger, sadness, disgust, shame, and guilt. How many do you see that are positive? It's no wonder society finds it easier to be negative than positive.

Verbal abuse is a very real thing, and the hurtful words toxic people use can have long-lasting effects. As we can't control what other people say, we can only learn to protect ourselves from this. Negative contractions like "You can't..." and "You don't..." are two obvious examples that don't appear to be that bad. However, after months or years of being told you can't do something, you start to believe it. Here are some other words that you need to prepare for so you can protect yourself:

- Dumb/stupid/fool
- Irresponsible/thoughtless/careless
- You're a failure/you're no good
- Ashamed/embarrassed by you
- You're a disappointment
- Weird/strange
- Mad/crazy/wrong in the head
- Boring/grumpy/antisocial
- Lazy/useless/inferior
- Ugly/fat/scruffy
- Arrogant/bossy
- The word "hate"

Decide now how you will respond to each of these words. If someone calls you lazy and you know it's not true, you might want to agree and ignore it. If a word hurts your feelings, like calling you ugly, you know this isn't true, but it's not fair that you should tolerate it, so stand up for yourself.

Master Your Conversation Skills

Anybody can talk, but not everyone has taken the time to master conversation skills. This is a vital skill not just for toxic people but for life.

As you start to free yourself from difficult people, you will start to create new relationships. The following conversation skills from experts will help you be the master of conversations with all types of people.

1. Really listen

We can all confess to a moment when someone was talking, and we were preoccupied with thoughts about what to eat for dinner. Listening is essential so that you can respond appropriately. Not listening leads to miscommunication and frustration.

2. Don't judge others

Everybody has their own story, their own sufferings, and their own reasons. Don't make judgments about others because we rarely know the whole story. Just as we don't like people making judgments about us, it's only fair to act the same way.

3. Be observant

It's amazing how many ways there are to start a conversation just by being observant. When you pay attention to what people wear, logos, or even colors, you can strike up a new conversation. For example, I once saw two women with travel mugs that said, "Seriously." It didn't make sense to me, but as soon as they noticed, a great *Grey's Anatomy* debate began.

4. Silence is okay

Don't feel the need to force a conversation just because you fear silence. It's perfectly normal to have breaks in a conversation, giving people a chance to focus their thoughts.

5. Have interesting things to say

On the other hand, watch out for that awkward silence! Awkward silence often occurs because people have run out of things to say. To prevent this, try keeping up-to-date on the latest news, but save the information for when the conversation runs dry. Be aware of your audience, especially when it comes to topics like religion and politics.

6. Ask for opinions

Asking for other people's opinions can give them a real confidence boost. People like to know that their opinions are valued. You can ask about restaurants, books, and TV. One word of advice, don't ask for an opinion if you aren't going to like the answer, and remember that it's alright if you don't agree.

7. Take care with humor

Humor is like conversation topics; you have to know your audience. Not everyone will share the same sense of humor, more so across different cultures. That being said, humor is a great ice-breaker, and you should feel comfortable using it. Look for some clean, politically correct jokes or stories that will please the crowd.

8. Expand your answers

One-word answers can come across as a little rude. If someone asks you a question or your opinion, expand your answer so that the conversation can be taken further.

9. Avoid question bombardment

Asking some questions can show a genuine interest in the other person. Question bombardment could make them feel like they are in an interview, and if you aren't careful, cross their boundary. As a general rule, ask questions that you would be comfortable answering.

10. Recognize the signs that the conversation is over

There is a little old lady at the end of my road, and I always take time to chat with her, but she will go on—to the extent that I am in my car and she is still talking. If you aren't capable of knowing when to end a conversation, people may be reluctant to start one with you.

Because the way we deal with difficult people will vary from relationship to relationship, we need to take a closer look at specific methods to handle parents, partners, and friends. In the next chapter, we will look at practical solutions to deal with the difficult loved ones in our lives.

Putting Chapter 11 into Practice

Don't make the mistake of pushing yourself out of your comfort zone and using phrases you wouldn't feel comfortable saying. Review this chapter and choose some powerful sentences or combine ideas to create new ones you would feel confident saying.

CHAPTER 12: DEALING WITH DIFFICULT PEOPLE

> *Peace is not the absence of conflict, it is the ability to handle conflict by peaceful means.*
>
> — *RONALD REAGAN*

In this chapter, we'll adapt the techniques from Chapter 10 for dealing with friends, partners, and family members. To recap on dealing with difficult people in general, remember to choose the right phrases for each situation. We'll look into more options for each circumstance.

Whether you're dealing with an impossible client, your overbearing parents, or your controlling partner, you'll have to think about those hurtful words they might use and prepare yourself. One of the biggest tips for dealing with difficult people is to avoid revealing your emotions, as they know just what words to use to get you to react.

Finally, becoming a master of conversation skills is going to improve relationships, particularly new ones. Your conversation skills are crucial for your personal and professional life and will increase your confidence. Keep in mind that these techniques may not always work on certain personality types. For this reason, we'll cover various personality types and the people you interact with regularly.

Powerful Phrases for Dealing with Challenging Personalities

Challenging personalities include those we have talked about, such as narcissists and manipulators, and these types of people require a special kind of treatment. If you're dealing with the most challenging types of personalities but they are making an effort to improve their behavior, these phrases may also help.

It can also be the drama queens in our lives, the suffocators, the pessimists, and the controllers. Each of these challenging personalities can appear in any area of your life. We will start with some useful phrases that can be used in a multitude of situations:

- I understand that you didn't do it on purpose, however...
- I apologize if I didn't explain myself well.
- I'm sorry that you misunderstood me.
- I do see your point of view.
- I appreciate your opinion.
- I think that we should talk about this more.
- Perhaps we can find a time to talk about a compromise.
- What do you think about this idea?
- How would you feel if we did X instead of Y?
- Let's look at the facts and keep opinions to one side for a bit.
- I respect that we see things differently, but we need to find a way to overcome this.
- I want to come up with a solution with you without interrupting each other.
- I'm glad we talked. Is there anything else you want to say?

As with the phrases we have seen before and subsequent phrases, stick to the ones that you feel comfortable with because you need to sound assertive, confident, and natural. If a phrase like "Perhaps we can find a time to talk about a compromise" is over the top for you or the person you are talking to, you could rephrase it to "Maybe we can chat and find a middle ground."

6 Steps to Effective Conflict Resolution and What Not to Do

Conflict can be both a verb and a noun. As a verb, it means to be incompatible or have differences in opinions. As a noun, it refers to a dispute or an argument. We can't shy away from conflicts or avoid them.

It's healthier to handle the conflict at the moment so that the situation doesn't escalate. Like communication skills, conflict resolution is a valuable life skill to master. To resolve conflicts, you can follow these six simple steps:

1. Put the brakes on and think

It all comes back to emotions. Someone may have said or done something that caused you pain and to feel upset. Our minds will naturally jump to the person and not the situation, and when you focus on the person, emotions have a habit of taking control over your logical side. This closes our minds and prevents us from being objective. Always pause before you speak so that you remain calm.

2. Expand your perspective

As we mature, we become better at evaluating situations from different perspectives. Putting ourselves in other peoples' shoes is a great way to get a better understanding of what is really happening and to try to see how the other person is feeling.

A great pro tip here is to play devil's advocate with yourself — disagree with your own opinion to come up with other ways of looking at the situation. Doing this might show you that, in the end, there may not even be a conflict. And if there is, you will be better equipped to handle it.

3. Agree on the problem

Next, it is time for both or all parties to define the problem. Until everyone agrees on the problem, it will be impossible for perspectives and solutions to be shared. Everyone needs to have the opportunity to agree or disagree on the definition of the issue without getting carried away with their opinions.

4. Share perspectives

The key here is to let everyone share their opinions and show they are being heard. Interrupting, checking your phone, or generally being distant is a sure way to aggravate others. Only when everyone is listening carefully to each idea you will be able to move on to solutions.

5. Respect each other's solutions

Much like the perspectives, people need to be given the chance to express their ideas to resolve the conflict. Going back to our basic human rights, everyone has the right to their opinion, and therefore, each must be respected. After solutions have been discussed, you can then look at the potential for compromise.

6. Agree on the final solution

Once everyone has been a little flexible, a solution to keep everyone happy can be reached. It's worth emphasizing the solution and ensuring that the person or people understand and have said all they feel they have to. End the conversation on a positive note, such as, "I'm really happy we worked this out, and I know we can do it again if necessary." (Everson, 2014)

Aside from what you should do, there are also a few things that you shouldn't do when trying to resolve conflicts:

• Avoid using extreme adverbs of frequency like always and never. They may come across as exaggerating and blowing things out of proportion.

• Don't stew on matters. The longer you think about something, the bigger it is likely to become, and then it becomes easier to drag irrelevant matters into the conflict.

• Pick a time that also suits the other parties. We often talk about choosing a time when you are calm, but it's only fair that you ask someone if you can have a few minutes when they are free to ensure they are in the right frame of mind too.

• Don't assume anything. When you assume you have understood everything or you assume that they have, there is a great possibility that everyone walks away thinking a problem has been solved when it hasn't.

Dealing with Difficult Parents

Take a moment to think about how you view your parents. I know this changes as we grow up, even more so when you have your own children. However, we tend to forget that our parents are actually only humans, just as we are. We set high expectations for them because, after all, they should know better. Aren't they always telling us this?

When you take away the parent element, they are subject to the same emotions, struggles, and conflicts that we are. The difference is that they have to live with the fear of their mistakes being judged by their children. The first step in dealing with difficult parents is to remember that they are human and to lower your expectations. If you know that a sociopathic friend isn't going to change, why would you expect a sociopathic parent to?

When it comes to our parents, one of the most common manipulative techniques they use is the guilt trip. They will likely ask you to do something, and when you say no, there will be some pushback. When you stand your ground, the big guns come out. You might have to put up with phrases like "It's okay! It's not like I raised you for over 18 years," or "Your cousin would never put your aunt in a home."

The most blindingly obvious are "You owe me" and "If you love me..." and yet we still fall for them. You need to put a stop to this emotional manipulation. They love you, you love them, and nobody needs to prove that. What you should do is tell them you know what they are trying to do and that it will no longer work.

If you're still looking for your parent's approval, it's time to overcome this. Parents often don't approve of the decisions their adult child makes; you may even feel like they are trying to relive their life through yours. They may withhold approval as a form of punishment or simply because they are unable to support their children because of a lack of emotions. As soon as you stop looking for your parents' approval, your dealings with them will become simpler, and asserting yourself will get easier.

On that note, be assertive with difficult parents. It's not rude or disrespectful because you can still be polite, even caring. At the same time, you can be honest and use "I" statements to express your feelings. Let go of any assumptions; they may listen, they may not. The point is that you stop allowing them to control your life—empower yourself and decide on the level of contact you are comfortable with.

Power Phrases to Deal with Difficult Parents

- I'll always respect you, but I have thought about this carefully.
- I feel suffocated when you won't give me space.
- It's great that you want to help me at home, but there should be limits.
- I know you're frustrated, but you can't take that out on me.
- I can't make plans this weekend, but I would like to do something next weekend.
- I will not tolerate you insulting me.
- If you keep crossing the line, I won't come over for dinner.
- It's fine if you don't agree with my opinions, but you do need to respect them.

Tips for Confronting Partners

Just because your partner is difficult doesn't mean the relationship is doomed. There are still reasons why you fell in love and plenty to look forward to once you have learned how best to deal with them while guarding your own happiness. This starts with being very clear about what your reality is, understanding your emotions, and realizing your boundaries.

Being clear on these matters will stop you from playing into their reality, allowing them to make you feel as if they are always the victim. Understanding your emotions better can help you avoid getting sucked into the same type of behavior. Your emotional intelligence will keep you on the right path so you don't join in with their negativity.

Take some time to talk to your partner about their feelings. They may have some bottled-up emotions that are causing their toxic behavior. While you are being compassionate, you have to remember that it's not your place to fix them. They have to want to do this! The conversation also has to be balanced, so you should also have the chance to talk about your feelings. As soon as your partner starts to raise voice, become aggressive, or you feel threatened in any way, it's time to walk away—at least for long enough to calm down.

You must resolve the conflict with a difficult partner. Don't just assume that the issue has been resolved now that you are both calm. Burying it only means that it may resurface in the next conflict.

You're going to need the thickest skin possible for difficult partners. We open our hearts up to them, we trust them, and it's incredibly painful when partners use words to break our spirits. I like to imagine it as a mental game of tennis, with every insult or lie being the balls, and my mind is the tennis racket hitting them away from me. You can also practice deep breathing to help the words flow away from you. Do not take this personally, and remember that it is not your fault.

Power Phrases to Deal with Difficult Partners

• I know we have both had a long day, but let's find time later to talk.

• I love that you want to spend time with your parents, but I need to spend time with mine too.

• If you are going to be home late, please let me know. That way I won't have to worry.

• You can choose between the laundry or vacuuming. Which do you prefer?

• I don't appreciate it when you disrespect my authority in front of the children.

• I have asked you not to raise your voice. If you continue, I will leave.

• I am here for you, and I want to help, but we have to be in this together.

• I want to see your point of view, but I can't when you're angry and shouting.

Handling Tough Talks with Friends

The first thing to consider is what type of friend you are dealing with. Friends of friends and acquaintances who are toxic, you should just walk away from. Life is too short to let these types of people impact your life. Our tips will help with any depth of friendship, but consider which friends deserve your energy.

The best thing about friendships is that there usually isn't such a close tie as there is with your partner or parents because you aren't living with them. It doesn't mean the relationship isn't just as important; it's like the middle path. More often than not, you have known them for years, even longer than your partner, but they know you differently from your parents. Friends are a great place to start practicing communication skills and setting boundaries.

Like with all conflicts, you need to begin by understanding how you feel and the cause of your unhappiness. Know what you want to say and practice it a few times, preferably in the mirror so you can see your body language. You need to check that your shoulders are straight and that you aren't hunched over. Your arms and legs shouldn't be crossed so that you appear open. Don't forget to smile! As well as coming across as confident, you want to seem approachable.

Call your friend to arrange a time and place that is convenient for both of you. This place should be free from distractions, so make it a coffee shop but not your usual spot. It's important that you meet rather than try to deal with the problem via text or call because it's easy to misunderstand each other.

Use the sandwich technique: start with something kind and positive, then address the issue directly. Your friend needs to understand the root of the problem and how it makes you feel, but they don't need to see you getting emotional. Getting angry will only make matters worse. Encourage your friend to respond with their perspective and feelings and pay attention! Finish your "sandwich" by ending on positives, making new plans, or talking about the good parts of your friendship.

Power Phrases to Deal with Difficult Friends

- I'm sorry if this seems insignificant to you, but...
- I love that I can speak honestly with you.
- I feel like you ignore me when I try to talk about my situation.
- I need some time before I make a decision.
- I have so much fun with you, but I get upset when...
- I know that you're angry, but shouting isn't going to help.
- It hurts when you laugh at my flaws.
- I see where you are coming from; however, I would like it if you could understand my point of view.

Tackling Family Conflicts

Family members who aren't parents are a little bit like friends. The conflicts that arise are still going to cause you stress, but it's somewhat easier to limit your contact and even break ties if necessary. It's always worth trying one more time to get the relationship back on track with the new knowledge you have. Begin by deciding if this difficult family member is caring and doing it in the wrong way or if they are just pure toxic. If you feel that they are toxic and manipulative, then follow the techniques we looked at before. If it's a family member trying to control you, smother you, or treat you in ways that hurt you or make you feel uncomfortable, it's time to work on strengthening your boundaries.

You may have already tried to establish your boundaries with family members, but it's possible that they didn't take you seriously. It might also mean that you weren't sure about your boundaries yourself, which is why others are crossing them. If you firmly believe that you know what your boundaries are and you have expressed them clearly, you now know that your consequences aren't in place.

One tip that works really well is to listen to family members as if it's the first time. After so many years of hearing the same thing, we tend to tune out the same nagging and complaining, and we start to switch off. Remember that even though they have said the same thing numerous times, you should listen like it's the first time because you are a different person now. You are mentally stronger, you are calm and in control of your emotions, and you will listen with a new perspective and new insights on how to handle the situation (www.harleytherapy.co.uk).

Power Phrases to Deal with Family Members

• I respect that you have more experience, but I am going to do things my way.

• I have explained before that I don't like it when you show up unannounced.

• When I say no, it's to the activity, not to you.

• I need some time to myself this weekend, but I can help you during the week.

• I need you to understand that if you insist on insulting me, I won't join in with your plans.

• If you are upset about something, I am here for you, but I won't listen if you are going to shout.

• My intention isn't to hurt you, but I don't intend to walk on eggshells.

• I am hurt by your nasty words, and I'm offering you a chance to talk about what is bothering you.

Tips for Confronting Difficult Colleagues

We often try to take on the attitude of walking out of the office and leaving work behind. If we are honest with ourselves, what goes on during those eight hours at work has a habit of following us and even impacting our personal relationships. I'm sure I'm not the only one who has experienced a colleague behaving in a toxic way at work, and then I go home and take it out on a loved one.

You may have dedicated years to your career, you have to put yourself first. Isn't it only fair that you put your career, your responsibilities, and your reputation first? Toxic colleagues will do anything to make you look bad so that they either look better or you feel bad about yourself. The end goal is to advance their own career.

As soon as you spot difficult people in your workplace, you have to put a stop to it right away before it escalates. Even if the behavior seems trivial —taking your stapler, for example—it could be the start of something more troublesome.

The most professional method of dealing with difficult colleagues is to strictly follow the six steps we mentioned earlier. So, stop and think, expand your perspectives, agree on the problem, and share perspectives. Respect the ideas that people put forward and agree on the final solution, remembering that some compromise will have to be made.

Timing is even more crucial when dealing with difficult colleagues. Although you have outstanding communication skills, your colleague may not. To avoid making a scene, you shouldn't call people out on their behavior, for example, in the middle of a meeting.

One thing that won't do you any favors is gossiping about the problem to others. Unfortunately, you are using toxic behavior to try and beat toxic behavior. If you need to communicate issues with management, do so in an informative way rather than gossiping. Take time to prepare what you need to say without any fluff.

Regardless of who you are dealing with, people are busy and don't need lengthy discussions for something that could be dealt with in five minutes. If you are doing it by email, reread the email before hitting send to ensure everything is included in one go to prevent frustration for the reader if a second email is needed.

You may have heard that in relationships, you should never go to bed angry with each other. Try to follow the same motto at work. Be the bigger person, and at the end of the day, let them know that it was great to clear the air or thank them for listening. Aim for both of you to go home as if the situation is resolved.

Don't forget to keep records of everything, especially when things start impacting other staff members. If you have a conversation with someone, following up with an email recapping the key points is a good idea.

This is a good way to double-check that you are both on the same page, but you should also have a digital copy in case your integrity is questioned later down the line.

Power Phrases to Deal with Colleagues

- I want to talk to you about a matter impacting the whole team.

- It bothers me when you criticize me in front of others.

- I don't find that kind of humor suitable for the office.

- I understand you might be comfortable bending the rules, but it's not fair to the others.

- Please avoid sending non-work-related messages and emails, as I'm too busy to read all of them.

- I like my colleagues, and I don't want to hear unkind things about them.

- I will not tolerate backstabbing and mind games in order to advance your career.

- I know you are very smart and experienced, but I also have valuable opinions that I would like you to consider.

Troubleshooting: Putting the Techniques into Context

Let's take a look at three different situations and how we could effectively resolve conflicts, even though efforts have been made before.

Laura suspects her partner, Anthony, is withdrawing emotionally. He often comes home late, citing work obligations, and their once vibrant conversations have dwindled to mundane exchanges. Feeling neglected, Laura's mind races to the conclusion that he might be involved with someone else. Rather than addressing her concerns directly, she starts suggesting activities to reconnect, which only makes her seem clingy and further alienates Anthony. As a result, Laura becomes more anxious and frustrated.

To address this situation effectively, Laura should first consider various perspectives, including the worst-case scenario. Instead of fixating on the possibility of infidelity, she should think practically about what separation would mean for her life. Preparing for a constructive conversation is crucial, so she should find an appropriate time to talk, ideally when both are relaxed. It's important that this conversation doesn't feel threatening or dramatic.

In the meantime, Laura can organize her thoughts using phrases like:

- "I've been feeling a bit disconnected lately, and I'd like to understand what's going on between us."
- "I realize I might not have communicated my feelings well, but I hope we can share our perspectives."
- "I appreciate how hard you're working, but I feel our relationship needs attention too."
- "I'd like to hear about what's been stressing you out so I can better support you."

There's a possibility that Anthony might respond by saying he feels overwhelmed with work and hasn't known how to share that with her. Conversely, he could express that he's feeling emotionally distant due to personal issues unrelated to their relationship.By jumping to conclusions and trying to read Anthony's mind, Laura has made a common mistake: assuming the worst without fully understanding his perspective. A healthy conversation, rooted in openness and curiosity, can help clear misunderstandings and strengthen their bond.

Jimmy is fed up with his loud-mouthed colleague who belittles everyone but then sucks up to management. He's like a real Jekyll and Hyde, and you never know which side of him you're going to see. Jimmy has made sarcastic cracks about his coworkers' behavior, but any criticisms are like water off a duck's back. As the boss starts to show favoritism toward the brownnoser, the tension in the office starts to rise. This colleague has no interest in rectifying his behavior because he has a strict timeline for his career advancement.

Sarcastic and even direct comments have no effect, so Jimmy has to find ways to make sure that tasks and responsibilities remain fair in the office so that even though the behavior may frustrate people, it won't affect the team's productivity. Obviously, there is little point in speaking to the boss as the colleague has manipulated how the boss views things. Jimmy comes up with a plan to introduce project management software and speaks to team members who are also looking to resolve this behavior. Using project management software, every team member is delegated tasks and deadlines, and it's easy to see who is doing what and when. The boss gets a complete overview, and there is a digital copy of tasks and communications.

Lisa has always enjoyed a close relationship with her brother, Mark. They share many interests and often hang out together. However, Mark has started making offhand comments about Lisa's career choices and personal life, which she initially brushed off as jokes. Over time, these remarks have become increasingly hurtful, leading to tension in their family gatherings.

After several uncomfortable moments, Lisa decides it's time to talk to Mark about how his comments affect her. When she first approaches him, he dismisses her feelings, claiming she's just being overly sensitive. This reaction leaves Lisa feeling frustrated and questioning whether she's overreacting. To prepare for a deeper conversation, Lisa reflects on their past interactions and realizes that Mark's comments have been consistent and unwelcome. She decides to approach him again, this time focusing on her feelings rather than accusations.

During their conversation, Lisa uses "I" statements to communicate her feelings: "I feel hurt when you make jokes about my job. It makes me doubt my choices." She also asks Mark if anything is going on in his life that might be causing him to act this way, opening the door for a more honest discussion.

Finally, Lisa sets a clear boundary: "I'm okay with light teasing, but if your comments continue to hurt me, I'll need to limit our time together." This way, Lisa not only protects her feelings but also encourages Mark to reflect on his behavior and consider the impact it has on their relationship.

With the majority of difficult people, these techniques will get to the bottom of the problems and allow you to move forward, with the option to readdress issues in the future if need be. It's up to you to decide whether these people are making efforts to improve their behavior or not. If some time passes and you see the same behaviors repeated, or your levels of stress have not improved, it's time to consider creating distance between you or breaking contact completely.

I know we are always hopeful that people will change, but it's essential to remember that the emotional strains you feel won't just disappear overnight. The longer the conflict goes on, the harder it can be to overcome in the long run.

Putting Chapter 12 into Practice

Think about some conflicts you have had in the past, preferably within different types of relationships such as romantic, work, and family. With the information you now have from this chapter, how would you have handled these conflicts? What would you have said for each response the other person gave you?

CHAPTER 13: EMOTIONAL ABUSE: YOUR GUIDE

> *Emotional abuse poisons a relationship and infuses it with hostility, contempt, and hatred.*
>
> — *BEVERLY ENGEL*

Our focus up to now has been on techniques and strategies for the difficult and toxic people in our lives. This is only the first half of taking back control of your life and becoming happy.

The impact these people leave on you doesn't just disappear because you have mastered how to handle them. There are both long-term and short-term effects of emotional abuse that need to be addressed.

This chapter marks the beginning of focusing on you to emotionally cleanse yourself and be ready for a fresh start.

It's possible you might not even be aware of the damage caused by this toxic behavior. Emotional abuse isn't like physical abuse. There are no cuts and scars to see.

Awareness of emotional abuse is essential so that you can focus your energy in the right direction for a positive change.

The Short-Term Side Effects of Emotional Abuse

Initially, you might be completely taken aback by your loved one's behavior, especially if something has happened out of the blue. You might feel shocked and confused. Male or female, you may find yourself crying frequently. It's important to be careful that this doesn't have a knock-on effect on your sleep. A lack of sleep can quickly become a physical problem and make it harder to take care of your emotional needs.

It's perfectly normal to feel anxious or even scared about not knowing what sort of behavior is going to come next. If the anxiety isn't controlled, it may turn into panic attacks, again a physical reaction to fear or anxiety. Signs of a panic attack include sweating, chills or hot flashes, dizziness or trembling, heart palpitations, and hyperventilation.

Short-term side effects of emotional abuse can go from one extreme to another. You might find yourself becoming aggressive (a defense mechanism after abuse), or you can end up feeling completely helpless as if you can't do anything right. Your confidence may be so shattered that you avoid eye contact or become more passive than usual.

Some people will feel a mixture of hopelessness and powerlessness. Though similar, they aren't the same. Being powerless means you aren't able to change a situation while being hopeless means losing all hope for change.

While unfounded, people who have been abused often feel guilty, as if it's their own fault. Or it's possible to feel shame and humiliation, questioning why you "let" the abuse happen, although your logical mind will tell you that you didn't let anything happen as the behavior is the responsibility of the other person.

Finally, in the short term, you may struggle with feelings of loneliness. If it's a partner, assuming you will remain alone for the rest of your life is common. If the abuser is a friend, you may also start to question your other friendships. Not surprisingly, abused people can feel unloved and unattractive.

You have probably taught yourself how to put on a brave face, to push those emotions down so that others around you can't see your suffering. Eventually, though, you won't be able to hide the emotional toll of abuse, nor should you. On the one hand, it's not fair to you. On the other hand, there are still people in your life who care about you and don't want to see you suffering in this way.

The strain of emotional abuse can lead to moodiness. I know from my own experiences that this only makes you feel worse because now you have the guilt of snapping at others who might not have done anything wrong. Aside from anxiety causing you to miss out on that all-important sleep, you might find yourself having bad dreams, even nightmares.

Because of the lack of sleep and the emotional strain you are under, it won't be long before you find it difficult to concentrate. No matter how hard you try to focus on, for example, work, your mind will shoot back to the problems you have been through.

Some people will suffer from headaches or muscle tension, particularly across the neck and shoulders. It's almost as if you can feel the emotional abuse building up in your muscles.

And, yes, these aches and pains may also affect your sleep.

The Long-Term Side Effects of Emotional Abuse

If left unresolved, the short-term side effects won't just disappear. It's more probable that they will escalate into something more serious. All of the short-term side effects can quickly manifest into heightened anxiety and/or depression. Sleep disturbances can lead to further emotional instability and also contribute to the lack of energy you may be experiencing. The first waves of low self-esteem can develop into more serious problems such as social anxiety and withdrawal. Difficulties in concentration can become more severe and impact your ability to remember things and make the right decisions.

Watch out for denial. This is a good one because so many people fail to understand the depression spectrum. You might experience a profound sense of sadness or emptiness and deny the fact that it could be depression. While many imagine depression as great bouts of heavy, pessimistic thoughts and feelings, there are various types, ranging from constant sadness to thoughts of suicide or attempted suicide. Let's take a quick look at some of the most common types of depression:

Major depression: Also referred to as clinical depression and is characterized by experiencing symptoms mentioned above for the majority of the time and on most days.

Persistent depressive disorder: A depression that lasts for two or more years is defined as persistent, which can also be broken down into dysthymia (low-grade persistent depression) or chronic major depression.

Manic depression: The preferred term today is bipolar disorder, but it involves feeling extremely energetic and positive one minute and then experiencing low moments of major depression.

Seasonal affective disorder: Appropriately abbreviated to SAD, this type of major depression occurs during months that have less light.

Psychotic depression: When the symptoms of major depression are accompanied by psychotic symptoms like hallucinations, delusions, and paranoia.

Postpartum depression: Postpartum depression is often related to giving birth, but that's not to say that toxic relationships won't contribute. It's also important to recognize that this is not just a type of depression that women suffer from. Approximately 1 in 10 men experience postpartum depression in the weeks and months after the arrival of a baby (WebMD, 2020).

Situational depression: Also known as stress response syndrome, certain major events in our lives can cause large amounts of stress and depression.

Atypical depression: As the name implies, this is not the typical depression of constant sadness or feeling low. Your mood will improve with positive things that occur in life, though this burst of happiness isn't permanent.

Regardless of the severity of your depression, you must visit your doctor. There are so many types of therapies available today, not just antidepressants. You aren't going to just "shake it off" or get over it, and the last thing you want to do is ignore depression so that it gets to the point where you consider ending your own life. Speaking from the heart, it is never as bad as you think as long as you are open to getting some help, and there is no shame in getting this help. It's almost impossible to see the silver lining right now, but it will only get better from here on because you have chosen it to be this way.

Traumatic events and stress can both lead to insomnia. To be diagnosed with a sleep disorder, insomniacs will have sleep difficulties for a minimum of three nights a week for three months. These sleep difficulties can be related to falling asleep, staying asleep, or both. It's estimated that one-third of adults show symptoms of insomnia, and 6-10% meet the criteria for insomnia disorder (American Psychiatric Association, 2013). Insomnia is very much linked to mood swings and irritability, and it's going to impact your ability to concentrate.

We all experience some unexplainable pain every now and again, and because it's physical, we don't relate it to the emotional abuse that we have been through. The nervous system keeps sending pain signals even though there is no reason for them. This can sometimes be in the same area as an old injury that healed a long time ago, or it could be completely random. Research shows that there is a connection between trauma and chronic pain. There is a theory behind this: the body has been so used to a heightened stress response because of the dangerous or toxic environment, and the response to the stress becomes abnormal and manifests into pain.

There are also many links between the long-term effects of emotional abuse. Chronic pain can be linked to depression, insomnia impacts concentration, and that overall feeling as if you have no energy or motivation. Both insomnia and chronic pain have connections to post-traumatic stress disorder (PTSD). Children who were exposed to abuse and went on to suffer from PTSD showed worse pain-related functioning and the ability to manage routine tasks. Between 60-90% of people with PTSD also suffer from insomnia (Ohayan, 2000). Those with PTSD are also more likely to attempt suicide, with one study showing around 27% of sufferers having attempted suicide at some point in their lives (Ramsawh, Fullerton, Mash, 2014).

The final long-term effect of emotional abuse is social withdrawal. Human beings are social creatures—pack animals, so to speak. We need social interactions to improve our mood, increase brain health, and boost our sense of security. When our emotional self has taken a severe beating, so do our confidence and self-esteem. You might find that you are no longer keen on doing your old hobbies and activities, closing yourself off from people.

The lack of energy discourages you from going out with friends, and overall, you are not comfortable in social situations. It might seem safer to stay away from people to prevent getting hurt again. However, the opposite will happen. We should distance ourselves from those who are toxic and surround ourselves with positive, supportive people to build up our strength and benefit from social interactions.

Both short- and long-term side effects are interconnected and may not neatly fit into specific categories. Many of the symptoms will be linked. You may experience only one or two symptoms or any number of them at once. In the next chapter, we will look into the different ways you can begin the healing process from emotional abuse.

Misconceptions About Emotional Abuse

Myths and misconceptions are extremely dangerous. They can make people think that emotional abuse is limited to a certain type of person or isn't as bad as other types of abuse. When you think of emotional abuse, it's easy to imagine a female being abused by her partner. With this misconception, people don't see emotional abuse in other situations. Though women are more likely to suffer emotional abuse, it's something that occurs in all types of relationships and all genders.

Without understanding the cycle of abuse, people think that the abused don't want to do anything about it, or worse, they actually like it. Breaking free from emotional abuse is complex, and myths about it can diminish the effects and question the severity of the abuse. These misconceptions take away accountability, letting the abuser get away with their behavior.

Another myth is that some behaviors with emotional abuse are attractive or affectionate. Some confuse controlling with BDSM (Bondage and Discipline/Domination and Submission and Sadism and Masochism), which only confuses our understanding of the culture. BDSM requires respect and above all, consent—abuse doesn't (National Network to End Domestic Violence, 2016). Constant calling and texting or needing to spend excessive time with someone isn't a sign of love, it's a lack of trust and an attempt at controlling another person.

It's essential that myths and misconceptions about emotional abuse are addressed so that behaviors don't continue to be normalized. Don't be scared to correct others who are confused about emotional abuse.

From Their Eyes

This is by no means a justification for abusive behavior, nor does it give them an excuse for the way they treat you. This moment to take perspective can help you understand more about your own experiences. There are various reasons why a person becomes abusive, and it might not be because they have a mental or personality disorder. It's possible that emotional abuse is caused by their own childhood and witnessing emotional abuse as normal. There could be a lot of pent-up anger, and they can't control it.

In some cases, the abuser may have issues with their own emotions. Aside from a lack of empathy, they might be afraid, and this fear could be fueling their need for control.

Their emotional abuse may be a defense mechanism. It's as if they feel they have been backed into a corner, and the only way involves being abusive—again, not your fault.

A lack of boundaries is another potential reason. Your abuser sadly may not understand your limits because they can't see you as a separate entity. It's hard for them to understand that you have the right to space and other boundaries.

I can't stress enough that this is not an excuse for abusive behavior, but they might just be at the end of their tether. Stress and exhaustion build up, and they lash out when they can't take any more. Nevertheless, we can all go through times like this. The difference is that the abuser doesn't have healthy coping strategies.

Finally, there are times when the abused becomes the abuser, known as reactive abuse. When someone is abused, emotionally or physically, their fight-or-flight response kicks in, and as a defense mechanism, they become abusive to protect themselves.

Paul had been in an abusive relationship where his girlfriend constantly made him feel worthless. He was never right, his opinions were belittled, and nothing he did was good enough compared to his girlfriend's ex.

Eventually, Paul ended up shouting at his girlfriend and even aggressively punching tables and walls, which was completely against his character.

In the case of reactive abuse, it's not entirely the fault of the person, and you may even find that you have also started reacting to emotional abuse. It's necessary to take a step back, accept responsibility, and make changes. This could mean discovering your own coping mechanisms as well as overcoming your emotional abuse.

I know I'm repeating myself, but it's that important—if you have any concerns, don't hesitate to contact a medical professional.

Nothing is too trivial, and with such a wide range of support available today, the benefits of taking better care of yourself and seeking professional help will speed up your healing process and make sure you stay on the right track.

Putting Chapter 13 into Practice

Spend some time tracking symptoms of emotional abuse. Notice how the abuse makes you feel, not just in the moment but also afterward. Jot down moments when you felt dismissed or drained after an interaction—what was said, how you felt, and how it affected the rest of your day or other relationships. Before you can start to heal, you need to understand exactly what needs to be healed!

Exercise: The "Three Strikes" Rule

Some people love to test your limits, but here's a simple policy to keep things clear: the "Three Strikes" rule. Each time this person behaves in a way that's dismissive, manipulative, or downright rude, give them a mental "strike."

After three strikes, make a conscious decision to shift the way you interact—whether that means setting tighter boundaries, reducing contact, or just treating them as a fascinating case study in what *not* to put up with. This rule isn't about punishing them—it's about protecting you.

CHAPTER 14: HEALING FROM EMOTIONAL ABUSE

> *Healing doesn't mean the damage never existed. It means the damage no longer controls our lives.*
>
> — *AKSHAY DUBEY*

This chapter will be short but highly influential. We have carefully looked at the impacts of emotional abuse and have compiled 20 tips on how to overcome these side effects as you start to put more and more distance between you and your toxic environment:

1. Acknowledge the abuse

The negative emotions connected with abuse can often lead us into a state of denial, shame, and even humiliation. Because of this, it's easier to ignore the symptoms of abuse rather than admit they are occurring. If you don't recognize that it's broken, you won't be able to start fixing it—or, in this case, healing.

2. Define a healthy relationship

If you have been trapped in an unhealthy relationship for a long time, it's hard to see clearly what constitutes a healthy one. Whether it's a partner, friend, or family member, you should be able to say no without feeling bad, express your needs and feelings openly, and be able to resolve conflicts. It's also true that there will be personal aspects that you would like to see in your healthy relationships, such as humor or equality.

3. Make a choice

Abuse is a cycle: we say no, and they apologize, although they never really mean it or fake change for a while before the abuse starts again. Only you have the power (and you do have this power within you) to stop the cycle. Make this necessary choice, own it, be proud of it, and above all, stick to it.

4. Be safe

If you fear for your safety in any way, even the slightest bit, you need to find a safe place. It's tough, but staying could result in you or your children ending up in the hospital, and that's never worth staying for. If you don't have a friend or family member you trust, you can reach out to the police and/or local support groups. Try searching for support groups in your area on Facebook.

5. Find your support group

Support comes in many shapes and sizes, even in places you might not imagine. Professional help is a great place to start for emotional healing.

If you aren't comfortable talking to people you know, Facebook groups are an excellent example of people coming together to help each other. Even your neighbors can provide a listening ear and sound advice.

6. Commit to not being a victim

Write a letter of commitment to yourself. I understand that some might feel this is a little corny, but you may be pleasantly surprised by the benefits.

A commitment letter can be a list of "I will not" statements. For example, "I will not let others dictate my life," or "I will not tolerate the silent treatment."

7. Remind yourself that you aren't responsible for the toxic person

We have said enough times that you are not responsible for a toxic person's behavior, but in fact, you aren't responsible for them at all. They are fully functioning adults who also have choices. Don't allow them to manipulate you into staying or doing things because they need you, or they can't survive without you, as this is not a healthy relationship.

8. Process and share your abuse

Some people like physical activities to process their abuse. I find swimming extremely mind-cleansing and makes me feel physically better. Others turn to art, music, or journaling. Sharing your abuse with your support group is a wonderful way to process what you have been through, with nobody judging you.

9. Be kind to your physical self

Your body needs you right now more than ever. Taking care of your body is all part of self-care, and it's often the simple things that will make a big difference, like eating well, drinking plenty of water, and resting when necessary.

Go for a walk and take in nature, meditate, or enjoy a relaxing bath. Take time to do the things you enjoy, whether reading a book or watching a movie. Don't forget to see a doctor about your physical and emotional symptoms.

10. Remember your triggers and boundaries

While we have discussed both at length, these strategies are essential for your recovery. Once you have recognized your triggers and determined your boundaries, remember to check in with them regularly to see if they need updating.

11. Speak up about what you won't tolerate

Another part of breaking the cycle of abuse is to stand up for yourself about the behavior you won't tolerate. Toxic people rely on the fact that you allow them to insult or hurt you so that they feel better. As soon as you put a stop to this, you will notice more balance in the relationship.

12. Understand that it is not your fault

You can admit to making mistakes in the way you have handled toxic people in the past, but that doesn't mean the situation is your fault. It's more than likely that the toxic individuals in your life have a mental disorder—you didn't create this, nor did you encourage it.

13. Let go of guilt and shame

Similarly to the situation not being your fault, there is no reason for you to feel guilt or shame. Processing your traumatic experiences will help you to work through these feelings, enabling you to move on.

14. Find things that make you happy

It has probably been a while since you took the time to do things that make you happy, and you may even have forgotten exactly what that is. Think back to a time in your life before the toxicity. What did you enjoy doing? Are there things that you have always wanted to try? You don't have to spend a lot of money. It could be something as simple as getting in the car and exploring a new area, learning how to cook, or starting a new series.

15. Decide who you can trust

It's normal to be in a stage where you don't trust anyone. While there are abusers and the abused, there are also many other people in the world who are neither. Create two lists—one with the people you can trust and one with those you can't. It won't happen overnight, but gradually, work on allowing yourself to trust these people.

16. Get comfortable with being alone

There is a fine line between spending some quality time alone and social withdrawal. The goal is not to learn how to do everything alone. It's to be comfortable doing everyday things alone before you build up to the bigger things. Time alone increases empathy, productivity, creativity, and mental strength. Enjoy the peace of going for a walk in silence, and work your way up to dining alone. I must say, one of the most empowering experiences in my life was going on vacation alone.

17. Discover ways to build your confidence

Every strategy you try is a step toward a more confident you. Finding your happiness will also start to boost your confidence, but for now, stop comparing yourself to others. Be careful of social media because people rarely post the real version of events, and we end up looking at other people's lives and wishing we were more like them. We never know what's really going on behind each post, so redirect your energy to your own life. Write to-do lists to track the things you are achieving.

18. Give yourself time

They don't call it long-term side effects for no reason. Your commitment and determination are commendable, and you should be proud of this. However, allow time for healing. For some, it could take a couple of months, and for others, it might be years. There is no race! The most important thing is that you are making progress.

19. Keep track of your decision-making skills

This is a great reminder of just how far you have come. You may have noticed that, in the early days, you would question everything, particularly if your abuser was a gaslighter. This would have caused you to doubt your instincts. A lack of sleep and emotional strain also impact your decision-making skills. But, as you start to let go of your emotional abuse, you will realize that your decision-making is more reliable, another way to boost your confidence.

20. Find what works for you

This book is full of advice for not only different types of abuse but also different types of personalities. I know people who have been helped by antidepressants and others who didn't experience any difference; for others, therapy was the solution. You might laugh at the idea of meditation, but the next person can't see how a 4-hour hike helps. We are all individuals and should respect that we will heal in various ways. Give each technique time before disregarding it, and take notes in your journal on the impact of the different strategies you try.

It might be that one technique has a different effect in six months, so it's beneficial to keep track.

Overcoming Anxiety and Depression After Emotional Abuse

People often forget just how complex anxiety and depression are. It's not a simple case of waking up in the morning and changing your mindset. There are techniques like deep breathing and mindfulness that can help relieve the symptoms and allow you the chance to find your strength, but at the same time, it's perfectly normal if you need additional help, and this is where your support system is vital.

When you think of a support system, your mind might jump to friends and family, and while this is a great starting point, it's not always the best for emotional abuse recovery. Our friends and family are some of the most intimate relationships we have, and this can mean that you aren't always comfortable opening up for fear of their reaction. The fear of showing your vulnerabilities to these people can be enough to put you off opening up.

A support system is a network of people who provide an individual with practical or emotional support (Merriam-Webster, n.d.). When you consider this definition, your support system could be made up of a wide range of people, even animals. Research has shown that pet owners are less likely to suffer from depression and have lower blood pressure when dealing with stress (Robinson & Segal, n.d.). That's not to say you should rush out and get a pet if you aren't in the position to take care of one, but spending time with animals can still be a part of your support network if it brings you relief from intense emotions.

When you don't feel comfortable discussing things with people close to you, there are still others who can form part of your support network. There are two main ways to do this: in person and online. For a more personal approach, you can try joining a group, participating in an activity you like, or starting a new hobby with like-minded people. The same can be said for volunteering for a cause you are passionate about.

There are support groups for anxiety, depression, and emotional abuse, and you can find information about them through local medical professionals. On that note, there is no shame in seeking additional support from medical professionals.

The internet can be an amazing extension of your support network. There are qualified therapists you can find online, whether that's in more formal sessions or even just online.

Chatting with a therapist is a way of getting things off your chest, knowing you are in a safe and confidential environment. It's also perfectly understandable if you don't feel like you are in the right place to talk to a professional, but that doesn't mean there aren't other options.

Forums with posts from people who are going through similar experiences can provide comfort. You don't have to share your own experiences.

Begin by reading what other people post without any judgment. It might seem they had it worse, but that doesn't invalidate or minimize what you are going through.

If you have been controlled, part of your recovery is learning how to take control again, and choosing when you are ready to share is a great start.

Regardless of where you find your support network, it's essential to make an effort to remain in contact with the people in it. I know that life gets busy and time passes without you realizing it, but any type of relationship requires effort from both parties. And fortunately today, there are so many ways to do this.

Send messages, forward memes that make you think of them, or call or video call. You may assume you're being a burden, but try to look at things from a different point of view. Reaching out to them also provides them with the opportunity to expand their own support network.

Moving Forward and Healing Social Connections

Something that people often struggle with after an abusive relationship is reconnecting with old friends and even family members. If a partner has successfully managed to isolate you from others, there could be feelings of guilt and shame for the distance created, as if you blame yourself for the breakdown in the relationship. The first thing to do is change this mindset because it's far from the case. The second thing to do is to reach out to these people because rather than thinking the worst of you, they are probably just generally concerned.

How you reach out is up to you. I know people who have made phone calls and others who have written a letter. The details you go into are also a personal choice. You may want to let them know that you were in an abusive relationship and that you are reconnecting with old friends. You may feel the need to apologize for the lack of contact. Just remember that genuine friendships don't have an expiration date, and although you might need to make an effort to rebuild these bridges, it will be worth it in the end.

There is an elephant in the room that needs addressing, and that is how you rebuild relationships when you are still with an abusive partner. Consider Tania, for example, who had a daughter with her abusive partner, left him once, but then went back. She lost contact with her mom because her mom obviously wasn't happy about her coming back. After getting pregnant again, the relationship with her mom was completely destroyed, and when Tania left for the second time, she was very much alone. It wasn't until after her second child was born and her mom saw that the relationship was definitely over that they were able to start repairing their relationship.

This is something to bear in mind when reconnecting. As much as they will want to be there and support you, they will be concerned about your well-being and your safety. Try to see things from their perspective and understand that they might be dubious if you haven't left the abusive person. It might be that the person has genuinely changed, but they may need time to see these changes for themselves.

On the other hand, it's these people who may be your greatest support if you do decide to leave your abusive partner. This is especially true if you decide to go for the "no contact" approach, as instead of reaching out to contact your ex-partner, you can reach out to these mended relationships.

The "no contact" approach is, as one would imagine, where you have absolutely no contact with your ex-partner, including calls, messages, and engagement in social media such as following or likes. This would also include avoiding social events and possibly social media where you have friends in common. The reason for implementing no contact is that after a breakup, there are bound to be moments when thoughts of the past can stir up emotions. No contact helps you reduce these moments.

If "no contact" is impossible, it's important to reduce the amount of contact as much as possible and perhaps even consider a mediator. Once again, this is where your support system and revived relationships can be helpful.

Navigating New Relationships

There will come a point where a new relationship appeals to you, but there will also be an immense amount of doubt. The first concern will likely be your ability to trust someone after what you have been through. Prior to starting any new relationship, you want to make sure you are in the right position both mentally and emotionally.

It will require time and patience, and during this time, you need to avoid judging yourself for needing this time. When you start to criticize yourself, remind yourself that this is all part of the process. Begin with small and low-stakes situations to start learning how to trust again. This could be opening up to a friend about a secret or asking someone for a favor and trusting them to comply. Reward yourself for each of these steps you take and the gradual process you make. With this ongoing process, you will not only have the necessary time to begin trusting others, but you will also have the time to start trusting yourself and your own instincts. It's your instincts that will enable you to decide when a person is worthy of trusting or not.

When entering new relationships, your boundaries will play a vital role. Know what you want from a relationship and how you want to be treated, and don't be scared to communicate these boundaries in an assertive way early on.

The moment something doesn't feel right, the behavior needs to be addressed and consequences clearly explained. You will be stronger this time, so expressing yourself won't be as daunting.

Always be aware of the following red flags:

- Name-calling
- Controlling time
- Controlling what you wear
- Gaslighting and questioning your reality
- Jealousy or possessiveness
- Withholding attention or affection
- Requiring you to ask for permission
- Not allowing you to work
- Public embarrassment
- Making you feel guilty when you say no to sex
- Love bombing

As we reach this point, you are now well aware of the red flags to watch out for, as well as your own limitations of what you will tolerate in a relationship. Remain strong and confident in these times, and please don't stay in a new relationship that is potentially abusive for fear of not finding the person you deserve.

Putting Chapter 14 into Practice

Before dating or entering a new relationship, ask yourself the following questions for better clarity:

- Why do you want to start dating?
- What personality traits are you looking for in a partner?
- What are you looking for in the short/long term?
- What worked in your past relationships?
- What are some non-starters that immediately turn you off?
- Are you happy with yourself?
- What are your core values and beliefs?

Exercise: The "Two-Word Mantra"

Choose two words that represent what you want in future relationships (e.g., *calm and respect, honesty and joy*). Repeat them to yourself whenever you start doubting or feeling pulled back into old patterns. This simple mantra will help ground you in what you're aiming for.

Exercise: The "Celebrate One Thing"

Healing is hard work, so each day, celebrate one small thing you did to prioritize yourself. Whether it was declining an invitation you didn't want or taking a walk alone, this exercise is about noticing and celebrating the little wins.

CHAPTER 15: NAVIGATING TOXIC NEGATIVITY

Like drama, some people just thrive on negativity. As we have mentioned, most of us will answer "How are you?" with a good or fine, but we all know at least one person who will start an in-depth discussion about everything negative they can think of. It's draining! However, it's also something we aren't able to completely eliminate from our lives, so it's necessary to learn how to steer through this type of toxic behavior. We will begin by looking inside and questioning our own negativity.

Even the Most Positive People Can't Escape Their Own Negativity

If you're completely honest with yourself, you can admit to having an element of negativity about yourself. That's not to say that you're spreading that negativity among others, but whether it's once in a while or more frequently, negative thoughts creep in.

You might have health problems or financial problems, and of course, we know there are going to be serious issues with your relationships. Any of these can lead us to questions like "Why me?" or "What did I do to deserve this?"

You may start to think about the "if-onlys." *If only I hadn't fallen for that person or taken this job.* After replaying the negativity, you might give yourself a shake and assume that it is what it is and that you have no choice.

If you think about things on a larger scale, life is a string of choices—some are easy, others more challenging, but everything is a choice you get to make. You get to choose what you want for dinner, what time you go to bed, where you go on vacation, and most importantly, the company you keep. From the moment you woke up this morning to now, how many choices have you made? None of them were probably that difficult.

When we listen to our bodies, the choices are actually easy. If you're craving coffee, you need a caffeine boost because your body is tired, so you choose to make a coffee. Logic will also help us to make choices. If you know you need to put gas in the car, you choose to leave earlier for work.

When it comes to our relationships, our emotions can get in the way, making the choices somewhat cloudy, but at the end of the day, the choice is still there. To overcome your own negativity, you need to take responsibility for your actions and accept the fact that nothing will change unless you make a choice. You chose to read this book, which is a giant step in the right direction. The next choice you have to make is what to do with the information.

> *Happiness is a choice, not a result. Nothing will make you happy until you choose to be happy.*
>
> — *RALPH MARSTON*

Negativity vs. Venting

The question you might be asking now is, "What's the difference between being a negative person and just getting things off your chest?" The answer will always go back to understanding that all emotions are there for a purpose, but how you handle them makes the difference.

Anger and frustration can be expressed in a healthy way with a simple "I need to vent. Can I talk to you?"

This way, the other person is not only willing but also prepared. If the moment isn't right, they will more than likely suggest another time. There is no blaming or victimization, nor is there any playing of broken records or multiple topics rolled into one. Venting can feel healthy, like unburdening yourself.

Negativity, on the other hand, is just a case of dumping issues. For the person on the receiving end, it can feel overwhelming or even traumatizing. There is no accountability as the person plays the victim, and any solutions that are offered are dismissed without consideration.

Here are some signs of negativity that can become toxic:

- Constant worrying
- Telling you what to do and how to lead your life
- Negativity is their default mode
- Secrecy is enjoyable
- They expose themselves to too much bad news
- They are overly sensitive, even talking compliments the wrong way
- Being stuck in a comfort zone
- Every sentence ends with the word "but"
- They aren't motivated by achievement
- They miss out on the good things in life
- Good news is spun into a negative

It's important to understand how negativity can quickly turn into full-blown spells of toxicity. If you worry about what others think about you and can calmly express these concerns, you are managing your emotions. If this fear turns you into a people pleaser, your behaviors may become toxic. If you don't learn how to take criticism, you risk becoming defensive.

The point is that the negativity in your life doesn't always come from other people. And, just like our moments of toxic behavior, recognizing this and holding yourself accountable is essential. To do this, you need to understand your triggers.

What Triggers Negativity?

Each of our emotions has triggers. The smell of puppies or freshly cut grass can trigger happiness while watching the news can cause us to feel angry or sad. Negativity can be triggered by some of our most intense emotions. To be able to get ahead of this negativity, you need to analyze what your triggers are. Some common examples include:

- Unfair treatment
- Someone questioning your beliefs or values
- Being ignored, excluded, or rejected
- Feeling emotionally drained by others
- A lack of control or independence
- Betrayal and lies
- Being criticized
- Being disrespected

Of course, negativity can arise from minor issues like traffic to major circumstances such as abusive relationships. Sometimes, our triggers can be from things that have happened in our distant past—parents who were distant can trigger a fear of abandonment.

Learning what your triggers are will lead you to a marvelous place where you are able to make a choice! In the first place, your trigger is there to warn you. You might start to feel negative emotions, or you may have physical symptoms like an increased heart rate, feeling sick, dizzy, or shaking. In between the trigger and your response, you have space. It might only be a split second, but it's still there. At that moment, you have a choice of how you react.

Let's say you have had an incredibly stressful day at work, your body is exhausted, and you are dreading the next day. Your reaction is to have a beer or a glass of wine, but before the negativity overwhelms you, you could choose yoga or meditation instead. If your reaction is to shout at people who frustrate you, you can feel the frustration building up, but before the outburst, you could choose deep breaths to calm yourself and refocus.

After discovering your triggers, it's time to deal with them. There will be some triggers that you can avoid. If you know that a coworker who can't stop complaining goes for a coffee at a certain time, you know not to go at the same time. Nevertheless, this isn't a healthy coping strategy for all of your triggers, as it's impossible to avoid all negativity or never experience negativity.

Space is crucial, and this is not the same as avoiding it. It can be a case of taking a few deep breaths and a mental break from the situation through positive visualization, or it could be excusing yourself for a moment and then returning. This space gives you enough time to manage the physical symptoms the trigger causes and not to react in a negative way—fire won't beat fire. Take this space and use it to pinpoint your emotions without any judgment.

Be aware of projecting negativity. You may find that someone drains you of all your positivity, and you find it all that much harder not to take it out on the next person. It's not fair on others, just like it's not fair to project past experiences onto others either. If you move on from a toxic relationship, though hard, it's not fair to project negativity because you fear the same will happen again.

Finally, watch out for making assumptions and not keeping an open mind. In my own experience, I have often walked away from someone who is so completely negative that spending time with them hurts, but they can't see it. They aren't out to try and make me feel bad; they just lack the same awareness that you now have. Try communicating your own frustrations and lead with a positive example to encourage them to communicate their intense emotions in the same way.

Naturally, this will take time to master, and you must be patient with yourself. Before expecting to control your response, take some time to look at different situations and note your physical and emotional reactions to really understand what triggers you.

How You Can Set Yourself Up for Success

Negativity from within can be controlled. Negativity from others can be avoided to an extent, but the rest will become much easier to handle when you are thriving.

There are two core ways that you can start taking care of yourself so that you can become more successful—whatever that means to you! Let's begin with what you can do for your physical self:

1. Embrace a routine: Routine provides structure and helps to create a more balanced, organized day. A great way to kick start any day is with a morning routine that makes you happy — perhaps a short cardio workout, walking the dog, or some stretching. These can all help to begin the day in a positive way. Having a plan for your day allows you to maintain control.

2. Focus on how you fuel your body: A healthy breakfast is an ideal way to increase your nutrients and energy intake. If you feel yourself reaching for sugary snacks throughout the day, try choosing things that will boost your mood, like berries, nuts, seeds, and even dark chocolate.

3. Choose the right time of the day for your challenging tasks: Some people thrive in the morning and feel a bit sluggish after lunch, while others are the opposite and take a little time to warm up. If you have a bunch of things that you know are stressful, get them out of the way first. Then, plan your day so that the most taxing tasks are scheduled for when you are at your best.

4. Stop multitasking: We are presented with images of multitaskers being able to achieve more, but the truth is that when we don't put all of our focus on one task, it can take longer and mistakes might be made. This doesn't only apply to work. If you are with your children, be with your children. If you are out for dinner, be in the present and not distracted by your phone.

5. Move, laugh, and play: Anyone stuck sitting at a desk should move around for a few minutes every 30 minutes or so. It's also a good idea to take a walk during your lunch break to increase the oxygen in your brain. Never forget the importance of laughing and having fun, even if it's just for a few minutes throughout your day. Choose an app with brain games, watch your favorite YouTube videos, or phone a friend who makes you laugh.

6. Get the right amount of sleep for your body: Whether you need 6 or 9 hours, make sure you go to bed on time so that your body and mind have the chance to rest and recuperate. Avoid caffeine and alcohol at night. As tempted as you may be to take your phone to bed, try and leave it in the other room. You may find yourself on social media, and there is bound to be some negativity online that you don't need before you go to sleep.

When you take care of your physical self, becoming emotionally successful is effortless, which will also be helped by setting boundaries and reinforcing them. Don't try to push your emotions away or ignore them. It's important to feel, recognize, and process your emotions. Journaling is a great way to get all of those feelings out without fearing judgment from others. Writing will allow you to gain objectivity about different situations and look at things from another point of view.

Envisioning Your Personal Power and Creating a Better Life for Yourself

Another great strategy for navigating your way around the negative is to increase the positive in your life. Although neither good nor bad, as we get older, we gain more and more responsibilities, and one way or another, we can lose our sense of identity and what we consider to be our true selves. It's also likely that we pay too much attention to what society thinks we should be, which is the worst way to lose personal power.

Your personal power is the ability to see yourself as an individual who has strengths, weaknesses, and potential. When we stop fighting who we think we should be, we can access our personal power and use this to work toward our goals and the life we want to lead. Begin by reflecting on your current situation by asking yourself why you are doing the things you do and what you get out of it. Evaluate your situation and your relationships so that you can use all of this information to plan for the future.

After years of dealing with toxic people, reminding yourself just how great you are is hard work. But, at the end of the day, you are amazing. You are a good person who is kind, caring, intelligent, and beautiful. You have your faults because we all do. You might feel like losing a couple of pounds, wishing there were fewer wrinkles, and watching the odd series on Netflix instead of doing something more productive, but none of this takes away from the fact that you are a good person. As you get better at establishing your boundaries and removing toxicity from your life, it will be easier to believe this. You will also turn your attention away from building up those who don't deserve your praise and start dedicating it to those who do. This will help you see what a great person you are, and you will find the personal power needed to create your vision.

Your life vision is how you see your life in the future. It's similar to goals but on a larger scale. It includes your goals and dreams, both personally and professionally, as well as a visualization of how you see your relationships developing over time. Imagine your life vision as a compass that you use to orient yourself in the right direction (www.lifehack.org). Without this vision, it's almost like you have handed your compass to others who will use it to control your life.

You might think it's as simple as asking what you want to do with your life, but it's actually a heavy question that doesn't have a quick answer. Much of the answer comes from the work we have already done, so you have a bit of a head start. Your vision will depend on your values and beliefs, which we examined when creating boundaries. You also need a great deal of planning, which we started with reflecting, evaluating, and planning. Let's start with questions to ask about the present, followed by ones about how you envision your future so that you can work on bridging the two.

Questions that look at your present life:

- What things matter to you at the moment? Disregard the expectations and focus on what truly matters to you!
- What do you want to achieve in your career?
- What do you want more of in life? Will this bring you happiness?
- What kind of relationships do you envision for yourself?
- What are you good at?
- What do you want to accomplish in life?
- What skills would you like to improve on?
- Do you have a passion that you would like to develop?

Pick a moment in the future. This could be 5, 10, or 20 years from now.

Questions that look into your future:

- What will you have accomplished?
- What will you be doing? What does a typical day look like?
- Where are you living? What type of home do you have?
- Who are the people around you?
- What do you look like?
- How are your emotions?

If your life vision makes you feel happy and excited about the future, you know you are on to a winner. If not, some of your ideas will need to be tweaked.

The next step is to plan how you are going to get from A to B. You will likely need to develop new skills or make certain choices you had not thought of before. If you imagine yourself in a big house in the country, you might need to adjust your financial situation in order to get there. If you picture a large family around you, it might be time to consider adopting. Rushing into a relationship just to have children will set your life on a different path.

Remember, there are always options and choices. Finally, break down each area of your vision and work out the steps you need to take to get there. Don't forget to recheck your compass as you meet each milestone so that you are confident you are on the right track.

Your Personal Power Needs a Power Phrase

One final tip for boosting your personal power is to create a power phrase. You have probably heard of mantras and affirmations, short phrases that help you remain focused on a goal or encourage the mind to start believing in what you wish to achieve.

For example, "I believe in my visions," "I love myself," and "I am proud of myself." A power phrase is similar, but as the name implies, it allows us to focus on our inner strengths.

A power phrase can be any short phrase, normally just three words that can be repeated any time you need it. It could be before an important meeting or a crucial conversation. It might be when you are feeling stressed or overwhelmed. Your power phrase is a great tool to use in between a trigger and a reaction to help you calm yourself and refocus as it helps you regain control.

To create your own power phrase, you should go back to your goals and visions of how you see yourself at your absolute best. Select three adjectives that relate to this.

The possibilities are endless, but I will give you some of my favorites:

- Beautiful
- Strong
- Powerful
- Independent

- Capable
- Intelligent
- Masterful
- Grateful
- Talented
- Joyful
- Energetic
- Creative
- Funny
- Loyal
- Brave
- Awesome
- Positive
- Confident

In addition to using your power phrase in times of need, you can incorporate it into your daily routine. Repeat your phrase a few times while you shower, prepare lunch, or drive to work.

Accept, Embrace, and Release Negativity

It's here, and it's not going anywhere! You have the choice to dwell on negativity or rise above it. Choosing to be happy and positive doesn't happen overnight, assuming it will lead to disappointment.

Even after practicing the techniques mentioned, you will still have to deal with the negativity of others. It gets easier when we take care of ourselves and practice self-love. However, learning the "accept, embrace, and release" method will help you protect yourself from the negativity that you can't escape.

Accept things for what they are. To do this, you have to determine whether you have control over the situation and whether or not it is your responsibility. Accept that your colleague just loves to look on the pessimistic side. It's not your responsibility to try and fix it, and you have a choice whether to listen or not.

Embracing negativity is about choosing activities that allow you to process it rather than burying it. Some people choose to write things down in a journal or talk to a friend. Meditation and mindfulness are excellent ways to embrace negativity in the right way so that it doesn't eat away at you. You learn how to inhale your life vision and exhale all that is negative.

If you reach a point when your negativity surrounds you, and you can't free yourself, it's important to get the support you need. Talking to a trusted friend can often help you to release some of these pent-up negative emotions. And there is absolutely no shame in talking to a professional if it means you can break free and take that all-important first step toward a brighter future and a stronger, empowered you.

Putting Chapter 15 into Practice

Identifying your triggers may take a little time, as they won't all come to mind at once. You may need to be with certain people or in specific places before they become apparent. Create a document on your phone where you can list your triggers and start working on accepting your emotions and overcoming negativity.

CHAPTER 16: TAKING BACK YOUR LIFE

At this point, I like to think that readers have a much stronger idea of what they are dealing with, the dangers of not dealing with it, and, of course, after some deep introspection, there is an effective plan in place to start eliminating toxic people and behavior. I also recognize that there might still be some nerves, and not all the techniques are fully mastered.

This final chapter is like the last push to the peak of the mountain that will enable you to see the amazing views all around you.

Why Don't People Support My Choices?

There are many answers to this question. It's amazing how many people in the world are incapable of seeing things from another person's point of view.

Your loved one might genuinely try to understand the choices you make, but they can't. It could be that they are just so concerned about you that the worry comes across as a lack of support. They may have a deep-rooted need to be right, so your choices are always going to be wrong.

As we have seen with toxic people, they are unlikely to support the decisions you make because the end result is that they lose control over you.

When people don't support you, even those closest to you who should always have your back, you have to accept this as part of normal life rather than fight it.

It's not your job to impress others or make choices that continuously benefit others. It's a shame, but even those who have known you the longest may never get their heads around you knowing what is best for your own life. And this is okay.

Try to empathize because this is one way for us to rise above people who don't support us. Maybe they are insecure, envious, or scared of the new things that you want to try.

Go ahead and attempt to explain things in a different way to see if this helps them understand, but know when to draw the line and accept it.

What you should do is remember that you have already wasted too much of your time pandering to the needs of the toxic people in your life. There isn't enough time or energy to spend another minute explaining your reasons to people who aren't going to respect them.

> *Your life is made of two dates and a dash. Make the most of the dash.*
>
> — *LINDA ELLIS*

What are you going to do with your dash? While you have decided to rid yourself of the toxic behavior, you also need to stop trying to please everyone else and start putting your passions and dreams first.

Doing the things that fill your heart with motivation, joy, and love will help you live a fulfilling life that isn't full of regrets and "what ifs."

It still might be hard to picture just yet, but you can do anything you want to do. There should be nothing holding you back—especially not self-doubt. Pick any inspirational person: Halle Berry once slept in a homeless shelter, J.K. Rowling was a single mom struggling to pay rent, Steve Jobs dropped out of college after one semester and became a millionaire by the age of 23, Ray Charles, Einstein...

I could go on. Each had massive setbacks and carved their own path away from their difficulties. You can do whatever you want with your dash, and you can do it without the support of others, and you certainly don't need them projecting their limitations onto you.

Why You Need to Own Your Own Life

Owning your own life is about focusing on yourself and being grateful for where you are at this point. It's about regaining control and then protecting it so that nobody else can take it away from you in the future.

Furthermore, you get to live your life by your own values, beliefs, and standards, which builds up confidence and the ability to love yourself.

Sometimes, owning your own life begins with accepting responsibility for where you are today and stopping blaming others. Yes, you may have had a rough childhood, but your parents did the best they could with what they had at the time.

Money might be tight, but you can take responsibility for your budget and make changes. You have made mistakes, been with the wrong people, tolerated too much, whatever it may be, own it.

What has happened in the past isn't a sign of what's to come in the future because every day is a new beginning with new opportunities.

Remember how we began by looking at our own negativity. Now is the time to check in with your attitude again and see if those negative thoughts are cropping up every now and again. You may have to keep forcing the positive thoughts until it gets easier to push past negative ideas before you eventually end up unaffected by most negativity.

How to Own Your Own Life

1. Be more intentional with your time and your outlook

While breakfast is the most important meal of the day, your mornings are also the most valuable time. When your morning starts well, the rest of the day tends to follow suit.

Having a morning routine ensures you can start your day with a healthy meal, some exercise, or meditation. It's a precious time for preparation and calm. For mental preparation, you can prepare your to-do list and check your goals.

You can be intentional about maintaining a positive attitude and keeping clear of negative people, even negative news.

When you are intentional about the information you share, it is easier to keep negativity out of your life.

2. Become more disciplined

Increasing your self-discipline is more than just a way to achieve your goals by removing distractions and temptations. It's about enhancing your resilience for different situations. When you are more disciplined, you have more control over your life, and this will have a positive effect on your levels of anxiety.

Setting goals is a great way to stay motivated and maintain discipline. Begin by setting small goals that are easy to achieve. Your confidence will build with every small goal you achieve, and you'll soon be tackling the larger ones.

Keep your goals where you can see them. I still prefer pen and paper, but I know others who create digital lists on their phone. Whether it's your to-do list or your goals, make sure you are prioritizing.

For those days when you can't find the motivation, you have to force yourself to get up and take action. There is no room for excuses or feeling sorry for your situation. Count down from ten, visualize yourself achieving your goal, and get moving.

3. Treat yourself like you are a guest

If you have ever had visitors stay, you will know that there is a mad rush of tidying, cleaning, and watering the plants. The best food is prepared, and the finest wine is opened. But why don't we treat ourselves in the same manner?

Even behavior like this shows that we place other people before ourselves. In fact, having a well-organized and clean home is extremely important for your self-care, and a decluttered home helps you develop a decluttered mind. Take some time to declutter your home, and every time you leave the house, leave it as if you were preparing for a guest. Coming home will be all the more rewarding.

4. Try new experiences

Not everyone has a passion for trying new things. It involves stepping out of our comfort zone. We might feel like we are destined to fail, we aren't good enough, or we don't have the skill or knowledge. Such beliefs will only hold us back from a world of so many amazing experiences, and we must get out there and explore the most amazing things in the world.

Again, start with baby steps. Plant some seeds and see what grows, ride a horse, eat new dishes. A famous weightlifting coach had some wise words, "Sorry, you just are not good enough to be disappointed" (Dan John). It sounds harsh, but as we venture into new experiences, there is no justification for our disappointment. If you've been gardening for ten years and your seeds still aren't growing, then it's understandable to be disappointed!

5. Embrace life's lessons

I've recently started growing my first peppers, so I'll stick to my seed analogy! I've tried growing so many things, but nothing ever turned out quite right. I learned that I had planted them in the wrong season, drowned the seeds, left them in the sun and then the rain, and so on. Finally, I got it right.

Wherever you look, life has lessons to teach that you have to embrace. Beforehand, you would have looked at your toxic relationships as a bad thing, and they certainly were. But you have been able to learn so much about yourself and dealing with other people that your life is going to do a complete 180. Keep calm in the face of change, know that you are getting wiser, and keep learning along your path.

6. Create a strategy for your goals

So many people fail to achieve their goals because they haven't planned. It's not enough to say, "I want to be mortgage-free in 15 years" or "I want to take that cruise in two years."

Both of these are significant goals, and writing them down makes them more concrete, but it doesn't automatically mean they are going to happen. Both short- and long-term goals need to be broken down into smaller, achievable steps.

Working on smaller steps is easier to achieve. You start to see progress with the bigger goals, and it helps to keep these bigger goals in sight.

7. Stop waiting for others

Remember when you were in high school, and you and your best friend had your parallel lives all planned out? In an ideal world, our paths would be in sync with our loved ones, but more often than not, you will find yourself waiting for others, preventing you from pursuing the things you want to do. Is it fair that your career advancement gets put on hold so that your partner can fulfill their dreams?

Discussing and agreeing on major life changes is healthy, but constantly waiting for others is unhealthy. To own your own life, you need to set a timeline for your goals and dreams and make this your priority.

8. Build a routine that is enlivening and keeps you centered

A good routine is essential for building healthy habits in your day. When we start practicing healthy habits regularly, stress levels are reduced, anxiety is controlled, and as time management improves, we will have more free time to do the things we enjoy.

Keeping fit has to be a priority if you want to feel good about yourself and stay mentally and physically sound.

Your fitness can include aerobic and muscular fitness as well as flexibility (American College of Sports Medicine). Nutrition, sleep, emotional and mental health will also impact fitness (Oken, 2019).

Here are some ideas you can incorporate into your daily routine:

- Give yourself plenty of time in the morning so that you don't start the day in a rush.

- Eat your fruits and veggies; take vitamin supplements if necessary.

- Make sure your diet is balanced so you are fueling your body with the energy it needs.

- Drink plenty of water; put slices of fruit in the water if it encourages you to drink more and have a glass of water with every other beverage.

- Avoid sugar and caffeine because although it gives us a quick boost of energy, you might find your blood sugar levels remain too high, and this can lead to complications with diabetes or heart disease.

- Increase your heart rate. It's great to start your day with a short cardio session to get the body moving and the oxygen flowing to the brain, followed by a refreshing shower. Start your day at your best.

- Move about during the day. For those who have a desk job, it's important to move regularly. Try taking the stairs instead of the elevator and don't feel guilty for walking away from your desk for a few minutes. The time you are at your desk will be more productive and your eyes get a break from the screen.

- Spend time doing something you love. This could be 20 minutes of reading a book, talking to a friend, scrolling through social media, or one of your hobbies.

- Take five minutes of me-time every day. This isn't the same as hobby time. This is five minutes of nothingness—no technology, no TV—just sit down and watch the world in a peaceful, calm state. Take in all of the positivity around you.

• Set time limits for your activities. Make sure they are realistic, or you will find yourself unable to complete everything, which is not motivating. Being strict with your time will reduce stress and allow you to achieve the most you can.

• Write your to-do list the day before to prevent yourself from worrying about it the next day when you should be relaxing.

• End the day by disconnecting from electronic devices. Instead, write down three positive things about your day.

9. Practice yoga and mediation

Neither yoga nor meditation is as hippy as it may seem. They are valuable tools to assist with both the body and the mind. Certain yoga poses will help you to detect imbalances in the body and increase energy flow.

It's the kind of thing you won't believe until you try, but even after just one session, you'll feel a difference, such as an amazing sense of calm and stretching your body, which is energizing.

I use the app FitOn for guided yoga sessions. And there are also lots of other short workouts that are great for the mornings. Meditation encourages a state where you detach from the emotional situation so that your brain guides you toward a state of tranquility.

Meditation can be used as a rapid response technique for times of stress or depression, but as you don't need very long, you can take just five minutes to meditate throughout the day.

It's not always easy to clear your mind, so I recommend apps like **Headspace** to guide you through meditation and help you focus on your breathing.

10. Own your life affirmation

Hopefully, you have created some affirmations for personal empowerment. If you are still playing around with some ideas, you might want to think about affirmations for owning your life:

• I am supposed to be where I am today.

- I am supposed to look the way I do.
- The events in my life have led me to the right place today.
- I am where I am for a reason.

You can be as creative as you want to be and even add some powerful adjectives to the ideas above.

Don't feel overwhelmed by all of these ideas. When you consider all the other tips and techniques we have looked at in this book, you probably feel that there is a lot to do. While this is true, it's always better to start making small changes that will last than to rush everything at once.

Putting Chapter 16 into Practice

Out of all the self-care ideas presented in this chapter, write a list of the ones you believe would be most beneficial. Which item from your list can you start today? Take a calendar or journal and now plan a realistic way to integrate all of the healthy habits you want to adopt.

CONCLUSION

Difficult people are everywhere. It doesn't matter how old you are, what you look like, who you love, or how you make a living—you will meet them. They might hide in plain sight, lure you with kindness, compliments, and love, and then reveal their true colors, but as the old saying goes, it's hard to avoid running into difficult people.

Fighting these toxic souls? Well, that's a losing battle, and you know it. You've spent months—maybe years—trying to mold something complicated into something healthy, only to find yourself drained, emotionally exhausted, or worse. It's not just time wasted; it's pieces of yourself you're trying to reclaim. You've given them the benefit of the doubt, only to watch your generosity evaporate into thin air.

Instead of repeatedly asking, "Why me?" or "What did I do to deserve this?" you've made the empowering choice to reclaim your life. Remember, you haven't done anything wrong. If this person hadn't attached themselves to you, they would have found someone else to mistreat. Now is the moment to transform these painful experiences into valuable lessons and let go of your suffering.

You may still feel fragile in the days and weeks ahead and might not be ready to confront the toxic people in your life. That's okay! The first crucial step is self-reflection and planning. Take the time to evaluate your relationships. Create three columns: one for good relationships, one for those that need work, and one for the people you want to eliminate from your life. Reassess your goals, identify what makes you happy, and envision how you want your life to look in one, five, and ten years. While it's hard to admit our faults, look within to see what changes you can make to foster a more positive outlook.

When it comes to the real heavy-hitters—the sociopaths and master manipulators—you're going to need more than a list. These people are Olympic-level in their ability to twist your emotions and wriggle back into your life. Make sure you're emotionally strong enough to stand your ground. Start with the changes you'd like to see in the difficult people around you, focusing on friends who will understand when you share your feelings. As you see progress, build confidence, and then firmly address those whose toxic behavior has hurt you the most.

Never forget that your safety comes first. If someone has been aggressive toward you in the past or you fear they might harm you physically, don't try to confront them alone. You are not responsible for their reactions but must prioritize your safety.

Practice what you want to say to a difficult person before you speak with them. Use "I" statements instead of "you" to avoid sounding accusatory. Preparation will positively influence how you deliver your message. Remember that any boundaries you set should have consequences you're willing to enforce. Expect pushback and harsh comments from them—this is on them, not you. You have the power to choose how you respond to difficult people and to rise above their negativity.

This is a process, not a sprint. There will be setbacks. Some days you'll feel on top of the world, and there will be days when you'll wonder if you've made any progress at all. But eventually, the bad days will fade. You deserve happiness, respect, and appreciation. You have the right to live your life as you wish. By removing toxic individuals who refuse to change, you'll make space for healthier relationships, and your newfound wisdom will guide you in nurturing these connections.

Don't be too harsh on yourself; you're still allowed to make mistakes. Learn and let go!

And let me leave you with this: just because someone else is determined to live in misery doesn't mean you have to pull up a chair at their pity party. Remember, there's only one dash between your dates—life is too short not to have fun. Smile, laugh, dance, sing, take pride in who you are, and most importantly, be happy!

Now, let's be honest—this isn't a magic solution. If one self-help book could fix everything, we'd all be walking around with perfect skin and halos, casually sipping cold brew in emotional equilibrium. The reality? Life is messy. Relationships are complicated. And toxic people? They're kind of like pigeons—impossible to avoid entirely.

But the good news is, you're not powerless. If you've made it this far, you've already taken a giant step toward reclaiming your life. Whether it's setting boundaries or finally telling that one friend (you know the one) that you don't need their constant passive-aggressive comments about your choices, you're now armed with knowledge, clarity, and—most importantly—perspective.

If you found this book helpful, I'd be forever grateful if you could take a moment to leave a quick review on Amazon. Who knows? Maybe together we can help a few more people navigate the wild and wonderful chaos that is life. Best of luck—you've got this!

RESOURCES

11 Warning Signs you are Dealing with a Workplace Sociopath. (2022, August 16). *www.marie-claireross.com*. https://www.marie-claireross.com/blog/11-warning-signs-you-are-dealing-with-a-workplace-sociopath

A study of the etiology of sociopathic behavior. (1974a, September 1). PubMed. https://pubmed.ncbi.nlm.nih.gov/17894069/

Alegria, A. A. (2013, July). Sex differences in antisocial personality disorder: results from the National Epidemiological Survey on Alcohol and Related Conditions. PubMed. https://pubmed.ncbi.nlm.nih.gov/23544428/

Altomara, D. (2023, December 26). *Sociopaths: warning signs and red flags*. WebMD. https://www.webmd.com/mental-health/signs-sociopath

American Museum of Natural History. (n.d.). Your Emotional Brain | AMNH. Retrieved July 5, 2021, from https://www.amnh.org/exhibitions/brain-the-inside-story/your-emotional-brain

American Psychiatric Association. (n.d.). What Are Sleep Disorders? Web Starter Kit. Retrieved July 2, 2021, from https://www.psychiatry.org/patients-families/sleep-disorders/what-are-sleep-disorders

Antisocial personality disorder - Symptoms and causes. (n.d.). Mayo Clinic. https://www.-mayoclinic.org/diseases-conditions/antisocial-personality-disorder/symptoms-causes/syc-20353928

A-Z Quotes. (n.d.). *Denzel Washington Quote*. https://www.azquotes.com/quote/1281937

Azam, S. (2019, December 19). Brain Chemicals. Peak. https://blog.-peak.net/2019/10/29/brain-chemicals/

Barberio, I. (n.d.). *Removing toxicity and letting go of self-limiting beliefs*. Inez Barberio - Emotional Intelligence and Diversity Inclusion. https://www.inezbarberio.-com/blog/removing-toxicity-self-limiting-beliefs

Barkley, S. (2023, May 5). *Am I The Problem? 6 Signs of a Person with Toxic Traits*. Psych Central. https://psychcentral.com/relationships/maybe-the-problem-is-you

BetterHelp Editorial Team. (2024, June 4). *Dating a Sociopathic Person: What to be aware of | BetterHelp*. https://www.betterhelp.com/advice/sociopathy/dating-a-sociopath-what-to-be-aware-of/

Bold, S. (n.d.). Emotional Healing with Meditation & Mindfulness | | Healing Holidays. HealingHolidays. Retrieved July 5, 2021, from https://www.healingholidays.-com/blog/emotional-healing-with-meditation-mindfulness

Brainy Quote. (n.d.). *Conflict quotes*. https://www.brainyquote.com/topics/conflict-quotes

Brooke, A. (2018, November 7). 4 Ways to Identify Your Own Toxic Behaviors in Relationships. The Temper. https://www.thetemper.com/4-ways-to-identify-your-own-toxic-behaviors-in-relationships/

Charuk, J. (2018, October 18). 6 Steps to Get Rid of Your Limiting Beliefs. Charuk Studios. http://www.charukstudios.com/blog/6-steps-to-get-rid-of-your-limiting-beliefs

Choi, C. L. Q. (2016, June 20). "Artificial Synapses" Could Let Supercomputers Mimic the

Human Brain. Scientific American. https://www.scientificamerican.com/article/artificial-synapses-could-let-supercomputers-mimic-the-human-brain/

Choose to Be Happy with These Happiness is a Choice Quotes. (n.d.). EnkiQuotes. Retrieved June 22, 2021, from https://www.enkiquotes.com/happiness-is-a-choice-quotes.html

Cikanavicius, D. (2018, October 14). *Dangerous dark traits among narcissists, abusers, and toxic people*. Psych Central. https://psychcentral.com/blog/psychology-self/2018/10/dark-narcissist-traits#1

Clear, J. (2019, February 19). You're Not Good Enough to Feel Disappointed. James Clear. https://jamesclear.com/good-disappointed

Cleveland Clinic. (2024, May 1). *Personality disorders*. https://my.clevelandclinic.org/health/diseases/9636-personality-disorders-overview

Collins. (n.d.). *Definition of "victim."* Collins Dictionary. https://www.collinsdictionary.com/dictionary/english/victim

Darcy, A. M., & Jacobson, S. (2023, March 6). *Traumatic Bonding – How to break free of trauma bonds*. Harley Therapy™ Blog. https://www.harleytherapy.co.uk/counselling/traumatic-bonding-break-trauma-bonds.htm

Dark Triad. (n.d.). Psychology Today. https://www.psychologytoday.com/us/basics/dark-triad

Dawn. (2021, January 29). *"Respond intelligently even to unintelligent treatment."* One Smart Fortunate Cookie. https://onesmartfortunatecookie.wordpress.com/2019/06/02/respond-intelligently-even-to-unintelligent-treatment/

Day, C. (2020, June 19). *I worked for a sociopath and here's what it's like. . .* https://www.linkedin.com/pulse/i-worked-sociopath-heres-what-its-like-christine-day/

Dialogues Clin Neurosci. (2010, March 1). The genetic epidemiology of personality disorders. PubMed Central (PMC). https://www.ncbi.nlm.nih.gov/pmc/articles/PMC3181941/

Doll, B. R. (2012, November 7). How to Recognize a Sociopath. Agnesian HealthCare. https://www.agnesian.com/blog/how-recognize-sociopath

Dombeck, M., PhD. (n.d.). Nature, Nurture and Psychopathy—Personality Disorders. Mental Health. Retrieved July 5, 2021, from https://www.mentalhelp.net/blogs/nature-nurture-and-psychopathy/

Dr. Ramani. (2020, July 13). 11 tactics for not letting narcissists into your life in the first place [Video]. YouTube. https://www.youtube.com/watch?v=UdcGsbcANj8

Evenson, R. (2013). Powerful Phrases for Dealing with Difficult People: Over 325 Ready-to-Use Words and Phrases for Working with Challenging Personalities (1st ed.). AMACOM Books.

Friedman, W. J. (n.d.). Developing An Inner Meter on Manipulation—A Critical Life Skill—Wellness, Disease Prevention, And Stress Reduction Information. Mentalhelp.Net. Retrieved June 21, 2021, from https://www.mentalhelp.net/blogs/developing-an-inner-meter-on-manipulation-a-critical-life-skill/

Habits: How They Form and How To Break Them. (2012, March 5). Npr.Org. https://choice.npr.org/index.html?origin=https://www.npr.org/2012/03/05/147192599/habits-how-they-form-and-how-to-break-them?t=1625241026390

Health Benefits of Social Interaction—Mercy Medical Center. (n.d.). Mercy Care. Retrieved

July 5, 2021, from https://www.mercycare.org/bhs/eap/resources/health-benefits-of-social-interaction/

How to Heal from Emotional Abuse: The Ultimate Guide to Recovery [Update 2023]. (2023, July 5). Eddins Counseling Group – Houston & Sugar Land, TX. https://eddinscounseling.com/how-to-heal-from-emotional-abuse/

Ifeanyi, D. (2022, August 22). Are you a people pleaser? [+ How to stop being too Nice in 3 simple steps]. *Pawns: Grow up - Level up - Step Up.* https://pawns.com.ng/people-pleaser/

Itani, O. (2021, February 28). You Are What You Think: How Your Thoughts Create Your Reality. OMAR ITANI. https://www.omaritani.com/blog/what-you-think

Janecic, P. (2020, June 1). How Your Perception Creates a Different Reality. Mind of Steel. https://themindofsteel.com/perception/

Journal of Women's Health. (2011, December). Sleep Disturbances and Their Association With Mental Health Among Women Exposed to Intimate Partner Violence. Www.Ncbi.Nlm.Nih.Gov. https://www.ncbi.nlm.nih.gov/pmc/articles/PMC3236986/

Katherine, C.-A. (2022, February 8). Healing Doesn't mean the damage never existed. *The Graceful Boon - A Guide To Women's Issues.* https://thegracefulboon.com/2022/02/08/healing-doesnt-mean-the-damage-never-existed/

Kass, A. (n.d.). How To Heal From Emotional Abuse [7-steps]. Go Smart Life. Retrieved July 5, 2021, from https://www.gosmartlife.com/emotional-abuse-in-marriage/emotional-abuse-healing

Khoddam, R. (2014, August 20). The Truth Will Set You Free. Psychology Today. https://www.psychologytoday.com/us/blog/the-addiction-connection/201408/the-truth-will-set-you-free

Kryger, K. (2023, December 24). *105 Toxic People Quotes to help get rid of the negativity in your life.* Parade. https://parade.com/living/toxic-people-quotes

Lancer, D. (2018, December 10). Beware of the Malevolent Dark Triad. Psychologytoday. https://www.psychologytoday.com/us/blog/toxic-relationships/201812/beware-the-malevolent-dark-triad

Lancer, D. (2023, August 1). *Myths about narcissism.* What Is Codependency? https://whatiscodependency.com/myths-about-narcissism/

Letting it go: getting past negative emotions. (n.d.). https://www.columbiadoctors.org/health-library/article/letting-it-go-getting-past-negative-emotions/

The link between serial killers and head trauma. (n.d.). Crime+Investigation UK. Retrieved July 2, 2021, from https://www.crimeandinvestigation.co.uk/article/the-link-between-serial-killers-and-head-trauma

Live Your Dream—Life, Business, Career & Health Coaching. (2019, November 28). Move Beyond | Live Your Dream. http://www.movebeyond.net

Lpcc, S. S. (2019, October 11). *Coping with Sociopaths (Antisocial Personality Disorder).* Psych Central. https://psychcentral.com/pro/recovery-expert/2019/10/coping-with-sociopaths-antisocial-personality-disorder#1

McAvoy, K., PhD. (2020, September 24). How to Survive Living with a Sociopath - Kerry McAvoy, PhD. *Kerry McAvoy.* https://kerrymcavoyphd.com/how-to-survive-living-with-a-sociopath/

Manipulation. (2019, March 26). GoodTherapy.Org Therapy Blog. https://www.goodtherapy.org/blog/psychpedia/manipulation

Main, N. (2024, March 18). The sociopath next door: Middle-class LA mom-of-two reveals what it's REALLY like living with. . . *Mail Online*. https://www.dailymail.co.uk/sciencetech/article-13196853/Sociopath-battling-personality-disorder.html

Marripedia. (n.d.). Effects of Divorce on Children's Future Relationships [Marripedia]. Www.Marripedia.Org. Retrieved July 2, 2021, from http://marripedia.org/effect_of_divorce_on_children_s_future_relationships

Martens, W. H. J., MD PhD. (2020, July 9). What Lies Behind: The Hidden Suffering of the Psychopath. Psychiatric Times. https://www.psychiatrictimes.com/view/what-lays-behind-the-hidden-suffering-of-the-psychopath

Matsumoto, D. (2019, December 4). The Seven Basic Emotions: Do You Know Them? David Matsumoto. Medium. https://davidmatsumoto.medium.com/the-seven-basic-emotions-do-you-know-them-66e6564b0208

Mayo Clinic. (n.d.). Narcissistic personality disorder—Symptoms and causes. Retrieved July 5, 2021, from https://www.mayoclinic.org/diseases-conditions/narcissistic-personality-disorder/symptoms-causes/syc-20366662

McGregor, J. (2014, December 2). Breaking Up With A Sociopath. Welldoing. https://welldoing.org/article/breaking-up-with-a-sociopath

Merriam-Webster. (n.d.). Support system. In *Merriam-Webster Dictionary*. https://www.merriam-webster.com/dictionary/support%20system

mindbodygreen. (2021, June 30). There Are At Least 8 Types Of Narcissists—Which Ones Are Dangerous?https://www.mindbodygreen.com/articles/types-of-narcissists

MindTools | Home. (n.d.). https://www.mindtools.com/axtfdfb/dealing-with-manipulative-people

Morin, A. (2017, August 7). 7 Science-Backed Reasons You Should Spend More Time Alone. Forbes. https://www.forbes.com/sites/amymorin/2017/08/05/7-science-backed-reasons-you-should-spend-more-time-alone/?sh=75a9bc711b7e

NNEDV. (2016, November 3). *Emotional abuse is anything but "Tender": Myths and reality*. https://nnedv.org/latest_update/emotional-abuse-anything-tender-myths-reality/

Pietrangelo, A. (2019, March 6). 10 Tips for Dealing with a Narcissistic Personality. Healthline. https://www.healthline.com/health/how-to-deal-with-a-narcissist

Psychology Today. (n.d.). *Trauma bonding*. https://www.psychologytoday.com/us/basics/trauma-bonding

The Power of Acceptance | Dylan Woon | TEDxKangar. (2018, March 30). [Video]. YouTube. https://www.youtube.com/watch?v=-mQKf3Fz5KA

Quoter, H. (2021, March 29). *Just Remember, We are All Toxic*. Fractal Enlightenment. https://fractalenlightenment.com/51182/quotes/just-remember-we-are-all-toxic

Quotes about people talking about you - DesiQuotes.com. (n.d.). https://www.desiquotes.com/quotes-about-people-talking-about-you/

Reader, L. (2023, April 16). *A classic Lovefraud story: I married a sociopath*. Lovefraud | Escape Sociopaths - Narcissists in Relationships. https://lovefraud.com/a-classic-lovefraud-story-i-married-a-sociopath/

Rebeca Zung. (2020, March 4). Phrases to Disarm a Narcissist [Video]. YouTube. https://www.youtube.com/watch?v=e6vJoq-6mXU

Rhein, W. (2022, November 3). The manipulative way narcissists turn friends & family against you. *Medium*. https://medium.com/heart-affairs/the-manipulative-way-narcissists-turn-friends-family-against-you-147e25149d61

Robinson, L., & Segal, J., PhD. (2024, February 5). The Health and Mood-Boosting Benefits of Pets - HelpGuide.org. *HelpGuide.org*. https://www.helpguide.org/wellness/pets/mood-boosting-power-of-dogs

Sapolsky, R. M. (2020, December 30). The teenage brain: Why some years are (a lot) crazier than others. Big Think. https://bigthink.com/videos/what-age-is-brain-fully-developed

Science Direct. (2014, May 1). Neurodevelopmental and psychosocial risk factors in serial killers and mass murderers. https://www.sciencedirect.com/science/article/pii/S1359178914000305

Shortsleeve, C. (2018, October 16). How to Tell If Someone Is Manipulating You—And What to Do About It. Time. https://time.com/5411624/how-to-tell-if-being-manipulated/

Sterner, S. (2018, January 30). 5 Questions to Help You Stop Being Manipulated. Steph Sterner. https://stephsterner.com/5-questions-help-being-manipulated/

Stillman, J. (2021, January 7). 10 Techniques Used by Manipulators (and How to Fight Them). Inc.Com. https://www.inc.com/jessica-stillman/10-popular-techniques-used-by-manipulators-and-how-to-fight-them.html

Terng, L. Y. (2020, June 6). 5 Things Toxic People Have In Common—Age of Awareness. Medium. https://medium.com/age-of-awareness/5-things-toxic-people-have-in-common-2d50a8723e7c

Tolles, J. (2017, January 9). How to Embrace True Power. Spiritual Awakening Process. https://www.spiritualawakeningprocess.com/2017/01/how-to-embrace-true-power.html

Tull, M. (2020, March 22). Coping With Isolation When You Are Suicidal and Have PTSD. Verywell Mind. https://www.verywellmind.com/ptsd-and-suicide-2797540

Types of Depression. (2008, May 22). WebMD. https://www.webmd.com/depression/guide/depression-types

Universidad Carlos III de Madrid. (n.d.). A study on human behavior has identified four basic personality types | UC3M. Www.Uc3m.Es. Retrieved July 2, 2021, from https://www.uc3m.es/ss/Satellite/UC3MInstitucional/en/Detalle/Comunicacion_C/1371223155576/1371216052182/A_study_on_human_behavior_has_identified_four_basic_personality_types

Wikipedia contributors. (2021, July 1). Narcissism. Wikipedia. https://en.wikipedia.org/wiki/Narcissism

Young, K. (2021, May 23). Toxic People: 12 Things They Do and How to Deal with Them. Hey Sigmund. https://www.heysigmund.com/toxic-people/

Zobolas, C. (2024, July 8). *Forming Healthy Relationships After Abuse | Denver, CO — Chadley Zobolas Therapy Group*. Chadley Zobolas Therapy Group. https://www.chadleyzobolastherapy.com/blog/forming-healthy-relationships-after-abuse

HEALTHY BOUNDARIES

HOW TO SET STRONG BOUNDARIES, SAY NO WITHOUT GUILT, AND MAINTAIN GOOD RELATIONSHIPS WITH YOUR PARENTS, FAMILY, AND FRIENDS

INTRODUCTION

What's the first thing that comes to mind when you hear the words 'healthy boundaries'?

Are you drawn to images of testing relationships and suffocating parents? Or is it a picture of frustration because your boss asks too much of you or your friends are demanding?

They are two words in the English language that so many of us strive for, but are often met by a brick wall. Every attempt to climb the brick wall results in a setback, pain, embarrassment, frustration, and fear of trying again. You know that if you could just get high enough to see over the top of that wall, life would improve. However, the idea of making another attempt prevents you from dusting yourself off and taking the next step.

Before you start to kick yourself when you're already down, think again. Struggling to establish boundaries doesn't mean that you missed this vital life lesson, or that you lack the intelligence to learn.

There are so many factors that contribute to setting boundaries, and none of them are your fault. We live in a bit of a dog-eat-dog world, and instead of supporting one another to the top, we are trampled on by the over-ambitious. Manipulation blurs the boundaries we are trying to set; not to mention the state of communication skills today.

Once upon a time we could have a face-to-face conversation, read body language, and understand tone of voice. Today, we often have to translate the meaning behind a combination of emojis. All of this culminates to make it harder to firmly establish our boundaries, and will be discussed in more detail later on.

The fact is, you do have to dust yourself off and learn how to set healthy boundaries. There's no way around this. Without them, you have no control over your own life. You end up doing things that make you unhappy, or even depressed. You can't say no for fear of hurting someone, and it's just easier to say yes despite hurting yourself. But deep down, you also know that it is neither fair nor right for you to continue to live a life that you can't enjoy to the maximum.

But it is far from doom and gloom! You don't have to continue living in a cycle that prevents you from reaching the top of your wall. From this moment forward, you can make the decision to learn new skills, master techniques, and show others that your boundaries do exist. Everything you need in order to do this is here in this book.

Several years ago, I was in the same position as many of you are now. I was working in the corporate world and had a lovely girlfriend, my parents were caring, and my friends were supportive. Or so it all seemed.

My life felt like a pane of glass. From a short distance, everything was as it should have been. But there was a tiny crack – my lack of boundaries. The problem was that this crack expanded, and it wasn't long before my entire life was broken.

I had reached a point where I couldn't keep feeling like I was the least important person in the room. I suffered too much when my girlfriend constantly put her own needs ahead of mine. I was doing the hard work, and my colleagues were getting the glory and the promotions. My friends and family looked at me in pity, and instead of helping, tried to tell me what to do and how to live my life. I was literally facing the very bottom, and all too often, the bottom of a bottle.

Depression led to health problems, exhaustion and weight gain, and the confidence I needed to set the necessary boundaries was draining from me.

One night I was scrolling through social media, and I saw a quote that just hit me. "A lack of boundaries invites a lack of respect."

I was truly feeling that lack of respect, but the quote also reminded me that while I wasn't asking for it, I wasn't preventing it either. So, I typed in 'healthy boundary quotes,' and the next one didn't just hit me: it woke me up. "Stop asking why they keep doing it, and start asking why you keep allowing it." I may not have realized it at the time, but this was going to be my turning point.

I started researching the power of the word no. I looked into how people pleasing was something we misperceived as being nice, but really, it was the core reason for unhealthy boundaries. The combination of these actions, through no fault of our own, causes us to lead an unfulfilling life. But this realization was only the first step.

I confess it took me about a year to transform my life. Psychology became my hobby and my passion. I tried out strategies, and read up on numerous theories. I read, listened and observed. Sometimes, I failed, but when I did, I could still see the progress I was making. I made it to the top of my wall, and it was awesome! A new me is just too much of a cliché, and it was not even the case – I was the real me.

My confidence grew so much that I started helping others. This was more rewarding than any corporate environment, so I decided to change my career. My goal became to help others, not by telling them what to do, but by providing them with insight into the techniques I successfully used to turn my life around. The only difference is that you don't need to take a year to achieve the same.

My book, *Stop People Pleasing*, briefly touched on the topic of healthy boundaries, and it sparked a lot of questions from readers. For this reason, we are going to take an in-depth look at boundaries. Not just the different types, but also boundaries within different relationships.

Some of you will read this book so that you can become more confident at telling others what is acceptable and what isn't, to free up your own time, or to stop taking part in things you don't want to. Others might be looking for more respect, peace and love.

The journey may be hard, and it will require a close look at yourself and why you do the things that you do. The changes that we make aren't just to establish your boundaries: we are going to make sure that you can maintain them, even when those you love insist on pushing them.

At the same time, we are going to learn how to let go of the guilt that arises when setting boundaries, and how to free ourselves from the fear of losing people in the process of creating these boundaries.

I want you to enjoy this journey, understand more about yourself, and celebrate each win. Let's begin with the fundamentals of healthy boundaries.

CHAPTER 1: BEFORE WE START: WHAT YOU SHOULD KNOW ABOUT HEALTHY BOUNDARIES

Boundaries are the limits that we set for ourselves in a relationship. Rigid boundaries can create distance. Porous boundaries are weak, and often get crossed or violated. A healthy boundary is one where you can feel comfortable expressing your thoughts, feelings, and the word "no" so that you can appreciate closer connections.

It is always good to start by taking a step back and considering how you see boundaries. If you look at the traditional sense of boundaries, you might see them as limits, or a line you don't cross. And this is correct.

Some people are very good at staying clear of other people's boundaries, and others know the exact point that they can reach before they have gone too far. Sadly, there are others who have no idea of people's boundaries, and the worst situations to find yourself in are the relationships where people don't care about your boundaries.

Meanwhile, we have others who feel the need to constantly push their own boundaries to succeed or to become a better person. Boundaries may also look like brick walls that we rely on for protection.

Before we go any further, ask yourself what your boundaries look like to you, and not what you think they should look like. If you're like I was at first, looking around trying to find your boundaries and realizing you don't have any, that's okay too.

This first chapter is about gaining an understanding of what healthy boundaries actually look like. So, regardless of what yours look like, from this point, we are going to give our attitude towards boundaries a clean slate.

We can classify boundaries as six key types: physical, emotional, time, sexual, intellectual and material (Earnshaw, 2019). Let's look at each one in more detail.

Your Physical Boundaries

Everything we need physically will have boundaries – from the food you need to the amount of sleep you require. These boundaries are defined by your personal space, as well as how much physical contact you're comfortable with. Physical abuse is an extreme violation of one's physical boundaries, but there is no question about when the line is crossed.

A physical boundary I had to work on personally was with food. I am what you could call a fussy eater, and although I'm happy to try new foods, I hate it when people try to force it on me. When someone started repeating, "Go on try it, you don't know if you like it unless you try it," I would always find myself caving in, and that would make me angry at myself.

Physical boundaries should include knowing when you need to rest or take some time to yourself. Peer pressure to go out in the evening or to attend family occasions on your day off are both examples of crossing boundaries. We are all entitled to take the time we need to recharge our batteries.

Personal space is high on the list of difficulties with physical boundaries. When Auntie plants a sloppy kiss on your cheek, she means well, but it makes you feel uncomfortable, and the line has been crossed.

This is a particularly important issue in the workplace. There are people who are naturally touchier – we call them huggers. Their physical contact is the same as another person's handshake. They might even find the thought of someone not liking a hug to be preposterous. Then there are the people who enjoy seeing you struggle when your personal space is invaded.

Your home is also important when you're thinking about your physical boundaries. Someone insisting on coming in is leaping over that limit.

Surprise visits can either be very welcoming or tread close to the line, especially if you already had plans but your visitor seems to feel they are more important.

Examples of physical boundaries:

- Being able to take rest when you need to
- People respecting your dietary needs
- Having the right amount of physical contact for the type of relationship
- Having personal space in your home

Your Emotional Boundaries

Our emotional boundaries need to be set with respect to how we are feeling, and this works both ways.

There will be emotional things that you will feel happy about sharing, and others that you would prefer to keep to yourself. Friends and family should be aware of exactly what you're comfortable talking about.

Parents and other family members have a wonderful habit of doing and saying things that embarrass us, whether that's getting out the baby photos, or reminding you that the clock is ticking and you should be settling down. Usually, this is fine but if it upsets you, there should be a boundary here.

Friends, too, need to know what you're comfortable listening to, but what's more, they need to appreciate your emotional state and whether you can handle taking on their emotional strains.

I am a firm believer in equal rights, equal earnings and equal housework, but we can't forget equal emotional rights.

This is another area we will be looking into further, but regardless of your gender, it is your right to be able to set emotional boundaries and to have them respected.

One of the things that hurt me so much with the relationship I had in my 20s was that I was laughed at for trying to explain that I was nervous or sad. It was as if, as a man, I shouldn't have these feelings.

When someone expresses their feelings, there shouldn't be any judgment, nor the need for justification. Emotions shouldn't be questioned or corrected.

If you're feeling angry, you should be allowed to express this, and not have someone say you are just tired or hungry.

Examples of emotional boundaries:

- Speaking openly about your views and opinions
- Not being told how you feel
- Sharing only what is appropriate
- Not having to justify your emotions

Your Time Boundaries

Once upon a time – and it really wasn't that long ago – we didn't all have cell phones to text and let someone know we were going to be late.

Don't get me wrong, I love modern technology, but time was more respected in the past. We made the effort to be on time. It might be picking your kids up, meeting your family or friends, or turning up at work, but time boundaries mean sticking to the agreed time.

It is rude and disrespectful to make someone wait. Every now and then, there could be a genuine reason, but if you feel that someone is constantly late or cancels on you regularly, they aren't respecting your time boundaries.

One action that you might not consider to be a violation of your time boundary is when you tell someone that you're busy, but then they continue to try to contact you. Again, as with being late, they might have honestly forgotten that you had plans.

If you feel like this is happening on purpose, however, then the other person is using manipulative techniques to play on your intentions, possibly trying to make you feel guilty for not spending time with them.

Another small gripe I have with modern technology is the lack of respect for time boundaries at work. The pandemic has certainly not helped.

Our regular working hours are very much blurred, and with email, social media, group chats and video conferences, so many people are struggling with the pressure of work, with little time to disconnect.

Employers shouldn't ask for more than the contracted time, and employees need to ensure that they're completing tasks within the deadlines.

Examples of time boundaries:

- Arriving on time
- Respecting other people's time limitations
- Accepting when people can't make an event
- Keeping planned arrangements

Your Sexual Boundaries

This is another boundary that I feel very strongly about, and it's a challenging one. Young people may struggle to have the necessary conversations to practice safe sex, both physically and emotionally.

Even adults can find themselves in situations they would rather stop, but lack the courage, or feel that there comes a point where they can't say no. It may surprise you to think that sexual boundaries change with life events such as pregnancy and menopause.

Thanks to some amazing support networks and better education, rape is becoming less of a taboo subject. However, society still seems to view sexual assault as a crime only against women.

Shocking statistics show that one in 33 men in America has experienced attempted or completed rape (RAINN). And that is only those who are brave enough to come forward. The same studies highlight mental problems such as PTSD, increased risk of drug use, and problems with personal and professional relationships.

Violating someone's sexual boundaries includes lying about contraception or sexually transmitted diseases. Complaining when someone doesn't want sex or about a person's preferences, likes or desires is also wrong.

Withholding sex as a form of punishment may not seem like you're crossing this imaginary line, but it is still a form of manipulation.

Whether you're walking down the road, or you're in a club, pub or at work, you must feel like you are in a safe environment, free from unwanted advances. If you choose to wear a short skirt, it doesn't mean you want men to leer. If you're a man without a shirt on, you shouldn't be subjected to sexual comments.

Examples of sexual boundaries:

- Asking for consent and respecting when the answer is no
- Talking about contraception
- Being open about sexual health issues
- Discussing likes and dislikes

Your Intellectual Boundaries

Have you ever met a person who is incapable of seeing things from your point of view? Or someone who fakes interest in your opinions, but always wants to be right and have the last word? Let's not mistake an education for intelligence. Anyone can read a textbook or watch a documentary and believe they are all-knowing about a subject.

Intelligence is a combination of intelligence quotient (IQ) and emotional intelligence quotient (EQ). A well-rounded intelligent person has the ability to share their learning, views and opinions, and then respectfully listen to others.

They are willing to spark a conversation and even to debate, but they will never cross the line that makes you feel stupid. I was constantly interrupted by my ex.

It was infuriating, but I was never able to set the right boundary.

My ideas were met with a look that told me I was just an idiot whose opinions didn't count, whether it was what take-out to get or the color of the wall.

I'm no Einstein, but I'm not stupid, and although I have come a long way, crossing intellectual boundaries can be devastating for someone's confidence.

Intelligence boundaries include knowing when it is the right time to talk about certain topics. Religion and politics are banned from my family dinner table – just because there are too many differing opinions, and it's not the right time.

If your partner does something to upset you, there's no need to shame them in public when you could talk about it privately at home.

You also need to be aware that setting intelligence boundaries means that you don't tolerate people's opinions on matters that are hurtful.

Laughing with the crowd at a sexist or racist joke will probably go against your core values. Nobody should have to pretend to be someone they aren't just to fit in.

Examples of intellectual boundaries:

- Accepting that everyone is entitled to their own opinions
- Agreeing to disagree
- Knowing the right time to talk about things
- Not belittling people for their beliefs

Your Material Boundaries

This is a tricky one. We are taught from a young age that sharing is good – let others play with your toys, or give your sibling a sweet. You let your friend borrow your car, knowing they will leave their trash in it.

The fact is, as adults, we have worked hard for our material possessions, and rather than seeing it as selfish and not sharing, it is more likely that we are protecting our investments.

Living with others brings up a lot of material boundary issues. If you're working from home, it's logical to set up a boundary regarding your computer. If someone breaks it, you could lose your income.

I feel a little weird complaining when someone uses my glass or my cup. It is enough to make others smile at what seems like a quirk. But these objects have meaning to me, and if they were damaged, I wouldn't be able to replace them.

Examples of material boundaries:

- Not taking things without permission
- Returning things in the proper condition
- Accepting a "no" when people can't or don't want to lend you things
- Respecting return dates

The aim of our first chapter is to awaken ourselves to the extent of boundaries. Take some time, and give yourself credit for those boundaries that you feel you have established. This might be the smallest thing like not letting your partner swear, or stopping your mom from packing up leftovers.

It's also about identifying the boundaries that you need to create. Now that you're aware of the different boundaries, we can start to assess which boundaries you need, and which ones you need to work on.

How to Practice Boundary Awareness

In your journal or on a piece of paper, draw seven boxes. Label each one as one of the boundary types, and the 7th as 'Other'.

You might want to take a week so that you have both working days and the weekend for a complete look at your relationships. Observe your week, and make a list of all the boundaries you can see that exist in your life.

Don't worry about looking at the boundaries you're missing: we'll start to work on this in the following chapter. Look at your relationships, and observe the boundaries you have in place.

CHAPTER 2: TESTING YOURSELF: DO YOU REALLY NEED TO SET BOUNDARIES?

Everyone needs boundaries. They are like our own little rule books. When you picture your boundaries as rules, it becomes easier to understand their importance. You can't play a game of Monopoly or football without rules.

Boundaries, like rules, help us to understand the thoughts, feelings and wishes of others, which in turn, allows us to maintain healthy relationships.

When our boundaries are clear, we are able to enjoy our personal and professional relationships. It is motivating to imagine saying no to someone and have them respect your answer.

Boundaries mean you will be heard and appreciated, and that your needs will be met. Healthy boundaries are mutual, meaning the other person will also feel safe within the relationship.

Needless to say, there are some situations when people aren't going to be aware of your boundaries and they might be violated. When a stranger stands too close to you, this is not on purpose. When you meet new people, they aren't going to be aware of where your limits are. Crossing them, again, is not intentional, and later on, we will look at how to establish boundaries in new relationships without causing offense. Then, we have those relationships that are well established but lack boundaries – often these the most challenging, as you may need to assert yourself more.

As I mentioned in the first chapter, we always need to go back to the foundations before we can start rebuilding. Now that you have discovered the extent of boundaries, it's time to figure out if you need to set them. It sounds like an obvious statement, but as a life coach, I have seen so many people who knew that they were in a toxic relationship, but they had never been able to put a finger on where it was going wrong. They were unaware of the need for boundaries.

What Do Unhealthy Boundaries Look Like?

After looking at what healthy boundaries are, you can imagine what unhealthy boundaries look like, some being more subtle than others.

- Giving inappropriate gifts
- Excessive texting, calling or emailing
- Ghosting
- Asking personal questions
- Repeating confidential information/gossiping
- Eavesdropping
- Imposing religious or political beliefs
- Demanding things of people instead of asking
- Interrupting
- Outbursts of uncalled-for anger
- Intimidating body language/communication
- Telling lies

- Saying yes to please everyone
- Feeling guilty about saying no
- Falling in love too quickly
- Not standing up for yourself or being afraid to disagree
- Trusting too easily
- Putting more into a relationship than the other person
- Expecting or needing others to care for you
- Pushing down your feelings or blocking them
- Letting others control your life

Let's take a closer look at some ways boundaries can be violated before further self-assessment.

What Do Boundary Violations Look Like?

- Physical contact that is not permitted
- Sex without consent
- Physical/emotional abuse
- Manipulation
- Taking belongings without permission
- Sharing confidential information without permission
- Posting photos on social media without permission
- Bullying, mockery, insults

Intimidating body language can be interpreted in more than one way, and it will depend on the other person's intentions.

Unfortunately, there are people in the world who are just terrible at communication and are unwilling to learn. These people are unaware that they're using too much eye contact and you feel uncomfortable.

This is still a violation of your boundary, but you need to look away in the hope that they mirror your example.

The person who purposely shakes your hand for too long or kisses your cheek too close to your lips needs to be stopped. It is not possible to list all violations of boundaries because it is something that is very personal.

You might feel like all lies are completely unacceptable, but your neighbor might feel that a little white lie is okay to protect someone.

This is the gray area we all need to explore until the black and white become clear.

What Happens When You Don't Set Boundaries?

Some of the consequences of not having boundaries are as clear as day, and you will find yourself nodding as you read on. Personally, I found that life just hurt. There is a weight that you can't shift, an exhaustion you feel all the time. It can be hard to get out of bed knowing that you are about to face another day of feeling used or hurt. Some people are amazing at putting on a mask so that from the outside, they seem fine.

Because we feel that the needs of others are more important than our own, it's easy for others to take advantage. This lack of balance causes the 'dominant' partner to feed on the weaker.

Here too, there is a spectrum of signs. Subtle signs could be controlling what people wear. It doesn't have to be phrases like, "You can't wear that." When you notice your partner making frequent comments about what they prefer you to wear or what they don't like, they're crossing a boundary.

Verbal abuse, physical abuse or sexual abuse is a clear line that cannot be crossed whether you are male or female. If a woman hits you or if a man insults you, it is abuse. It is unacceptable, undeserved, and a sign of a toxic relationship.

After an extended time of not having clear boundaries, you will start to see a negative impact on your health. This may include lack of sleep, eating the wrong foods, burnout, drug and/or alcohol abuse, depression, anxiety, and self-harm.

The scary thing I worry about is that we all have our breaking point. The moment when you know you can't cope with it anymore. We will learn how to set the necessary boundaries, and although your self-esteem is probably at rock bottom right now, you can do it. That being said, if you feel that you have reached your breaking point, please get professional help.

Setting boundaries isn't easy, and you need to start with the right mind frame and a can-do attitude. There is no shame in asking for support to get yourself in the right place to start working on these strategies.

How Do You Know if You Have Boundary Issues?

It's not always obvious, especially when it comes to those boundaries that are still a little gray or you haven't clarified your limits around just yet. Below, you will find 20 questions that you can use as a form of self-assessment. You can give each question a score from 1 to 5, 1 being never, and 5 being always.

There is no golden answer here. Mostly nevers might mean that there is just a small area of your life that you would like to improve. If everything comes back as always, it's time to wipe the slate clean and create fresh, strong boundaries. If you end up with a lot of sometimes, it probably means your boundaries are there, but you need to reinforce them.

Remember that nobody is going to correct your answers or judge you, or even see them, so be completely honest with yourself.

1. Do you regularly feel stressed, anxious or overwhelmed?

2. Do you feel like you aren't in control of your life or that others tend to control it for you – kids, partner, parents, etc.?

3. Do you feel like there is always something that needs to be done or that you are always behind on things?

4. Do you feel like your loved ones take advantage of you, your time, your generosity, etc.?

5. Do you go out of your way to prevent others from being hurt?

6. Are the needs of your loved ones more important than your own?

7. Do you feel that people won't want to be with you unless you meet their needs?

8. Do you attend to the needs of your family and friends before your own?

9. Do you resent your loved ones when they ask too much of you?

10. Do you feel like you need to justify your needs, whether that's to others or to yourself?

11. Do you feel obliged to say yes because you're the only person who can help?

12. Does it upset you or hurt you when you think you have let others down?

13. Do you worry that people will leave you if you say no?

14. Is it easier for you to just say yes to avoid confrontation?

15. Do you doubt your feelings, assume you don't have the right to these feelings, or feel that your feelings aren't as important as those of others?

16. Does it make you anxious when you think people don't like you?

17. Does it make you anxious when people don't approve of you?

18. Do you believe other people's criticism, without considering the circumstances?

19. Are others able to control how you feel by playing with your emotions?

20. Do you find yourself making excuses for others or covering for them?

I love to use these questions for general boundaries. Further on in the book, we will look at specific types of relationships, and this will enable us to look more closely at whether you need to work on your boundaries.

If you still feel like you're unclear on your boundaries, don't worry. In the next chapter, we're going to dive deeper into defining your boundaries to provide complete clarity before creating strategies to set them.

CHAPTER 3: 7 DEEP QUESTIONS TO HELP YOU DISCOVER YOURSELF AND CREATE BOUNDARIES

> *"Life wasn't meant to be easy. The difficult things we go through are the things that make us stronger."*
>
> — *KOMAL KANT*

We can find 100 quotes about the necessity of doing the hard things in life. The lesson is normally that life is better once you have mastered a skill, and the difficult task then becomes easy. Mastering your healthy boundaries starts with some difficult questions, but the sooner you start, the better off you'll be. This is because, as time passes, the people around you become accustomed to treating you in a particular way – the way you don't like.

If you feel like you're facing an impossible challenge and have no idea where to start, it's time to take a deeper look at yourself and what the real you looks like.

This is not supposed to be a session where you look at all your negative qualities so that you feel worse about yourself. If you find yourself starting to get frustrated with yourself or upset, take a step away, or you will find that your discoveries won't be constructive.

Rather than overwhelming you, we are going to look at different types of boundaries, but in each situation, you will be able to see three clear stages.

We will follow the 3 C system – Create, Communicate and Control. It is wise to make sure you have the 3 Cs in your plan before enforcing boundaries, but we will look at each extensively.

Learning to Define Your Boundary Limits

These questions are designed to help you clearly identify the thin line between what matters to you and what you are comfortable accepting.

It is the first stage of our 3 Cs in creating boundaries. You are the only person who can create healthy boundaries, but starting with the answers to the following questions will help you find your limits. Only when you know what is valid to you will you be able to explain these validations to others.

Take a piece of paper and a pen so that you can make notes. Don't feel like your answers need to make sense straight away. Take two shots at deep questions. The first time I write down what immediately comes to mind. I call this the unfiltered stage, or the raw answers. Sometimes, it doesn't seem that my thoughts make any sense. Then I take a little more time to really delve into the question.

It's a good idea to try to find a peaceful moment to ask these deep questions. Don't feel like you need to do this all in one sitting. It's better to take a day or two rather than to rush through. Revisit the questions when you're in different places or when you're with different people. Make a note on your phone, and then add it to your piece of paper later. The more ideas, thoughts and opinions, the better – as long as they're honest!

1. What are the positives and negatives of your relationships?

This in itself is quite an extensive question because there are numerous relationships to consider, each with its own boundaries. Your list of relationships could include your partner, children, friends, parents, other family members, your colleagues, your boss, etc.

Try to keep your list quite specific because your relationship with your best friend might not be the same as with other friends. You may prioritize their needs differently – just as you might be comfortable with a kiss from your mom but not so much from cousins or aunts.

2. Do you do things out of love or fear?

This is a great question. Look back at the last 10 or 15 things you did for other people. It doesn't matter who these people are or the size of the task. Decide your reason for saying yes.

Was it because you wanted to, because you love that person and doing it made you happy? Or did you do it because you feared the repercussions of saying no?

3. What makes your blood boil?

The answer to this question will help you to define your hard boundaries. These are the boundaries that will not be crossed no matter what.

Most typically, these actions go against your core values. They might be racist comments or jokes, unfaithfulness, inequality, or breaking the law. It could also be things like people telling you how to raise your children, or arguing with you about topics that you feel passionate about.

4. If you had unlimited time and money, what would you do?

This is not a question to spark a daydream. The reality is that you will have to get up for work tomorrow, and winning a lottery is unlikely.

The idea behind this question is to consider the daily things that make you happy, whether that be reading more books, going to the cinema, or going out for dinner more often. It is these things that you frequently don't get to do because you are unable to say no to helping others.

5. What's on your bucket list?

I've seen people pull a strange face when I ask them this question. They seem to think it's depressing thinking of things that they want to do before they die. Realistically, it's just the list of things you want to do and achieve in life.

Your bucket list could include travel, a fitness goal like running a marathon, extreme sports, learning how to cook, overcoming a fear, or seeing the Northern Lights – the list is endless, and it should be motivating. Having a list of your own goals will help you to see the importance of putting your own needs and dreams before those of others.

6. What did you love doing as a child?

Children have hobbies. For so many of us, adulthood can mean sacrificing our hobbies for responsibilities. Those long bike rides become evening routines. Movie nights are replaced with working overtime. The list goes on.

The moment when I realized I had no hobbies was quite shocking for me. How do we get to this point? To fix this, go back to the things that you used to love as a child. Which hobbies would you like to start again, or do you have others in mind that you fancy trying?

7. Are you a human being or a human doing?

This is deep, but the answer is one or the other. There is a wonderful Buddhist proverb, "When is more enough?" Our lives are filled with things we need because we think they will make us happy.

You have to say yes to your boss because you need the money. You allow your friends to decide what the plans are because it is easier than rocking the boat. This is a human doing (Saviuc, 2020)!

You are defined by what you do. By the end of this book, you will be able to enjoy life as a human being, be who you really are, and start to live life to the fullest.

Let's look at how one person answered these questions and how he used the answers to start developing his boundaries.

Example Answers to Help You Put the 7 Questions Into Practice

Luke has been struggling with understanding his boundaries for a while. He has attempted to set some and enforce them, but people either assumed he was joking, or they just brushed off his requests. Here are the notes I took after reviewing Luke's answers:

Question #1 - What are the positives and negatives of Luke's relationships?

Luke is single. He knows that he doesn't want to start another relationship until he is stronger. He has a daughter with his ex, and sees her once a week. Her mom has a habit of changing the day to suit her, and he is scared that by saying no, he won't be able to see his little one.

His parents are generally understanding, but every now and then, he feels like they still treat him like a child, which prevents him from wanting to do more with them.

His best friend is his rock, and is always telling him to stand up for himself. He has distanced himself from other friends, and regrets this slightly.

Question #2 - Does Luke do things out of love or fear?

His biggest fear is not seeing his child. The other things he has done for others recently have been in order to have an easy life: neither love nor fear.

Question #3 - What makes Luke's blood boil?

It is his work environment that makes his blood boil at the moment. There is a toxic atmosphere where certain employees can break the rules, and the others just have to pick up the pieces. It's not enjoyable, and he knows that he wants to do something but is unsure of what steps to take.

Question #4 - If Luke had unlimited time and money, what would he do?

Luke would love to spend more time exploring nearby cities and cultural areas, perhaps take some day trips to meet new people. In general, he would like life to slow down a little bit, perhaps be able to sit in a coffee shop and watch the world go by.

Question #5 & 6 - What is on Luke's bucket list? What did he love doing as a child?

Luke wants to swim with dolphins, walk part of the Great Wall of China, and go on a short cruise. As a child, he loved playing football in the street with his friends, and he loved his pet fish.

Question #7 - Is Luke a human being or human doing?

Luke is definitely a human doing. He felt that each day of his life was a process to be completed. He had fallen into a routine, and couldn't see a way of breaking it.

From this incredibly deep look at his life, Luke could see that his feelings were not valid. Despite having tried to talk to his ex and his parents, their behavior continued. He knew that his best friend would be there to support him, and he was interested in reconnecting with other friends if could be sure the boundaries would be in place and respected.

Work would be a challenge. Answering the question reminded him of how much he loved his job. He didn't want to look for another job because that would feel like running from the problem. He would still need boundaries in a new work environment, so although he was nervous, he was determined to find a solution for work. He decided to use the items on his new hobbies and bucket list as rewards for achieving various steps throughout his journey.

Turning These Questions Into Practice for You

Finally, with all of your newfound information about yourself, draw a line straight down the middle of a piece of paper.

This line is your boundary. It is your absolute no, and from this moment, you can no longer make exceptions. To the right of this line, write a list of everything that is crossing your new boundary. Don't hesitate. If you don't feel that people respect your emotions or needs, it goes on the list. If your boss doesn't respect your weekends, it is written down.

To the left, you can now place ideas in relation to the line. If your mom insists on you taking home Tupperware lunches, think about this for a second, or even ask her. Is she doing it because she thinks you can't take care of yourself, or is it because she simply has leftover food not to be wasted, and thinks it will save you time?

Suddenly, what you saw as overstepping a boundary might just be a case of a mom being a mom.

There will be some things you don't mind doing. If your friend needs you for an emergency, you can put this closer to your line. The idea is to create a visual image of what is acceptable and what is not.

For many of us, understanding our boundaries is hard because it is not something that we can physically see. This paper provides a visual tool. You can always edit it, add new boundaries as new situations come up in life, or adjust one, as long as it is a decision you want and not something you feel like you have to abide by.

We're still at the point where the work we're doing toward our healthy boundaries is just for you. I think this is an important thing to keep in mind because if you start to worry that others will see your notes or your boundary line, you won't be completely honest.

Even if it is subconsciously, you will start to create new boundaries that will make others happy instead of yourself. You may even start to feel guilty at the idea of someone reading your thoughts and feelings; you might feel like you are being selfish.

Negative emotions such as guilt and the fear of saying no are huge influencers on our ability to create healthy boundaries. So much so that the next chapter is dedicated to finding your inner strength to overcome these negative emotions and to actually look forward to creating boundaries.

CHAPTER 4: POWER WITHIN: HOW TO STOP FEELING GUILTY, OVERCOME FEAR, AND FIND ENERGY

This is one of my favorite stages in the journey to enforcing healthy boundaries. It requires a change of mindset, meaning that you must expand your ideas on common issues that often prevent us from putting ourselves first. Often, we know what our boundaries look like, especially after the previous chapters, but there is still a stage in the middle that is essential if we are to succeed with these boundaries – the strength and power to say no without feeling guilty or selfish.

The Real Reasons That Some People Don't Have Boundaries

#1 Reason: People call me selfish when I try to set boundaries.

Solution - Changing your mindset will help. The reason we need boundaries is so that we can take care of our health. You wouldn't be called selfish if you went on a diet or saw a doctor when you needed antibiotics. Selfish is when you constantly put yourself ahead of others, not when you put your wellbeing first.

#2 Reason: It is just easier to say yes.

Solution - In the short term, it is easier to say yes. But, in the long run, you will continue to suffer mentally and physically, and probably worse than you are now. At first, it will take more energy to assert yourself, which is why it is essential to take care of yourself. However, once you have passed the initial stress, you will find it gets easier to say no.

#3 Reason: Even though I know the relationship is bad, I am scared of ending it.

Solution - Ending a relationship is always going to cause fear. You might fear being alone or fear the idea of being independent. The fact is, you deserve better, and the fear is often about the act of ending the relationship rather than what comes next. Take some time to plan how you will achieve your goals and the rewards.

#4 Reason: I don't set boundaries because I worry that my family will love me less.

Solution - Establishing your boundaries isn't about creating distance. It's about communicating your wishes and needs in the right way so that your family don't take offense, but understand the importance of your boundaries.

When boundaries are set in the right way, you have the chance to experience greater love.

#5 Reason: People will see me as boring.

Solution - The word 'boundaries' does have a mature sound to it, but that doesn't mean you're boring or that you're uptight. Without boundaries, you may end up without the strength or energy to enjoy any time with your friends and family. Saying no to the things you don't want to do will provide you with the energy to enjoy the activities that you want to do even more.

#6 Reason: I can't set boundaries because people need me.

Codependency will often prevent people from creating their boundaries, and unfortunately, this leads to others taking advantage of them.

We will look closely at codependency for different relationships, but it's important to understand the difference between supporting others and doing everything for them.

I feel that a large part of this problem starts in childhood and follows us into our adult lives.

Even though it was almost three decades ago, I can still remember the pressure in high school to make friends, to be popular, and to be liked. It is part of human nature and the way we are wired, so there's nothing wrong with this.

It goes back much further than this – it is a survival tactic. It's hard to deny that babies are just adorable and cute. They need adults to see them this way so that they are taken care of.

Research on parenting styles also impacts our view of boundaries from a young age. In the 1960s, Diana Baumrind noticed that there were three major parenting styles: the authoritative, the authoritarian, and the permissive (Parenting for Brain, 2021).

Authoritarian parents have extremely strict rules and a somewhat black and white approach, which can result in children growing up with low self-esteem. Permissive parents are often over-indulging, and there are few or no rules.

A child's behavior can be egocentric, leading to problems in relationships. It is the authoritative parents who are warm and supportive, yet have clear rules and high expectations. This parenting style creates higher self-esteem and improved social skills.

Social media has taken the need to be liked to an extreme level, with people defining themselves by the number of likes they have. When people say that social media has become a drug for them, they aren't exaggerating.

Dopamine is a chemical that is released when we do something that feels good, and it will motivate us to do it again. It is produced when we have sex, when we exercise, or when we do any other enjoyable activity.

Cognitive neuroscientists have shown that receiving likes on social media causes an influx in dopamine.

Racheal S. Heslin, transformational author and speaker, likens our need for approval to the small part of us that still fears what we did as a child

– the need for our parents' love and approval. It is only when you are able to provide yourself with the approval that you need that you can start to forget the recognition you crave from others.

The need to be liked and loved becomes a problem when you have to do things that you don't want to do for fear that someone will like or love you less.

This causes us to do things we wouldn't normally do. If you think about it, it's probably the worst thing we can do when starting any kind of new relationship.

I remember on one of my first dates, my then-girlfriend insisted that I tried fish in a restaurant. I hate fish, but I wanted to impress her, so I tried it. From that very moment, the boundary had been crossed, and it would be hard to undo the behavior.

To be liked, it can often feel as if we need to be this chilled out person who goes with the flow. You don't want to come across as the party pooper, so you say yes to everything. The price you pay for not being boring is people taking advantage of you.

It's also true that some of you have been able to say no, but the reactions from people have left you feeling worse than you would have if you'd just said yes.

I've been called selfish, mean, and even heartless after trying to say no. My ex had fits of rage followed by tears. I would have to back down because I felt responsible. She would smile, and only then would I realize that it was all an act.

It is often similar in the workplace. Have you ever tried to say no to your boss or colleague and then experienced micro-actions that feel as if you're being punished?

By definition, they are so small – being left out of a group email or having ideas dismissed in a meeting – that you might think you're being paranoid.

Being liked and loved is no different for an empath. The difference is seen in the degree in which they experience other people's emotions in a relationship.

Highly sensitive people will experience love in a different way. It might be deeper, rawer and more beautiful, yet more painful at the same time.

On the contrary, narcissists seek out those who they can get the most from. It is still a need to be loved and liked, but it can almost come across as though it is their right, often not caring that their partner (often an empath) also has needs.

To overcome these challenges, we have to break down this stage and first work on our confidence and skills to express our needs.

We are also going to learn that setting boundaries isn't selfish at all; in fact, on the contrary, you are helping those in your life to have more meaningful long-lasting relationships.

Taking Care of Yourself to Boost Your Energy and Inner Strength

We all know that it takes an awful lot of energy to deal with certain people.

Unfortunately, dealing with them results in burnout, anxiety, stress, and a whole handful of other potential health problems.

It is likely that you aren't sleeping properly, and you wake up extremely tired.

It's easier to grab an energy drink for that boost of energy you need rather than looking for long-term solutions. There's no judgment here: I have been there.

However, all of these health problems cause us to look at ourselves in a different light.

The extra pounds we might be carrying all of a sudden make us think we're fat and ugly. The bags under our eyes make us look drained.

Every negative knocks our confidence, and we start to tell ourselves that we don't deserve to be happy. For this reason, it's time to start taking better care of yourself.

Don't panic! No strict diets or hour-long sessions at the gym.

Here are some ideas that you can easily add to your day so that you start increasing your energy and boosting your confidence:

✔Drink more water.

Start the day with hot water and a slice of lemon. It is a great cleanser. For every coffee you drink, have a glass of water first, and another glass with each meal.

✔Try to add more fruit and vegetables to your day.

I confess, I love a chocolate cookie, but I made a rule where I could only have one if I had a piece of fruit with it.

✔Increase your mood-boosting foods.

Things like Omega 3, dark chocolate, bananas, berries and nuts can help you to feel more positive about life.

✔Exercise is essential.

I promise I'm not a fitness freak, and I'm not pumping weights at the gym every night.

Exercise makes me happy, even if it's a short walk each day or 20 jumping jacks and a few yoga stretches to start the day.

More oxygen is delivered to your organs, including your brain. You will have more energy and better concentration.

✔Start meditating.

Meditation is no longer the same hippy concept from the 70s. Scientific studies are continuously showing the health benefits of meditation, including managing stress, reducing negative emotions, and increasing patience.

If you find meditation hard, you can find excellent guided meditations online. I absolutely love this guided meditation for confidence.

Marisa Peer includes some wonderful phrases that relate to our boundaries, such as "You matter," and "You are significant."

SCAN ME

Scan the QR code above to open the meditation

I recently added the **Wim Hof Method** to my daily routine, and the results were outstanding. Today, we aren't so in touch with our basic survival needs. We have resources that help us when it comes to food and clothing. Not being in tune with the need to survive reduces our ability to connect with our inner self, where so much of our power lays dormant.

Here is another guided video that will teach you the Wim Hof Method. If you feel that this method is going to help, it's worth downloading the Wim Hof Mobile App. The free version lets you watch videos, practice exercises, and monitor your progress.

SCAN ME

Scan the QR code above to open the Guided Wim Hof Method Breathing video

✔**Create to-do lists.** I have a daily to-do list that I write with my first coffee of the day. It helps me to organize my thoughts and prioritize. Crossing off completed tasks shows the progress I have made, and it helps to motivate me throughout the day.

✔**Take 5 minutes for yourself every day.** I know you're busy and there are plenty of other things that you can do with those 5 minutes, but it is doubtful that those things are more important than your health.

Step away from the technology, read a couple of pages of your book, or stand outside and breathe in the fresh air. Just 5 minutes all to yourself is a small step to allowing your needs to matter.

✔**Create a bedtime routine.** In order to get a better night's sleep, be strict with your evening routine. Needless to say, you should avoid caffeine, but try to keep your phone away from your bed too.

Overcoming Negative Emotions to Establish Boundaries

The two main negative emotions we feel when setting boundaries are guilt and fear.

Guilt arises because we have put our own wishes before others, and the second we do this, we begin to feel as if we are selfish. It is possible to feel guilty because the other person needs you, or just because you have come across as being mean and not caring.

Fear can be brought on by short-term consequences, like someone is going to get angry with you or insult you, or long-term consequences, like fearing losing the person from your life.

Let's tackle the two separately.

Tackling Guilt Head-on

Never have I seen a worse case of the guilt trip than the Rolo advert from the 90s. You know, the round caramels covered in chocolate wrapped in a tube. The voice would say, "Do you love someone enough to give them your last Rolo?"

And this resonates through our entire lives as we live with this idea that we have to walk on burning coals to prove our love for someone. Anything less, and we feel guilty.

It is just as bad when we are able to say no without guilt, but then the other person says something or acts in a way that causes us to start feeling guilty. Neither situation warrants this guilt.

Why should you feel guilty for doing exactly the same thing the other person's doing when they don't feel guilty about it? What makes their needs more important than yours? Is it just because they are better at dramatizing their needs?

Setting boundaries is nothing to feel guilty about because it is teaching others that there has to be a balance in the relationship, some give and take. It is what successful relationships thrive on. You're entitled to your thoughts, opinions, beliefs and emotions, just like the next person. You are no less worthy.

You also can't feel guilty for putting self-care ahead of the wishes of others. An important part of having boundaries is to recognize that we all have our limits, both physically and emotionally. You need to dedicate time to yourself so that you're in a better position to help others when they need it.

This is a very common problem for parents. Parents could spend 24 hours a day taking care of their children, making sure they're healthy, safe and happy. The thought of taking some time to do an activity they want to do is impossible because of the guilt.

Logically though, we all know that a 10-minute shower, a glass of wine with friends, or sneaking in an episode of your favorite series without the kids screaming at you would be enough to recharge your batteries. When you're able to see that self-care makes you a better person for those around you, it is easier to leave the guilt behind.

You will also find that freeing yourself from guilt is something that requires practice. As you begin to start setting your boundaries, if you start feeling guilty, follow these steps:

1. Take a step back, and stop talking. Take a deep breath, and give yourself a second to compose your thoughts.

2. Remind yourself that setting boundaries is a good thing. Find an affirmation that empowers you, a short phrase to help you remember that there is no need to feel guilty. Try sentences like, "I have done nothing wrong," "My boundaries are a good thing," or "My boundaries are important."

3. Don't apologize or feel you have to justify your words. The more you talk, the more ammunition you give them to try to change your mind.

4. Keep in mind the activity you would rather be doing instead of what the other person is asking of you: it will help you to stay focused.

5. Smile. Smiling helps you to express your thoughts confidently, and without coming across as being mean.

6. Don't punish yourself if you still feel guilty. Time is going to help, but the initial goal is to have other people respect your boundaries. The more success you have, the less guilt you will feel.

7. Don't let setbacks put you off trying again. Sometimes we win, sometimes we lose, and sometimes the actions of others are so strong that it might not be possible to avoid guilt. This is on them, not on you, and it doesn't mean that you aren't able to set boundaries without feeling guilty.

As with so many of the techniques we master throughout this book, it is going to take strength and perseverance to overcome guilt. However, you will experience such an amazing rush with even the smallest progress that you will be motivated to keep going.

Getting to the Bottom of Your Fears

When breaking down the process of setting boundaries, it's important to discover which stage makes you afraid. So far, we haven't done anything that should cause real fear because we're still in the planning and preparation phase. You probably haven't put anything into practice. It's very rare to feel fear when creating your boundaries.

So now it's down to two other sources – expressing your boundary or the consequences of doing so. Even when you're expressing your boundary, the fear begins because you're already thinking about the reaction you might get. To take this one step further, we need to identify the type of fear (Levin, 2021).

Are you scared that the other person is going to get angry? Could it be because they might get upset? You might fear hearing the word 'no' or them rejecting you in some other way. And what if they were to simply just walk away?

This is the best thing about fear! We are afraid of something that doesn't exist, and this is how we need to rewire our brains to think. The moment that fear starts to fill your body, you have to tell yourself that the consequence of your boundary isn't set in stone.

The only sure thing is you expressing the boundary, and this is what you can control. By placing all of your focus on explaining your boundary, there will be no room for fearing what is yet to happen, if it even will.

Let's look at some methods for overcoming certain types of fear:

Fear of aggression - If you are in the extremely difficult position of trying to express your boundaries to an aggressive person, you might freeze in fear because of their possible reaction. It is essential that you deal with this type of person in a place where you feel safe. Ensure that others are around you, but they don't necessarily have to be people you know. Even being in a public place will reduce the likelihood of a violent outburst, and there will be help if you need it.

Fear of abandonment - Some of your loved ones won't like the idea of you creating boundaries you intend to keep. They might have lost their control over you, or they might not like the fact they are no longer the focus of your life. In some cases, they will threaten to leave, and in the majority of these cases, it is just a threat. They are hoping to create this fear of abandonment so that you revert to being your more submissive self.

Even though you can see that your relationship is toxic, it doesn't mean it is easy to end. You may start to worry about the possibility of being alone forever, or that in reality, you need this person. The truth is that you don't need this toxicity in your life. You are stronger than you realize, and with time, you will see this. Removing people who manipulate you will provide you with the space and energy to focus on who you want to become, and make way for better relationships.

Fear of shame and embarrassment - Worrying about being shown up in front of others is a frequent reason for delaying boundary setting. If you're out with friends and you say no to your partner, the moment they start to ridicule you is mortifying. All eyes are on you and how you react, which is something that people with our personality are generally uncomfortable with.

As you work through the stages of this book, you will start to see your confidence grow, and you will feel more empowered in these situations.

Remember, all eyes might be on you, but people are actually highly attuned to shaming, and as a society, we are becoming less tolerant. The audience will feel embarrassed for the other person's behavior.

Fear of stress - We already lead incredibly stressful lives. According to the American Institute of Stress, 75% of Americans experience moderate to high levels of stress. Stress infiltrates every area of our life. Avoiding it is a way of protecting our physical and mental health.

The stress we fear when developing our boundaries is a necessary evil. We need to work through this stress because the result will be less stress in the long run.

Taking care of yourself is critical, which is why we closely examined ways to make yourself stronger in Chapter 4.

Simple Steps to Overcoming Your Fears

The following steps are very simple. However, that's not to say that you will wake up one morning and your fears will have just disappeared. It might take just a couple of days, or maybe a few weeks, but practice is the key.

- Get to the bottom of your fear. Understand the type of fear and where it is coming from.

- Listen to your fear. You can't just block it. Take time to address it. Don't feel like you have to take action straight away – a few minutes for reflection will help to calm your subconscious.

- Focus on your goals. Your goal is a firm boundary, but beyond that, it is a more fulfilling life. This positive visualization can gradually replace the fear and provide you with motivation.

- Make a decision to learn from your fear. Fear causes pain, but this pain offers us a chance to grow. Learning to let go of the pain helps to overcome present and future fears.

- Understand that, on occasions, you will fail. Not everything in life is about winning or succeeding. Failing is not the same as being a failure. It is a minor bump in the long road. When fear rises up, concentrate on deep breaths, and never give up. The rewards will far outweigh your little setbacks.

The majority of our fears are based on experiences from our past. It might be that you have tried to tell a co-worker that you won't pick up their slack and they ignored you, and now you fear that any time you attempt to assert yourself, you are going to get the same reaction.

And here is the beauty: you will now have the skill and confidence to establish your boundaries, so the chance of people reacting inappropriately is greatly reduced.

Furthermore, as I have said before, you are only able to control your actions and emotions. In the case of others reacting the wrong way, you have to accept that this is their problem rather than your failure.

How Can Empaths Protect Their Energy and Create Boundaries?

Empaths or highly sensitive people (HSPs) aren't just highly sensitive to physical and emotional stimuli. It is believed that they have a more sensitive central nervous system, which enables them to literally take on the emotions of others, making boundary-setting especially difficult. Not only do they have their own emotions to handle, but they also take on the reactions of those with whom they wish to create boundaries.

An empath can already feel stress and fear; expressing their needs can lead to them absorbing the upset or anger of the other person. It is estimated that approximately 20% of the population is highly sensitive (Scott, 2020), so you aren't alone.

While it is easy to see the downside of being an empath, you have to remember that there are positives. You have the ability to appreciate things at a much deeper level, whether that's the emotions felt watching a movie or documentary, or the more profound connections you can make with friends and family.

At the same time, creating boundaries is also going to be much more difficult... but it's not impossible. Here are some things that empaths should take into consideration regarding healthy boundaries:

- Certain social situations may be more stressful, as you will be able to pick up on a huge range of emotions that others may not.

- A busy schedule can cause you to feel extremely overwhelmed, unlike others who are able to thrive on the stress. The thought of not being able to achieve everything generates stress.

- Since you are more aware of others' feelings, it is incredibly hard to say no and feel the disappointment of your friends or family.

- Empaths will avoid conflict whenever possible.

- Empaths may struggle more to end a toxic relationship. You might feel that there is more to be done before walking away.

- Empaths are prone to rumination, continuing to think about a stressful situation, with thoughts turning more and more negative.

Many of the techniques we have looked at will help highly sensitive people, but there are specific things that you can incorporate in your life to make you feel more comfortable about creating boundaries.

1. Protect your energy

The first thing is to protect your energy. If you have taken the steps to start boosting your energy, it is important that you don't let others drain it away. If you know certain people who we call energy vampires, keep a distance from them. If you are in a social situation where you pick up negativity, politely move away.

2. Use visualization techniques

At this stage, you can use visualization techniques to create an image in your mind of the boundary issue you have. Take a look around the situation – what is happening, and how do you feel?

Think about the changes in your energy and the energy of others. Repeat this activity for a few days. Each time, you will start to notice more details. This self-awareness will help you to face challenging situations in the real world.

3. Consider your boundaries

We have already done this. Take the notes you have made previously, and now focus on the energy concerning these boundaries. Because you will be more sensitive to the energies surrounding a boundary, you might need to adjust them.

4. Say no to the big ones

There are probably lots of cases where you want to say no, but of course, it's going to be hard taking on all of those emotions. Reserve your energy for the no's that matter.

Depending on the situation, you might use phrases like, "I see your point of view, but I don't agree," or a simple "no."

There will be plenty more on how to say no later in this book when we look at specific relationships.

5. Have faith in your instincts

It is easy to not trust your gut feeling when so many thoughts and feelings are swirling around. Listen to advice, but always remember that you know yourself better than anyone else does.

6. Create a safe space in your home

I call this your charging dock. A space that is full of positivity and warmth. This happy space is where you can go to escape the stress of the day or the world. Take 5 minutes to meditate or practice mindfulness to balance your energy.

7. Self-love is even more essential

Absorbing other people's emotions is going to be extremely draining. Whatever it is that helps you to relax must be part of your daily routine. It could be cooking, listening to music, dancing, drawing, fresh air, or anything under the sun that means you are your own priority.

Please don't think that this is the end of the help for empaths. As we continue on our journey, I will make sure to include specific tips and strategies related to the topic we are discussing.

How to Deal With Codependency

Codependency is a complex learned behavior (Gaba, 2019) , often developed in our early years. We have watched a parent or family member who has displayed codependent traits, and more often than not, they were matched with a narcissistic partner.

It is the codependent who goes out of their way to satisfy the needs of the other partner. So much of the attention is on the needy person and the efforts to please them that other people in the family learn quickly that their needs will always be the lesser priority.

Many of the struggles we have discussed ring true for a codependent – they will fear loss and confrontation. They might not be aware of their own needs, or they may feel that their needs aren't as important.

Codependents can also feel quite isolated. People outside the relationship will tell you to stop being a doormat, but it is just not the case. A learned behavior takes time and practice to reverse.

If you have grown up in a verbally, emotionally or physically abusive family, you might need cognitive behavioral therapy (CBT) to help change the negative patterns that codependency has created. This is a great way of discovering the difference between your needs and problems, and the needs and problems of the other person.

Relationship dynamics may determine the way you face your boundary-setting, so in the next few chapters, we will look at how codependent people can successfully create boundaries for various relationships. For now, here are some general guidelines for setting boundaries in a codependent relationship:

- Be explicitly clear when communicating your boundaries
- Let others know how their codependent behavior makes you feel
- Be there to support codependent people, but don't do everything for them
- Wait for a request for help rather than offering
- Don't tolerate any form of toxic behavior
- Teach others the importance of self-care by being a great role model
- Make codependents take responsibility for themselves and their actions

---

This chapter has focused on the need for self-care and self-love. We have looked at the importance of understanding that it is not only okay to put your emotions and needs ahead of others in your life, but it is also your right to do so.

Gradually, you will start to feel more confident within yourself, and more determined about maintaining your boundaries. What is going to help even more is knowing exactly what to say so that your loved ones respect your words and don't get upset by them.

CHAPTER 5: POWERFUL BUT KIND WORDS FOR EXPRESSING YOUR BOUNDARIES TO PEOPLE

If you have read any of my other books, you will probably remember that I am an advocate for teaching soft skills in school. I know there's so much that teachers already need to include in their curriculum, but how can we forget the importance of communication skills? We are still working on the assumption that we pick this up naturally; however, it is far from the case.

There are two factors to consider when understanding why we all need help with communication, neither of which are bad things. With increased globalization, the world is becoming smaller. It is far easier for us to travel, and people are more comfortable with living and working in other countries.

We are exposed to a wide range of cultures, which is fantastic when it comes to expanding our knowledge and understanding of the world. But each culture has its own mannerisms around communication. Some men would be shocked if another man from a European country gave him two kisses on the cheek. It would most definitely be a violation of a boundary. But the European man might find this shocked reaction offensive. There are hundreds of examples of cultural differences that have changed the way we communicate.

Technology is another. It is such a shame to see people in cafes and bars all on their mobiles instead of having a face-to-face conversations. I worry that we're heading towards a world where we forget how to express our feelings in person because it's easier to hide behind a text message.

This chapter is going to teach you how to master communication, the second of our 3 Cs, in a way that allows you to explain to people your boundaries using kind words, and not feeling the need to be aggressive.

We're going to look at the fine line between passive and aggressive, and look at the most effective ways to say no. Our aim will be to improve our communication skills in person. Nevertheless, throughout the book, we will also discuss situations where modern technology can help us to communicate our boundaries.

What Does Healthy Communication Look Like?

I like to break communication down into three sections. Naturally, our words are going to have a huge impact on how we communicate our boundaries and how the other person reacts. Next, we need to learn just how much our body language impacts our communication. Finally, we will understand the importance of listening, rather than hearing what we think is being said.

How to Successfully Communicate Boundaries

The whole book has tips and techniques for very specific situations, but here we will look at the guidelines to communicate your boundaries in a way that leads to the desired results.

Step 1 - Know exactly what you want to say. You need to remain specific and clear. Your statements shouldn't be long, or contain any type of hidden meaning; nor should the conversations start to wander off topic.

Step 2 - Use I statements. There are two core reasons for this. First, you need the conversation to be about your emotions and not the actions of the other person. Second, I statements prevent you from making assumptions about the other person's feelings.

Step 3 - Listen to what the other person has to say. Don't interrupt them, and don't assume you know how they're feeling or what they're thinking. Repeat what they have said so that they know you're listening.

Step 4 - Be aware of each other's triggers. When people start to swear, I get mad. This is my trigger, and I have to be careful not to react negatively when others swear. Being aware of triggers will help to prevent the conversation from taking a wrong turn.

Step 5 - Make your expectations clear. Half of the boundary is how you feel; the other half is the behavior you would like to see changed.

Step 6 - Apologize when necessary. Saying sorry isn't a sign of weakness. It is admitting a mistake has been made, and showing that you would like to put things right.

Step 7 - Accept that people are going to have different opinions and it isn't possible to agree on everything. You might need to take a break from the conversation and come back to it when you have both had a chance to think.

To put these steps into practice, you could try some of the following clear examples of communicating your boundaries:

- I don't like it when you won't let me finish what I'm saying. I need to feel like we're equals.

- I feel like you're obliging me to do things when you start a sentence with "You have to..." I think there are better ways you can ask for my help.

- I'm sorry that you feel this way, but I need to be able to express my feelings without you taking it personally.

- We're both entitled to our thoughts on this subject, but I don't think we're making progress. Perhaps we can talk about it again tomorrow.

How to Set Limits and Still Be a Loving Person

This is another case of what might seem like a fine line. The word "no" can sound very harsh, and perhaps too direct for some people. On the other hand, if your words are not firm enough, the other person might not respect your boundary.

First, let's look at some ways that you can express a boundary in the wrong way, and some of the ways you can express it the right way.

Sarah has a boyfriend who is constantly interrupting her. It makes her mad, and she admits it's hard to control her temper. She will often use phrases like, "You're impossible when you're like this, and it's not worth talking to you." This comes across as an insult, and naturally, her boyfriend often throws an insult back.

Instead, Sarah could say, "I'm listening to what you're saying, but I feel disrespected when you don't listen to me." The emphasis is no longer on his behavior, but on her feelings.

James has a colleague who takes all the credit for joint projects. He has used sarcasm to try to keep the tone light, but still express his dislike. His colleague has taken the sarcasm as a joke, and continues to reap the rewards.

His kind words to set the boundary would be, "I really enjoy teaming up with you, but I don't feel that there's a balance. What can we do to fix this and work better together?" This is a great sentence because the colleague has heard the positive and the problem, and James has asked for feedback towards the solution.

Eli's friend wants her to commit to a plan every Saturday morning. She already has a 50-hour job, and her parents aren't in the best health. She is exhausted, and has told her friend that she can't. Her friend might complain and call Eli selfish, but this is very much out of character.

In this case, Eli should ask her friend if there's an underlying problem. If this is typical behavior of the friend, Eli could say, "I'm not selfish. I love you, and I am happy to do X activity on Y day. But I'm not going to commit to Saturday mornings." The boundary has been set, the insult has been corrected, and an alternative has been provided that they can both be happy with.

Question: I'm not sure about how to set boundaries so that we both get what we want and need and still be happy.

Answer: Communicating your boundary isn't just about expressing your needs and then ending the conversation. In order for both parties to be happy and to feel that there is a healthy balance in the relationship, it's important that you listen to the other person's response and maintain positive communication until you find the middle ground.

How to Say No Without Being Rude

A fellow life coach once said, "If you want more time, freedom and energy, start saying no." In essence, it is that simple. Nevertheless, this tiny word can pack a lot of punch. Even the idea is enough to make some people feel nervous and stressed – even sick to the stomach.

For many of us, it is the word "no" that makes us feel as if we're being rude. It is hard to go from someone who constantly says yes to a person that comes out with a straight no. The good news is that not all boundary setting is going to require a firmer hand, and a lot of people will respect your answer without having to use the word "no." For example:

- Now isn't a good time.
- I have a full schedule today.
- I can't.
- Right now, that isn't possible.
- I'm available tomorrow.
- Today isn't going to work for me, but how about next week?
- I need time to think about it.
- I'll think about it.
- Sadly, I have plans.
- It sounds great, but maybe next time.

There will be times when people don't accept this answer, or they have a more dominating personality, and will require you to be firmer with your boundary-setting. Always remember that no is not a bad word when used in the right way. You can use any of the phrases above, but start it with a no. Also, don't forget things like "No, thank you," or "No, sorry."

Question: When I say no, people look at me as if I don't have the right to. Then they insist on me explaining myself or justifying my answer.

Answer: There will be times when people insist on pushing against your boundary. Stand firm. You are not obliged to defend your no or explain your words. Choose phrases like:

- I don't appreciate it when you insist on me explaining myself.
- You should accept my answer and not badger me for more details.
- What I do with my free time is my business.
- I'm not obliged to explain myself to you.
- I'd prefer not to say.
- I have my reasons

For those who aren't used to seeing you stand up for yourself, you might need more than one attempt for the boundary to sink in. It doesn't mean you've failed or that you're destined to back down. If you do feel yourself wavering under the pressure, this is perfectly normal, but don't give in for an easier life.

One good way to prevent a yes from slipping out when everything in you wants to say no is to ask for more time or information.

Ask questions about what the other person is asking of you. Then tell them that you'll think about it. Once you walk away from the pressure of the situation, you can decide whether it's something you want to agree to.

Explanations are dangerous ground. I have a general rule where the fewer words said, the better. The longer we talk, the more we say, and the more we say, the more opportunities the other person has to change your mind.

Imagine a conversation where you start listing all of the things you need to do. The other person is going to start organizing your time. All of a sudden, you have to run errands after work, the kids can go with their grandparents, and the ironing will just have to wait.

If you had kept your response to a simple, "No, I can't," you would have maintained control of your own time. At the end of the day, it is exactly that – your time!

How to Handle People Getting Upset With Your Boundaries

Not everyone is going to get angry with your new boundaries. Some people might get upset because they assume that you don't want to spend time with them. It can be particularly difficult if they become so upset that they start to cry, and even more so if you're an empath.

In this case, it's important for you to remind people that the boundaries are not because you want to end a relationship or to create distance. Let them know that it's the opposite. Having healthy boundaries is the key to continuing a healthy relationship built on honesty and respect.

Be wary of those who turn on the waterworks to make you feel guilty. This is a manipulative technique they're using in the hope that you'll change your mind. Regardless of the authenticity of their upset, you still shouldn't allow people to disrespect or cross your boundary.

A Sound Check for Your Tone of Voice

It's worth bearing in mind that only 7% of communication is based on the words we use (Albert Merhabians' 7-38-55 Rule, 1971). That's not to say that there's no point in carefully selecting your phrases. Being confident in what you want to say will help you to come across as more confident in your decisions. A massive 38% of our communication is down to our tone of voice.

As we go through some different tones of voice, have a think of people you know, and see just how accurate the description is.

A deep tone of voice, whether the speaker is male or female, implies that the person is more mature. You might find that once the voice becomes too deep, there is an element of darkness, even depression. It weighs heavy on your ears.

A very quiet tone of voice shows that someone is lacking in confidence, they are shy, or they are nervous about something.

When a person's voice is incredibly high-pitched, it is difficult to take them seriously. People who speak slowly show a lack of interest, whereas rapid talkers might be trying to hide something.

A tone of voice that is neither too high nor too low, too loud nor too quiet, with calm breathing, suggests confidence.

To practice your tone of voice, record yourself on your phone. It can be reading a few sentences from a book, or some of the boundary phrases we have looked at.

When you play back the recording, the first thing that comes to mind is, "Oh... that's what I sound like!" But everyone has this moment.

Now bring your attention back to the descriptions, and see which areas you need to tweak.

How Small Changes in Your Body Language Can Reinforce Your Boundaries

Our words are only going to be as effective as possible if we're able to match our body language to the same message. Mixed messages are when your words plant a firm boundary, but your body language is submissive. 55% of our communication comes from our body language.

There is a great amount of psychology behind body language, and I must admit I find it fascinating. One of the best things you can do before putting these ideas into practice is just to spend some time watching other people's body language. Often, people say what others want to hear, but body language can paint a more honest picture.

Another thing to practice is self-objectification. This is when we try to imagine what others think when they look at us. Empaths may have an advantage here.

Really, it is something we all do at some point. When you look in the mirror, you're checking to see how you look, but as you don't look at yourself all day, really, you're looking at what others are seeing. This is a good technique to check that your body language is relaying the same message as your words.

However, be careful not to get stuck in self-objectification mode. Studies show that self-objectification can take us out of the moment and make it harder to concentrate. When expressing your healthy boundaries, you definitely want to remain in the present.

Have a look at the following questions to see if you are mastering positive body language.

Do you know what *iHunch* is?

The "i" refers to smartphones, the hunch is a slouched position. When you look at someone on their phone, you'll notice that their head is down, they're leaning forward, and their shoulders are slumped. If you have the iHunch position, you're suggesting that you're disengaged, but it's also a very submissive position.

How long are you holding eye contact for?

Too little, and you are not showing confidence; too much, and the other person might feel like you're flirting with them. The difference is a matter of seconds. Thanks to much research, psychologists have come up with the ideal level of eye contact for a confident appearance. Eye contact should be made before the conversation begins. The ideal amount of time is 4 to 5 seconds (Schulz, 2012).

The perfect ratio is to maintain eye contact for 50% of the time when you're speaking, and 70% of the time when you're listening.

Are you knitting your eyebrows?

Knitted eyebrows doesn't mean that they're tightly joined. It means that they're lowered and centered, but in a natural way. A little too far, and you will be frowning. Knitted eyebrows are a sign of focus and determination.

Is your head in line with your neck?

Nobody likes to see a person with their nose up in the air as if they're superior, but keeping your head down is another submissive gesture. Your head should be in line with your neck. Be careful that you don't nod in agreement without realizing it.

What are you doing with your arms?

Arms that are crossed show a lack of confidence, while folded arms are likely to portray a lack of interest. Your hands will also play their role. Closed palms or hands behind your back are signs that you're hiding something. If your palms are open, it shows that you are too.

Are you aware of the relationship between breathing and body language?

There are more advantages to deep breathing than bringing about a sense of calm and control. Breathing from your diaphragm is seen as more relaxed, and again, confident. As you're probably aware, when you're nervous or anxious, your breath becomes shallow and rapid.

Some of our body language is innate: we are born with it, and we can't control it. Blushing, for example, is going to happen whether we like it or not. Micro expressions occur at a fraction of a second, and also can't be controlled.

Everything on our list can be learned, which is excellent news because everybody has the ability to learn new things.

The first step to learning how to control your body language is to be aware of it, so after some time watching other people, turn your attention to yourself.

Focus on the way you stand in a supermarket queue, how you sit at your desk, and your position when you're in social situations.

Start by making small adjustments. You could change the habit of crossing your legs and arms so that you appear more open. Or you may feel that your shoulders need to be less slouched.

Make the changes now, before expressing your boundaries, so that your body language backs up your powerful but kind words.

Why Should I Listen When I Want Them to Hear Me?

We have two ears and only one mouth for a good reason (Epictetus AD55-135)! The 60-40 rule suggests we should listen for 60% of our communication and speak for 40%. This might sound bizarre when we're working so hard on what we want to say, but listening is still an essential part of establishing boundaries that will last.

Imagine a conversation where you tell someone that you don't like it when they insult your taste in music and try and get you to listen to their favorite songs.

You have expressed your boundary correctly, and are revisiting the conversation in your mind while the other person is speaking. They might be trying to explain the reason why they think you would like their music.

Some people also have the habit of assuming what the other person is thinking, and therefore don't actively listen. Either way, not listening can cause the other person to feel hurt and disrespected – the exact thing we don't want for ourselves.

Listening to the other person's thoughts and feelings doesn't imply that you have to go back on your boundaries. It provides you with an opportunity to strengthen your relationship by addressing their concerns, and essentially, finding a middle ground.

You might tell your friend that you will listen to some of their music but you'd like them not to force it on you when you're not in the mood. Then reinforce the fact that everybody is entitled to their own tastes.

If you're the type of person who feels selfish because you're setting boundaries, effective listening will help you to overcome this: you are not making it all about your needs, but understanding the two sides.

Just remember that even listening should have its limits.

If a person starts to shout, swear or become aggressive, it's time to let them know that you aren't going to listen to them while they're speaking in this way, and that you can have the conversation later on when they've calmed down.

What Not to Do When Setting Boundaries

• Never rush to set a boundary. You will find that your emotions are not under control, and you might not be fully prepared for the response.

• Don't lie. It sounds obvious, but we might tell lies in order to protect other people's feelings. It won't help because your boundary won't be true to yourself, and it won't be very clear.

• Try not to be inflexible with your boundaries. You will have your list of absolute limits, but remember there might be times when the boundary was crossed for a good reason.

• Remember that people are not perfect. Rather than focusing on mistakes people make with regards to your boundaries, check to see if they're making an effort to learn and respect them.

• You cannot forget to reinforce your boundaries. As we aren't perfect, it's likely that people will either intentionally or unintentionally cross your boundary. You will need to be both patient and determined in order to reinforce your boundaries.

How to Practice Communicating Your Boundaries

Before jumping into practicing communicating your boundaries, take some time to practice successful communication. Apart from watching other people's body language and listening out for different tones of voice, start taking some notes on your communication skills. Answer these questions:

• Do you think you're an active listener? Can you remember everything that people say in a conversation?

- Are you able to spot other people's triggers? Watch for tension in the body as a reaction to things you say.
- Do you interrupt?
- Are there any parts of your body that fidget or distract the listener when you get uncomfortable?
- Can you stop a conversation before it gets heated or out of control?

All of these are essential skills for communication, and for successful boundaries, effective communication is a must.

There is a huge amount of information in this chapter, and I hope you're motivated to start putting it into practice. Don't overwhelm yourself with too many changes at once. After some time of observation and self-reflection, make a list of things that you'd like to improve, and begin by making small changes. The small wins will encourage you to keep going.

We have looked at improving your lifestyle so that you feel more energized, and we've got to the bottom of our inner-selves, and are now fully aware of the boundaries we wish to introduce. With the tools to express your boundaries in a kind but firm way, you are now ready to bring everything together and start setting boundaries with your family.

CHAPTER 6: HOW TO DISCUSS YOUR BOUNDARIES WITH FAMILY

People around the world have their own definitions of family that often go beyond the traditional blood relatives. Your family might include parents and siblings, a partner and/or children. We have aunts and uncles, cousins, nieces and nephews. Some of our best friends can be more like family... and then there are the in-laws!

For this chapter, we are going to take parents, partners and friends out of the equation. This is because the dynamics of these relationships are quite complex, and we will focus on them in individual chapters.

The core boundaries we're going to look at are with siblings, in-laws, more distant relatives, and our children.

Siblings Who Overstep the Limit

Generally speaking, it is your sibling who knows you the best. At the very least, this was the case for the majority of your childhood. The massive amount of time you spent together provided them with the chance to know exactly what you like, how to tell what mood you're in, and of course, what annoys you.

Empaths, like twins, are likely to have an even stronger bond with their siblings. So why is it hard to create boundaries with the people who know you inside out?

As you're growing up together, the role model for boundaries is typically the parent. Children follow the words of Mom and Dad, and little attention is aimed at the siblings developing their own boundaries. As you get older, parents might start to say, "Figure it out yourselves," meaning that whatever problem you have, you need to deal with it together. This is the first stage at which you and your sibling establish boundaries.

The teenage years hit, along with rushing hormones and new sets of problems. Certain things that were acceptable no longer are – in particular, the concept of personal space and privacy. Younger siblings who have always just walked into a room are not used to now being shouted at and told to get lost.

The boundary is there, but it isn't expressed in the right way, and because it isn't expressed in the right way, problems will continue to not only occur, but increase in severity.

Things can quickly become toxic when a parent favors one child over another. In our minds, we tell ourselves that this isn't possible, but favoritism is very real.

A 2005 study showed that 74% of mothers favored one child over the other, and 70% of fathers had a favorite child (Journal of Marriage and Family, 2016). The study was relatively small, with just 384 families and an age gap of fewer than 4 years. Nevertheless, the percentages are quite high.

Favoring a child is extremely dangerous, as the favorite learns that they can manipulate the parent, while the sibling is left feeling second best and less significant.

Whether or not your parent has a favorite child, you probably feel as if you weren't treated as an equal when you were younger, and your sibling has the ability to cross all boundaries. There's little point in playing the blame game, as it's unproductive. It's time to get to the core of the issue and change the behavior.

Before dealing with a toxic sibling, it is necessary for you to have your emotions under control. They're probably more than capable of knowing what to say in order to upset you or make you angry. You can't allow them to have that control over you anymore. Once they see that they don't get that rise anymore, you may find that they completely back off and move onto the next person.

Let your sibling know that you will no longer accept their behavior towards you. They shouldn't be allowed to think it's okay just because they're your sibling. It could be that they aren't aware of how much they're hurting you. This could lead to an open conversation about your relationship where you can both express your feelings.

Keep reminding yourself that you aren't the villain, even if they make you out to be. Explain how you respect their boundaries, and give clear examples like, "I don't call and gossip about you to the rest of the family," or "I respect that you need time for yourself."

Tell them that you love them, and you want them in your life, but not as the relationship is now. Paint a positive picture of the relationship with clear boundaries so that they can completely understand your reasons.

When siblings continue to break boundaries, you will need to have a more serious conversation. It might be that they weren't listening the first time around, or that they didn't feel that you were serious enough.

Change your vocabulary to make it more powerful, rather than angry or infuriated. Let them know that their actions will lead to consequences. Be careful that your consequence doesn't sound like a threat, as this can lead to confrontation.

Try to avoid phrases like, "If you don't do this, I will do that." You should try to phrase it more along the lines of, "If you keep crossing these boundaries, I don't feel like we're going to have the close relationship I want to have with you."

Finally, give your siblings a chance to improve their actions, and trust that they will make an effort. You might want to choose a time frame for this so that it doesn't go on for a long time.

After, say, a month or two, you might need to create some distance between you and your sibling. That's not to say that you should cut off all contact: the longer this goes on, the harder it will be to make things right. Some space will give you the time to feel stronger and give them a chance to think about what life would be like without their siblings.

Phrases to practice:

- I know you need my car, but you can't borrow it today. Next time, ask in advance.
- You know I'd love to, but today's not going to work for me. Rain check?
- I don't like it when you play Mom and Dad against me. It hurts.
- I would appreciate it if you didn't talk to the family about my private life.
- I can see that you're angry. I'll come back at a better time, and we can talk.

The Wonderful World of In-Laws

You might be one of the lucky ones who get on well with their in-laws, or you might not. Regardless, boundaries still need to be made. This relationship is often a complex one because of the subtle competition for attention.

As the most complex relationship is normally between a girlfriend and her mother-in-law, we will use this as an example, but this isn't to say that the same boundaries won't apply to other in-law relationships.

When a girlfriend comes along, the son's attention moves away from the mom, who had been the most important female in his life, to the girlfriend. Mothers often feel saddened that their son doesn't need them as much, and it can lead to jealousy.

Other moms might feel that the girlfriend is never going to be good enough for their son, or that they aren't going to be as capable of taking care of them. There are several issues with this, but the biggest is that girlfriends aren't supposed to be replacement moms, and it is not a girlfriend's job to take care of the son.

Caring is mutual and equal. Some moms have such tight control over their sons that their interference is a serious violation of boundaries.

The silly thing is that both parties have the same goal – the happiness of the loved one. And this is the key to enforcing the right boundaries with your in-laws.

While you have already concentrated on the boundaries you need for a happier, healthier life, you will need to start with the reasons for establishing these particular boundaries. Your in-laws might have a habit of making you feel bad about yourself, insulting you, disrespecting your opinions, or ignoring you. The tension could be so much that it's causing problems within your relationship with your partner.

If you're having trouble with your partner, you need to sort this out first. Any sign of a divide between you could be seen as a weak point and fuel the problems with your in-laws.

A good way to start looking at what boundaries to set is to create two lists: one for what you need, and another for what the family needs. It might be your wish to see your in-laws less, but that's not fair on your partner, and even less fair to the grandchildren. Once your two lists are complete, talk with your partner to create a set of boundaries that work for everyone.

You don't have to do everything together, so one solution would be for your partner to take the children for some visits, and you all go together for others.

When you and your partner are comfortable with the boundaries, it's time to have a conversation with the in-laws.

You can use the same short phrases we've seen before, but it's crucial that you use the word "we." If you use the word "I," your in-laws may feel that the boundaries are only coming from you, and they will feel as if you're controlling the relationship.

The stressful part comes when you have to maintain these boundaries. Watch out for your in-laws having conversations with your partner without you in order to persuade them to see things from a different point of view.

Also, be careful they don't use grandchild to tug on your heartstrings in order to cross boundaries. To prevent this, be prepared to adjust boundaries to accommodate their wishes, while making sure that you and your partner are still happy.

It's also worth considering your partner's relationship with your parents and whether there should be boundaries put in place to ensure your partner is happy. Don't assume you know the answer – communication from both sides leads to healthy boundaries for everyone.

Phrases to practice:

- We're so grateful for your advice, but we've decided to take a different direction. Your input means a lot to us, and we hope you're okay with our decision.

- I would truly appreciate it if you could give me a call before coming over. It would make me feel more respected. Thank you for understanding.

- My job isn't to replace you. I'm his partner, and there's room for both of us.

- It would mean a lot to me if you could give me a heads-up before spoiling the kids. I'd really value that. Thank you!

Having the Right Boundaries for Other Family Members

It's hard not to love your grandparents. I love how grandparents do all of the things that they would never have done with their own children, but feel fine doing it with the next generation. They're wise and have a different perspective on life.

Aunts and uncles are like parents, but again, they have a unique perspective and relationship with your parents. Then we have cousins, and if you're lucky enough, they're almost like extra brothers and sisters.

This isn't to say that setting boundaries is easy. It's true that you probably don't spend as much time with them as you do with your close family, and it's easier to break ties with those who constantly cross the limit.

But they're still family, and the one thing you notice as you get older (and go through pandemics and other life changes) is that you need your family. Let's look at some of the ways that family members can overstep boundaries:

- Talking down to you
- Disrespecting your values, ethics, or religious and political views
- Treating you like a child
- Nagging about you growing up, getting a job, or starting a family
- Trying to control your relationships
- Talking about you behind your back
- Showing up at your house unexpectedly
- Expecting you to go to family occasions
- Requesting too much from you
- Sharing your photos on social media

You can probably think of plenty more specific to your situation. While it's tempting just to accept that they're family and they only do it because they care, this isn't a healthy attitude, and it isn't going to help you on your journey to a better life. That would be like going to your favorite restaurant and having a glass of water – not really the point!

Choosing the right time to bring up your boundaries is critical to your success. At this point, family members may have pushed you to such an extent that you're a ticking time bomb. It might be that the next violation of your boundaries will cause you to explode.

The sad fact is that the attention will be on your explosive outburst rather than the behavior of the family member. And this is going to be worse if you're at a family gathering. Every excuse will be made for your outburst – the pressure of your job, your inappropriate relationship, or the fact that you aren't getting enough sleep.

Never do we hear, "I've overstepped a boundary, and this has caused your upset." Unwanted advice is a classic example. After all, they were "only trying to help," as we hear so many times.

So how do you find the best moment?

First of all, the frustration that leads to the moment when you can't handle more of your family takes time to build. Don't fall into the pattern of, "I will mention it next time." The next times keep building up until you can't take it anymore.

It's important not to let it get this far because it might not be the right moment to establish your boundary, and you need to know that the problem hasn't got to the point where you might lose control. Let's look at an example.

Joe has an uncle who keeps calling him a player because of the girlfriends he's had. In reality, Joe hasn't had an excessive number of girlfriends, but naturally, his issues with healthy boundaries are also affecting his relationships.

During his early 20s, this was kind of an acceptable joke that his uncle would bring up at every event. As the years went on, it was no longer the case of a young man sowing his oats, and the joke became quite hurtful when his uncle mentioned he couldn't keep a good woman.

Joe didn't laugh at the jokes anymore. His mom had picked up on Joe's sadness at being the butt of the family joke, and had also attempted to reign in her brother's seemingly harmless comments. Joe was able to control his emotions during family occasions, but each time, he dreaded these get-togethers more.

One day, while talking to his parents, he lost his cool, and this upset him further, so he decided that it was essential to enforce a boundary with his uncle.

At the next family occasion, Joe was prepared for the jokes. He had prepared what he wanted to say, and was prepared for the necessary conversation. Because he wasn't at his complete limit, he was still in control of his emotions and his ability to use the right words with the right body language.

As expected, the jokes were made. Joe was in the perfect position to take his uncle to one side at the right time, and explain how he was feeling. He said that although it was funny, it was causing him pain.

Boundary preparation was what enabled Joe to succeed, and it can do that for you too. His uncle apologized, and said he was unaware of the pain he was causing. Still, after years of habit, Joe did have to remind him of this boundary now and then, but each reminder became easier, to the point where just a look was enough for his uncle to stop.

If a family member gets mad because you've set a boundary, this is proof that the boundary needed to be set. Constantly remind yourself that you aren't a doormat for family members to walk on.

You shouldn't be the tool they need to achieve their goals, and you're certainly not the little child they still see you as. Look at the achievements in your own life to remind yourself that you're a responsible adult now. You have experiences and knowledge that you can contribute to your family.

It's a shame that there are times when family members don't respect our boundaries. It's not quite the same as a sibling or in-law.

If a family member insists on crossing the limits you've clearly set, it's time to create that space for your own wellbeing. It doesn't have to be forever. But if they aren't willing to understand the importance of your needs, happiness and life, you're better off removing them from the equation so that you can look after yourself.

Phrases to practice:

- It upsets me that I'm the butt of the family joke. If this continues, I don't feel like I can come to these occasions.
- This is not the time to discuss my love life.

- I know Granny isn't well, but she's not asking me to drop everything: you are.
- This conversation is inappropriate for a family dinner.
- I'm an adult, and capable of making my own decisions.

Getting Your Parenting Style Right for Healthy Boundaries With Children

Years ago, I was scrolling through Facebook, and came across a story of a mom who had reported her son to the police. Not knowing the woman on the street was his mother, he had come up behind her and mugged her. His intention was to use the money to feed his drug habit.

The mother had done plenty of research on codependency and setting boundaries, but nothing had worked. Her son had violated a boundary that was beyond acceptable, and the only solution was to report him. I found her story to be inspiring, and a sign of just how strong parents can be.

Hopefully, if you need to establish boundaries with your children, it won't be quite so extreme. Nevertheless, even pushing the limits can be exhausting. If you're living with your children, it's a problem that you can't escape from, and you may find that it impacts your health more.

We briefly talked about authoritarian, authoritative and permissive parenting styles. Now we're going to look further into the benefits of authoritative parenting and why this style is not only the middle ground, but also the most effective when setting your boundaries.

Don't think that it's too late. Adapting your parenting style can be done whether you have a two-year-old or a 20-year-old.

Before we get into the details, you need to know that what you've been doing up to now may not have been working, but that isn't to say you're a bad parent. Absolutely nobody in this world is a perfect parent: there are just too many factors. What does matter is that you want to improve.

A parent who is authoritative is one who actively listens to their child without dismissing thoughts, feelings and ideas. At the same time as respecting a child for who they are, an authoritative parent will set and maintain boundaries. They will understand the importance of give and take with a child, instead of setting rules that can never be broken.

Think back to when you were a child. It's natural to try to break the rules – it's what happens afterward that matters. The idea is to allow a child to explore rules and boundaries so that they can learn about limits and what happens when they're crossed.

If you think about an incident from your own life, you can agree that you learn more from trial and error than you do from what someone tells you. What's more, when someone tells you that you can't do something, you become more determined to do it. Children are no different.

It is this definition of an authoritative parent that allows for happy children who are comfortable in social situations and have better mental health.

To adopt this style of parenting, you need to start by listening to your child, no matter how old or young they are. When children express their feelings, be sure not to belittle them. It's true that their problems are probably not as important as finding the money to pay the utility bills, but to them, it's a big deal.

You need to have clear rules in your home, and it's common to have to remind children of the rules regularly. What's even more important is that any breaking of the rules, even minor, needs to have consequences. You have to remember that parents should punish the behavior and not the emotion.

A child expressing anger should be allowed to explain how they feel. But if they throw something in a rage or become physically violent, there has to be a consequence.

On the other hand, good behavior has to be rewarded. Don't mistake this for the permissive parent who overindulges.

Small rewards appropriate for their age motivate children to improve certain behaviors, and the parent is given the chance to help with support and positivity, rather than nagging and punishment (Morin, 2020).

Children are going to test boundaries. However, there are some cases where the problem gets out of hand. Family violence is on the rise, and it is not only child abuse and violence against women.

Studies in 2019 showed that between 7.2% and 22% of adults had experienced physical aggression from their adolescent children. For psychological aggression, it was between 65.8% and 93.5% (International Journal of Environmental and Public Health, 2019).

If, for any reason, you feel that you can't set boundaries with your children and they're physically or emotionally causing you pain, you should seek professional help.

When looking at establishing boundaries with different family members, begin by making sure you're clear of what these boundaries look like and if there's room for give and take, depending on your relationship and their expectations.

Prepare yourself so that you're in the right frame of mind and are feeling as confident as possible.

Finally, start with the people who you know will understand, and who are more likely to react appropriately and respect your wishes. You can use this experience to learn, praise yourself for what you did well, and look for ways to improve before tackling more challenging family members.

Phrases to practice:

- I/we want you to feel confident in your decisions, but I would like you to respect my opinions.
- I/we will not tolerate any activity that breaks the law.
- We really care about following our family rules, but please know that your thoughts and ideas are also important.
- I/we respect that your room is your space, but you need to respect our joint efforts to keep our home clean.

Practicing Boundaries With Different Family Members

Choose a family member with whom you need to establish a boundary, but with whom you also have a close relationship.

This is a family member who will give you a little push back when you set your boundary, but not necessarily so much that it will hurt or cause you excessive stress.

These people value you, and will understand the importance of your needs. They're the perfect family members to talk to about the boundaries you wish to set in general, as well as with them specifically.

Take advantage of these relationships to help you not only establish your first boundaries, but also to talk through and practice with.

CHAPTER 7: 10 GRACEFUL TACTICS TO SET BOUNDARIES WITH PARENTS

Most of us have so much to be thankful to our parents for. They brought us into the world, protected us, put clothes on our backs and food in our stomachs. They have probably lent us their car, money, and a shoulder to cry on.

There are some parents who just love to bring this up at any possible opportunity, whether that's to guilt us into doing something we don't want to, or to dissuade us from doing something that we do.

Who has ever heard something like, "30 hours of labor just to have a son who abandons his mother," or, "I didn't raise you to be selfish."? Both statements may well be true, but they shouldn't be used to manipulate you.

If you're having problems with any of the following parental boundaries, we're going to work through 10 tactics that are graceful, but will firmly get your message across.

- Suffocating love
- Codependency

- Interfering with your personal life
- Too opinionated regarding your love life
- Unsolicited advice on your parenting style
- Obsessive purchasing of things for your home (or children)
- Unnecessary or hurtful comments on your body, image, clothes, etc.
- Turning up unexpected
- Constantly disagreeing with your views
- Planning your schedule or free time

As older people, parents are often stuck in their ways. You might find that they're also from a generation of authoritarian parents, where there was no other choice but to listen to and obey the rules of the parents. If your parents never set boundaries with their parents, it could be harder for you.

Also, many times, parents are completely unaware that their actions are upsetting you. By now you have probably tried having a conversation, but your parents continue to break your boundaries. I know that I used to get angry with my parents, and this would only make me feel guilty afterward.

Whatever your emotions were in the past, don't assume that the same will happen this time. Just because they're your parents, it doesn't mean you should give up on your boundaries and accept that this is how life is going to be.

Why Are Boundaries With Parents More Complex?

In the first place, it is down to the way we feel about our parents and what our relationship should be like with them. They've probably made a lot of sacrifices for us, and to an extent, we feel like we owe them for this.

The other major issue is that parents find it almost impossible to let go of their control. From your parents' point of view, you are, and always will be their child.. You are an extension of their own lives.

Some parents don't want you to make the same mistakes as they did, and others may have missed out on opportunities and are trying to relive their life through yours. All of this creates a very controlling environment.

As the child, we assume that things will change when we turn 18 or move into our own place. Oftentimes, our relationships with parents can take an even more negative turn because this fear of losing control causes them to try to control us even more. It is this need to control that leads parents to overstep boundaries continuously.

This attempted control can be very obvious as they repeatedly tell you what to do or how to do it. You can spot this because they will have quite dominating words and body language.

It could also be more manipulative: making you feel as if they need you to be able to survive is a form of playing on your kindness and generosity.

Finally, they can use silence as a form of control. Purposely creating space, not contacting you, or ignoring your calls and messages is a psychological game designed to make you come running to them.

There is a gigantic spectrum when it comes to dealing with challenging parents. One person might not be able to cope with a mother who is constantly asking them questions.

The pressure can be so much that they turn to drinking and drugs as a form of escape.

Others won't see this as a huge cause for concern because they have to deal with verbally and physically abusive parents, even well into adulthood.

It's okay to love your parents despite their control. It's normal to have a love-hate relationship, and in some circumstances, it is okay to hate your parents.

What's most important right now is that you do what you feel is right for your own situation.

Nobody but you knows how you feel, what boundaries you want to set, or the type of relationship you hope to get out of it.

You're in a vicious cycle of control, and it is up to you to break it. Once the control is broken, the boundaries become clearer for both parties.

10 Techniques to Assert Boundaries With Your Parents

Our focus now is going to be on 10 things you can do to enforce boundaries. Just remember that you have to adapt them to match your needs and goals.

1. Break the Control

It's pointless trying to establish boundaries with your parents when they still have the control (Karuna, 2020). Any attempts you make will be met with ridicule, anger, temper tantrums, or just the word "no." They will continue to manipulate you and use your emotions to get what they want.

To break the cycle of control, you first have to be in the right place: a good place. You need to be aware of your emotions, and know how to manage them in all types of situations. You might not be as confident or as strong as you want to be just yet, but you know you're going in the right direction.

Whatever your parents throw in your direction, you need to be able to handle it. This is critical because as soon as you react, whether that is floods of tears or anger, you're putting yourself back into the cycle of control.

Don't be surprised if this causes parents to push further or up their game. It's going to be a shock for them not to experience the same reaction as normal.

You might hear hurtful insults, like, "You're selfish," or "You're ungrateful." They could try to regain control by reminding you that they're the parent, and you're "just" the child. They may even kick you out.

The harsh lesson of "realizing how lucky you were to have parents that cared for you" might come up, which is another reason why you have to be prepared for any outcome. The truth is, they are only creating this space in the hope that you will return to your placid people-pleasing self.

Keep telling yourself that you aren't a child anymore, and that you are an independent human being who deserves respect from everyone, including your parents.

If it gets to a point where you can't cope with your parents' reaction, you must walk away. You aren't abandoning them or running away from your problems. You're protecting yourself.

You may have to go for a walk, or you may have to stay with a friend for a while. It could take a couple of weeks. Have faith in your own instincts because you will know when the time is right.

Phrases that will help you to break the control cycle include:

- I won't allow you to use guilt to control me.
- My feelings are as equally important as yours.
- As an adult, I'm no longer scared of you.
- If you choose to ignore me or not love me, that's your issue, not mine.

2. Start With a Conversation

Now that the control cycle has been broken, the dynamics of your relationship will have changed. Contact your parents, and let them know that you would like to talk to them about a few things.

Choose the right time: a time when you're mentally and physically strong, and when you don't have a ton of other things on your mind that could impact your stress levels.

Knowing that they don't have the same control over you, your parents might have seen a side of you that they hadn't before. Hopefully, they will now see you as the adult you have become, and treat you as such. For some families, this break in control is all that's needed for boundaries to be discussed, and together, agreed upon.

For example, if you're comfortable with them having a key to your home, you can agree to give them one, but on the condition that they message or call the day before and don't just show up.

For parents who are all over your love life, you can let them know that they can show interest and ask questions, but they can't keep trying to set you up with every single person they know.

To start your conversation, you can try sentences like:

- I would like to have a conversation with you about my feelings.
- It would be nice if we could sit down and talk about things without getting angry or upset.
- I want to talk to you about this, but I won't stay if I feel threatened.
- It is not that I want to create distance between us. I just want you to understand that there are some areas of my life I don't want to talk about.

3. Empathize With Your Parents

This is incredibly hard, particularly if they have driven you to a point of anxiety or depression. If you're able to see things from their point of view, it will be easier for you to understand their behavior.

A great example is a single parent who projects their fears onto you and your relationship. If your dad was cheated on and he categorizes your girlfriend as "all women," it can be very hurtful. Being able to imagine the pain he went through and his fear that the same thing will happen to you can help you to understand his actions.

A lot of interfering in your life could come down to a parent's fear of being alone. When parents reach a certain age (often closely linked to retirement age) they have an enormous amount of free time that they aren't used to. It has been known for moms to go to their adult child's home and clean, or even do the laundry. Dad might pop round to fix up those DIY jobs that have been on your to-do list.

This sounds quite heavenly for a busy person, but it isn't just a step over a boundary – it is a leap into your personal space. Yet the only reason they've done it is that they wanted to help, and their lives were a little empty.

This is not to say that empathizing is the same as accepting or permitting. You still need to have a conversation about the correct boundaries. However, if you can approach the conversation having thought about their intentions, your words will be kinder.

There is a fine line between being empathetic and appearing weak.

Below are some phrases that meet the balance:

- I can see that you're worried about me, but I know that I've thought about it from every perspective.
- I understand that you're angry, but you can talk to me instead of shouting at me.
- If we just talk about it, you'll see that I agree with you, but I want to do it my own way.
- I need you to respect the fact that after a hectic week, I have to have some time to disconnect.

4. Teach Your Parents; Don't Do It for Them

This one often goes unmentioned with parents, but it's becoming a growing concern, especially with new technology.

I learned very quickly that if I popped over to my parents' house to fix something, they would have no issues calling me for every tiny problem they couldn't resolve.

Alexa was talking to the TV, the printer was jammed, the kitchen sink was leaking, the dog was chewing its tail, and so on.

It started small, but it got to the point where I couldn't make plans because I was expecting my daily call to solve a problem they could find the answer to online.

I love the proverb, "Give a man a fish and you feed him for a day; teach a man to fish and you feed him for life."

In my case, if I taught my parents how to fix their own issues, they wouldn't feel as if they needed me. The times that I did then go to visit were much more enjoyable.

Some skills you aren't going to be able to teach. If your parents don't drive and they have errands to do, of course, you should help. Just make sure that you're arranging a time to help them that suits you.

It's important that you tell your parents that you're going to show them how to do things. For example:

- I'm happy to come over and show you, so you'll know how to do it yourself next time.
- I can explain to you over the phone, or I can come over to explain, but not until the weekend.
- Have you tried to do it yourself?
- I'll send you a video that shows you how to do it.

5. Set Consequences for Your Parents' Behavior

Yes, parents need consequences too. Let's say you broke the control cycle and had a meaningful conversation about how your mom resorts to crying every time you assert yourself. She promised not to do it again, and for a while, you could see the effort she was making. But then there came a time when the tears started again.

This is perfectly normal because to maintain boundaries, you need to keep working on them. If reminding your mom isn't working, you need to explain what will happen if her actions continue.

You don't want to come off as condescending or as if you're treating her as the child in the relationship.

You should also keep in mind that the attention should be on how you're feeling – "Mom, I'm emotionally drained, and I can't cope with you crying when it isn't necessary. If I say no to you, it's not because I don't love you; it's because I need to take care of myself. If you can't see this, I won't be able to visit as often, and I don't want that."

Alternatively, if you feel you need to be firmer, you could say something along the lines of, "Mom, we've discussed this. I'm not going to keep visiting if you can't respect my boundaries."

What's equally important as establishing boundaries with your parents is to follow through with the consequences. Empty promises will only encourage parents to cross other lines. With this in mind, never explain a consequence without being fully confident that you can go through with it.

A healthy boundary is to only let your parents buy your children sweets once a week. If you have to enforce a consequence like only being able to see the grandchildren once a week because they don't listen, you can't then call them up and ask them to look after your kids. You need to be able to stick to the once-a-week consequence.

Aside from the sentences we have seen, consequences might look like this:

- In moments when our approaches to parenting differ, I think it might be a good idea to hold off on visits for now. Your understanding would mean a lot.

- I don't think it's necessary for us to exchange hurtful words. If we can't have a calm conversation, maybe we could take a break and talk another time.

- I'll do my best to join the lunches I can. But if there's pressure to attend every single one, I might have to skip them altogether.

- I love you, but if you can't find anything positive to say about my relationship, I'd rather not talk about it right now.

6. Don't Feel Like You Have to Do This Alone

Establishing boundaries with your parents isn't a competition, but you can feel slightly outnumbered if you're planning to have a conversation with two people on your own.

If you've tried to have these necessary conversations and they didn't go as planned, you can't give up. First, take some time to practice exactly what you want to say with a friend or an understanding relative. Ask them to be very honest and provide you with their feedback, not just on how you present your boundary, but also on other aspects of your communication, such as your tone of voice and body language.

Even with practice and confidence beforehand, the idea of trying to express the boundaries again can bring up fear and anxiety.

Ask a person you trust to come with you for support. It won't be their task to have the conversation, but just knowing that someone is there next to you can help to keep you calm and confident, and also prevent the situation from spiraling out of control.

7. Respect Your Parents' Values, Beliefs, Culture and Opinions

Your parents are the source of the problem, so don't feel guilty or put the blame on yourself. Nevertheless, it doesn't hurt to see if there are things you can do to ease particular situations.

Politics and religion are two examples where we have to tread carefully, as even though your parents raised you, as an adult, you may have developed your own views. These are also two topics that people can often feel very passionate about.

Part of the controlling behavior from parents is going to follow through into your religious and political views, from how you choose to raise your child and the diet that you want to try, to pretty much anything that goes against their traditional beliefs.

As an adult and a human being, you're entitled to your own opinions. You might be well-read on a subject or have no interest in it at all, but you have the right to express this, just as they do. Modeling behavior is one way that you can educate your parents on beliefs, especially if they continue to disrespect boundaries that you've set.

Generally speaking, in my family, we avoid talking about politics because of our strong opinions. I was so shocked when one year, my mother-in-law at the time asked me who I had voted for, and then told me that she hoped it was her party because they were obviously the best.

I didn't agree with her, but I was so blown away that I couldn't answer. Her continuous asking eventually led me to explain that in my family, we don't talk about politics. I could see that this wasn't an acceptable answer for her, and she looked at me as if I were the one in the wrong or I just didn't know anything about politics. I had to remember that this was her problem, not mine.

When parents bring up topics that you don't want to talk about, simply say, "I don't talk about topics like this." Full stop! You don't need to explain why. You can also use phrases like, "I can see your point of view and I respect that, but as you aren't willing to accept that I have my own opinions, I won't talk about the subject." Naturally, it won't be the last time your parents bring up a subject that you won't agree on.

Stand your ground, and keep repeating that you aren't going to get into a debate about something you both feel strongly about. You might also have to set a consequence if they continue to upset you.

When it comes to our values, we often feel even more strongly about them. Two lines I will not allow people to cross are racism and (this probably sounds strange to some) speaking ill of the dead.

Ironically, these are values I share with my mom, but my dad will cross the line. My mom puts up with it, and I used to. I have clearly expressed this boundary, and I've said that I won't tolerate it. If my dad crosses the line, I stand up, give them both a kiss, and say goodbye. Then I remove myself from the situation that's upsetting me.

Cultural differences can be extremely challenging, but that's not to say that you don't have the right to establish your boundaries as you see fit. For those who come from a culture where close relationships and intrusive behavior are part of the norm, it's hard to see your friends enjoy a more relaxed and less controlling relationship with their parents.

The one things you should avoid saying are things like, "All my friends..." because your parents will come back with the all-time classic, "If all your friends jumped off a bridge, would you jump?"

Instead, use sentences that remind them that you aren't abandoning your culture and you completely respect where they're coming from, but that you need to find a middle ground that includes aspects from your culture and the new one you're living in.

More ideas for phrases would be:

- I know you favor this political party and I respect that, but you need to respect that I have a different opinion.

- Our culture holds a special place in my heart as well. Rest assured, I'm not turning my back on it; rather, I'm navigating my own path while keeping its significance close. Your understanding truly matters to me.

- I don't feel comfortable discussing this as we have different beliefs.

- I will gladly listen to your opinion if you're willing to listen to mine.

8. How to Deal With Parents Who Insult Your Choices

Do you have parents who hate your partner, your job, your house, or your hair? Do they complain that your clothes aren't right? It's a cruel world, and unfortunately, some people are used to listening to their parents calling them fat, ugly or stupid. This doesn't always represent the entire relationship.

Together, you could have other times that are great, but the times it gets dark are extremely painful, and something nobody should have to deal with.

There is only truth in their words if you choose to believe them. I've had moments when I've felt overweight and known I needed to do something about it. There have been other times when someone has said, "Look at the tummy on you!" when I was actually feeling better about myself. You're not stupid, and nobody is ugly because it should only matter what's on the inside.

There are some important facts to remember when dealing with cruel parents:

1. They are unlikely to change, and you can't fix their issues.

2. Their insults are a sign of their own emotional immaturity.

3. It's unlikely you will ever gain their approval.

4. This is emotional abuse.

Emotional abuse takes many forms aside from insults.

They might give you the silent treatment, threaten you, withhold their love or affection, set unreasonable expectations, play mind games, check your phone or computer, or isolate you from people you love. Some emotionally abusive parents think it's okay to belittle your achievements or highlight your mistakes.

If you've tried to implement boundaries and your parents aren't making any effort to change, or you've reached the point where you mentally can't take any more, it's time to step away and limit the contact as much as possible.

If you aren't ready for a complete cut off, keep your interactions short.

If you're still living at home, this is more of a challenge. Find friends and other family members who you can spend time with, and when you're at home, try to limit the time you have with them.

After this much time with an abusive parent, you have probably discovered that there are certain triggers that cause your parents to hurt you.

And no, you are not a trigger, and triggers aren't excuses for behavior. Alcohol, drugs, or an abusive partner are examples of what may trigger your parents' abuse. It is a good idea to look out for these triggers so you can avoid the aftermath.

As hurt as you feel, you need to be the emotionally mature person in the relationship.

Rather than fighting back, choose from the short phrases below to end the conversation:

- That really hurt.
- You're allowed your opinion.

- It's a shame you feel that way.
- Please stop insulting me.
- No, I'm not going to do that.
- Thank you for letting me know that.

Walking away from this horrible treatment is the healthiest thing for you to do. Whether you feel that you need to be alone or with someone you trust, take some time to process your emotions instead of bottling them up.

Talk to other people, or keep a journal. Use the deep breathing techniques we've worked on, or use a guided meditation video.

Don't get trapped in a place where you're hurting. Revisit your goals, and make plans that are going to make for a better future.

9. Try the Loving Approach

This is not going to work in every case of controlling parents. Firstly, you might not feel like you're capable of showering your controlling parent with love. Secondly, they just might be too wrapped up in their own feelings and needs to appreciate the step you are taking.

The loving approach could work for those parents who don't have enough going on in their own lives to keep themselves busy, or who are feeling lonely with their empty nest.

They might just require enough reassurance that they've done an amazing job raising you, and that you're still going to be there for them and love them, even if you do have to say no or if they can't keep up their smothering love.

Kind words and kind actions can not only reassure a parent who feels they're losing control, but they can also open up the door to a closer and more loving relationship.

When it comes to narcissistic, codependent, and toxic or abusive parents, it's still worth trying the loving approach. It could be a way to break down the incredibly hard wall they've built up around them.

However, in more cases than not, this reassures you that you've tried absolutely everything to develop a healthy relationship with your parents.

10. When It's Time to Walk Away

Sometimes, words and consequences are not going to have the impact we had hoped for. This is most often going to be the case with toxic, abusive and/or codependent parents. You may feel that you've tried everything possible and your parents are still treating you in a way you can't cope with. Let's look at what constitutes everything possible:

- You've taken a very long hard look in the mirror and decided the changes you want to make.
- You've had an open conversation about the boundaries you wish to implement, using kind words and sentences that emphasize your feelings rather than their behavior.
- If your parents react badly to your boundaries or continue to disrespect them, you have used firmer vocabulary and introduced consequences.
- When your parents still don't respect your words, you follow through on your consequences.
- You've asked a friend or family member to support you while you explain the boundaries and stricter consequences.
- You've asked for professional help, but you still feel like there's no progress.

After so many attempts, and probably months of effort, your parents are obviously not going to appreciate that you're an independent adult who's capable of making their own way in life.

This is a very individual decision depending on the situation, but for your own welfare, it might be time to walk away. When we talk about walking away, it could be for a few weeks, a few months, or more permanently. It might mean that you walk away and only have limited contact when you decide so that there's still an element of contact. Or it may be that you have to leave this relationship behind completely.

It's a heart-breaking decision for lots of people, but there also comes a huge sense of freedom when the decision is made. The pressure of trying to please impossible people, the fear of abuse, and the constant demands just disappear, and all of a sudden, your life becomes your own.

The fact that you have had the strength to say no once and for all will give you the confidence and power to create balanced, fulfilling relationships with people who love you for who you are.

It's also possible that this separation causes your parents to change their behavior. They might get the help they need and reach out to you. This opportunity to restart the relationship is going to be up to you, but take it slowly and with caution. Take the time to see that they're genuine before opening your heart up to being hurt again.

If you feel that some professional help is necessary but you aren't sure where to turn, you can have a look at HAVOCA (Help for Adult Victims of Child Abuse). The site has a forum, support group, and the chance to find a suitable therapist, as well as some amazing resources.

Some parents will learn very quickly that you're determined to maintain your boundaries. Others will test the limits you have in place in the hope they're able to find your weak spot and regain their control, which is why persistence and determination are critical.

If you're someone who has to break away from their parents, don't feel guilty or regret your decisions. You haven't made them lightly, so have faith that you made the right ones.

As your life starts to quickly fill up with happiness, the pain will fade.

Practice Setting Boundaries With Your Parents

Take a few minutes to think about how you would respond to your parents in these situations:

1) Your parents turn up at your house at 9am on a Saturday morning with plans for your day.

2) Your mom insists you come over to pick up a curry she's made you, but you're going out for dinner.

3) Your parents go absolutely silent when you express your boundaries. All you get are some grunts and huffs.

4) Your dad mocks you in front of everyone at family gatherings.

CHAPTER 8: BOUNDARIES WITH YOUR PARTNER

We start each new romantic relationship wide-eyed, eager and positive. We learn from our past mistakes, and as we mature, we feel more comfortable that this is the right person. At first, the relationship blossoms, and it seems like nothing could go wrong. We call this the honeymoon period.

Life starts to throw the usual challenges at us, stress rears its ugly head, and we start to show and see sides of us that were dormant during the honeymoon phase. You might have the first argument or just start to doubt your original positivity.

As problems escalate, it's hard to tell if the problems are things that can be fixed or if this is how life is going to be. Ending a relationship, even a bad one, is never easy, and can cause you to feel like a failure, so sometimes we put up with certain behavior because it's easier.

However, there comes a point when the relationship becomes so toxic that your life becomes depressing, your partner expects too much from you, and you wake up each day just to go through the motions.

Boundaries within a romantic relationship are probably some of the most important to establish in your life. Your partner is the person who you likely spend the most amount of time with – you could live with them or even work with them. They may know things about you that nobody else does, despite not having known you for as long as your family members have.

As with boundaries and our family members, there's a wide spectrum with regards to the need for boundaries. There could be niggly things that cause arguments or more severe issues such as narcissism, codependency, and abuse. We will look at the dynamics of these relationships separately, as well as examples of how couples have managed to set their healthy boundaries.

Before working on boundaries, it's necessary to have a check of your own mental health to ensure you're not confusing other issues with the need for boundaries.

What Does a Healthy Romantic Relationship Look Like?

Each person you ask will give you a different answer to this question. Some will say it's trust, others a sense of humor. It's possible that you feel physical intimacy is more important, while others need space. All of these are very true. But there are still key aspects that make for a healthy relationship.

Inter-dependent is an excellent description of a good relationship: it is one where you depend on each other for support, but you are strong enough to remain an individual. So, as an example, you have plans together, but you're still able to do things alone if necessary. You can meet with your friends and have your own hobbies, which relates to time apart and personal space.

Healthy relationships make you feel like you're a part of a team. You can learn new things from each other and take an interest in each other's hobbies and goals. You may even be able to support your partner in achieving their goals without taking over. Arguments will come up, but together, you need to have the communication skills to resolve them.

Naturally, intimacy is a large part of a healthy relationship, but that doesn't mean that you need to have the same (often unrealistic) passion we see in the movies. Aside from the sexual boundaries we discussed in Chapter 1, intimacy will include hugs, kisses, cuddles and handholding.

Why Is Your Mental Health Important?

In 2012, a study was carried out on couples in those first stages of love. They displayed significantly higher levels of oxytocin than in those who were single. This rush increases relaxation, our ability to communicate positively, trust, empathy, and psychological stability.

Meeting a new partner and enjoying those first stages of a new romance makes us feels like we've been fixed, often mentally and physically.

So, what happens when the real world comes crashing back down to reality?

We soon realize that our own mental problems are still present, and will have an impact on the relationship.

Stress, anxiety and depression will cause you to see things in a different way. It's so much harder to enjoy time together when all you want to do is be alone. After a time, your partner may struggle with your mental issues, and this can create tension in the relationship.

We've spent some time looking at how to create boundaries with codependents, but you might be the person with codependent issues. This is not your fault: it may be due to problems from your childhood or past relationships. If you're the type of person who is needy or starts to rely on a partner for their own happiness, you may end up suffocating your partner.

Mental health problems are nothing to be ashamed of or anything to hide. Johns Hopkins estimates that 26% of Americans over the age of 18 suffer from a diagnosable mental disorder annually (Johns Hopkins, 2021).

Many mental health disorders are diagnoses that do not go away, and we have to learn how to deal with them before expecting another person to be able to understand the disorder. It is essential that you know who you are, and you are able to love yourself for who you are.

If you know you're in a good place mentally and physically but still feel that the issues in your relationship could be greatly reduced with boundaries, don't worry: we're going to dive deeper into various problematic relationships and what can be done.

Relationship Type #1 - New Relationships

Those first few weeks and months of a new relationship are essential for setting the tone for a long-lasting and happy relationship. As we've mentioned before, it's also a trickier time because of the flood of love hormones.

It's common to feel that boundaries aren't necessary because everything's perfect. It's actually these moments that lay the foundations for the future.

While you're tempted to change your behavior to please the other person, in many cases, the other person will be doing the same, and to an extent, that's nice.

It's good to be open to new concepts and experiences, but there has to be a limit. If there isn't, you'll find that lots of small changes soon lead to looking in the mirror and not recognizing who you are.

If you're unfortunate enough to be dating a narcissist, allowing boundaries to be crossed at this stage makes it easy for them to find your weak spots and then play on them.

Just because you want to establish boundaries in a new relationship, it doesn't mean that you're boring or that you aren't a good partner.

Let's take, for example, a new partner who sends too many messages or calls you constantly. You can put this down to excitement, but there will come a point when it becomes too much.

You might start to feel suffocated, or that you can't do anything without your partner checking in. The excitement of those messages soon becomes dread as you feel like you're being controlled.

It would be healthier for you to establish a boundary in the first moment that the excessive contact starts to upset you.

You can start with a simple message like, "I love your texts, but I'm busy right now. Talk later!" –and don't forget to add your kisses or usual emoji so they don't read in emotions that aren't there.

If the behavior continues, you might need to be firmer: "I can't talk – I'm working."

If you feel that a text isn't enough for them to refrain from the continuous messaging, you will have to have, at first, a light-hearted conversation.

Again, remind them that while you love hearing from them, you're often not in a position to be able to reply.

You need to focus on your work, or that you need time to be with your friends or family. You could talk about times that are convenient for both of you to text or call.

Don't forget that a consequence might have to be put in place. Letting someone know that you can't be in a relationship with someone who can't respect a communication boundary isn't a threat: it is honesty.

As a general rule in new relationships, it's often not until a boundary issue arises that you become aware of it.

A new person in your life is allowed to express their likes and dislikes regarding how you dress, or even your opinions. But they don't have the right to expect you to change for them.

Seriously consider what your limit is, and deal with it straight away. It's easier to enforce a boundary earlier than to leave it for later down the road. Not only that, but you also increase the chances of the relationship thriving.

Here are some examples of boundaries to communicate in a new relationship:

- I don't like it when people abbreviate in text messages.
- I'm happy to try new things, but I won't have them forced on me.

- I'm not necessarily looking for long-term commitment, but I'm happy to see where things go.
- I need one hour a week to be alone and catch up on my favorite series.

Relationship Type #2 - Established Relationships

If you've been in a relationship for a while, you probably feel quite comfortable around your partner, and you know the good and bad sides of each other. Still, if you weren't able to implement boundaries early on, there will probably be things that your partner does that irritate, frustrate or upset you.

You may have recently moved in with each other, and seen a side to them that you hadn't seen before. Even life-changing events like births, moving house, or the death of a loved one can add stress, sometimes leading to problems that last longer than expected.

The fear of not being liked may have subsided, but only to be replaced by the fear of someone leaving you. If you've tried to express your boundaries previously, it might have caused an argument, and now you may think that it's not worth bringing up the subject again. Falling into this way of thinking only leads to a miserable relationship and life for you. You may even start to resent the other person – and yourself for not standing up for yourself.

As with all boundary-setting, the first stage is to be exceptionally clear about the boundaries you wish to create and where there is room for negotiation. If your partner constantly complains because you work overtime, do they have a point?

Try to see things from both perspectives because sometimes in a long-term relationship, we want to create a boundary that we think we need but isn't necessarily good for us. You're working overtime so that you can save for a new home together.

Your partner complains, not because they're jealous of the time you spend at work or the fact that you aren't home. It might be expressed the wrong way, but they're just genuinely concerned for you. If you go back to check your communication skills, some of the problems can be resolved with an open conversation.

How you start the conversation is crucial for setting the right tone. Regardless of your gender, when you hear the words, "We need to talk," after a long day, you're just drowned by a feeling of dread, and possibly even annoyance. The word "boundaries" can also stir up negative ideas about what's to come.

Remember that just because you know what you want to say, it doesn't mean that the other person is ready to listen. Make sure that neither of you is tired, and that the atmosphere is positive. There shouldn't be any other underlying problems that can be dragged up in a new conversation.

In order to not turn a conversation into an argument, you need to keep your sentences focused on your emotions rather than the actions of your partner.

There is quite a difference between, "You make me so angry when you complain about my overtime," and, "I feel angry when you complain about my overtime." The first sentence implies that they are the cause of your emotions, while the second shows that you're taking responsibility for your feelings rather than blaming your partner.

After you have expressed the behavior you want to change, wait for a response, and actively listen. You should always have a backup conversation if your partner is unable to see or understand the boundary you're trying to establish. But that doesn't mean that it's the only direction the conversation will take.

Listening to what your partner says rather than assuming you know what they will say is how the boundary will be fully accepted. If your partner explains that they're worried about your health, you can decide on a time limit for your overtime. If your partner is upset because there's nobody home to cook dinner, then you can see that they're more concerned about their needs than your wellbeing.

It's important that you control any anger that may arise, and explain that resolving financial issues is more important than who will cook the dinner. If you're willing, you could suggest that one or two nights a week, you will finish early to cook if they can stop complaining.

This is only one of numerous examples in a well-established relationship. A bugbear for so many couples is the housework. Your partner might be more than happy to let dishes pile up or leave clothes all over the floor.

Remember that every time you do the dishes, pick up the clothes, or do anything that you don't want to do, you're teaching your partner that it is okay for them to act in this way.

Creating new boundaries after so much time together isn't unnecessary, and it's not necessarily a sign of deeper issues. It's normal to fall into a routine when things become assumed instead of spoken.

To make boundaries easier, keep working on your communication. Why not try some of these ideas:

- I need time to spend with my friends, as do you.
- I feel like I'm being treated like the cleaner rather than your partner.
- My career is just as important as yours.
- I'd like there to be more balance between the time we spend with your family and the time we spend with mine.

Relationship Type #3 - The Codependent Partner

There are two sides to codependency, and they are related. Someone who is codependent might have issues with addiction, whether that's drugs, alcohol, work or sex.

A codependent partner is someone who relies on the validation and emotions of others. Codependency in women is widely talked about. We need to be careful because men are just as likely to become codependent, and less likely to discuss it (Lancer, 2020). Many use addiction as a means of escapism or as something they see that they control.

For example, a codependent man might use an addiction to work as a form of providing for his family. The hope is that his partner and children are taken care of, and this way, his family won't leave him. This example doesn't seem too painful, but in reality, his work is a cover for identifying the real needs of his family.

Similarly, drug and alcohol abuse allow people a break from stress and anxiety, but the problems are still very much there.

Addiction is rarely a problem that you can overcome alone. If your partner is an addict, valiant as it may be, it isn't healthy for you to be the solution. Part of sobriety and recovery is to gain self-esteem, a feeling that you have this ability to control your habit yourself. If your partner needs you to be sober or clean, the codependency deepens.

Please, if your partner has an addiction of any kind, talk to them about it and encourage them to seek professional help. You can lead a horse to water, but you can't make it drink. Provide leaflets and contact information, but it is up to them to take the first step.

On the other hand, codependency doesn't have to stem from addiction (Glass, 2020). A lot of people will say that their partner is too needy, which is the polite way of saying they're codependent. This could look like a person who always seeks your approval. They might struggle to spend time without you, and will not actively make plans alone, but instead, wait to see what you're doing and 'tag along'.

Codependency can cause jealousy, and even violence. You may start to change the way you dress before you go out, or just give up on the idea of going out at all. Jealousy isn't limited to friends. Codependent partners can become jealous of colleagues, and even family.

The first thing to remember is that codependency isn't your fault or your partner's. There is often childhood trauma that leads a person to become dependent on others. In some cases, professional help will be needed, especially if you've tried establishing boundaries and your partner won't accept them.

The second step is to decide what's important for you. What are your hobbies and goals? Where do you see yourself in 6 months or a year?

Don't feel selfish about creating plans for your future. Next, discuss these plans with your partner. You may want to avoid the word "boundaries" as they could see this as a harsh way of trying to create distance between you. Instead, lead by example. Show them how excited you are about your goals, and encourage them to do the same. Help them to discover hobbies and interests that they'd like to do individually. Also, find interests or make plans for things to do together.

You will need to learn how to say no to your codependent partner. You can use the gentle phrases we have practiced like, "It sounds lovely, but I can't," or the firmer approach of, "No, not today." Remember that "yes" and "no" are just words. There are no feelings attached to these words unless you express them in such a way.

If your no is loud and harsh, it sounds angry, but when you say the right way, it can sound loving. It will be a gradual process, and your partner will need to rebuild their confidence so that they're able to do things without you, therefore, giving you the time you need for yourself.

Use these sentences as you create boundaries with a codependent partner:

- I truly understand that you need assistance, and I would like to help you. However, today happens to be quite hectic for me. Please know that I'd be there for you if circumstances were different.

- I think it's a good idea if we each try this activity on our own first and then come together to do it as a team. This way, we can both enjoy it to the fullest!

- I'm going to take some time for myself this weekend to focus on my goals.

- It's tough for me when I notice jealousy, as I've always been open and honest in our relationship, giving you no reason to doubt my trustworthiness.

Relationship Type #4 - You Are the Codependent

Codependency and empathy are also closely related. Codependency could also mean taking on a large part of other people's emotions and feeling responsible for them.

It is impossible to say no, as you can't stand letting your partner down. This goes back to the need to be wanted, needed and loved. There is a heart-breaking reality here.

Do you love the person, or do you love that they need you? If you came home and the laundry was done, the kids were fed, and your dinner was on the table, would you feel happy, or would you feel disappointed?

Being codependent doesn't mean that you can't have a healthy relationship. It just means that rather than trying to fix others, you need to work on fixing yourself. This might include getting help for substance abuse or mental health issues. You might need to focus on your diet, and start looking at hobbies, interests and goals.

Get to know what your triggers are. You might accept emotional or verbal abuse because it's something that was considered normal in your family when you were growing up. Taking care of a family is ongoing.

Have you ever noticed that you can't sit still and read a book because you feel that there's always something you should be doing?

In this case, you need to work on taking time for yourself. Start small, just 5 minutes a day for a coffee in the garden or meditation.

Slowly build on this so that you don't start to feel guilty when you want to introduce a new hobby. Keep telling yourself that this crucial time for yourself isn't abandoning those who need you.

Your partner will still need you, but instead, it will be for the right reasons – because you are their best friend and they enjoy spending time with you.

Let's look at some phrases to use if you're codependent:

- I'm working hard to make sure I take care of myself and my needs.
- I would appreciate your support in this matter.

- I'm going to take some time for myself, but that doesn't mean I don't love you.
- I really care about our connection, and I hope we can make sure that my kindness is valued and not misused. Your understanding is something I deeply appreciate.

Relationship Type #5 - The Narcissist

You might think that a narcissist is easy to spot. Traditionally, we see them as the person in the room who has all eyes on them. They need to be showered with attention; they believe they're more important than others and that they're generally better than everyone else in the room.

A narcissist lacks empathy and will not be able to see any need for the boundaries that you wish to foster. That would mean seeing things from your point of view, which they're incapable of. This is what psychologists call a covert narcissist (Clarke, 2020).

A covert narcissist will also see themselves as superior and lack empathy, but their behavior is more subtle. Sadly, many covert narcissists are masters of manipulation.

A covert narcissist:

- Constantly looks for reassurance regarding their skills or achievements
- Will play the victim rather than outright criticize you or blame you
- Can cause you to doubt your own ideas or question your perspectives
- May use the silent treatment to get what they want
- Might allow you to feel like you're 'winning', but the end goal is what they wanted all along
- Have a habit of being late or not showing up to reiterate your lack of importance in their life

Studies from Washington University have shown that narcissists aren't aware of their behavior. One study showed that while a group of narcissists ranked themselves as being more intelligent and more attractive, they were also tougher on themselves with regards to their negative qualities (Kaufman, 2011). Some people firmly believe that everybody has the ability to change. Others feel that the only reason for a narcissist to change would be if they could see the greater good for themselves.

Whether your partner is capable of change or not will be up to you. If you try the following techniques and your relationship doesn't improve, the healthiest thing to do for you is to walk away.

If you're determined to try everything first, let's look at how you can implement new strategies in your relationship.

- **Remember who you are**

A narcissist will project their own expectations onto you. If they're the best runner, you are unfit.

If they work more hours than you, you're lazy. If you struggle with your finances, you're an idiot. None of this is true.

When your partner expresses their opinions, you can tell them that these words hurt you, but as they are unlikely to empathize with this, you're better off using your energy to protect yourself emotionally.

- **Focus on your own independence**

You may feel like your partner has the ability to drain all of your power and energy from you. Their intimidation prevents you from standing up for yourself.

Turn your focus onto yourself and what you need to start feeling stronger.

As your strength grows, so will your confidence, and you will start to feel more independent.

- **Be aware of the manipulation**

Whether it's in your face (like shaming you in front of your friends) or subtle (like the bottom lip shaking when you say no), stand your ground.

No means no.

I know from experience that this is far easier said than done. But I promise that the rush of empowerment you feel after the first no is worth all of the anxiety leading up to it.

- **Escape the silent treatment**

The whole point of the silent treatment is that you feel left out in the cold and have to go rushing back to them.

If they decide to cut off all communication, go out. See a friend or visit relatives. There's nothing more empowering than going to the cinema or out for dinner alone.

You get to enjoy a lovely experience, while your partner has to consider the fact that their tactics aren't working.

- **Control your emotions**

Whether you need to breathe deeply, count to ten, or walk away, never let your partner see that they've got to you. Part of them feeling better about themselves is to make you feel worse about yourself.

If the only thing you can bring yourself to say is "Okay," that's fine. It's better than playing into their emotional game.

- **Keep control of your own money**

Many couples have a joint account. It makes it easier for you to pay bills. But being together doesn't mean you merge into one being.

As you strive to maintain your independence, you need to maintain control over your own money. Have a joint account and pay equal amounts into it to cover your joint expenses, but don't give up your main account.

Don't allow yourself to get into a situation where you don't have the financial resources to leave if you want to.

- **Never give up**

A narcissist is going to test every single limit you have. They will try to cross your boundaries, and they'll probably continue to make you feel inferior.

You're going to have to be determined not to give up on yourself. That's not to say that you need to put up a shield to block out your emotions.

Learning to listen to what your emotions are telling you is the best way to start your emotional healing and give you the strength to face the consequences of your boundaries.

Determination will only take you so far.

If you don't see the changes in your relationship that you want to see, it's time to end it.

Deciding to end a toxic relationship isn't giving up on you: it's giving up on the relationship so that you can live the life that you deserve.

For narcissistic relationships, your phrases will need to be firmer:

- My reasons are personal, and I don't have to explain them to you.
- I'm confident in my choices.
- If you aren't going to respect me, I'll walk away.
- No means no.

Relationship Type #6 - The Abusive Partner

First of all, I'm sorry that you're in this place. It's not your fault, and nothing you have done makes you deserve this treatment. Before we go any further, I urge you not to put yourself in any situation where you're in danger. I commend your bravery, but it's not worth your safety.

If your partner is physically abusive, or you're worried that they might turn abusive, don't try to enforce boundaries alone. You can have the conversation in a public place, or make sure that a friend or family member is with you.

Sometimes, a partner suffers from a mental health disorder that causes them to lash out. This isn't an excuse for their abuse. The chances are that you're an empath and completely understand why they're abusive. But you also need to realize that your feelings are valid.

You have the right to be upset when someone hurts you, and you have a right to express this. Burying your feelings is like feeding the ticking bomb inside you with more explosives. You might hear the words, "I'm sorry," and forgive the behavior.

Abuse is only forgivable if your partner is willing to get the help they need and to put the effort into the relationship.

Victims of both verbal and physical abuse are caught in a nasty cycle. The abuser will abuse, and they will say sorry, perhaps telling you it won't happen again or it was the last time. After this, the victim often forgives. For a short time, the abuser will make an effort, but a trigger will cause them to repeat the behavior. Similar to controlling parents, this cycle has to be broken.

As with before, think very carefully about what your limit is. Is it a verbal insult, a physical threat, or physical contact? Remember that physical abuse doesn't have to leave a bruise. Once your boundary is clear in your mind, decide on the consequence of them breaking this boundary. In other relationships, you might be more inclined to be slightly flexible with your boundaries, and even with your consequences.

With abusive partners, there is no room for the same flexibility: this is your mental and physical safety, and possibly even that of your children.

Let's use the example of a partner who verbally abuses you and has raised a hand, but has never actually hit you. You understand that they have their own problems, and are willing to support them while they get professional help.

While their emotional insults hurt you, you can cope for now. The absolute limit is raising their hand to you. If this happens, you'll leave, and there will be no looking back. Tell your partner that you do love them, and that you want the relationship to work, but only if there's mutual respect and care from both sides.

As there is little room for gray, one of three things will happen. Your partner will deny that there's a problem, call you dramatic, and basically show no signs of respecting your boundary, in which case you have to hold your head high and know that you've tried everything you can.

Your partner may agree to get help and things will go well until the point that they violate your boundary. As tempted as you are to give them one more try because they've been working so hard to improve, take care: they're learning that your boundaries can be broken.

The third possibility is that your partner continues with their therapy and/or treatment, while gradually you become stronger and your partner respects you for this. You can work together at establishing and maintaining new boundaries as your relationship grows.

It would be wrong to imply that there is a one-size-fits-all approach to establishing boundaries with your partner when there are so many factors that influence a relationship. In summary, there are certain stages that will apply to all of us. Let's recap on those:

- Know who you are and what you want from the relationship
- Understand that you're entitled to your own space, time, hobbies, interests, goals and friends
- Decide where there's room for give and take and where the absolute no is.
- Don't feel guilt for expressing your boundaries and expecting respect from your partner
- Find the right time to have a conversation when neither of you is tired, stressed, or preoccupied
- Make sure clear communication is your goal, and this includes your own words as well as what your partner has to say
- Accept that sometimes, we all need a little help, and seeking professional help is not a sign of weakness

Remember that it's okay to walk away from a toxic relationship. Don't despair and start to tell yourself that you're doomed to a life of being single.

Take time to learn more about yourself, and become stronger and happier so that you have the right foundations to start a new relationship when you're ready and if you want to.

To keep the focus on your feelings rather than aggravating your abuser, try to remember "I" sentences such as:

- I feel scared when you shout at me.
- I feel personally attacked when you insult me.
- I want to feel important and respected in our relationship.
- I will leave if I don't feel safe in our relationship.

Practicing Your Boundaries With Your Partner

To identify exactly what your relationship boundaries look like, write five sentences that start with the words, "I'm not comfortable with..." and another five that begin with, "I draw the line at..."

You may find that when you look more closely at your relationship, there will be more. Start with at least five for each, and then be clear about your consequence for every point.

CHAPTER 9: GENUINE WAYS TO SET BOUNDARIES AND SAVE FRIENDSHIPS

We all need friends. It's been proven scientifically. Experts at the University of Exeter explain that, aside from releasing these wonderful happy hormones like oxytocin and dopamine, there are evolutionary reasons why we need friends.

Sociability is in our genes. Humans have evolved in large groups containing both family members and non-family members. Early friends would have been there to protect other humans from predators, or they would have helped each other to find food (Mandel, 2019). These connections are still important to us, but they have evolved as we have.

Today, we might need support when we have an argument with a relative or partner. Spending time with your friends releases happy hormones that allow us to feel good. But what can you do when these friendships are not quite as balanced as you had hoped?

Friendships are different to other relationships in the sense that they aren't blood, and your friends aren't your life partner. Nonetheless, a friendship that doesn't have boundaries will show the same issues as other relationships. Without boundaries, you might experience:

- A lack of empathy
- Inappropriate amounts of sharing
- Disrespecting each other's time
- Disrespecting religion or values and beliefs
- Controlling decisions rather than supporting
- Putting a friend's needs before your own
- Not saying no when you need or want to
- Putting up with behavior that you don't agree with
- Being too physically close or suffocating
- Toxic friendships

There's also a friendship spectrum, encompassing people who you would call acquaintances, others who are part of a regular circle of friends, and those that you can't imagine life without.

How you go about setting these boundaries will depend on the closeness of your relationship.

You might also have a niggly feeling about a friendship, but you can't identify the source of the problem. It might be as simple as identifying why you need to create these boundaries.

Why Would You Need to Set Boundaries With Friends Now?

If you've just met some new people, it's essential that you establish your boundaries straight away so that your relationship doesn't suffer in the future.

For those friends who've been in your life for some time, don't assume that it's too late. Without sounding like a broken record, boundaries are there to enhance friendships and not to push them away. See if any of the following situations ring true for you.

1. You are overwhelmed. Your family could be putting pressure on you,

or you have additional work deadlines. Your boss is going on at you, and the last thing you can handle is your friend adding to the pressure.

2. Your life has changed. Certain events in our lives mean we aren't as available as we used to be. This is often seen when we have children, and that Sunday afternoon beer has been replaced with afternoon naps and diapers.

3. You no longer feel that it's acceptable for you to put more into the relationship. Friendships have to be mutually beneficial so you both put in equal amounts and get equal benefits.

4. You can't trust your friend. Whether they've never been particularly trustworthy or they've recently broken your trust, you need to feel safe to share.

5. You can't accept some of their extreme views. We all have that one friend who is a political buff, or perhaps you have someone whose opinions of illegal immigrants breaks your heart.

6. You can't do anything without your friend asking what you're doing or where you're going. It has come to a point where their keen interest makes it feel like you have another controlling parent.

7. They are in constant contact or don't appreciate your communication style and technique. A quick meme from a friend midday can boost your mood. 100 texts and half an hour phone calls aren't necessarily productive, and can cause annoyance.

8. Your friendship has turned nasty. It could be a combination of one or more of the above. They might be picking at your personality, making fun of you, or bullying you. This toxicity can lead to manipulation and other unhealthy friendship traits.

Two Amazing Techniques for Setting Boundaries With Friends

Before we look at some specific cases of friends who break boundaries, I want to look at two techniques that will help you to determine and establish boundaries. Don't forget: you can use these techniques for boundaries with any person in your life, but they're nice to use with friends as a practice.

The Compass

Sarri Gilman shared a unique way in which she created boundaries in her TED conference. You can either draw a small compass on a piece of paper, or you can visualize one on the palm of your hand.

This compass has just two words: "yes" and "no." It goes back to the idea that yes and no are only words, and there are no emotions attached to these words.

When you enforce your boundaries in your friendships, they will react with their feelings, but you have to remember that this is on them. Your compass has no feelings, and its sole purpose is to take care of you.

So you go about your day, and any time a friend asks something of you, you look at your compass and decide if it is yes or no. Remove the emotions, remove the what-ifs and buts – just answer yes or no. Once you have your answer, you can then choose the right words.

It's not uncommon for your compass to get "clouded over". It's not always clear whether it's a yes or a no. We can't blame the compass: it's just an object. Normally this happens when we don't agree with the initial answer.

Imagine your friend wants you to help them move house. You look at your compass, and it says no because the last thing you want to do is spend your one free day shifting boxes.

Then the tiny voice in your head says, "But it's the nice thing to do, and they helped me when my car broke down." But your answer is no, and you should have faith in that. If your compass is only there to care for you, the answer is no because your body and mind need time to disconnect.

That being said, your compass won't provide you with any details. It doesn't have the ability to see the middle ground. The idea is that it provides you with the initial answer that you can then work on.

In the case of moving house, you could say, "I can help for 2 hours, but then I have to go." Your boundary is clear, so it's crucial that after 2 hours, you go. If you don't, you have ignored your compass and your own wellbeing.

Sell Your Time

This is an excellent technique to help you visualize your limits. Break down your day into 30-minute slots - so logically, in 24 hours, you have 48 slots.

If we're lucky, we can take away 16 slots for sleeping, and most will have to take away around 16 more for work. You have 16 slots left.

Be precise here: do you need a slot for showering? Do you need two slots for dinner? Once you've delegated your slots to everything you need to do on that day, you'll be left with, let's say, seven slots.

You're now left with the things you want to do and the things your friends want you to do. I'm going to take away two slots because I want to go to the gym. My friend wants to have a drink. Okay, I'll sell two slots to my friend. A different friend wants to go to the movies. This will require at least my remaining five slots, and therefore, I have to say no.

As you get better at saying no based on the number of slots you have available, you will soon start to feel like you have more control over your own time and that you have more time for yourself.

This time alone is energizing, and makes the activities that you do with your friends that much more enjoyable.

You can even combine these two techniques. Use your compass to decide if you say yes or no to selling a time slot.

You can even explain your technique to your friends. When a friend hears, "I don't have time," they assume you're exaggerating or just making things up.

If you say, "Sorry, I only have three slots left today," they can see that you've calculated your time precisely.

They may come back and say, "Can I have one slot?" Well, that's something that may work, depending on whether you want to say yes or not.

There are so many potential issues with friends that all require some form of boundary. We're going to look at some of these with examples of how to be firm and fair.

Your friend laughs at your attempt to set boundaries

Within a friendship or a group of friends, you each develop a role that's hard to break free from. You have the joker, the carer, the planner, and so on.

You probably feel like you don't have a role established, and that you're the submissive one who lets others carry out their roles.

The moment you try to form an opinion, the friend or group is shocked, and find it funny that all of a sudden you have a voice. They may laugh or ridicule you, and this will hurt. While you shouldn't excuse their behavior, consider whether, on some subconscious level, they're fearful of your boundary, as it means they might have to give up part of their role.

The planner is organizing a dinner for the group. You have always said yes to everything, but this time you don't like the location, and suggest somewhere else. You can imagine the shock on their face, and then they reply with a laugh and ridicule your idea. It was probably a good idea, but deep down, they fear that you'll have more good ideas, and that you'll start to take on the role of planner, leaving them feeling redundant.

Setting boundaries doesn't mean that you're no longer an empath. You can still understand the root of your friends' laughter in order to express boundaries in a way that reassures them.

For example, "I know you love planning, and you've always done such a good job. I just think that the atmosphere is better there." This gives your friend some reassurance in their abilities, and tells them that you have a valid opinion.

Here are some other phrases you can try:

- Please don't laugh at me.

- It hurts me when you ridicule my ideas.
- You know that I get upset when you laugh at me, so why do you keep doing it?
- I feel like your joking has crossed a line.
- No, I don't want to do that because you've hurt me by laughing at me.
- Did I miss the joke?

There's a combination of phrases that emphasize your feelings, and others that highlight bad behavior. Which ones you want to use will depend on how you're feeling at the time.

Friends who never pay

Thanks to technology and payment apps, there's little excuse for someone not paying their way anymore. If you're out for dinner and you pay the bill, they should be able to send a transfer for their share. Still, we all know that one person who never seems to open their wallet.

The solution to this problem is rather simple, regardless of if you're better off than they are or vice versa. You work hard for your income. You want to be able to enjoy your time with friends, but should your 40-hour week really enable them to enjoy their lives that little bit more?

The other way to look at it is that you aren't actually helping them to be responsible with their finances if you're constantly paying.

First of all, prepare yourself for a frank conversation with them. They might not even be aware that they're doing it, so avoid subtle digs. "I love our Saturday lunches together, but I need you to start paying for half."

You shouldn't have to feel like you need to justify this, but you might want to explain that things are tight, or that you're saving for something. If your friend takes offense at this or becomes angry, then it's time for the consequence, and that would be to stop meeting them for lunch.

Your friend dominates conversations

Still bearing in mind that everyone is entitled to express their own opinions, conversations among friends have to have balance. If you feel like your friend chooses all of the topics, voices their opinion, and then doesn't bother to listen to you, you're lacking a boundary.

Being a constant listening ear is exhausting and draining. You can feel undervalued and disrespected. A healthy friendship is one where you can both unload when you need to, or you can both share stories from your day.

The irony is, if you've tried to interrupt your friend to get a word in, you've probably been called rude. Never interrupt: it won't achieve your goal.

What you can do is control how you react to the friend's constant chatter. You probably try to show interest in what they're saying in the hope that they will ask you a question.

From now on, we're going to do the opposite. That's not to say that you're going to start rolling your eyes and huffing and puffing. Instead, remain neutral; only respond to things that you feel are important and keep your comments relative.

While this will help to reduce the extended chatter from your friend, it's likely that you'll still need to make it clear that the conversation needs balance. For example:

- I don't feel like I have a chance to voice my opinion.
- I'd like to feel heard.
- It's important to me that I contribute to the conversation.
- I feel shut out when you hog the conversation.
- I don't feel like you care that you never let me speak.
- I feel like there's distance in our friendship because I don't have the chance to talk.

Once your friend is aware of the problem, it's time to introduce the solution. While it might sound dramatic, a code word is an ideal way to remind your friend that they've slipped into talkative mode: a single word that relates to you both that you can say to pause and remind your friend that you need to have your say.

Friends call you mean when you try to establish your boundaries

It's hard enough to overcome your own fear and worries about coming across as selfish. When a friend calls you mean, selfish, unkind, or any other insult, it should reassure you that this is exactly why boundaries are needed.

Secondly, think about what these words actually mean to you. Your friend won't realize that their insults more accurately describe their own behavior, as they can't see the importance of your needs.

Let's look at the word "mean". It means to be cruel or unkind; however, people throw the word around for situations that really are far from cruel.

If you can't pick your friend up or taxi them around because you already have plans with colleagues, wouldn't it be crueler to cancel on your colleagues?

We've probably all had that moment when we've asked a friend to keep their mask on or wanted to be socially distant, only for them to call us mean.

You aren't being mean at all. You're protecting your health. So remind yourself that you're not mean. And selfish? We aren't talking about sharing your chips or a bag of sweets.

Allowing your friends to manipulate you into doing things you don't want to by insulting you will slowly chip away at your health and your happiness. So again, constantly remind yourself that you aren't selfish.

Tell your friends that you won't tolerate insults because they don't get their way. Explain that there are certain things that you can do, and others that you're not willing to do.

You can explain that you can see their point of view, you understand that they need help or want to do things with you, but there's a right way to ask and a wrong way: "Insulting me is not going to encourage me to say yes to you." You can also point out that they wouldn't like it if you treated them in the same way.

Be confident in your words and body language. Make an effort to ensure that you're facing the person and making eye contact.

Your tone doesn't have to be negative or forceful, but it does have to be direct. Avoid the word "sorry" as it isn't you who should be apologizing.

Put it into practice:

- I'm not mean. I'm taking care of myself.

- I've been hurt too many times by your words. Right now, I feel it's best for me to take a break from our friendship.

- This is difficult for me to say, but I've noticed that our interactions have been affecting my health negatively. Considering that, I think it would be best for both of us if I took some time away.

- If you feel so strongly, I don't see a future for our friendship.

The friend who is always late

I have a friend who is always late. I think in 10 years she has been on time once. There is absolutely no malice in this. She's incredibly disorganized, and talks to everyone in her path. As frustrating as it is, she means no harm. She's also from a different culture where they tend to be more laid back about everything. To handle this, I calculate a half hour difference.

On the other hand, I had a friend who was always late because they wanted their entrance to be dramatic. They wanted the whole room to see that they were more important, that their lives were busier than anyone else's, and their responsibilities were more important. Classic narcissism!

For people who are narcissistic and don't respect boundaries, your phrases will likely fall on deaf ears, but that's not to say that you shouldn't have a frank conversation and implement consequences: "I feel that you don't respect the importance of my time when you're constantly late or don't show up. From now on, I won't wait."

It's short and to the point, and clearly explains that you won't stand for the behavior. Of course, to maintain your boundary, you'll have to leave as soon as your friend is late.

Put it into practice:

- If you arrange to meet me at a certain time, you need to stick to it.
- I don't appreciate being left to wait. I feel it's very inconsiderate.
- It takes less than a minute to send a message and let me know of the change of plans.
- My time is just as important as yours.

Learning how to trust in a friendship again

Breaking someone's trust is incredibly hard to fix. Depending on the degree, it may be impossible to completely overcome. Once bitten, twice shy doesn't only apply to existing friendships: the experience stays with you when you make new friends. When it comes to new friendships, be open about your feelings and past issues.

Many people have had problems with a friend gossiping or talking about them behind their back. This becomes a fear that we assume will happen in all other friendships, but you should always give people the benefit of the doubt.

On that note, if you have a friend who likes gossiping to you, it's more than likely that they gossip about you. If a friend starts to talk about others, tell them straight away that you aren't interested, and bring up a new subject.

Also, look for particular patterns in the friendships you create. You might realize that you tend to form friendships with people who are untrustworthy. There will be a reason behind this, and you should explore it in order to break the pattern.

Don't just look at trust issues within your friendships: also look at your relationships with your partner and family members. You may find that talking to a professional will help you to get to the root of your trust issues.

Now, if your issues are because friends have hurt you, you need to make sure they're aware of the depth of your pain.

Let them know that you're not going to be able to trust them again for some time, and that if they want the friendship to last, they will have to prove their trustworthiness.

An amazing quote I once read was, "Trusting you is my decision. Proving me wrong is yours."

It's your choice to trust someone, and it will take time. If the behavior continues, even after several attempts to establish your trust boundaries, the friendship has become unhealthy, and even toxic. These people are doing more harm than good, and you should consider walking away.

Put it into practice:

- I don't gossip, and I don't listen to gossip.
- I'm not comparing you to my past friends, but I've had problems in the past, and I'm learning to trust again.
- I'm incredibly sad about what you've done. I need time to process it.
- I need you to stick to your promises if you want me to trust you again.

The big one - friends who don't respect boundaries

You've taken a look at yourself, and you clearly know what you want from your friendships. You've asked your compass and decided what is a firm yes and what is a firm no, and you've identified the areas that can be negotiated. You've used the right language and short phrases, and you've set the consequences.

Even after reiterating boundaries and following through with the consequences, your friends still try to push the limits.

Imagine you can only have five foods for the rest of your life. Are you going to choose the unhealthy or the healthy?

If you only had room in your world for five friends, would you still hang on to the toxic friendships, or would you be more willing to break the contact knowing that you now have room for friends who have your best interests at heart?

As we grow up, our life circumstances change. We mature, we learn, and we see things from different points of view. Sometimes, our friends do the same, but in opposite directions.

There's no rule that says you have to remain friends with someone no matter what.

Put it into practice:

- I have said no, and I mean no.
- I'm taking steps to prioritize my own needs, and I hope you can support that decision without any feelings of guilt.
- If it's hard to accept me as I am, I'm finding it tough to see a future for our relationship.
- Your actions have left me quite upset, and at this moment, I feel it would be best for both of us if I could have some space.

Initially, setting boundaries will cause you stress, but it's not permanent. Once you've set your boundaries, your friends will respect them, or they won't. You will notice that once you end the friendship, or at least distance yourself from these boundary-breakers, your stress will ease.

There is still one other group of people that we need to form boundaries with. A group of people that we spend the biggest part of our day with – our colleagues. The next chapter is going to be dedicated to those workmates who know exactly what buttons to push to get a reaction.

CHAPTER 10: BOUNDARIES IN THE WORKPLACE FOR A MORE POSITIVE ENVIRONMENT

Hollywood has a habit of romanticizing workplace boundaries. Don't get me wrong, I love a rom-com as much as the next, but they tend to turn very real issues into a humorous situation where inevitably, two boundary breakers fall in love.

Take *Two Weeks' Notice* with Sandra Bullock and Hugh Grant. Grant's character calls his assistant (Bullock) at an inappropriate time for an "emergency": he couldn't choose a tie!

Unfortunately, for many of us, there isn't a Grant or Bullock for us to fall in love with, and we don't have to suffer a negative or even toxic environment day in and day out.

The harsh fact is that we spend approximately half of our waking hours in the workplace. Today, 50-hour weeks are becoming the norm, and even 60-hour weeks aren't uncommon (Business News Daily, 2020).

Problems at work and with colleagues are going to have a knock-on effect in other areas of your life. Workplace stress has a huge impact on employees and employers.

83% of US workers suffer from work-related stress, and a massive 1 million workers miss work each day due to stress. The cost to businesses in the US is up to $300 billion, and $51 billion of this is due to absenteeism caused by depression.

Naturally, there are various reasons for workplace stress. That being said, boundaries could help the 39% of people whose workload causes them stress, and the 35% of people whose boss is the main cause of their stress (The American Institute of Stress, 2019).

When there are no boundaries at work, stress builds up. You wake up in the morning, and you dread starting your day. Tasks are more challenging, colleagues are more annoying, and not even the end of the day makes you any happier.

Many people also have to take work home with them. The constant strain of having to answer the phone, reply to a text, or check emails takes its toll.

Tiredness turns into exhaustion, anxiety, and often mental health issues, physical health issues, and even substance abuse. The lack of strength makes it more difficult to set and maintain boundaries with your friends and family.

What Are Workplace Boundaries?

Workplace boundaries are a set of legal and ethical practices that allow employees to feel safe, both physically and emotionally, in a work environment.

Some workplace boundaries are very clear, especially when they're the law.A relatively new boundary that we must all comply with is around privacy laws. Sexual harassment is now a hot issue, especially since the #MeToo movement. There are others that we still need to consider, as well as people who don't seem to understand how close their actions come to breaking the law.

Workplace boundaries include:

- Bullying
- Racism
- Discrimination

- A narcissistic boss
- Flirting
- Asking personal questions
- Working without pay
- Not using your vacation days
- Working through your breaks
- Taking on other people's responsibilities
- Taking on too big a workload
- Saying yes to jobs you don't have the skills for

An element of common sense will be required. For example, when asking personal questions, if your boss asks you about your family, they might be showing a genuine concern. If a boss starts to ask about your kids' grades, where your partner works, and what you had for breakfast on Saturday, it becomes intrusive. You may also have a tight deadline or a meeting that can't be changed. On this occasion, you don't mind skipping your break.

The need for workplace boundaries will come when the action starts to make you feel uncomfortable or unhappy. If I saw a woman looking at me and smiling, I would take it as a compliment. The next man might find it uncomfortable. The law is clear to a degree, but there is still a gray area that you need to navigate your way round based.

The Benefits of Establishing Boundaries in the Workplace

When you decide to implement boundaries in the workplace, it's not about being right or wrong, nor is it about asserting your dominance. Your boundaries won't make you unpopular or the party pooper of the office. On the contrary:

1. Boundaries allow for a respectful workplace. Not just respect for the superiors, but for people in every position.

2. Employees will be able to clearly see what behavior is considered acceptable in the workplace. Not every location or industry will have the same rules, so boundaries make it easier for people to follow acceptable behavior.

3. Creating boundaries promotes positive communication. When people feel safe to talk about their concerns, you can start to have more open and direct conversations, which is incredibly productive.

4. Not having boundaries makes it harder to discuss and manage expectations. Without expectations, the entire company seems to just float along rather than striving to achieve goals as a team.

5. You can enjoy your work. Many people agree that they love their job but hate their toxic workplace. There is a huge sense of relief when you can go into work and not have to fear the atmosphere.

How to Form Boundaries at Work

In the first place, you need to understand what your personal boundaries are.

What type of jokes do you find funny, and where is the line that makes them offensive? How much physical contact is enough for you, and similarly, how much of your personal life are you willing to share?

Next, it is time to communicate them. I have included some simple phrases that you can use in a variety of settings, but have the confidence to adapt them to suit your boundary.

If you aren't ready for a short "No," you can use the softer versions. Just never say more than you have to.

Your boss wants you to come back to work on a Friday night.

- No, I can't.
- Sorry, I can't, but I'm available tomorrow morning.

• I'd love to help you, but I have plans.

You co-worker has sent you a demanding email – all in capital letters.

• Thank you for considering me, but that's not going to work for me today.

• I wish you'd asked sooner.

• I'll check my schedule for later.

• No, I'm afraid not.

• I understand your urgency, but I'd appreciate it if you didn't email in this way.

Your co-worker keeps insisting you go out with them.

• I don't date colleagues.

• I'm flattered, but no, thank you.

• I'm dedicated to my work.

• I'm not available.

Your manager is manipulating you into giving a presentation you aren't ready for.

• This is John's area, not mine.

• I'd be happy to if I could have a day or two to prepare.

• This isn't in my job description.

• My workload is already full.

A colleague makes discriminatory jokes.

• That isn't funny.

• That type of humor disgusts me.

• If you continue to tell jokes like this, I'll report you.

• Wow, I thought that humor went out with the 80s.

Your colleague has recently been promoted and is on a power trip.

• Congratulations on your promotion, but I still know how to handle my role.

• I feel that you're abusing your power and not respecting my experience.

• You're truly deserving of this promotion, and I believe we can handle this situation without any unnecessary negativity.

A person in your office invades your personal space.

• I feel uncomfortable with personal contact.

• I'm sorry, but I'm not a touchy-feely kind of person.

• Would you mind taking a step back?

The new kid is trying to reinvent the wheel.

• I'm more than happy to listen to your ideas, but at a more appropriate time.

• We're on a tight deadline. Let's focus on the task at hand, and then look at your suggestions.

• Your enthusiasm hasn't gone unnoticed. Perhaps you can draft an email so I can take a closer look.

• I appreciate your recent qualifications, but experience is just as crucial.

A co-worker is disrespecting the janitor.

• I find your behavior unacceptable for a positive working environment like ours.

• There's nothing wrong with earning a decent living.

- Not everyone has had your opportunities.

(It will very much depend on the type of comment, and it doesn't have to be the cleaning crew. The point is, when you see other people being treated unfairly, stand up for them.)

It's always better to address work boundaries as they come up. If you've ever had something on the tip of your tongue and not been able to say it, you'll know how frustrated you feel afterward. This frustration leads to self-tormenting, regret, and wasted time.

Don't force yourself when you aren't ready. With practice, it will become more natural for you to enforce the boundary in the moment.

You can take a couple of minutes to compose your thoughts, or wait until the other person is on their own. But the longer you leave it, the more likely your colleague is to cross the boundary again, and the harder it becomes for you to deal with it.

Make Technology Part of Your Boundaries

It's true that I've complained about the effects of modern technology on communication, but in the workplace, it's an absolutely amazing tool to help with boundaries.

Project management tools are fantastic ways for your colleagues to share tasks and update progress. The team can see exactly what needs to be done and what different people are working on at the time. Individual deadlines and team deadlines can be posted. Delegating becomes easier, as you can see who already has too much to do and who could pull their socks up a little.

With built-in communication tools, you can also keep everyone in the loop. If a meeting has been canceled, everyone gets to find out at the same time instead of someone wasting their time waiting because they didn't receive the memo.

Make sure that your digital tools also have their boundaries. Limit chat to professional comments only, and make sure it's only used within office hours.

Social events at work are very important. They provide us with the opportunity to get to know each other better, and most importantly, to learn about personal boundaries.

That's not to say that the office BBQ should be used as a show and tell for boundaries. It's a chance to relax and enjoy time without the stress of work. Though it is a social event, remain professional at all times, regardless of whether it is your first wheel or you're the CEO. It will be almost impossible for you to assert your boundaries in the office if your colleagues are imagining you doing karaoke after too many drinks.

Practice Your Work Boundaries

It's a good idea to first write a list of the areas you would like to see change. Play out conversations where first you play the boundary violator, and then you play yourself.

Even if you feel a little crazy, use a mirror so that you can focus on your body language, and in particular, your facial expressions.

If you have had success setting boundaries with a friend or family member, ask them to role play with you. Even better, if you know someone in the office who is having the same difficulties as you, practice together.

Expressing your boundaries in the workplace may require a different kind of confidence, as you aren't as close to co-workers as you are to your friends. The more practice you can have, whether it's with the mirror, your pet, or another person, the greater your confidence will be.

Finally, take time off. Take every day and every hour you're entitled to. When someone emails you or texts you when you're in yoga or taking your kids to soccer practice, send a quick message back saying, "Let's talk about it on Monday morning," or, "I don't take work calls/texts/emails out of hours."

Remember that as more of us are working remotely nowadays, it doesn't mean to say we're on call 24/7. It's essential for your own wellbeing that you have a chance to disconnect from both your job and your colleagues.

Nobody can afford to let work stress make them sick. Without this break, you'll remain in the already large percentage of people suffering from work stress.

CHAPTER 11: DEALING WITH DIFFICULT PEOPLE: HOW TO MAINTAIN YOUR BOUNDARIES WHEN SOMEONE VIOLATES THEM

In a perfect world, you will have expressed your boundaries to the people you love, and they will have understood completely, allowing you to lead the life that you imagined. We live in a far from perfect world, and you are going to get pushback, and this is where our final C comes into play – control.

You may have already experienced this painful experience, and are starting to wonder if there's any point in continuing. Our focus has to be on maintaining your boundaries, but even before that, it's about remembering your decision and standing by it.

It's about keeping the image of you in a place where you are free to make your own choices without fear of repercussions.

It is this image that's going to help you to cope with the reactions of those who aren't going to accept your boundary easily.

Before looking at how we're going to deal with difficult people, I think it's important to learn how to stick to our own decisions.

Whether you have made the decision to establish one boundary or 10, keep these small steps in mind:

- Don't wait a long time in between making your decision and executing it. The longer you wait, the more time you have to doubt it.

- Get excited about your decision. Visualizing the results is one way, but you might also want to be a little more creative.

Make a board showing some of the things you want to do with the spare time you create, like new hobbies you wish to start or other new goals.

- Wake up every morning and remind yourself about your decision. Think of a powerful mantra like, "Today I will carry out my decisions."

- When you have moments of doubt, pull yourself back to the present and think of the result you're going to achieve.

- Take time to give yourself a pat on the back. There will be more celebratory moments when your boundaries are respected, but for now, don't forget to celebrate the fact that you have made this life changing decision.

- Share your decisions with someone who will not only support you, but also get excited about your decision. These are the people who are going to motivate you to keep going when someone violates your boundary.

When Is It Really a Violation of Boundaries?

Throughout this book, we've looked at a number of boundary-crossing scenarios that one person would say are okay, and the next would agree that are unacceptable. We began in the initial chapters with the importance of understanding your own boundaries, and the subsequent chapters have been about learning to deal with boundaries related to specific types of relationships. In each type of relationship, there are going to be people who either push your boundary or just completely disregard it.

You will feel like this is your fault, and that you haven't expressed the boundary clearly. Truth be told, you have executed your boundary to perfection, but by definition, there are two sides to a boundary – your limit and the ideals of the other person.

If people are still pushing your boundaries, it's not because you're doing it wrong. It's on them and their beliefs, views and ideals.

You will have to get tougher. Your communication will have to be clearer, and your consequences more extreme. You can't feel bad about this in any way because you are only responsible for your own emotions.

On that note, you need to turn all of your negative emotions, such as fear, worry, guilt and selfishness, into positive energy and strength. Give yourself a stern talking to: "Hang on a minute, I expressed a wish, kindly and respectfully, and the other person has reacted as if I don't exist. That's wrong!"

Remember that this isn't the same as establishing your boundary. We have already considered what needs to be achieved and set boundaries.

Many people won't have been aware of these personal limits you had, and now that they are, they'll respect them. However, violating boundaries is when you have set them, and people continue to disrespect them.

Whether it's unintentional or not, at this point, there should be no excuses, and no letting people off because they didn't realize. Even if it was unintentionally, you have expressed your wishes, and they haven't taken them seriously enough to remember.

A boundary violation is when you have asked someone to stop swearing in front of your children, but they continue to use foul language. You've told your partner repeatedly that you don't like mushrooms, but they add them to every meal. Your boss asks you every weekend to work overtime, even though you've told him that you can't. Perhaps it's your family: Mom and Dad still think it's okay to show up unannounced, or despite being perfectly happy single, your best friend just doesn't stop matchmaking in the most embarrassing way.

It could be any situation where you have clearly stated your discomfort and people continue with the actions that hurt you. Again, name-calling or mocking you might seem relatively small to someone else, but it's having a negative impact on your life, and has to be stopped.

How to Deal With Negative Responses to Boundaries

To put things in perspective and context, we have 10 examples of negative reactions to boundary setting, and examples of what can be said.

#1 But you always help me.

"I have always helped you in the past, but this has taken a toll on me. I'm not saying that I'll never be able to help you, but this time, I'm saying no."

Notice that you have changed 'always help me' to a past action to reinstate that there is a change. For a short answer, use, "That was then. This is now."

#2 I can't believe you're being so selfish.

I was so fed up with someone constantly calling me selfish that I turned around and said, "I can't believe you're being so ironic." I had to explain this to them because they weren't able to see that they were being selfish by not considering my needs.

You can also use phrases like, "I'm not selfish: I'm taking care of myself," or, "Stop calling me selfish. It's unkind and not true."

#3 Ghosting/Silence

When someone gives you the silent treatment, it's because they want a reaction from you, so in this case, you shouldn't say anything. Take some time to see what life is like without this person in your life. Is it better or worse?

If they're a true friend, they will contact you. If they're a person that you can't simply remove from your life, send a message such as, "Giving me the silent treatment isn't going to make me change my mind. I'm willing to talk to you about it when you're ready."

#4 I hate you.

Take a deep breath, and don't react with anger. These words hurt, but it's unlikely that they mean it. Ask them if that's how they really feel because they will probably say, "No," and you can reply with, "I understand that you don't like what I'm saying, but it's important to me." If they say "Yes," then walk away, at least until they reach out to you with an apology.

#5 If you don't do it, I won't talk to you again.

It's a very immature thing to say, and again, this response is probably lashing out because they don't like you asserting yourself. You may feel the most appropriate response is, "Okay, if that's how you feel." If you don't feel ready to walk away, say something like, "Threatening me isn't going to make me change my mind. If you like, we can look at finding a compromise so we're both happy."

#6 I'll find someone who does want to help me (guilt trip).

Like ghosting, it's a manipulative response, and if you don't stand your ground, it will be that much harder to establish boundaries with this person in the future. They will be expecting you to say that you'll do it.

The best way to reinforce the boundary is to say, "Okay," or, "That's great." You might feel that a phrase like, "It's not that I don't want to help you; it's that I can't," is kinder, but be prepared for the other person to come back with further pushback.

#7 You will never get a promotion if you keep saying no.

This person is trying to scare you into doing things you don't want to do. If they're a colleague, then they have no weight behind the empty threat. If they're a superior, report the issue to human resources.

Your responsibilities and hours are clearly defined in your contract, and they can't not consider you for a promotion for not taking on more than is required of you.

#8 Why do you have to be so cruel to your mom when she's only trying to help you?

Again, we have this word "cruel" that implies you're killing puppies or stealing from old ladies. Your parents still haven't seen that you're only trying to live your life independently. Review the steps for breaking the control cycle.

Phrases you can use could be, "I'm not being cruel. I love all you do for me, and I'm grateful. I'm setting boundaries because I need to focus on my health," or, "I feel very hurt when you call me cruel, and I would appreciate it if you didn't insult me and try to make me feel guilty."

#9 My last partner never complained.

Comparing your partner with a past partner is an absolute boundary violation. You are two completely different people. You have to clearly state that you won't tolerate being compared. "Don't compare me with your ex," "I'm not the same person as your ex," or, "Your ex was entitled to their opinions just like I am," are three examples.

#10 Shouting, insulting. or any sign of physical abuse.

The aim is to calm the person down before reiterating your boundary. If you continue, you run the risk of their temper escalating. Try, "I want to have a conversation with you, and I want to see your point of view, but I can't when you're shouting," or "Let's take a little time to cool down, and then we can talk about it." Don't stay in any situation where you don't feel safe, and I can't stress this enough. It is always better to walk away than to stay and risk being hurt.

How to Protect Your Boundaries

If you're worried about protecting your boundaries, you need to understand that the process is much easier when you're taking care of yourself.

Enforcing boundaries causes stress. The stress is temporary, and each step will get easier, but in those first few weeks and months, take time to do the things you enjoy and to physically experience the benefits of the boundaries you've begun to enforce.

Seeing small improvements is the greatest motivation to protect your boundaries. We'll start with the people who are going to be more open to your boundaries because not everyone is going to push back.

Let's imagine a friend who keeps talking about their sex life, and it's way too much information for you. They're easy to talk to, and the rest of your relationship is great, so you set your boundary by saying, "I love that you have an amazing sex life, but could you please tone down the details?" The problem is solved, and you can reward yourself for a fantastic job. The relief is encouraging, and it will help you to not only protect this boundary, but also the others that you're preparing.

What If Your Boundaries Are Pushed: How to Stand Up for Yourself

Standing up for yourself is very similar to not having boundaries in the first place. There's often a deep-rooted reason for why you can't stand up for yourself. It might be that your parents were overly strict and you didn't have the chance to stand up for yourself, or you've learned over time that your standing up for yourself means putting your needs before others, and society has taught us that this is wrong. The first thing to do is to get to the bottom of this and ask yourself why you don't feel you can stand up for yourself.

Look at all of the situations in which you wish you'd stood up for yourself. Use these as practice scenarios. Imagine what you would have said. Think about "I" statements you could have used:

- I don't appreciate it when...
- I would like it if...
- I feel...when you...
- I'm not prepared to...
- I need...

Initially, you will feel guilty, but that's not to say that you're doing the wrong thing. You need to keep telling yourself that guilt is just an emotion that has no place in this process.

If people don't respect you for standing up for yourself, it's time to decide whether they're toxic people in your life and if the relationship is worth saving. The toxic people in your life may need special treatment. Here are a few more specific tips.

How to Deal With Difficult People

- Be empathetic, and try to understand where they're coming from.
- Actively listen to what they're saying.
- Don't engage with people who yell or shout.
- Highlight someone's inappropriate behavior, such as the silent treatment or passive aggression.
- Decide if you want this person in your life.

A co-worker invited you out on a date and you kindly declined. They have now started spreading rumors about you to overcome their rejection. You can see that their ego has been damaged, but also understand that their behavior is both passive-aggressive (playing the victim) and socially aggressive.

You can take the person to one side and say, "I'm sorry that you were hurt by my no, but that's no excuse to speak badly of me. I'd like to find a way for us to work together in a friendly way. If your behavior continues, I'll have no option but to talk to human resources."

How to Deal With Manipulators

- Ignore all manipulative behavior. Don't fall into their trap.
- Don't feel the urge to fit in with them.
- Trust yourself and your judgment.
- Resist compromising.
- Decide if you want this person in your life.

You tell your aunt that you can't make Christmas dinner. She starts with some overly dramatic statements that play on your emotions – your parents are going to be devastated, it's the first family Christmas in years, and who knows if dear old Granny will be around for the next one, or something along those lines. You need to tell your aunt, "My parents are my problem. It might be the first family Christmas in years, but we're together every month, and dear old Granny's only concerned that her family is happy." This is the end of the conversation, so change the subject.

How to Deal With a Narcissist

- Remember that narcissists rarely change.
- Remember that a narcissist will go to any length to make you look bad.
- Don't play their behavior down.
- Don't try to compete with a narcissist.
- Decide whether you want this person in your life.

You cook dinner for friends, and the narcissist finds every reason to complain and belittle your efforts. "Oh, paper napkins — classy!"

They constantly watch your reactions, waiting for a reaction, each comment becoming harsher and more obvious than the next.

Every snarky comment has to wash over you as if it was no more than a raindrop. Take control of the conversation with your other guests, and bring up positive, entertaining topics so that the narcissist can't ruin the evening.

If it becomes too much or your guests are becoming uncomfortable, keep a smile on your face, and say, "If you aren't enjoying the evening, you're more than welcome to leave."

How to Deal With a Toxic Person

- Speak up and let them know that you don't accept their toxicity.
- Don't take their behavior to heart.
- Be compassionate but don't excuse.
- Be careful of toxic mood swings where people run hot and cold – this shouldn't be tolerated either.

- Decide if you want this person in your life.

You're talking to a group of friends about the *Black Lives Matter* movement. Your friend interrupts you and says, "They're all being dramatic and need to find something better to do with their lives," and they know this attitude will hurt you.

You can say, "Everyone's entitled to their opinion, but I find yours insensitive and offensive. This is now a topic I won't discuss with you." If they continue, say, "No." Stand up, and walk away. Toxic people will often cross hard boundaries related to your ethics, and you need to be true to yourself.

How to Deal With Emotional Drainers

- Limit your contact with them, especially when you're exhausted.

- Explain that you're there for them, but that you also need to take care of yourself.

- Teach them about boundaries.

- Find ways to recharge your batteries.

- Decide if you want this person in your life.

Your friend complains about everything – the weather, their partner, their job, the last thing they watched on TV – and nothing makes them happy. Every time you meet them, you come away feeling depressed and deflated.

Here's a great quote to get them thinking: "The grass isn't greener on the other side. The grass is greener where you water it."

You have to teach this person that you too have problems, and sometimes you want to talk about them. You also need to explain that complaining only gets them so far in life; they have the ability to change their own situation.Stop answering every phone call and every text. Say, "I'm here for you, but I need some time to myself to recharge."

How to Deal With a People Pleaser

- Empathize with them.

- Ask for their opinions and ideas.
- Encourage them to make decisions about what you do together.
- Encourage them to get professional help.
- Decide if you want this person in your life.

It might sound ironic because more often than not, we are the people pleasers. However, it's still difficult to establish boundaries with someone who says yes to everything.

Imagine you're planning a party for your parents, and your sibling says yes to every idea. Having their input would make the party so much better. "I know you're happy with anything, but I would appreciate your ideas."

Instead of asking yes/no questions, ask questions that require an opinion. Replace, "Does Mom like purple flowers?" with "What color flowers does Mom like?" Praise them for making choices.

You will notice that with each type of person, you need to decide if you want them in your life. It's a decision only you can make, and it will be a hard one, but ask your compass, and have faith in it. You aren't mean, cruel or selfish; you're making an essential decision that will improve the quality of your life.

Boundary-Setting Troubleshooting

Finally, we will look at real life situations that people have struggled to overcome.

Troubleshooting #1: My family is an enmeshed family unit. None of us have boundaries, and any time I try to express mine, people call me selfish and say that I only think of myself.

Solution: Enmeshment is a complex family dysfunction. First of all, decide if there is another family member who is inclined to agree with you. It will be easy to have an open family conversation with someone who shares your feelings.

Create a safe environment for the conversation at a time that is suitable for everyone; make sure there's no rush. Speak openly about how you feel and the changes that you want to make: "I understand that this is something you don't agree with, but I need to make some changes so that I can feel happier in our family. I love you all, and this is the main reason for my decision."

Listen to how your family feels, and if they insult you, say, "This is exactly my point. I feel hurt when you call me selfish, but you don't appear to care about my feelings." Always keep the conversation on track, but stay calm.

Troubleshooting #2: I hate feeling like a nag all the time. I've tried explaining the problem, but it doesn't sink in.

Solution: Consequences. I had a friend whose partner went out, and at least once a month, would come home drunk at 6 am. There were no trust issues, but he was drinking and driving at nearly 40, and with a baby on the way. He didn't understand that this behavior was unacceptable. She had so many conversations and arguments, and even took his keys away, but it didn't make a difference.

One day he said, "You're such a typical woman: always nagging." She said, "I'm not going to nag anymore. If you aren't home by 3 am, you're locked out until 6 pm the next day because you aren't treating our home like a hotel."

And the next time, he was locked out until 6 pm the next day. He came home, and there was no fight because everything was clear. Stop nagging, set your consequences, and follow through with them.

Troubleshooting #3: I've been direct about it, and even explained why it bothers me, but it hasn't made any difference.

Solution: The problem here is that although you feel you've been direct, you may not be using the right words to express your feelings and how much you're suffering.

Try having another conversation, but use more powerful adjectives. Instead of bother, use hurt, pain, anger and frustration. Remind the person that you've been patient and already tried to have this conversation.

Tell them that it's not right that you have to put up with such behavior. Find a consequence that is appropriate, and stick to it.

Troubleshooting #4: My family gets mad at me when I set a boundary. They shout and yell, and I always end up in tears.

Solution: On the one hand, your family may be looking at you as an emotional wreck who's not mature enough to set their own boundaries and live independently. If this is the case, to the first thing you need to do is work on some techniques to recognize your feelings and then learn to control them.

Try keeping a journal to work through your emotions. When you become better at controlling your emotions, you'll be more prepared to handle their anger. "I want to talk to you, but I'm not going to get involved in a fight, and I won't stay if you start getting mad."

As you have set the consequence, you need to follow through. As soon as someone raises their voice, leave. It may take a few attempts, but your family will learn that they're going to have to control their tempers if they want a relationship with you.

Troubleshooting #5: I'm an adult but still living at home. My family are toxic people who won't respect or even listen to my boundaries.

Solution: If you've tried all of the techniques we've worked on so far and nothing has worked, the safest thing for you to do is to create distance.

Find a hobby that takes you out of the house. Exercise will help you to start feeling better about yourself and provide you with more energy.

Make your room your safe place so that you're happy to spend more time there. Get excited about financial goals so that you can save up for your own place. If things get really bad, stay with a friend or another family member.

Troubleshooting #6: My partner is toxic. I feel like if I end the relationship, I'm the failure, but I'm not sure what else I can do.

Solution: Ending a toxic relationship is not a sign of failure: it's a sign of strength. It's not an easy decision to make, but take a close look and see if the negatives outweigh the positives. Is your physical or mental health suffering?

If you still feel there's hope, try writing down your feelings. Sometimes, when we have the chance to read them out, we don't get angry or start to shout. You have time to gather your thoughts and speak the truth without the fear of a reaction. You don't get interrupted, and the other person can re-read what you have to say as many times as necessary.

Troubleshooting #7: I'm fed up with feeling like I don't have the right to say no, or that I need to explain why I'm saying it.

Solution: You're halfway there already. You have recognized that you shouldn't have to explain every decision you make. Take this feeling of frustration, and use it as energy and confidence.

Try saying, "Because I said no," "No, is my final answer," "You don't have the right to ask me," or, "It's private." Then change the subject. If people continue to question your no, walk away.

Troubleshooting #8: I can't shake the feeling of guilt because I ended an unhealthy friendship. I feel bad because they might need me, or I worry that I could have done more.

Solution: It's perfectly normal to feel guilty, but instead of trying to bury this guilt, accept it and put it to one side. Try to remember that, sadly, they don't need you, and they've probably moved on to the next person.

Know in your heart that you made the right decision and that you will continue to take the same approach. Don't let your past experience with friendships make you fear creating new ones.

Troubleshooting #9: I don't know how many times I should keep trying to establish my boundaries.

Solution: There's no magic number: it will depend on the importance of your relationship with the person. For general acquaintances and colleagues, I have a three-strike rule before creating distance from them, but the number is a personal choice.

Rather than a number, think of your emotional limit. At what point do you feel that you can't take any more? Stop before you reach this limit so you know that you're protecting yourself.

Troubleshooting #10: I feel like my superiors at work are unprofessional and don't respect boundaries. I don't want to come across as boring, but I feel extremely uncomfortable.

Solution: Document everything. Not in an emotional or snitching way, but stick to the facts. Don't go back on your boundaries or feel that you need to compromise. Reinforce them every time, but when you feel like you're close to your emotional limit, take your concerns to human resources.

If you have a co-worker who shares your concerns, it will help if they could do the same. However, be proactive, and don't just complain about the situation together.

Every boundary you establish will require your determination to follow it through, but not until you have driven yourself into an unhealthy place.

Your boundaries will only survive if you know your own limits and when to say no to toxic people and toxic relationships. There's still a hurdle to overcome, and that's letting go of this toxicity that others have created so you can go forward on your road to recovery.

CHAPTER 12: EMOTIONAL DETOX: HOW TO RELEASE TOXICITY AND RECOVER FROM A BOUNDARIES CONFLICT

I've met with so many people who have set their boundaries and worked incredibly hard to maintain them within their relationships, and there's always a moment of limbo.

There's a time in between establishing a boundary and the moment when the other person, or people, actually accept it. You may feel like you're walking on eggshells, waiting for the person to explode or revert back to old ways. The people in your life might treat you differently as they are not used to seeing you stand up for yourself and then stick to your decision.

There are other emotionally draining situations during the boundary-setting process. You may have taken some time away from the strain of life to focus on yourself, build up your energy, and learn more about yourself and the boundaries you want to set.

Stepping back into the real world can highlight just how desperately boundaries are needed, and you might have to adjust your expectations, adding more boundaries to your list than you had first thought necessary.

Of course, if you have had to end relationships, there's still going to be a huge amount of pain that has to be dealt with before you can hope to create new, meaningful relationships.

We've looked at how to build up our energy before expressing boundaries. Practicing emotional control during difficult situations will help you to manage boundary conflict. Now we're going to look at how beneficial an emotional detox is in order to move on with your life in the most positive way.

How to Stay Calm and Control Emotions in Boundary Conflict

There will always be times in our lives when we experience conflict, before, during and after enforcing our boundaries. This isn't necessarily a bad thing. It's good to feel passionate about things, and others are allowed to feel the same passion.

However, how we handle this conflict speaks to our emotional intelligence, our ability to recognize and manage our emotions, and our ability to recognize the emotions of others while appreciating that we can only control our own feelings.

This is a life skill that will help you in so many different situations.

1. Take a few deep breaths and concentrate on what your body is telling you.

Deep breaths prevent us from reacting to the other person's emotions. We have all been in situations when someone snaps as we snap back. Controlled, deep breaths help to reduce the stress hormones, adrenaline and cortisol. This is also an essential few seconds when you can focus on the parts of your body that become tense, and relax those areas.

2. Listen with both ears.

A boundary isn't just expressing what you want. It's about strengthening a relationship. To do this, you need to listen to the other person's point of view. Not listening may irritate the person you're talking to and increase the tension. It's not until they've said all that they have to say that you'll have all of the information to continue the conversation.

3. Stick to questions that require more than a yes or no answer.

Most yes and no answers don't give you more information. More often than not, we tend to ask questions that we want to hear the answer to. Questions that begin with why, what, how, etc. will encourage dialogue.

4. Don't shout.

Don't raise your voice. When we raise our voices, our tone changes.

A change in tone and an increase in volume can appear like aggressive behavior, and the other person is likely to retaliate with more conflict. Calming your voice will encourage the other person to mimic your behavior.

5. Appreciate that there are times you won't agree.

You won't agree with everyone all the time, and they won't always agree with you.

While it's great to see a point of view and accept it, sometimes you just have to say, "Okay, I love where you're coming from, but I don't agree. Let's agree to disagree."

Both parties have expressed their opinions, and the conversation has ended before things get heated.

Quick Tips for Dealing With Confrontation

- Act as soon as you feel emotionally and mentally prepared. The longer you wait, the bigger the issue becomes.
- Give yourself time to feel your emotions before acting.
- Try to deal with the issue in person, and in a neutral environment.
- Choose a time when neither of you is in a hurry or stressed about another issue.
- Keep your goals in mind so that you can focus on the change and not the person.
- Smile, but make sure it's a genuine smile. A smile shows others that

you aren't looking for an argument, and that you're positively looking for a solution.

Putting It into practice

If you feel that the boundary you're about to establish is likely to cause a conflict, practice beforehand. Begin with a few minutes of calm breathing to centralize your thoughts. Imagine your conversation going well, the phrases you use, and the reactions of the other person. Play out different reactions and your response to each one. Get comfortable role-playing how you handle conflict.

The best preparation is to imagine the worst-case scenario, and practice how you will handle this. This isn't about assuming the worst or thinking negatively. It's about having every angle covered so you feel more confident in handling conflict, whether it is just a little bit of grumpiness or full-blown rage.

The All-Important Emotional Detox After Conflict and/or Emotional or Physical Abuse

Barbara Ford Shabazz, a clinical psychologist at South University in Savannah, Georgia, has described an emotional detox as the activities and behaviors that allow us to remove any emotions that negatively impact our mental health and physical health. The seven steps below will help you to carry out your emotional detox.

1. Emotional detoxing requires honesty

There's a strong link between our bodies, hearts and minds. There are good connections, and there are negative connections. It's the negative emotions that are connecting to our bodies that we need to understand: this will enable us to find the paths we need to clear.

2. Create a step-by-step plan

A plan of what you want to achieve will keep you focused on specific goals, both in the short term and the long term. Include the triggers that cause stress, hurt, rage, etc.

3. Take a break from social media

Scrolling through people's feeds leaves you wide open to posts that can greatly affect your mood.

Furthermore, it's easy to start comparing your life with the lives of others based on photos that often don't reflect the truth.

4. Know your vices

Some people turn to food; others turn to alcohol or drugs, and some people exercise as a way of combating stress. Before heading for your go-to stress vice, take a moment for self-reflection.

5. Learn how to forgive yourself

We make mistakes, and this is normal. Mistakes are how we learn. Take the lesson with you to become a better person, but forgive yourself and move on.

6. Mentally declutter

A full mind is exhausting, and it can prevent us from getting a good night's sleep, concentrating on our work, and engaging in meaningful relationships.

Use your journal to take everything that is on your mind and feel the weight lifting off you.

7. Take time to enjoy the good

Gradually, as the pain starts to fade, there will be space in your life and emotions. As you start to recover, you will be able to experience positive experiences: a moment of uncontrollable laughter, the excitement of meeting new people, etc. Relish these positive emotions.

Controlling your emotions and an emotional detox isn't about not feeling. We need negative emotions to help us survive. They are the keys to identifying other health issues.

This chapter has taught you the importance of accepting your negative emotions, taking time to process them, using them to your advantage and then letting them go. It will take practice and perseverance. It's all about the temporary stress of boundary-setting that clears the way for the next stage.

CHAPTER 13: LIFE AFTER BOUNDARIES: HOW TO KEEP LOVE IN YOUR RELATIONSHIPS WITH PEOPLE

Not everything in your future is going to be focused on boundaries. It will become a natural part of who you are. You will start to find it easier to express your boundaries without feeling awkward, or as if you're demanding too much from others. You will notice this when you feel the need to readdress your boundaries and adapt them for different stages of your life.

In this final chapter, we're going to look at life after creating boundaries. We'll focus on making sure we don't go from one extreme to the other, and being the best person we can possibly be in order to take our existing and new relationships to a whole new level.

Balance Our Boundaries

If you've been badly hurt in the past, you might find that you go a little over the top with your boundaries. You won't be alone because it's a form of self-protection, and many of us do it.

Imagine a woman who has had several bad relationships because she falls in love far too quickly and then gets called easy. Her new boundary is to date without any form of physical contact until after at least 4 weeks.

What happens here is that she meets a perfect man, but because of her extreme boundary, the dates don't move on as they would have naturally. He feels that she isn't attracted to him, and the relationship is over before it even begins.

She would have done well to explain her boundary to her date, but she was unsure of how to do it without making it all about her ex.

I've seen cases where friends are too scared to ask a person for help because they're worried about crossing a person's new boundary. So, while they have established the boundary well, the communication still needs to be improved so that the friends can appreciate the balance.

Relationships will improve, and you'll both be able to get to know each other on a deeper level, and this is a great moment as you work together to discover your middle ground and to respect the new boundaries, but also to appreciate the freedom that comes with it, the new sense of love, regardless of what type of relationship it is.

Knowing When to Say Yes

If you're having trouble reading your compass for a yes or no answer, there are some other questions to ask yourself before making a decision.

If you are put on the spot, never feel pressured into making a choice straight away because nine times out of 10, you will give the answer others want to hear. Remember: if you aren't sure, ask for more time. During this time, ask yourself the following questions:

- What will you need to sacrifice if you say yes – your free time, or a plan with someone else?
- Find out if the question needs an answer straight away. If you're offered a promotion, will the offer still be there next month?
- Does your yes come with any risks?
- Are there any hidden motives behind the question?
- If the shoe was on the other foot, would this person do the same for you?

With the answers to these questions, you'll be able to decide if you really do want to say yes, and if it's for the right reasons. Learning how to say no is crucial, but don't make it your only answer. It's great that you've mastered how to put your own needs first, but in a successful relationship, it's about both people's needs having equal importance.

Two-Way Boundaries to Keep Relationships Healthy

Now that your relationships are starting to settle and you can see the benefits of your boundaries, it's worth taking a moment to look at things from another perspective: the boundaries of other people. Helping others to express and maintain their boundaries is an excellent way to emphasize a safe environment for both of you.

- Make sure you're giving the other person enough personal space. It's great that you've identified when you need time alone, but don't let your loved one focus so much on your wellbeing that they forget to take care of themselves.

- Get excited about their interests and achievements. Showing someone you care about the things that excite them allows them to feel like you genuinely care about them. It's not the right time to tell them about your exciting news, as it will take away their special moment.

- Ask permission before borrowing things. Until a person tells you that you don't have to ask, it's respectful to ask first. Siblings have a habit of taking things, and this can stick with them into adulthood, but it's not okay. You should also ask permission before entering personal space, even if it's just a knock on the door.

- Don't criticize the people you care about. Body shaming is a massive problem that both men and women suffer from. If someone asks you for advice, choose your words and your tone carefully so that it doesn't come across as offensive.

- This stage might seem like you've rebooted your relationship and it's similar to those first moments. You're more tempted to send messages and call, but make sure you aren't overdoing it.

- Checking someone's phone is the equivalent of reading their journal. Aside from showing that you don't trust them, you also risk breaching privacy and confidentiality if they use their phone for work.

- Always check with people before you post images of them on social media. Not everybody has the same boundaries when it comes to their personal life online. In the case of social media, asking before posting can prevent conflict.

- Protect your independence. As you start to become closer again, check that this closeness doesn't convert into dependency. If you feel like you can't make decisions without them or you don't want to do things alone, take a step back, and reassess your emotions.

- Don't be a snooper! By paying close attention to what people are saying, you can get an idea of what they're comfortable talking about and what they aren't. It's natural to want to ask questions to start a conversation or learn more, but try to keep them general. Asking someone about when they're going to settle down or start a family looks like prying rather than caring.

- Keep every promise you make. Breaking promises leads to distrust and a feeling that you don't care. If you aren't sure you can do something, don't promise it.

- Never go to bed on an argument, even if it isn't with your partner. First of all, the chances are, you won't sleep well. Secondly, the issue won't just disappear: it will fester.

Recreating Love for All of Your Relationships

If you've had to take some space away from people you love, the first few interactions might be straining or tense. It won't be like this forever. After a few visits, you'll both start to relax and feel more confident with your interactions.

Don't bring up the past. It has been dealt with, and it is now time to move forward. If the other person brings it up, you can choose to listen if they feel that they need to communicate their feelings.

If you feel like the conversation isn't productive, don't interrupt, but just say, "I think we discussed our problems in the past, and now I would love to focus on getting things back on track for the future." In the first few interactions, keep the conversation quite light and positive.

It's really important at this stage that you listen and read their boundary signs, while making sure that yours are protected. Keep visits and activities short so that nobody outstays their welcome. Gradually, you can plan activities that last longer.

It's the comfort and security that you both feel while being able to communicate openly that will lead to having fun together, and when you're having fun, love is soon to follow.

Put It into Practice

Think about the following questions and how you would answer them:

- Your best friend wants you to be their bridesmaid/best man – yes or no?
- Your kid wants to borrow your car but never fills up the tank – yes or no?
- You want to meet your parents after a few months of little to no contact. Will you agree to lunch at their house or coffee in a neutral location?
- Your sibling has posted photos of you on Facebook. How will you react?
- What would you say to the colleague who got promoted before you?
- Your partner doesn't feel that your boundaries are fair or balanced. How will you work on compromises?

TYING IT ALL TOGETHER

Reaching the end of a book like this is just the beginning. There has been plenty of information, techniques, tips, and things to start practicing. Some people feel motivated, others overwhelmed by what might lie ahead.

While you should feel prepared to begin, remember that the first step is reflection. It's likely that you have been through some extremely stressful, and possibly traumatic, experiences.

Don't rush into making any changes before you've taken some time for self-care and to gain your strength. This is the key to getting the next stages right.

You don't need to be fit for a marathon or feel that you have all the confidence in the world. But you do need to be in the right place, both physically and emotionally.

To summarize all of the information, we can look at the 3 Cs – create your boundaries, communicate your boundaries, and then control them.

To create your boundaries, look hard at yourself and your life to decide where you need to see changes and when you want them. The changes that you need are your first priority because they're things that are affecting your wellbeing. The things that you want are the smaller boundaries that will allow you to enjoy your life to the fullest.

Write a list of your boundaries, and be clear on those that are an absolute no, and those that you would be willing to compromise on. The planning stage is so important because it will help you to feel prepared before communicating your boundaries.

When you're confident, your loved ones will see that you're calm, collected, and above all, serious. Prepare some short sentences, keeping the focus on your feelings rather than the person's behavior. This is where the "I" statements will help. Have backup phrases in case there's some push back from the other person.

You will know when you're ready to communicate your boundaries. It could be at the time of a boundary violation. If you don't feel like the circumstances are right, wait for the time that is.

You should try to keep the time between the boundary violation and the communication as short as possible, but if the room is full of people or if emotions are too high, ask to speak to the person a little later. Take a few minutes for deep breathing, meditation, or even just watch your favorite YouTube video – whatever helps you to get into the right mindset.

Don't push your emotions down: take this time to feel them and understand their roots, and then leave them to one side. Keep your head high and your shoulders back, make eye contact, and keep your tone at the appropriate level.

Once you have communicated your boundary, bear in mind that you have done the right thing in the right way. It's now up to them to control their emotions. Stand by your decision, no matter what. Don't let people try to manipulate you or make you feel like you don't have the right to express your boundary. At any point that you don't feel comfortable, walk away.

It will be easier to control your boundaries with some people than it will with others. Mom might not accept your boundary straight away because she could think you're being dramatic.

Toxic people may insult, threaten, manipulate or scare you. You neither deserve this, nor have to put up with it. You have every right to put your needs first. Ending a toxic relationship can be harder, and it is a personal decision.

Professional help is nothing to be ashamed of. Sometimes, our traumas are so deeply rooted within us that it takes a professional to help us untangle them. And, please, remember that your safety must come first.

The stress caused by creating boundaries has to be controlled. You might want to dance, scream, do yoga, talk to a friend, or curl up with a book.

Notice your emotional triggers, and when stress becomes too much, go to your stress releasing place. This stress will not last forever.

Soon, you will be able to see the amazing impact of your boundary setting, even if it's just small steps. Celebrate every win, take each day one at a time, and remain determined to achieve the wonderful life you have envisioned.

RESOURCES

3 Tactics of Controlling Parents . . . and Ways to Handle and Heal. (2020, January 1). [Video]. YouTube. https://www.youtube.com/watch?v=I8Nd2pCP4UQ

10 Ways to Deal with a Toxic Sibling – Psych2Go. (2017, October 29). Psych2Go. https://psych2go.net/10-ways-to-deal-with-a-toxic-sibling/

A. (2020, August 5). 7 Boundary Exercises for Empaths and Sensitive People. Kind Earth. https://www.kindearth.net/7-boundary-exercises-for-empaths-and-other-sensitive-people/

Abrams, A. (2017, October 1). Overcoming the Need to Please. Psychology Today. https://www.psychologytoday.com/us/blog/nurturing-self-compassion/201710/overcoming-the-need-please

Anderson, M. (2020, October 14). Setting Strong Boundaries When You're Codependent. Love Over Addiction. https://loveoveraddiction.com/boundaries-for-codependents/

Atanacio, A. (2016, February 8). 11 Ways to Handle Confrontation. SUCCESS. https://www.-success.com/11-ways-to-handle-confrontation/

Boundary Setting and Healthy Communication | The Georgia Way. (n.d.). Thegeorgiaway. https://thegeorgiaway.com/project/boundary-setting-and-healthy-communication/

Business News Daily Editor. (2020, May 6). 50-Hour Workweeks? How to Cut Back on the New Normal. Business News Daily. https://www.businessnewsdaily.com/8357-longer-work-weeks.html

Carver, C. (2019, December 26). Quotes About Boundaries to Help You Set and Honor Them. Be More with Less. https://bemorewithless.com/quotes-about-boundaries/

Chui, A. (2019, February 28). The Desire to Be Liked Will End You up Feeling More Rejected. Lifehack. https://www.lifehack.org/634716/the-desire-to-be-liked-will-end-you-up-feeling-more-rejected

Clarke, J. (2020, July 27). How to Recognize Someone With Covert Narcissism. Verywell Mind. https://www.verywellmind.com/understanding-the-covert-narcissist-4584587

Cole, T. (2021). Boundary Boss. T. Cole.

Contessa, C. (2021, January 5). How to Establish Healthy Boundaries at Work. Career Contessa. https://www.careercontessa.com/advice/healthy-boundaries-at-work/

Earnshaw, E., LMFT. (2019, July 21). 6 Types Of Boundaries You Deserve To Have (And How To Maintain Them). Mindbodygreen. https://www.mindbodygreen.com/articles/six-types-of-boundaries-and-what-healthy-boundaries-look-like-for-each

Gaba, S. (2019, August 4). Boundaries and the Dance of the Codependent. Psychology Today. https://www.psychologytoday.com/us/blog/addiction-and-recovery/201908/boundaries-and-the-dance-the-codependent

Glass, L. J. (2020, November 29). Codependents & Boundaries: Why Do They Struggle? PIVOT. https://www.lovetopivot.com/what-cause-triggers-codependency-boundaries-recovery-coaching/

Good boundaries free you | Sarri Gilman | TEDxSnoIsleLibraries. (2015, December 17). [Video]. YouTube. https://www.youtube.com/watch?v=rtsHUeKnkC8

Haynes, T. (2021, February 4). Dopamine, Smartphones & You: A battle for your time. Science in the News. https://sitn.hms.harvard.edu/flash/2018/dopamine-smartphones-battle-time/

Heckman, W. (2019, September 25). 42 Worrying Workplace Stress Statistics. The American Institute of Stress. https://www.stress.org/42-worrying-workplace-stress-statistics

Hoskin, M. N. (2021, March 23). What's an Emotional Detox and Do You Need One? The Healthy. https://www.thehealthy.com/mental-health/emotional-detox/

J. (2018b, June 18). What Does Your Tone of Voice Convey? Exploring Your Mind. https://exploringyourmind.com/what-does-your-tone-of-voice-convey/

Jodi Schulz, Michigan State University Extension. (2021, March 9). Eye contact: Don't make these mistakes. MSU Extension. https://www.canr.msu.edu/news/eye_contact_dont_-make_these_mistakes

Katherine, A. (2000). Where to Draw The Line. Fireside.

Kaufman, S. B. (2011, March 25). DO Narcissists Know They Are Narcissists? Psychology Today. https://www.psychologytoday.com/us/blog/beautiful-minds/201103/do-narcissists-know-they-are-narcissists

King, P. (n.d.). How to Establish Boundaries. P. King.

Lancer, D. (n.d.). Dilemas of Codependent Men. Whatiscodepencency.Com. https://www.whatiscodependency.com/dilemmas-of-codependent-men/

Lancer, D. L. (2020, April 11). Dilemmas of Codependent Men. What Is Codependency? https://www.whatiscodependency.com/dilemmas-of-codependent-men/

Levin, N. (2020, January 17). How Your Fears Prevent You from Setting Boundaries. Nancy Levin. https://nancylevin.com/how-your-fears-prevent-you-from-setting-boundaries/

Li, P. (2021, April 22). 4 Types of Parenting Styles and Their Effects. Parenting For Brain. https://www.parentingforbrain.com/4-baumrind-parenting-styles/

Mandel, L. (2019, June 13). Why We Need Friends, According To A Scientist. The FADER. https://www.thefader.com/2017/03/08/science-of-friendship

Marketing. (2020, November 29). Codependents & Boundaries: Why Do They Struggle? PIVOT. https://www.lovetopivot.com/what-cause-triggers-codependency-boundaries-recovery-coaching/

Morin, A. (2020, October 26). Strategies That Will Help You Become More Authoritative to Your Kids. Verywell Family. https://www.verywellfamily.com/ways-to-become-a-more-authoritative-parent-4136329

Newman, L. (2015, March 6). When To Say Yes: What To Ask Before You Agree To Something. HuffPost. https://www.huffpost.com/entry/when-to-say-yes-agree_n_1930507

Patterson, E. (2020, November 6). Stress Statistics. The Recovery Village Drug and Alcohol Rehab. https://www.therecoveryvillage.com/mental-health/stress/related/stress-statistics/

Psychologists Explain How to Stay Calm In An Argument. (2020, September 25). Power of Positivity: Positive Thinking & Attitude. https://www.powerofpositivity.com/psychologists-explain-stay-calm-argument/

RAINN. (n.d.). Victims of Sexual Violence: Statistics | RAINN. Rainn.Org. https://www.rainn.org/statistics/victims-sexual-violence

Raypole, C. (2019, December 12). What Makes a Relationship Healthy? Healthline. https://www.healthline.com/health/healthy-relationship#characteristics

Rees, C. (2020, November 3). Setting Boundaries in a Codependent Relationship. THE LOVE BRAIN. https://thelovebrain.com/2020/09/28/setting-boundaries-in-a-codependent-relationship/

ROBBINS RESEARCHINTERNATIONAL, INC. (2020, December 17). <i>10 steps for how to overcome fear and achieve goals. Tonyrobbins.Com. https://www.tonyrobbins.-com/stories/unleash-the-power/overcoming-fear-in-5-steps/</div>

Saviuc, L. D. (2020, January 7). On Living Life like a Human Being, Not a Human Doing. Purpose Fairy. https://www.purposefairy.com/82716/living-life-like-human-being-not-human-doing/

Setting Boundaries. (2019). The Therapist Aid. https://www.therapistaid.com/work-sheets/setting-boundaries.pdf

Shebloski, B. (2005, December 1). APA PsycNet. APA PsycNet. https://doi.a-pa.org/doiLanding?doi=10.1037%2F0893-3200.19.4.633

Siefert, R. (2020, February 10). Relationship Boundaries You Might Not Realize You're Violating. The Active Times. https://www.theactivetimes.com/violating-relationship-boundaries/slide-6

Stines, S. P. (2019, August 18). Setting Boundaries with a Narcissist. Psych Central. https://psychcentral.com/pro/recovery-expert/2019/08/setting-boundaries-with-a-narcissist#4

Tawwab, N. G. (2021). Set Boundaries, Find Peace. TaracherPerigee/Piatus.

Touroni, E. (2020, August 6). How to stand up for yourself (and why you find it so difficult). The Chelsea Psychology Clinic. https://www.thechelseapsychologyclinic.com/uncate-gorised/how-to-stand-up-for-yourself/

Vision Psychology. (2020, October 22). Setting Boundaries with your Mother-in-Law - Hannah Jensen-Fielding | Vision Psychology Brisbane. https://www.visionpsychology.-com/setting-boundaries-with-mother-in-law/

Well, T., Ph. D. (2018, January 29). How to Nonverbally Communicate Openness and Set Boundaries. Psychology Today. https://www.psychologytoday.com/us/blog/the-clarity/201801/how-nonverbally-communicate-openness-and-set-boundaries

Why Setting Boundaries with a Verbally Abusive Partner Is Okay | HealthyPlace. (2020, June 3). [Video]. YouTube. https://www.youtube.com/watch?v=TI8d0DE3NzM

wikiHow. (2021, May 6). How to Cope with Mean Parents in the Long Term. https://www.wikihow.com/Cope-with-Mean-Parents-in-the-Long-Term

Wikipedia contributors. (2021, May 8). Body language. Wikipedia. https://en.wikipedia.org/wiki/Body_language

STOP BEING TOXIC

HOW TO QUIT NARCISSISTIC AND MANIPULATIVE BEHAVIORS, OVERCOME NEGATIVITY, AND BUILD HEALTHY RELATIONSHIPS

INTRODUCTION

If I had a dollar for every time I said something toxic and regretted it, I would have retired to a remote island where no one could call me out on it.

It was the group message that sounded harsh or the overly sarcastic remark at a dinner party that caused an awkward silence. I would scold myself time and time again with phrases like "What were you thinking, you idiot!?" only to repeat the same mistake later.

Regardless of how much we try, *it happens.* A snippy comment, a passive-aggressive text, a conversation that goes sideways because we just couldn't let it go.

If we are completely honest with ourselves, we all either have a little toxicity in us or the potential of it. When you think of toxic behavior, you might think of the most evil of people—the abusers, the narcissists, and those who go out of their way to inflict harm.

But the truth is, toxic behavior exists on a broad spectrum, from giving someone the silent treatment to gaslighting that leads them to question their reality...and everything in between. Some toxic behavior is intentional; however, for many, it's unintentional and the only coping mechanism they have.

Nevertheless, your words and actions can cause others significant pain, and that needs to change. It's likely that your toxic behaviors are causing a strain in your relationships, and it's possible that some of them have ended prematurely due to regrettable words and actions you feel you have no control over.

Nobody is born with skills such as empathy and effective communication. The other harsh fact is that we are under immense stress and pressure in more than just one area of our lives today. This means it can feel like our blood is constantly boiling, ready to explode at any moment. When you combine this with poor communication skills and difficulty seeing things from other people's perspectives, toxicity is pretty common.

As if that's not enough, your toxic behaviors can create a cycle of anger and frustration. Your anger may have caused you to slam a door with more force than you intended, but then you become upset at your reaction.

Aside from anger, you also have to deal with waves of guilt. You watch the smile disappear from your loved one's face and see their eyes cloud over with sadness. This guilt only adds to your anger, shifting it toward yourself. Instead of having the strategies to tame your anger and express your concerns, more toxic behaviors slip out. But where did it all begin?

The root cause of anger is often injustice, including the feeling of unfairness or wrongdoing. However, in your situation, the root cause of your anger stems from the frustration of not understanding, feeling pain, and being afraid. At this stage, it's hard to see this, but your toxic behaviors are deeply rooted in the fear of appearing weak, vulnerable, and not being good enough.

As a result, you overcompensate as a defense mechanism to protect your self-esteem. Few people realize that defensive or manipulative behaviors stem from intense emotions. It's not about waking up in the morning and plotting to ruin someone's day. More often than not, you're fighting a battle to protect yourself and remain in control, and unfortunately, this can hurt others along the way.

Let's clarify something incredibly important to remember—not just now, but for the long term: you are neither a bad person nor the villain in the story. If you have gotten this far, it's because you want to change, grow as a person, and heal and strengthen your relationships. You might be hung up on your past, but I urge you not to feel guilty about the things you can't change, especially those you weren't even aware of at the time.

Even if you feel you have pushed your loved ones away, they will still be there to support you but probably on one condition. You have to be accountable, own up to your flaws, and take those steps to make positive changes in your life. You might be surprised to learn that you have already achieved the hardest step. Self-awareness and recognizing that something needs to shift are 90 percent of the battle. The other 10 percent is where we dig into the practical stuff.

Only you can commit to this, but there is a shining beacon of hope and help to keep you committed. *Stop Being Toxic* takes a fresh approach to removing those personalities holding you back. It's not about sugar-coating things or providing temporary quick fixes. It's about deep exploration that may even feel more painful at first, but the darkness starts to clear, and the changes will last a lifetime. As you work through the pages, don't expect a dull self-help manual. We will use a mix of actionable strategies, practical exercises, a few "Oh no, I have definitely done that" moments, and even a few laughs along the way.

I have dedicated my career as a life coach and social interaction specialist to unraveling the complexities of the human mind and behavior. If there's one key takeaway, it's this: the path to growth is one of self-discovery, whether you're dealing with a toxic person or addressing your own toxic tendencies.

As you work through the process, you will embark on challenges as you uncover things about yourself that you would never have considered before. Each challenge you overcome will provide you with personal growth, meaningful relationships, and a more positive life.

Through my work, I have encountered some of the most incredibly toxic people. The combination of more than ten years of research and working with people who were determined to change their ways enabled me to come up with proven strategies that have opened pathways and opportunities. These strategies, which incorporate mental attitude, emotional resilience, and assertiveness, are going to be the foundations of your transformation.

The transformation won't occur overnight, and you will likely slip up along the way, not because you are a failure, but because you are human. As long as you keep going, you will master essential skills to reduce or even eliminate toxic behavior.

With them, you won't just underpin the manifestations of your toxic behavior. You will also develop a greater sense of personal well-being as you learn to empathize, communicate, and master your emotions. You will have the tools that prevent knee-jerk reactions that blow up conversations. You'll learn how to handle stressful situations without resorting to sarcasm, defensiveness, or pressing your favorite passive-aggressive emoji.Best of all, this transformation won't end when you close this book; it's a change that can last a lifetime.

Before diving into these empowering strategies, let's begin our journey of self-reflection by discovering exactly what we are dealing with in terms of toxic behavior. It's a "rip the bandage" off moment that might sting, but I know you've got this!

CHAPTER ONE: MORE THAN JUST VANITY

> *I tell you, my dear, Narcissus was no egoist... he was merely another of us who, in our unshatterable isolation, recognized, on seeing his reflection, the one beautiful comrade, the only inseparable love...*
>
> — *TRUMAN CAPOTE*

In Greek mythology, Narcissus was a hunter known for his attractiveness. He turned away the advances of all women, as the goddess of revenge, Nemesis, claimed it would be impossible for Narcissus to love anyone who fell in love with him. One day, when leaning into a pool of water for a drink, Narcissus fell in love with his reflection. He was so drawn to his own beauty that he couldn't leave his reflection, and upon realizing that his love couldn't be reciprocated, his body melted away by the burning flames of passion inside.

Unfortunately, Greek mythology simplifies the complexities of narcissism today, and as Capote noted, it's not just about being a selfish person. The word narcissist is thrown around too liberally today, so before we get started, it's crucial to understand that toxic behaviors are not the same as narcissism. Before delving into narcissism as a central theme, it's necessary to understand that toxicity can arise from various emotional issues.

The Roots of Toxicity

While it's true that narcissists often show some of the most toxic behaviors, if we only focus on this, there is a risk that you overlook your own behaviors.

For example, you may be confident that you aren't a narcissist, and because of this, you might not see your words or actions as toxic, while others may. At the same time, your emotional struggles may appear unrelated to narcissism, but with a deeper understanding, you will be able to see a connection between them.

So, where does it all come from? Babies aren't born with toxic traits. They start with a fresh slate, and time and experiences can quickly scar this fresh slate. I firmly believe that in most cases, parents try to do their best but don't always get it right, so as we explore learned behaviors, please don't assume I am blaming the parents.

Children often grow up admiring their caregivers and seeing them as role models. When one parent withholds love and affection, it teaches the child that this is normal, acceptable behavior.

It's not just the parents. Siblings displaying toxic behavior that isn't corrected implies it's acceptable for a child to do the same.

I used to be guilty of a particular toxic trait with my own children until I saw things from a different perspective. It's common for us to say things like, "Go and give Granny a kiss" or "Go and hug your aunt and uncle," but sometimes your child may be reluctant.

Panic sets in because it seems like your child doesn't love them, so you urge them a little more, perhaps even resorting to statements like, "If you don't give them a kiss, there will be no..."

The problem with this is that we are teaching children that they don't have the right to say no. A lack of ability to say no can lead to pleasing people. Though it might not seem like it at this point, people pleasing is also a toxic trait.

Learned behaviors from childhood can impact toxic traits in your own early relationships. If you have witnessed toxic traits in your parents' relationship, it's possible that they will be displayed in your own.

Unresolved trauma is a common root of toxic behavior.

Past traumatic events, whether from childhood or relationships, may be filled with mistrust or hypersensitivity that you end up in a cycle of toxic behaviors—and relationships.

There is also the case of reactive abuse. This is when the person who has been abused becomes the abuser, not necessarily because they are a toxic person but because it's the only way they feel they can defend themselves. Reactive abuse applies to both physical and emotional abuse (Lux, 2023).

At times, toxic behaviors stem from our own lack of emotional awareness and not knowing how to handle intense emotions. This is nothing to feel guilty or ashamed about.

Like most adults, you have probably never been taught these valuable skills.

Instead of being able to talk about emotions such as fear of being abandoned and jealousy, you react in the only way you know how to, which could be anything from anger to jealousy.

We have been taught that exposing our vulnerabilities and letting others see our weaknesses is a negative thing, but this is the cornerstone of a healthy relationship.

Instead of being completely honest with those we love, you may become defensive and resist emotional honesty. A lot of this boils down to insecurity and low self-esteem.

Low self-esteem has a surprisingly strong connection to narcissism, which will be discussed in more detail soon.

Unpacking the Cycle of Toxicity

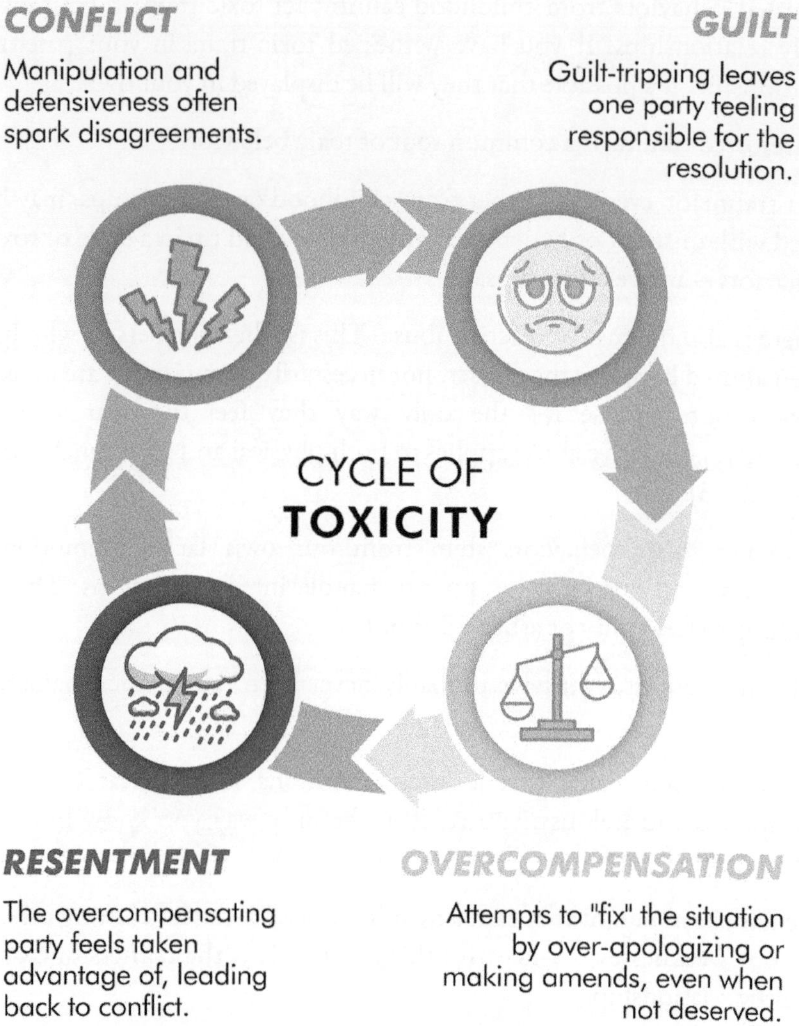

Imagine life as a yo-yo. You start with the string wound and the yo-yo in your hand (the fresh slate as a baby), and when you let go, the yo-yo spins up and down a few times, mirroring the passing years and accumulation of experiences. All of a sudden, the yo-yo stops bouncing, and the string gets tangled. The moment when the string gets tangled is when your mind and body can no longer cope with the pain and suffering, causing your emotions to freeze.

This is a psychological phenomenon known as age regression when you are emotionally stuck at the age a traumatic experience occurred. This can lead to behaviors such as adult temper tantrums, clinginess in relationships, or a lack of impulse control (Marie, 2022). Age regression can have a horrendous impact on the cycle of toxicity because, like the yo-yo, if it isn't unraveled, emotions will remain stuck.

Let's look at what the cycle of toxicity would look like in real life.

Mia was emotionally abused in a relationship when she was 20 years old. In her following relationship, she fell into the habit of people pleasing and going out of her way to make sure her partner was always happy, even though he never expected anything from her. Her constant fussing became too much, and the relationship ended. Mia couldn't understand where things had gone wrong.

In her second relationship, Mia also ended up overcompensating for the abusive relationship, but this time, she found herself desperately trying to take control of everything. Her subconscious told her that if she were in control, she was protecting herself from being let down and other sources of pain. Once again, the relationship ended.

Subsequent relationships all ended, but looking back, Mia can see how she self-sabotaged these relationships because she was convinced they were doomed from the start.

Mia had packed her abusive relationship into a tiny box and pushed it deep down inside to avoid confronting how all the emotional pain that was technically in the box was causing her toxic behaviors in other relationships. Just because the box was buried, it didn't mean it wasn't still there, and as painful as it was, she needed to unpack all that pain to break the cycle of toxicity.

This is a good moment to raise some awareness about the danger of labels. Just like there is a difference between toxicity and narcissism, there is also a difference between a toxic person and toxic behaviors, as well as a narcissist and narcissistic behaviors. Mia suffered an immense trauma that led to both toxic and narcissistic behaviors.

However, it would have been wrong for Mia to label herself as a toxic person. This is because her behaviors weren't set in stone. Mia was able to change her behaviors with the right tools and strategies. Labeling yourself is unjustified because you too can change.

To kickstart that change, consider the following questions to better understand what triggers your behaviors:

- When do you feel most insecure in your relationships?
- Do you tend to react defensively when someone gives you feedback?
- Are there moments when you feel compelled to control a person or situation? What's driving that urge?
- Does the idea of fully opening yourself up to someone scare you?
- Is there a painful experience in your past that you acknowledge but still try to deny its impact or dismiss its significance?
- Being completely honest and keeping in mind that nobody is judging you, is there a time when you have manipulated someone to fulfill your own needs?

Toxic behaviors, whether stemming from insecurity, anxiety, or trauma, are often linked to deeper emotional struggles. While many people may not identify with the term "narcissist," understanding how narcissism fits into the wider picture of toxicity can help illuminate behaviors we may not be aware of in ourselves. So, let's explore narcissism—what it is, where it comes from, and how it can shape not just our lives, but the lives of those around us.

What Really Is Narcissism?

When you hear the word narcissist, you picture a person who has an overly inflated ego and is self-centered. They need to be the focus of attention, especially in terms of recognition and praise. While this can provide a general description, there are different types of narcissism, and behaviors can vary between individuals.

Overt Narcissism

This is the most common view of narcissism. A person is incredibly outgoing to the point of being overbearing. They have a sense of entitlement and will exploit others to get what they want. They need praise, and this often makes them compete for admiration.

An overt narcissist is arrogant and tends to feel good about themselves. They often overestimate their abilities, intelligence, and emotional intelligence. This is especially true when it comes to how they avoid uncomfortable emotions and lack empathy.

Covert Narcissism

This type is also known as closet narcissism because the traits don't align with the usual perception of a narcissist. These people seem to possess low self-esteem, lack self-confidence, and an introverted nature. They have a habit of playing the victim or being defensive, and criticism will be hard for them to accept because they will take it personally.

One study showed a link between covert narcissism and higher neuroticism, the tendency to experience uncomfortable and unpleasant emotions (Miller et al., 2017). This puts them at greater risk of anxiety and depression.

Antagonistic Narcissism

This is actually a subtype of the overt narcissist, where the person is more competitive and driven by rivalry.

They are still arrogant and will attempt to take advantage of others, but they are more prone to arguing and less likely to show forgiveness. Some antagonistic narcissists have a harder time trusting others.

Communal Narcissism

Communal narcissism is another subtype of overt narcissism and perhaps trickier to spot. Individuals with this trait have strong morals and intense reactions to anything they view as unfair.

They consider themselves to be empathetic and giving. While this doesn't seem like a bad thing, their own behaviors don't match the beliefs they feel so strongly about because they crave social power and a sense of importance.

Malignant Narcissism

As a severe form linked to overt narcissism, this type can cause serious problems in a person's life. They can have the same traits, such as the sense of grandiosity and need for praise, but it's often combined with vindictiveness and aggression. Some experience sadism (the enjoyment of others' pain) and paranoia. It's also possible for malignant narcissists to share traits with antisocial personality disorder. They can lack remorse, be reckless, and are more likely to have problems with money, the law, and substance abuse.

Even with a clearer understanding of narcissistic types, it's still not cut and dry. It's not a case of being an overt narcissist or a covert narcissist. A covert narcissist can have phases where overt narcissistic traits are more dominant and vice versa. At the same time, like most personality disorders, narcissistic traits lie on a spectrum, and it's not entirely negative!

For a long time, a lack of self-esteem, confidence, and self-love has been a huge problem for many. It's as if society went to the other extreme of narcissism, and it was seen as a bad thing to put our own needs above those of others. This is certainly true for parents who risk burnout in an attempt to balance work with their family responsibilities. Taking care of yourself is selfish when there is so much else to get done. We end up people-pleasing, unable to say no as we drown in responsibilities and ultimately feel like we aren't worthy of anything more. It's almost as if we fear standing up for ourselves and our needs in case we are wrongly labeled as narcissists.

The term "healthy narcissism" was coined by Paul Federn in the late 1920s and refers to a person's healthy self-love, which is necessary for creativity, empathy, confidence, and self-acceptance. Traits of healthy narcissism include:

- **Assertiveness:** The balance between passiveness and aggression in order to express needs and desires.
- **Self-love:** The ability to truly accept and love yourself while embracing strengths and areas for improvement.
- **Pride in abilities and achievements:** Recognizing that achievements require effort and hard work and appreciating the outcomes without boasting or trying to impress others.
- **Healthy boundaries:** Communicating boundaries shows self-respect and that you value your own time and resources.
- **Admiring others:** People have a healthy respect for others and their achievements without feeling threatened.
- **Goals:** Healthy narcissism includes having realistic goals and a solid plan to reach them. Self-awareness and confidence enable them to achieve their goals.
- **Compromise:** In a relationship, there is a balance of giving and receiving to ensure that both individuals' needs are fulfilled.

On the other end of the spectrum, narcissistic personality disorder (NPD) is a diagnosable mental health condition. Because people with NPD don't consider themselves to have a problem, it's difficult to know the prevalence, but different research has shown it to be as low as 0.5 percent of the general U.S. population (Ambardar, 2023) to up to 6 percent of the general population (Ronningstam, n.d.).

To be diagnosed with NPD, you need to meet five or more of the criteria outlined in the *DSM-5 (Diagnostic and Statistical Manual of Mental Disorders Fifth Edition)*. The criteria are:

- A grandiose sense of importance (exaggerates talants and achievements and expects to be recognized as superior even without achievements)
- Having fantasies of endless success, power, brilliance, beauty, or ideal love
- Requiring excessive admiration

- Having a sense of entitlement (refers to the belief that one deserves favorable treatment or that others should automatically comply with their expectations)
- Exploits others and takes advantage of others for their own gains
- Lacking empathy, unable to identify the needs and feelings of others
- Is often envious or thinks others are envious of them
- Shows arrogance, disdainful behaviors and attitudes

The major difference between having NPD and having narcissistic traits is that the traits a person suffering from NPD shows are consistent across all areas of their life. As mentioned before, at some point, we all have narcissistic moments. Who hasn't dreamed of the perfect partner or experienced a moment of road rage, expecting the other driver to back down? The above traits are fundamental to the personality of someone with NPD. What's more, these traits will have a significant negative impact on all areas of their lives, especially when it comes to relationships.

You are not a pathological narcissist! The main reason for this is that you have recognized your problems and need for change. Though these traits impact your life because they come and go, it doesn't feel like healthy relationships are impossible, and certain relationships may be more affected.

Because of the lack of self-awareness, it is impossible to self-diagnose NPD. Furthermore, NPD and narcissistic traits can overlap with symptoms of other mental health disorders such as bipolar disorder, PTSD, and antisocial personality disorder. If you are concerned about your traits and their impact on your life, please talk to a professional medical practitioner for support and guidance in managing symptoms.

From here on in, when we refer to narcissism, we will be discussing the traits rather than the diagnosable disorder.

Roots of Narcissism

The exact cause of narcissism is unknown, and experts continue the nature versus nurture debate when trying to understand the development of such traits. In reality, narcissism is more likely a combination of genetics and biology (nature) and a person's environment and upbringing (nurture).

Let's clear one thing up: children aren't little narcissists despite any tendencies they may show. If you are a parent who is worried that your child's behavior is your fault, don't panic because it's never too late to make necessary changes. Children are naturally a little narcissistic as they learn about the world around them and their relationships. It is pretty common for a child to want to be the center of attention or seek more praise for their achievements. These normal behaviors in children are not signs that they will grow up to become narcissists.

That being said, childhood is an incredibly important stage for development, especially personality. It was once thought that narcissism was due to a lack of love and attention from parents, but it is now agreed that this isn't necessarily the case. Without placing all the blame on parents, let's begin with nurture.

While there are many parenting styles, there are three that can lead to a greater risk of narcissistic traits in adults. As originally thought, neglectful parenting may cause some children to develop narcissistic traits as a way to cope with parents being unresponsive to their needs. Their greater sense of self-importance may be a way of compensating for neglecting to validate thoughts and emotions. Abuse and maltreatment, whether emotional or physical, are high-risk factors.

An authoritarian parenting style may also encourage children to develop defense or coping mechanisms against feeling unloved or that they are never good enough. Strict rules and overcontrolling children push away the room for love, warmth, and open communication. The pressure parents put on children through high expectations may cause adults to chase endless dreams of success. It may also be possible that adults develop controlling behavior because it is what they were accustomed to during their upbringing.

On the other end of the scale, the indulgent parent may shower their child with love and praise, but often without justification. For example, if a 2-year-old puts their shoes on by themselves, they deserve a little celebration, a hug and kiss, and some words of encouragement. They don't deserve an expensive new toy.

If you are a parent who has had the fortune of watching *Bluey*, you may have seen the episode where one character tells his daughter that she is the most special girl in the world. Needless to say, the daughter breaks all the rules because she thinks she is special enough to get away with it. There is a difference between being special to you and being the most special. These inflated views can lead to children growing up assuming they are entitled.

The indulgent parent may also cave into rules that can manifest as weak boundaries. A child who has never learned how to establish boundaries isn't going to magically start as an adult. What's more, aside from not having their own boundaries, they will be more inclined to disrespect the boundaries of others.

Before giving your parents (or yourself if you are a parent) a hard time, remember that there is no one parenting style that has been concretely linked to narcissism, and it's not easy getting the right balance between love, boundaries, respect, motivation, and encouragement. Nevertheless, children mirror their parent's behavior, so if you feel like narcissistic traits run in your family, find peace in the fact that you can be the person to break that cycle.

Culture can also increase the risk of narcissism. There was a fascinating study on the differences between East and West Germany when the country was split after the Second World War. In West Germany, the culture was more individualistic compared with the collectivistic culture in East Germany. Results from an online survey showed that those in the former West Germany displayed higher levels of grandiose narcissism and lower self-esteem than those in the former East Germany. Yet, there was no difference in those who started school after the country reunited (Vater, 2018).

With regard to nature, certain narcissistic traits have been linked to genetics, specifically entitlement and grandiosity. NPD is one of the least studied personality disorders, so there is no certainty that these genetics are passed on to children.

Finally, in other cases, narcissistic traits may be due to a different brain structure. Brain scans carried out on people with NPD showed less gray matter in the brain (Jauk & Kanske, 2021). Gray matter density in the brain is associated with empathy. Other research has shown a link between NPD and increased levels of oxidative stress (Lee et al., 2020). Oxidative stress refers to the imbalance between free radicals and antioxidants in the body, and although this is biological, environmental factors can also lead to an increase in this imbalance.

Before you start to tell yourself that your narcissistic traits aren't your fault, which they may well not be, it's still important to hold yourself accountable for your actions today. To help with this, it's necessary to examine the extent to which these traits can impact your life.

The Ripple Effect

A true narcissist can spend their entire life immune to the ripple effects of their behaviors. For two years, Emma and Oliver doted on each other, but Emma was heartbroken when she discovered Oliver was having an affair. He promised her it was over and proposed, assuring Emma that there was a future for the two of them. Each time after that, Oliver had the most perfect excuse that made Emma feel sorry for him. The ripple effect of Oliver's narcissism destroyed Emma's life, and it took years to regain any sense of self. However, Olivier continued as if nothing had happened, even questioning what he had done wrong when Emma finally left!

Oliver was a true narcissist. However, since you are not, the consequences of your actions will deeply affect most, if not all, areas of your life. Despite the image of grandiose and an exaggerated sense of self, at the core, you will probably feel shame, worthlessness, and possibly self-hatred. The drive for social status and to achieve goals may seem like the need for attention, but deep down, it's a way of avoiding fears, a lack of control, failure, and humiliation. After all, your narcissistic traits likely developed as a coping or defense mechanism. Regardless of overt or covert traits, your self-esteem is incredibly fragile.

In your relationships, you may find your angry outbursts are only exasperated, knowing that you are hurting your partner. Your empathy skills might not be as well developed as you like, but you can still see that they are in pain. But it's easier for you to ignore problems or avoid situations than to face your potential role in this. When conflicts arise, you may struggle to recognize facial expressions or emotions, which leads to feeling isolated in the relationship.

In the workplace, you may not notice how your need for praise and admiration leads to you taking credit for tasks and projects that others warranted credit for. It's hard for you to accept feedback, and it's possible you have gained a reputation for being arrogant, especially if you tend to overestimate your abilities. Again, the reality is that you don't genuinely feel like you are above criticism, but it's the fear of not feeling accepted that causes this.

Everybody's situation will be very different, but people with narcissistic traits can all relate to the sheer emotional turbulence they go through every day. Unfortunately, this is often something that others nearby don't understand. They may assume that as long as you are the center of attention, then you are okay.

The truth is that low self-esteem, the envy of others, and the lack of emotional regulation all contribute to an extreme sense of loneliness. Any attempt to explain how you are feeling comes out as an angry outburst rather than an expression of your sadness and anxiety.

Sadly, it's more than likely that your narcissistic behaviors don't just impact your life but also the lives of those around you. Please don't take this as a personal attack. As you read on, keep reminding yourself that you are here because you want to make a change. And part of this change is taking the time to consider the perspectives of others. Here are some ways narcissistic traits can cause ripple effects:

- Your partner may feel like you are using them in order to gain something, whether that's making others envious or having your needs met.
- It's likely that your partner feels that their boundaries are constantly being crossed.
- They might feel like they are always being lied to or gaslighted, causing them to doubt their perception of reality.
- Your children might feel obliged to behave in a way that ensures your needs are catered to.
- They could feel as if their thoughts and feelings aren't valid or are being ignored.
- Colleagues are probably fed up with working in a toxic environment, walking on eggshells, and frustrated by your attitude.
- If you are in a position of authority, people may fear saying no to you, causing them to take on more than they can handle and impacting their health.

The ripple effect continues. The partner complains to their parents, and now the parents are worried. The child goes to school and picks on another child because they don't have the skills to process what is happening. The colleague goes home, and in the little time they have with their family, they are angry and frustrated.

In any type of relationship, both parties will find it hard to trust. From your point of view, trust is a challenge because opening yourself up can lead to disappointment. For other people, they just don't know what they are about to face at any given moment.

I've seen friendships survive long distances and even couples without physical intimacy, but the hard truth is that no relationship can survive and flourish without trust. Vulnerability is the foundation of trust, and showing your weaknesses and true emotions can be simply terrifying!

Before your mind goes down the metaphorical and very dark rabbit hole, take a breath and remind yourself again that you are here for a change.

While you will develop the ability to influence other people's emotions (without manipulating them), your first goal is to work on holding yourself accountable for your actions and emotions. Everything else will fall into place.

Time to Shift Gears

How often have you heard that a leopard never changes its spots and that narcissists are incapable of change? Technically, this is not true because someone with narcissistic personality disorder doesn't see a reason to change. The next doubt to cross your mind is whether you are able to change, especially if you feel quite set in your ways.

It's easy to consider the brain the source of your problems, in particular, your negative view of the world, but in doing so, we overlook what a marvelous organ it really is. Did you know that during pregnancy, it was estimated that the average brain develops approximately 250,000 nerve cells per minute? (National Academies Press, 1992). It was once thought that the brain reached a certain age and stopped developing.

Today, we know that the human brain has around 86 billion nerve cells, or neurons (Caruso, 2023). These neurons receive information and communicate with other neurons by sending chemicals through a tiny gap called a synapse. It's estimated that a single neuron can have thousands of connections with other neurons, putting the total at over 100 trillion connections.

Imagine each of these connections as a muscle. The more it is used, the stronger the connection becomes. Neuro connections that aren't used or no longer needed eventually die, a process is known as synaptic pruning.

This process of connections strengthening and weakening is called neuroplasticity, which means that anyone is capable of learning new things and changing.

Suppose you have a narcissistic trait of envy. Whenever you see someone with something you want, the neuro connections fire together, and your response is automatic.

Replacing this thought with joy for the other person is hard at first because neurons need to make a new connection, but the more you practice this new strategy, the easier it becomes, especially as the "envy synapse" weakens.

I always find the science of neuroplasticity fascinating and reassuring. No matter what has happened in our past, there is a way to shift from the cloud of negativity to a life more positive.

Positivity isn't just about enjoying life with a smile on your face. A positive outlook leads to higher motivation and greater productivity. You become more resilient to tougher times and bounce back stronger.

Stress and anxiety become easier to deal with and even less consuming as relationships become more fulfilling.

Positivity is contagious, and your acts of kindness and gratitude have a knock-on effect on society!

To achieve this personal growth and increased life satisfaction, I have a straightforward yet highly effective REFLECT framework that guides you through seven steps to overcoming your narcissistic traits and leading a more positive, fulfilling life. We are going to:

- **R:** recognize toxic traits
- **E:** explore perspectives
- **F:** face your fears
- **L:** learn healthy patterns of interaction
- **E:** empathize with others
- **C:** cultivate positivity
- **T:** trust the process

Attempting to make this transformation on your own can leave you feeling more frustrated than before, especially without proven strategies. You are probably feeling that your narcissistic traits have already taken up too much of your life, so the last thing you want to do is waste time on anything that doesn't empower you.

This chapter has focused on narcissism, but there is more to toxic behavior than this. The next chapter will undoubtedly be challenging, but the first step is understanding what actually needs to change by discovering your toxic traits.

CHAPTER TWO: RED FLAG ALERT

> *Owning our story can be hard but not nearly as difficult as spending our lives running from it.*
>
> — *BRENÉ BROWN*

In my experience, pain normally comes in one of two forms. There is the pain that blindsides you at the moment, like the sudden loss of a person, the end of a relationship, or losing a job.

The second type of pain follows us around, stemming from past experiences that we think we have dealt with but cause more damage than we realize.

Every painful moment caused by toxic traits adds to the pain that follows you around, and it makes running from the pain so much harder as if it's physically weighing you down.

Self-discovery and owning your story are indeed going to hurt, but it's a little like antiseptic cream—know that the pain is what will lead to healing.

As we embark on the first step of the REFLECT method, it's time to recognize toxic traits, some of which will be more obvious than others. But beyond this, we will also look at how to face these negative traits and even own them!

What Does Toxicity Look Like?

Toxic traits are patterns of behavior that cause emotional harm, and the key word here is patterns. If someone makes a mistake, apologizes, and doesn't repeat it again, it's not the same as someone who continues to damage a relationship with the same behaviors. Narcissism is a form of toxic behavior, but not all toxic people have NPD.

However, like narcissism, toxic behavior often comes from a lack of self-awareness as well as insecurity, past trauma, or fears. Without self-awareness, people with toxic traits aren't aware of the pain they cause themselves or others.

Let's look at some of the most common toxic traits, and please bear in mind that they are not listed in any particular order.

Lying and Insincerity

Not telling the truth can be an outright lie or even the omission of truth, and both can break the trust in a relationship.

Even if you begin with the truth, you may find yourself deviating from it. You may also feel compelled to tell lies to cover up previous lies.

Words can be insincere, but an insincere person is someone who isn't authentic. Examples include self-censoring during a conversation or craving attention over genuine connections. The roots of insincerity are often a fear of being vulnerable.

Example: Your partner asks about who you went out with, and you purposely leave out someone you have a history with.

Judging Others

Judging others is closely linked to another toxic behavior: comparison. You might find yourself comparing your actions, behaviors, achievements, and even things like morals and beliefs to those of others and judging the people who don't match your comparisons. Essentially, this is a reflection of how you feel about yourself, and you might criticize the actions of others to validate your own decisions.

Example: You observe another parent and wonder why on earth they would let their child eat candy so close to dinner.

Negative Self-Talk

There is a fine line between recognizing your flaws and falling into the trap of rumination. Because it's human nature to look on the negative side, it's easy to take a flaw and catastrophize it, making it worse than it could actually be.

The loop of negative self-talk can impact your sleep and mood, increasing anxiety. In turn, this can put added strain on relationships.

With neuroplasticity in mind, replaying negative thoughts strengthens the connections to the point where your brain may actually begin to believe these untrue thoughts.

Example: Your friend is trying to give you some feedback, and they tell you one good thing and one thing to work on. You completely ignore the good feedback and replay the negative feedback in your mind until you convince yourself your friend must hate you.

Destructive Pessimism

Seeing the glass half empty can have a paralyzing effect for all involved.

For you, it brings your morale down, possibly causing a defeatist attitude, such as telling yourself, "Why bother trying if it'll only end in failure and giving up sooner?"

A pessimistic outlook quickly rubs off on others, bringing them down too. Those looking to maintain their positive attitude may start to avoid you.

Example: You walk into an interview thinking you are going to mess up and not get the job despite your qualifications and experience.

Attention-Seeking

Excessive attention-seeking can involve catastrophizing events, making self-deprecating comments, or oversharing on social media just to get likes. People seeking attention may resort to making others feel uncomfortable, embarrassed, or irritated in order to get their attention.

Example: You post political memes on Facebook, knowing it will annoy your mother-in-law enough to get a response.

Manipulation

Manipulation is a form of influence in order to gain control, power, or personal benefit. Some manipulation is more obvious, such as lying, placing the blame, judging, or ridiculing others. It can also be far more subtle, like knowing someone's weaknesses and taking advantage of them or encouraging people to give up meaningful relationships so that they depend more on you.

Example: You ask a team member to stay late to complete a task and explain it has to be them because nobody else would be able to do the job as well as they can.

Gaslighting

This is a form of emotional manipulation where you say things to confuse people and question their reality, even sanity. It often starts with smaller incidents but can often lead to the other person suffering from emotional abuse and isolation.

Comments that are a sign of gaslighting include "You're imagining things," "You're too sensitive," "You're overreacting," and "You're crazy."

Example: Your partner mentions how you were slightly rude to their sister, and you reply, "It's all in your head."

Playing the Victim

Someone who has a habit of playing the victim will always blame someone else for their problems and are unable to get themselves out of difficult situations. They tend to expect others to come to their rescue instead of trying to solve the issue on their own. This behavior is often accompanied by a lot of negativity and manipulation.

Example: You cheat on your partner but blame them because they were never around.

Guilt-Tripping

This is a form of manipulation where emotions are used as a way to control others, and guilt is an incredibly powerful emotion. People often feel guilty about their choices or actions, which can lead them to believe they are being selfish.

Example: Any phrase that involves "If you loved me, you would..." is a form of guilt-tripping another person to change.

The Dramatics

Drama is used as a way of seeking attention or gaining control. There are several ways a person can revel in the dramatics, but it's commonly through exaggerated stories, lies, rumors, or gossip. In some cases, the dramatist will start arguments. For others, the constant drama is draining.

Example: Your boss tells you something in confidence that is necessary for your role as a leader, but you can't resist telling others to show off your status of having "insider knowledge."

Holding on to the Past

Our pasts are good for wonderful memories and learning experiences. Hanging on to painful experiences and unresolved issues only causes you suffering and, by extension, those around you. Holding onto grudges is a sign of chronic unforgiveness!

Example: Your brother scratched your car ten years ago, and since then, you have never let him drive one of your cars.

Conversation Hogger

While this can also be about not giving others the chance to talk, it's more about ensuring the conversation is always about you. If someone starts telling you about a problem they have, you redirect the conversation back to your own issues. It's rare for you to ask other people questions during a conversation.

Example: Your partner starts telling you about their day, and you interrupt with things like "That's nothing compared to my day..." or "Wait until you hear about what happened to me..."

Competition

Similar to judging, unhealthy levels of competition only lead to comparing your life with others. While a small amount of competition can increase motivation, the need to win all the time takes the fun out of activities and creates tension with others. Competitiveness can be made worse by perfectionism.

Example: When you are playing games with your children, you never let them win, even when you see how discouraged they are.

Clinging

Clinginess is subjective, so what one person feels is clingy could be different from the next. It refers to a constant need for reassurance or support, which is often observed in relationships. Even if your partner shows plenty of love and support, you may still feel insecure and fear being abandoned.

Example: You call your partner multiple times in a day and send numerous messages. When they don't reply, you start overthinking, convinced they are doing something wrong.

Control Freak

Being a control freak means having an obsessive need to be in charge of everything and everyone. You try to micromanage other people and their lives, which can be very suffocating for those around you. Control freaks will even try to manage situations that are out of their control or can't be changed.

Example: You insist on everything being done a certain way in the office, and when people don't follow your plan, you get moody, agitated, and snap at your coworkers.

Apathy

Someone suffering from apathy has a persistent absence of emotions and a sense of detachment from the world. Nothing seems to matter to you, whether that's spending time with people or your favorite pastimes. There is little enthusiasm for making plans or setting goals.

Example: You work in a job that requires empathizing with others, but you have recently noticed that you are feeling lethargic, which prevents you from connecting with others. Your supervisor warns you that if you can't find a way to regain your empathy, you will need to look for another job. But you don't even care about this warning.

Greed

Selfishness is a common trait of narcissists; however, greed is about wanting more than you need at the cost of others. Even when you gain more than you need, you won't feel satisfied.

Greed can also be displayed through stinginess, such as refusing to share time or possessions.

Example: Despite being financially comfortable, you raise the rent of your tenant's rate without considering how this might affect them.

People Pleasing

People pleasing is a toxic trait that causes harm to yourself more than others. This habit involves saying yes to doing things you really don't want to do and apologizing excessively even when you did nothing wrong.

It's also likely that you don't speak out or stand up for your beliefs and values for fear of repercussions. People pleasing also means that self-care is often neglected.

Example: You need a quiet weekend at home but your parents invite you for dinner. When you try to say no, your mom tells you that your siblings have all agreed.

Perfectionism

Toxic perfectionism can cause yourself and others pain because of unrealistic expectations and high standards.The need to be perfect can cause constant dissatisfaction and impossible levels of pressure. There is an intense fear of failure that comes with perfectionism.

Example: You spend 30 minutes obsessing over a 3-sentence email, writing and rewriting it, fearing that there might be a mistake or that the message will be misinterpreted.

Flexibility and Inflexibility

A person or a company with too much flexibility will struggle to stick to rules and structure, and there will be minimal clarity in their lives.

On the other end of the scale, inflexibility can come across as extreme rigidness with no give or take. Even when evidence to the contrary is presented, an inflexible person will still stand their ground.

Example: A flexible parent would let their teenage child stay out partying all night. An inflexible parent won't let their teenage child out without them.

Love Bombing

In the early days of a relationship, love bombing is an excessive amount of affection and attention in order to manipulate a person into a relationship.

It's a form of emotional abuse that is difficult to recognize because the other person is receiving a boost of self-esteem and may not see the warning signs. Love bombing can involve the overuse of flattery, showering your new partner with unwanted and unnecessary gifts, and over-communicating feelings.

Example: You have been seeing someone for a couple of months, and they are your soulmate and the love of your life. You give them a key to your place and insist they move in because you couldn't possibly live another day without them.

Perspectives have to be taken into consideration here, which is a challenge if you don't feel like you can rely on your empathy skills.

In the instance of love bombing, one person might be more than comfortable with adorable messages every hour, but the next person could find this suffocating. At the same time, a random gift to show appreciation shouldn't be feared as a sign of love bombing.

This brings us back to the spectrum of traits. Everyone has moments of toxicity, whether that's a moment of greed when you really don't want to share your favorite dessert with your children or when you wake up one morning and everything looks sad and dreary.

It's when these traits become continuous and impact your daily life (like the traits of narcissism) that you need to take the necessary steps.

Facing the Truth About Yourself

There is no point in feeling bad about yourself or getting frustrated. Having toxic traits doesn't make you an inherently bad person. Like many others, your behaviors are unintentional, and you might not even be aware of them. Everyone has negative traits, even the most successful people in the world.

What makes all the difference is knowing exactly what the problem is before attempting to fix it. If any of the narcissistic or toxic traits sound familiar to you, it's now time to take responsibility for those actions.

Owning up to things is so much more complicated than it seems. It's like a trip down memory lane, waiting for someone to tell us off or punish us for our actions.

Again, it's not about blaming the parents, but if you grew up in an atmosphere where apologies were forced, and mistakes were punished, it's normal not to appreciate the benefits of taking responsibility. As adults, taking responsibility for our actions also means acknowledging our flaws as human beings!

Taking responsibility isn't the same as blaming or looking for a scapegoat. It's about being responsible for your part in a situation or experience and, therefore, some responsibility for the outcome.

If you have ever been on a date and the person spends the entire time complaining about their ex, there are several red flags. First, they are stuck in the past and are portraying their ex as crazy without taking responsibility for their role. People don't act out for no reason. Your date may have had other toxic traits that caused their ex's behavior and, ultimately, the demise of the relationship.

Responsibility is crucial in relationships. If someone comes across as if they never make a mistake, it's impossible to relate to them and build bonds. If you can own up to your part in something, it enables others to see a little bit of themselves in you (the flawless human).

On the contrary, by denying all responsibility, you can expect to create a barrier between other people as you seem less trustworthy. You will gain more respect by owning up to mistakes and moving on from them rather than hiding from them.

At the same time, these mistakes are ideal learning opportunities. Imagine not paying attention to your child's problem and having them come home from school the next day with even greater stress and trouble. It's an invaluable lesson that we can't ignore our responsibilities if we don't want our loved ones to suffer. It's part of your personal growth that will prevent smaller problems from escalating into bigger ones.

Finally, taking responsibility actually improves your decision-making skills. When we don't take responsibility, we can end up making self-justifications or excuses for our actions.

The harsh reality is that these self-justifications are distortions of the truth, and one can lead to another, firing off a domino effect. The information used to make decisions is now warped. To make the best choices in life, you need to ensure your information is accurate and without prejudices.

Some of the decisions you make will have a direct impact on those around you. Though making tough decisions can be challenging, it's unfair for others to delay or make choices based on inaccurate information.

Being responsible means you have the strength to make the best decisions, follow through with them, and admit if things don't go as planned so that adjustments can be made.

The only way you are going to fail in life is by not taking responsibility and action after making a mistake. It's scary but also quite liberating.

Here are some examples of how people can take responsibility.

- Accept that you are the driver of your life, not a passenger.
- You recognize your part in different situations, the good and the bad.
- You don't make excuses when things go wrong.
- You don't blame others for your part in things that have gone wrong.
- If you hurt someone with your words, you can genuinely apologize and take steps to improve your communication.
- You don't delegate your responsibilities to others.
- When things don't go well in your personal and professional life, you look for solutions rather than burying your head in the sand.

Knowing why you should take responsibility for your negative traits isn't quite the same as recognizing and fully owning them.

Let's take that one step at a time!

Step #1: Identify Your Negative Traits

Here is where self-reflection begins to kick in, and there is no rush to achieve this all at once. You may want to take a few days to make sure you have taken the necessary time to fully consider all of your negative traits. This can be done by journaling your thoughts, feelings, and actions.

The best way to get to the roots of your negative traits is to use the Why Technique and keep asking yourself why until you have a lightbulb moment that reveals a negative trait. For example:

My colleague doesn't want to work with me.

Why?

Last month there was a bit of a disagreement during a project.

Why?

They disagreed with my idea.

Why?

My idea may have been one-sided.

From here, I can see that one of my negative traits would be to assume I know better and not respect the input of team members.

Another way to discover more about your negative traits is to look at your triggers and what makes you react in ways you don't like. If you tend to lose your temper or go into a mood, consider who you were with and what you were doing before the change.

You may also want to journal this so you can keep track of patterns. Pay close attention to the things that irritate you in others because they are often a reflection of what we don't like about ourselves.

It's always beneficial to get different perspectives on your negative traits by asking those you trust for feedback. Tell them you are looking for genuine personal growth, so you need them to be honest about any behavior you could change.

Step #2: Step Outside Your Traits

Once you have a list of traits, it's time to take a closer look at each one. Be blunt, and don't hold back as you write (or at least consider) a complete version of that trait. Imagine yourself as a bystander. What does your negative trait look like to them?

Step #3: Consider Those Around You

Next, take each of your negative traits and consider how they affect the people around you. Follow this up with how you feel, knowing that your behaviors are causing these secondary effects.

If you start to feel overwhelmed, take a break, but don't give up. Knowing how your behavior affects others and your own life will provide you with greater motivation to change.

Step #4: Monitor Your Traits

Real change takes knowledge and time, so don't try to rush the process and change everything all at once. At this stage, it's important to note every time negative traits arise and the reasons behind them.

Keep as much detail as you can to increase your awareness. This can include times of the day, locations, and even how exercise and diet may impact your mood and behavior.

But what if you have done all this and still struggle to identify your negative traits? In that case, you may be troubled by blind spots!

The Power of Ownership: Taking Responsibility for Your Actions

We saw in the previous chapter that there is a significant difference between toxicity and a toxic person, as well as the difference between narcissistic traits and a narcissist. But what defines that difference?

Accountability! Full-blown toxic people won't take responsibility for their actions and, therefore, will rarely change. You have taken the fundamental step toward recognizing your toxic behaviors, and although the next step is incredibly hard, it's a necessary part of the healing journey.

Here, we will look at the consequences of toxic traits and how to own them.

The first thing to be aware of is making assumptions. As the old adage goes, it only makes an "ass" out of "u" and "me". Take, for example, someone who has cheated on their partner; they know they have caused pain and broken all trust, but have they actually listened to how that person feels and the extent of the consequences?

To begin the process of making amends, you need to genuinely listen. This means you have to avoid interrupting the other person and especially avoid becoming defensive or blaming the other person. In the previous example, if the person blamed their cheating on the other person because they were never around, it's deflecting and not taking responsibility.

At the same time, you need to make sure your emotions are under control. It's going to be painful to hear the suffering you have caused someone else or the damage you have done to a relationship. It's natural to feel angry at yourself, but if you don't control that anger, the other person might think it's aimed toward them, which means you aren't owning up to your faults.

A part of the process that some may skip is to thank the person for explaining how they feel. From their perspective, it would probably have taken a lot of courage to do this, more so if they fear repercussions. They may also be struggling with their own past demons and how to express their emotions the right way. A simple "I appreciate you sharing this with me" can go a long way in opening the doors for communication. The next step would be a genuine apology.

The process of taking responsibility for your actions is a good place to start showing your vulnerability, even if it's just a small glimpse in these early days. Use this opportunity to ask for help if you need it. Your loved one may be willing to listen to you as you try to open up about your feelings and explore the roots of your pain. They might also have resources that can help you.

If you are in a situation where you can't listen to the consequences of your actions, this doesn't mean you should skip this stage. You can still take time to consider what the other person felt and even read the experiences of others who have gone through the same treatment online to gain a clearer understanding.

Also, try writing a letter to this person, recognizing the pain you have caused. While you don't necessarily have to send it, writing is an excellent way to process your thoughts and feelings.

If you are left in a situation where you have no idea what you have done and are unable to understand the consequences, you may need to go back and revisit your blind spots.

Seeing the Unseen

Blind spots refer to areas of your character that you are not aware of or don't know about yourself. As much as we like to think we know who we are, there are certain unknowns that are only visible to others, and you might have reached a point where others aren't completely comfortable being honest with you.

There are four types of blind spots, all related to assumptions or misjudgments:

1. **Knowledge blindness:** We think our cognitive abilities are higher than what they really are.

2. **Beliefs bias:** Also known as confirmation bias, this means we only believe information that supports our beliefs.

3. **Emotional blindness:** Our emotions cloud our view of reality and judgments.

4. **Thoughts blindness:** Like emotions, if you only look at things from your thoughts, your judgment will be clouded. What we think of ourselves isn't necessarily true.

Blind spots are going to vary from person to person. They will be greatly influenced by an individual's emotions as well as the person's character and the situation. Nevertheless, there are some common blind spots that people with toxic and narcissistic traits may suffer from:

- A lack of empathy
- Difficulty with feedback
- Overestimating one's abilities
- The expectation of special (unwarranted) treatment
- Intentional or unintentional manipulation

- Blaming relationship problems on others

The previously mentioned steps to identifying negative traits will increase self-awareness, and this, with time, will help uncover blind spots. This can happen faster when you take advantage of the Johari window.

The Johari Window, created by psychologists Joseph Luft and Harry Ingham, is a tool for understanding gaps in your reality and assumptions. The model is divided into four areas: the arena, the mask, the blind spots, and the unknown.

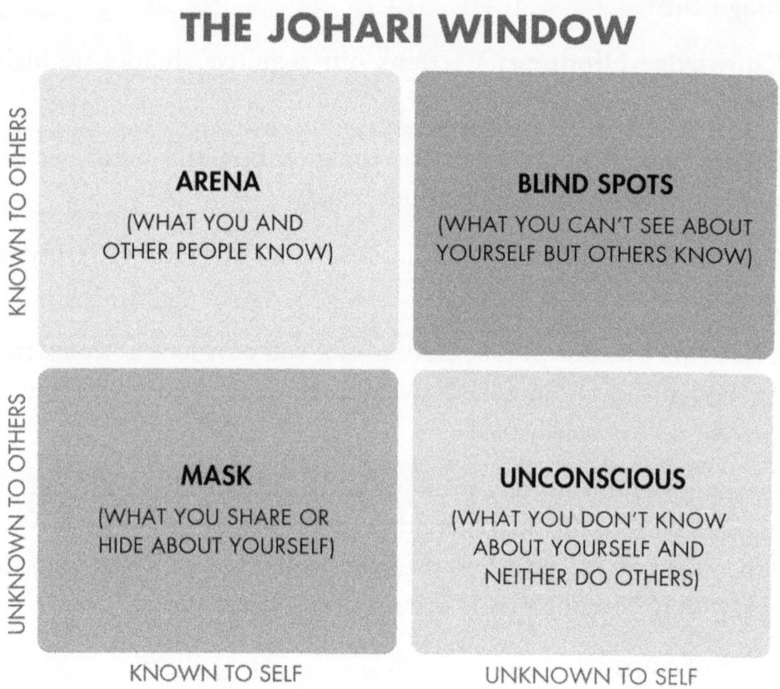

The goal of the Johari window is to expand the arena because this is the area that builds clarity and trust. And, as the arena area grows, the blind spots and the aspects you hide behind a mask are reduced.

The simplest way to do this is to start sharing more with others. This doesn't have to be all of your deepest, darkest secrets, but even gradually letting people in will make it more comfortable for both of you when it comes to asking for feedback, which, in turn, will reduce the blind spots. When these two things start to happen, what neither you nor others know about you becomes more clear!

Alternatively, you can record yourself to get to know yourself better. At first, you may find yourself more "on guard" as you are recording, but even then, this will still give you insights into your microexpressions, those you can't control, and how you react in different situations. The more information you can gather, the more objective you will become!

You can do a simple activity to expand the arena area of your Johari window. Begin by writing down five words that describe you. Now, ask nine other people to do the same, ensuring that three are friends, three are family members, and three are coworkers or from a different social setting to the first six. Let them know that the idea of the activity is to discover more about yourself, not to inflate your ego!

Once you have everybody's words back, start comparing the similarities and differences. What things do you like about yourself, and what words come under areas for improvement? It will be interesting to see if there are certain traits that are more apparent with different people, indicating how your behavior changes in different situations.

Don't forget to thank people for their efforts in helping you. It's not easy providing constructive criticism, especially not to someone who has been less than willing to accept it in the past!

As we move on to the next chapter, it's time to take the first step toward better empathy as we discover the wonderful advantages of seeing your own world through different lenses and perspectives.

CHAPTER THREE: LIFE IN HD

> *If you change the way you look at things, the things you look at change.*
>
> — *DR. WAYNE DYER*

How individuals view things can be quite fascinating! There are plenty of images on social media that explain just how different our perspectives can be. The image of the rabbit and the duck is a classic example, with some people seeing a duck first and others seeing the rabbit.

There are some images where, no matter how hard you look, you cannot seem to see the same image as another person. In this chapter, we will remove the rose-tinted glasses as we cover the E in the REFLECT framework and explore perspectives.

Perception vs. Perspective

Your perception is the physical sensations you interpret as a result of observation. Your perspective is the mental view of your perceptions. Both contribute to the way you view the world and, essentially, your reality. Each person's perspective will differ due to many influencing factors involved. Understanding these factors is often enough to appreciate a newfound respect for other people's perspectives.

One of the biggest influences on our perspective is our past experiences. Imagine if two people went to a party, and one found it super boring while the other had a great time. The first person is likely to dread the next party, while the second would be more inclined to look forward to it.

Rather than reading through the following list, take a moment to think about each influencing factor and how your perception could be shaped:

- **Education:** The way individuals interpret and organize information varies based on their country and cultural background.

- **Expectations:** Your subconscious tells you what to look for. The brain has a habit of creating patterns of expectations that are hard to shut off.

- **Circumstances:** Circumstances provoke different expectations. Think about how you perceive an alleyway at night versus during the day.

- **Senses:** People's senses react definitely to stimuli. A blind person may hear things that the next person doesn't, just as someone who has a highly sensitive sense of smell will interpret information differently.

- **Age:** As we grow older, certain things become more or less important. As teens, your perspective on retirement will differ greatly from what it is as an adult.

- **Mood:** A tiny annoyance can either be seen as a huge issue or a walk in the park, depending on your mood.

- **Emotions:** Perceived negative or perceived positive emotions can influence how stimuli are interpreted.

- **Motivation:** We are more likely to notice things that interest us.

- **Personal beliefs and values:** How you view issues like equality, racism, politics, and religion can cause you to see things differently

• **Media:** The cultivation theory proposes that media can alter attitude and behavior of people.

Take the following image as an example of how easily perception can be influenced.

The Bruner and Minturn study consisted of two groups of students. One group was shown a series of numbers, and the other, a series of letters.

Afterward, both groups were shown an ambiguous figure.

The group that was shown the series of numbers viewed the figure as the number 13, whereas the group that was shown the series of letters saw the letter B. This may seem insignificant, but imagine how many images we are exposed to on a daily basis and how easy it is for others to shape our perspective.

It's our responsibility to broaden our own perspectives and ensure that we have all the necessary information not to allow others to negatively sway our perspectives.

The Power of Perspective

According to an Indian folk tale, there were once six old blind men living in a village. They spent ages debating what an elephant was like based on stories they had heard from others. Their opinions ranged from the magical to the terrifying, with one man claiming elephants didn't exist. Tired of arguing, they went to visit a palace one day where an elephant stood on the grounds.

Each blind man touched a part of the elephant and came up with further opinions. The elephant was like a wall, a snake, a spear, a cow, a carpet, and a rope. After more arguing, the palace owner interrupted and asked how each man was so certain they were right. Each man had only touched one part of the puzzle, and it wasn't until they put those pieces together that the truth about the elephant would be understood.

It's hard to imagine how many conflicts arise simply because one person is unable to see a different perspective. It can start with something so innocent, like the ambiguous figure and whether it's a B or a 13. But then the argument gets sidetracked, and other situations and emotions get dragged into the discussion. Before you know it, you have forgotten about the figure and are debating why you have to spend the holidays with your in-laws again.

Perspective is fundamental for learning, creativity, and problem-solving. Imagine having a problem and only having your knowledge and past experiences to solve it. As soon as you speak to one other person to gain their perspective, you have doubled your chances of finding a better solution.

It's important to consider whose perspectives you are also taking in. If you ask five white middle-aged businessmen for their perspectives, their viewpoints are likely to be relatively similar. Once you expand your scope and ask people from different age groups, cultures, and backgrounds, the perspectives become far more open and less biased.

Because your perspective determines your thoughts, which are directly related to your actions, having a diverse range of perspectives can help your communication and interactions immensely. Taking in such a range of information enables you to challenge your own and other's preconceived opinions, making biases more apparent. This openness leads to increased inclusion and equal access to opportunities, which improves society as a whole.

Perspectives give us firsthand experiences of the lives of others and their struggles. Speaking of senses and stimuli, people with neurodevelopmental disorders, such as autism or attention deficit hyperactivity disorder (ADHD), often have trouble with sensory processing. You may have heard about how some people find lights to be too bright or sounds to be too loud, but it's only when you actually listen to the perspective of these people that you can truly understand what their lives must be like. This is when empathy truly starts to develop.

A word of warning, though! In a world that desperately needs diversity, different perspectives, and empathy, technology is not always helpful when it comes to personal growth. If you have read any of my other books, you will know that I am not against technology. However, I am cautious of the potential downfalls, especially in our ability to communicate.

Aside from the media having the power to shape our perspectives, the more and more common use of personalized content can also limit our exposure to different perspectives. Whether it's streaming platforms or social media, algorithms suggest content to see based on our preferences, and unfortunately, this can often exclude anything that could cause discomfort. It's these uncomfortable things outside of our comfort zones that spark curiosity, learning, and acceptance.

The 'Recommended for You' feature is convenient, but every now and again, make an effort to scroll past these recommendations and explore new content to broaden your horizons.

A Different View

Expanding your perspectives is an excellent start. The more open-minded you are, the easier it will be for you to appreciate the perspectives of others, a process known as perspective taking or theory of the mind as we attempt to understand the mental states of others. This requires the activation of many areas of the brain as you set aside your own mindset and shift into the state of mind of someone else.

This isn't the same as mind reading or having a psychic connection. But as we have seen how perspective is unique, it does take a certain amount of cognitive capacity and emotional intelligence to intentionally distance your own perspective from that of others. To understand the perspective of others, you need to be able to consider their thoughts, feelings, and motives without judgment. This is an active process, unlike your own perspective, which is something automatic.

Perspective taking is highly beneficial because as you consider someone else's perspective, you start to see more of yourself in them. Imagine a coworker who had recently lost a parent. From an outside perspective, it is clear that this is a painful experience. But when you stop to reflect on what it feels like to go back home to a place where your loved one is no longer there, and you remember how it felt when you lost someone, there is a deeper connection that wouldn't have been established without perspective taking.

Nevertheless, there are a few barriers to perspective taking. Since your perspective is deeply ingrained and occurs naturally, you have to activate the ability to consider someone else's perspective. This has to be a deliberate action that takes time. Considering another person's perspective is more difficult and takes longer compared to considering your own point of view. You won't always have the complete information to understand another person's perspective, and our assumptions and inferences aren't entirely accurate.

During a conversation, there may already be a lot going on if you are working on active listening. If you can't take a moment to think about how a person is feeling or what they are thinking during an interaction, make a commitment to do so later on. You could even reach out to them through a phone call or message once you have thought about their point of view.

If you feel like you are missing a part of the picture or you need clarification, ask the person questions rather than assuming.

Let's finish up with some tips and exercises to improve perspective taking:

1. The Movie

Besides a movie, this exercise can be done with a book or a series. Choose one character, preferably someone you can relate to, as this will be easier to start with than someone whose perspective may differ greatly from yours. Also, fictional characters are easier to understand because you aren't as emotionally attached to them as you are to people in your life.

During the movie/show/book, pause a quarter of the way through and again halfway and three-quarters of a way through. Ask yourself what your character is thinking about at that point and why. Think about why they are behaving in a certain way and what emotions they could be experiencing.

When you have finished, ask yourself how well you understood the character and their actions. Could you see the events in a similar way to the character? Were you accurate in your emotional understanding?

2. Your Imagination

Take a photo or an image with at least two or three people. Don't make it an image where you know the people or a photo of a past experience; it has to be an unknown snapshot. Spend a few minutes writing down a story about what is happening in the image, including the lead-up and the outcome. Naturally, this is your perspective.

Next, spend a few minutes rewriting the story, but this time, from the perspective of one of the people in the image. Don't forget to consider what they might be thinking and feeling at that particular moment. Repeat the same process for other people in the image.

Once you have finished, take a few final minutes to think about whether you were able to differentiate between the perspectives. Because perspectives are so unique for each person, the narratives for each story need to be different.

3. Using Your Past Experiences

Think about a recent conflict you had. You can also write about it if this helps your brain process information better. Begin with one sentence summarizing the argument. Now, put yourself in the other person's shoes. How did the conflict play out in their mind? Write about what they were thinking and feeling, as well as how they perceived your words and actions during the conflict. Finish the activity by thinking about what you could have done differently but from the perspective of the other person. Don't worry if this one is a little more challenging and may require more patience with yourself and practice.

4. Role Reversal

For this, you will need a willing partner to switch roles with. Role reversal is a great exercise for creating empathy and understanding by stepping into someone else's shoes and experiencing things from their point of view firsthand.

Take, for example, a toxic couple where one partner comes home from work every night and spends a couple of hours on their hobby while the other partner is at home taking care of the children, helping with their homework, preparing dinner, and other chores. Role reversal would have the toxic partner stay at home while the other person would go out to enjoy themself. The toxic partner would have to take on the same chores as the other partner and appreciate the stress and hard work that they go through each night.

There is no end to the possibilities of role reversal. Doctors can be treated as patients, teachers become students, parents become the child, and so on. However, it's important that both people involved set guidelines and goals before initiating role reversal. It should be treated as a learning opportunity rather than a chance to throw blame and guilt at each other, so schedule time afterward for feedback and reflection.

5. Pre-Interaction Perspective Taking

Imagine you are about to meet someone for a coffee or step into a meeting. Before you open the door, take a brief moment to think about how the other person might be feeling at the same moment.

Reflect on their values, beliefs, and motives and how they can impact everything that is about to occur during your interaction. Be sure to practice this exercise with various relationships, such as colleagues and family members, and in different settings, even with the same person, but in other settings. Just like yours, their perspective will change depending on their environment.

Exercise: Role-Reversal Dialogue

Think of a recent situation where you and another person have clashed and argued. It can be your partner, friend, family member, or colleague. Write down both sides of the conversation on a piece of paper in the middle of the sheet. Look at your side of the conversation and think about your emotions. Try to be as specific as possible and consider where these emotions came from. In the beginning, you might think an emotion arose because of something the other person said, but there could be underlying causes. Make notes next to your side of the conversation. Next, take a moment to gain some perspective. Beyond just the words of the other person, consider their emotions and look deeper than the surface level.

The idea of this exercise isn't just to see things from the other person's point of view, but it's also about considering what they might have been expecting from your interaction. Once you have thought about these factors, how do you now see the conflict, and what could you have done differently with this new perspective?

Understanding another person's point of view is not easy, especially when there is a lot of history and painful emotions involved. It also requires putting one's ego aside. No matter how right you think you might be, it doesn't mean that other people aren't entitled to their own perspective. When you are able to see insights into this, your ego may even be a little bruised. That being said, the improvements in relationships will far outweigh the damage to your ego!

Seeing things as others may give you a glimmer of what they might be feeling because of your toxic traits, but it won't necessarily stop these behaviors. In the next chapter, we will embark on confronting and overcoming the fuel of your toxic behavior!

CHAPTER FOUR: FACE THE MUSIC

> *Fear is not your enemy. It is a compass pointing you to the areas where you need to grow.*
>
> — *STEVE PAVLINA*

Take a moment to consider what the most powerful emotion is.

If you scroll through forums, answers vary from lust to hope, but one that creeps up more frequently than others is fear.

Movie makers have profited from it, marketers have used it to influence buyers, and parents have manipulated children with it!

But is fear something that should be dreaded, or have we got our perspectives wrong?

What Is Fear Exactly?

I have always felt that understanding more about how emotions are formed is an essential step toward overcoming personal struggles, especially when it comes to fear. It is interesting to note that some of the same chemicals that lead to happiness and excitement are also used in the fight-or-flight response when we are exposed to a threat or fear. So, what makes fear such a powerful emotion?

Our senses pick up stimuli in the environment and send messages to the amygdala, a part of the limbic system, which is responsible for processing emotional stimuli. When the amygdala detects danger, it sends signals to the rest of the body to prepare for action. This preparation includes an increase in heart rate, breathing, and blood pressure, while some functions, like those in the digestive system, slow down to preserve energy. Fear is powerful because it is programmed into our nervous system.

Why would seeing a tiger in the wild cause a different response to seeing a tiger in a zoo? This is because the hippocampus, the information-processing part of the brain, reassures the amygdala what is a real threat and what is only a perceived threat.

But fear goes beyond imminent danger. Fear can also be caused by things that make us feel unsafe or unsure, such as when someone leaves us. In turn, these fears can lead to avoidance and the development of toxic behaviors, like leaving conflicts unresolved. Avoiding the source of fear doesn't cause it to go away. Instead, it can only reinforce it and make it stronger.

Behind the Mask

Considering everybody's past is different, which means everyone's perspective is different, it would be wrong to assume that everybody's fears are the same.

A practical exercise would be to go through typical causes of fear and rate on a scale of 1 to 5 how relevant each fear is, with 1 being not at all and 5 causing a physical response such as anxiety and increased heart rate.

Fear of Abandonment

Growing up in a home where there is little or no emotional and physical care can wreak havoc on an adult's self-esteem. Though this might imply that a child may have lost a parent through death or divorce, it also applies to those who were absent because of long hours at work or other responsibilities despite doing the best they could.

As an adult, you may not realize that you felt neglected or abandoned during your childhood, but these experiences can still cause you to feel as if you aren't good enough as an adult and push those close to you away.

It's easier not to let anyone close than to risk the fear of being abandoned. Naturally, rejection of any kind can increase fear of abandonment.

Fear of Being Ordinary

A narcissistic trait is to feel special and superior. They are above having flaws, being weak, or making mistakes. Feelings of loneliness, self-doubt, and looking bad are for the ordinary. Your fear of being ordinary may not be as extreme, but it's still possible that perfectionism causes you to feel terrified of being anything but amazing. The fear of being ordinary can also relate to the need for important positions, power, and extreme competitiveness.

Fear of Commitment

Commitment in a relationship requires letting your guard down and letting others see that you have faults and imperfections that may even be embarrassing. There is a phenomenon called sexual narcissism, where a person creates an unrealistic image in their head by believing they are better at sex than they actually are. The fear is that a long-term relationship will expose the truth about their abilities. In some cases, commitment can feel like a loss of freedom, which can prevent you from acting on your impulses.

Fear of Insults

With an already fragile self-esteem, any insult you receive can be a crushing blow that you hold onto for much longer than usual. In some cases, people never get over a particular insult, which can exasperate the fear of receiving more. This fear can even lead to paranoia, for example, when a person makes an innocent comment, but you take it as an insult. The same applies to criticism.

Fear of Having Lies Uncovered

Imagine lies, even small exaggerations of the truth as building blocks, each one adding to the next. Remove one block and the whole structure could come crashing down. It's the same principle as lies. A lie uncovered can bring immense amounts of shame and reveal that you aren't as good as people assumed you were. In this world of lies, you are the focus of attention and admiration, and it's scary that others may find out that it's fake. They may also be paranoid about someone revealing the truth.

Fear of Remorse

Experiencing remorse can be a challenge, and the fear might be more related to remorse for a costly mistake you made rather than the hurt caused to others. Remorse might be seen as an emotional weakness or vulnerability, as it means admitting to making a mistake, which damages pride. For some, apologizing can be fearful because it can feel like the ego is threatened by admitting you have done something bad.

Fear of Gratitude

At the other end of fear of remorse, a fear of gratitude can feel like admitting help is needed. Gratitude can feel like a weakness because, in the act of needing someone, you have handed over your power. When someone does something of value or that we need, it can remove the sense of being all-powerful. Gratitude is the act of expressing appreciation for what you have, and sometimes, this can cause a fear of being judged for what you are grateful for.

Fear of the Loss of a Partner's Admiration

In many ways, the fear of losing a partner's admiration is related to previous fears. When someone you love stops admiring you, it can cause feelings of abandonment and make you realize that you aren't the most special person in a relationship and that you are ordinary.

This fear can lead to toxic behaviors such as trying to win back their love through love bombing or grand gestures.

Fear of Being Laughed at

Gelotophobia is the official name for fear of being laughed at or mocked and involves misinterpreting someone's laughter as malicious and feeling like the target of a joke.

This fear can make you feel ridiculed and lead to not trusting others and even social withdrawal. In relationships, it can cause avoidance of intimacy. This fear tends to be more common with people who have covert narcissistic traits.

Fear of Failure

Everyone, to some extent, has a fear of failure, and it goes back to the fact that it's hard to accept that we are flawed human beings. The problem for those who are struggling with toxic behaviors is that the fear of failure can be taken out on others. In such situations, they may blame those around them who don't deserve it. Additionally, they may also blame others for their lack of success.

Fear of Loss of Control

For a narcissist, a loss of control can be feared because it will expose their weaknesses, but even for those without NPD, not being in control can be terrifying because it leaves you open to negative consequences. In most cases, this will be a form of coping mechanism or defense mechanism stemming from your past. Although maintaining control can help you feel calm, it can be suffocating for those around you.

Take this opportunity to consider anything and everything that sparks fear in you. It doesn't necessarily have to be on the list above. You may fear the future or fear your own emotions. Apart from asking yourself what fears you have right now, use your journal or at least think about the following questions to know your fears better.

- Why do you fear what you fear?
- Is your fear valid, or could negative thinking get in the way?

- Are you afraid of the process or the result?
- Are you trying to protect yourself from a certain outcome?
- Have you adopted someone else's fear as your own?
- Are you scared because feelings are overwhelming?
- Do you fear uncertainty or not knowing what could happen?

Until you can accurately pinpoint your fear, you won't be able to take the steps to overcome it. Don't feel rushed to answer the questions, and know that although exploring fears can be uncomfortable, you are safe!

Quick Fixes for Managing Emotional Reactions

In the next section, we will discuss how to handle fear, but for now, let's focus on the other emotions that are caused by fear.

If we are honest about our lack of emotional intelligence, we might experience any number of emotions, but when examined closely, we often discover that those feelings actually stem from fear.

A simple example would be jealousy. The issue may not be that your partner is talking to someone else, but it's that you fear losing them. In a conversation, it's possible that you start to feel frustrated, but could this frustration be rooted in a fear of not being in control? The results are often the same—lashing out.

Once you acknowledge that fear is in the driving seat, the next step is to manage the emotional surge before it crashes into toxic territory. Here are some quick and effective techniques you can use in the heat of the moment.

1. Check your facts

There are so many influential factors within each of our interactions, and unfortunately, many are biases or assumptions. Sticking to the example of jealousy, if a partner has been unfaithful in the past, it's easy for you to assume the same is about to happen. Allowing our emotions to steer our thoughts can be dangerous when there is no evidence to support the situation.

Always ask yourself if you are responding to an actual fact about something happening or whether your response is based on the fear of a distorted reality. Rather than reacting to someone who seems to be ignoring you, consider whether they might just be lost in their own thoughts, and your insecurities may lead you to fear that they aren't interested in you. By challenging each of your emotions, you are creating space between your fear and your response.

2. Label your fear

We often think of fear as a negative emotion, so why on Earth would you want to label it and make it all the more real? Fear is actually a helpful emotion that is there to protect us. Fact-checking and looking for evidence gives you a chance to not only uncover your fear but also consider if this fear is real.

Once you have confirmed that the fear is real (one conversation with another person doesn't mean they are going to leave you), you can say your fear out loud, reminding yourself that it's there to protect you. For example, you might say, "I'm scared that I'm going to make a fool of myself." or "I'm scared this person won't love me if they knew the real me." This step isn't about overcoming the fear yet. It's more about making sure you are creating space between the fear and a toxic reaction.

3. The "Text-Yourself Trick"

Here's a fun fact: we think at a speed of around 1,000 to 3,000 words per minute and that information can flow as fast as 268 miles per hour (ECG Coaching, n.d.). Take a couple of minutes to test how many words you can type or write in a minute. It won't be anywhere near 1,000! The point of this exercise is to encourage you to slow down. Take a piece of paper or grab your phone and write yourself a message. It doesn't have to be very long—something like, "I'm scared right now because I feel like I am about to fail." By chance, that was 13 words, about the average amount a person can write in a minute.

One minute can be all it takes to calm your mind and help you understand that you've got this instead of ignoring it. At the same time, when you are distracted by sending yourself a message, you reduce the risk of blurting out your emotions, especially if you can't physically remove yourself from a situation.

Once you've mastered these quick fixes for fear-based emotions, you'll find it easier to approach stressful situations with a clearer mind. Now, let's take a closer look at how confronting these fears head-on can create deeper, more lasting changes in your behavior and relationships.

Staring Down the Fear

We know that avoiding fears may only fuel them and make them stronger, but at the same time, it's not as simple as just facing your fears. Before beginning any technique to overcome fears, it's essential to have the right frame of mind, and for this, you need to have some coping mechanisms prepared.

Imagine you are faced with a fear, and your body starts to react as your mind races. If you continue to stare down at the fear, the response is going to get stronger until full-blown panic kicks in. The first thing to do is gain control of the physical response by taking some time out. Try doing another activity, such as deep breathing, making your favorite drink, or walking around the block. Some people benefit from a calming playlist, which doesn't have to be slow music but any songs that put your mind in a good place.

Visualization is a great technique for putting you in the right, calm mindset for facing fears. Find a quiet, comfortable place, take a few deep breaths, and close your eyes. Picture a scene where you feel most at peace. This could be in the mountains, on a deserted beach, or by a trickling river running through a forest. Immerse yourself fully in this scene, using all your senses.

When you are ready, imagine your fear next to you in this calm place. Don't react to it. Just allow it to be present with you while you focus on your breathing and your senses. Now it's time to flip the switch! Each time you have previously pictured your fear, you will have come up with the worst possible outcome. As you remain in your calm place, imagine you have all the tools and skills necessary for a positive outcome. Create a vivid image of this positive outcome!

Susan feared talking to her parents about her personal life because the conversations usually ended up with her parents reminding her that she wasn't getting any younger and it was time to sort her life out. This resulted in Susan lying to her parents about a perfect relationship and a perfect career. During her visualization, Susan pictured herself in her parents' kitchen, where she had many fond memories of growing up. She pictured her parents sitting across from her as they sliced the fresh banana bread from the oven. She explained that her life wasn't perfect, but she was okay with that, and instead of pressuring her into taking actions that she wasn't ready for, they could support her and her decisions.

Visualization has been proven to help anxiety and can help reprogram the brain to reduce the response to fear. Remember, the more you practice, the stronger the neuro-connection becomes!

Now that your mind and body are calm, it's time to take the first step to overcoming fear.

Gradual Exposure

If you are petrified of snakes, the last thing you want to do is visualize handling one and then allow someone to wrap a 6-foot python around you! Gradual exposure breaks down a fear and enables you to take small, manageable steps to overcome it.

Gradual exposure or exposure-based interventions is a core concept of cognitive behavioral therapy (CBT) and is typically carried out in one of four ways: in-vivo, imaginal, virtual reality, and interoceptive. In-vivo exposure involves real-life confrontation of fears. Imaginal exposure uses a person's imagination or narrative, such as a written description. This type of exposure is generally used when in-vivo exposure isn't possible, for example, past traumas or feared disasters that are unlikely. Virtual reality exposure relies on technology and is often used when real-life situations are difficult to create. Finally, interoceptive exposure focuses on triggering the physical response to fear so you learn that discomfort does not cause any harm.

It's possible to practice gradual exposure by yourself, but if you notice that you experience extreme anxiety or panic, it might be a good idea to enlist some support, whether that's a professional or someone you trust.

Let's break gradual exposure down into steps!

Step #1: Create a list of your fears

You are a step ahead because previously, we looked at potential types of fears and questions to uncover your fears. It's advisable to write down all of your fears and use this list as a brainstorming session to ensure the list is complete. Missing a fear may hinder the next steps. It may also help to group certain fears together. You may have particular emotional fears and, at the same time, a fear of spiders and dogs. Fears related to animals can be grouped together. Grouping fears is especially useful if you have many fears.

Step #2: Turn your list into a fear ladder

Use a scale of 1 to 5 to rank your levels of fear, with 0 being slight anxiety and 5 being complete panic. Next, organize these fears into a ladder where the first rung represents your least terrifying fear, while the biggest fear is placed on the top rung. Once your fears are visually organized, take the first fear on the ladder and use it to create a new ladder. For each rung on the new ladder, create steps to overcoming the fear, so every rung will be a mini-goal toward overcoming the fear. To keep the steps specific, include how long you will attempt each step, the environment you will be in, and who will be there.

Step #3: Face the first fear on the ladder

Be sure to plan your exposure to fear in advance. Know exactly what to expect and when so that you have a sense of control over the situation. Don't feel the need to rush the process, and be patient with yourself.

Face the first fear on your ladder and rate the level of anxiety or fear response. Remain with your fear until you are no longer anxious. This might mean fears that are short in duration and can be repeated multiple times so that you confront them several times.

As your body adjusts to the fear, each time you repeat the first rung, your mind starts to fear it less. Keep repeating the same fear, noticing how the fear response diminishes each time. When you can face this fear, and there is no reaction, you are ready to move on to the next fear on the ladder.

Step #4: Keep practicing

Practice the steps to your fears regularly. The more often you practice, the faster you will get over them. Even once you reach the biggest of your fears and there is no longer a response, it's essential to keep practicing so that fears don't come back. If you notice this starts to happen, don't be too hard on yourself.

For example, in times of stress, it may feel like you are taking one step forward and two steps back. Frequent practice will help you stay on track. Also, monitor your progress so that you can see how far you have come.

Step #5: Reward your progress

Just like any goal, every mini-goal in the process should be celebrated. Rewards should be relative to the progress made, with larger rewards given for overcoming the main fear. That's not to say that overcoming those smaller fears along the way shouldn't also be celebrated.

Step #6: Reassess your fears

As time passes, some of your fears may evolve. Some may disappear, and others may appear. The severity of fears may also change. Take your original fear ladders and reorganize them based on new levels of anxiety or fear response. If you have successfully conquered some of your fears, keep a separate list to remind you that you still need to confront them...

Tanis was terrified of showing her vulnerability and was scared that anyone who knew her weaknesses and fears would have too much power over her. Those close to her knew the bare minimum about her life, and her social withdrawal got to the point where she lacked the confidence to even say hello to people she didn't know. The first rung of her ladder was to make eye contact and say hello to her regular bus driver. The next was to talk to a friend about her day. After getting comfortable with this, her next challenge was to speak to her sister about some of the problems in her life. Finally, she was able to open up to her partner about her fear of being vulnerable.

Chris's fear of losing control caused him to micromanage every aspect of his relationship to the point where his partner was ready to leave. As two perfectly capable adults, she felt it was only fair that decisions in the home were for both of them to make. Though this may not sound like much to others, Chris began by letting his partner plan meals. It took a few weeks for him to get comfortable with this and not interfere. He then moved on to allowing his coworkers to handle more responsibility in the office. After time for reflection, Chris grew to understand that it wasn't necessarily a fear of losing control but a fear of losing financial stability that was causing his toxic behavior, so his final stage of the ladder was to hand the household budget over to his partner, which, with time and practice, he was able to do.

Cognitive Restructuring

There is no question that our thoughts can contribute to fears, especially negative or automatic thoughts. One thought can cause an emotion, and this emotion determines our behavior. In many cases, this is extremely useful. For example, we have a thought in the form of a goal, and this causes excitement, which, in turn, motivates our actions. However, when the thought is an irrational belief, where many fears stem from, it's necessary to work on these negative thoughts so that emotions and behaviors don't spiral out of control.

Automatic negative thoughts (or irrational beliefs) are also known as cognitive distortions. Cognitive distortions can apply to all areas of negative thinking patterns, but one that is particularly relevant is catastrophizing. Imagine your biggest fear is being laughed at while giving a presentation to coworkers. The cognitive distortion of catastrophizing means you think the situation will be far worse than it really is. Your coworkers will laugh at you, at the way you look, and at your ideas. Because of this, your project won't go through. As a result, your boss is angry, and you end up losing your job and becoming a failure. The reality is that your coworkers may have no reason to laugh at you and may actually find you amusing and be laughing with you rather than at you.

While catastrophizing and other cognitive disorders aren't recognized as mental health conditions, they can be symptoms of anxiety and depression. So, it's important to get this unhelpful thought pattern under control. This can be achieved through cognitive restructuring, another component of CBT, and other forms of talk therapy.

Use the following steps to learn how to reframe thoughts about your fears. You can also use the same structure to reframe any negative thoughts about toxic traits you may possess.

Step #1: Identify the situation

Take a moment to understand exactly what was happening that caused your negative thoughts. What happened leading up to the thought, and what were the triggers? How did this situation make you feel? Be sure to accurately identify your emotions at the time. It's easy to say, "I feel angry," and this is probably true, but would the words frustrated, humiliated, or furious be more accurate?

Step #2: Pinpoint your automatic thoughts

Automatic thoughts are those that pop into your head regularly, and you may not even realize you have them. Common automatic thoughts include:

- Nobody likes me
- Today is going to be awful
- It's all my fault
- I will never be good enough

- I shouldn't have done that
- It's all too much for me

With these examples, you can spot words associated with catastrophizing, such as nobody, all, and never. If one person doesn't like you, it doesn't mean everybody dislikes you!

Step #3: Look for evidence to support your automatic thought

Using the examples given earlier, cognitive restructuring isn't about blocking out the things we don't want to acknowledge. It's about reframing a thought so that it's based on the truth and more constructive. If you are constantly telling yourself that it's all your fault, where is the evidence? It's more likely that X was your fault, but Y wasn't.

Step #4: Look for evidence that doesn't support your automatic thought

A classic example here is when we tell ourselves we are stupid. Again, it's very possible that there was something that we shouldn't have done, and you could even go as far as saying it was a stupid thing to do. However, we are only human, and it's okay to make mistakes. This doesn't make us stupid. On the contrary, you could have a long list of qualifications, run a successful business, or have a set of skills that allows you to save lives...any of which confirms that you are not stupid.

Step #5: Rephrase your automatic thought for a balanced outlook

Based on the evidence you collected, you can now rephrase the automatic thought so that you aren't denying the truth but are representing it more accurately. For example:

- I made a mistake, but it's not the end of the world, and I can learn from it.
- What I said was accurate, but it's true I could have said it in a better way and an apology is warranted.

- Right now, my thoughts and fears are getting the better of me, but this isn't permanent. With practice, I will improve.

Robert was terrified to receive any form of criticism at work. Even the slightest feedback would be taken personally, and he knew that not only was his reaction impacting his mental health, but it was also affecting his relationships in the office. After cognitive restructuring, Robert understood that feedback wasn't a personal attack but actually, people who were trying to support him with his personal and professional growth. From here, he was able to remind himself that feedback was about his actions and not his character.

Because these types are so automatic, you need to make a conscious effort to work through the steps. Knowing that thoughts can be changed (and neuroplasticity will help this process) won't automatically change a habit you have probably had for years. I understand it's not always practical to drop everything you are doing to consider each step in detail but commit to going back to the thought when you have time.

Mindfulness and Meditation to Confront Fears

To understand how mindfulness and meditation can aid in overcoming fears, you should first consider how they help in dealing with stress. Right now, at this very moment, what is causing you to feel stressed?

It's almost guaranteed that any stress you are experiencing is due to something that has happened in the past or something you are worried about in the future. Fears are the same because, in this present moment, there is nothing to fear.

Learning how to spend more time in the present with mindfulness and meditation can help overcome fears as well as manage stress and anxiety. This is because they both help to calm the mind and emotions. It's excellent practice for self-control, and with a greater awareness of what is happening, it becomes easier to see reality more clearly.

Mindful meditation can be used as a way of exposure therapy when using your imagination for fears. Find a quiet, comfortable position and close your eyes. Begin by taking a few deep breaths, making sure your exhale is longer than the inhale, as this promotes more calm.

Once you feel the tension leave your body, picture your fear. If it gets too much at any time, go back to focusing on your breathing and revisit the fear once you are calm again.

Break your fear into smaller pieces and ask yourself if the fear is related to a past experience and what the likelihood is of the same thing happening again, knowing that you are now wiser than you were in the past.

Is your fear about a future event, and which aspects can you control?

Pay attention to how the fear feels in your body.

Are there moments when the physical sensations are more intense? If you redirect your attention to your breathing, can you control the intensity of these sensations?

Tom started practicing mindful meditation when his fear of being ordinary led to his competitiveness becoming aggressive.

Though observing his fears without judgment was hard for him, he soon found inner peace and greater self-acceptance.

He discovered that his constant need for attention wasn't necessary because his worth wasn't based on standing out from or being better than others.

Mindful meditation isn't easy, especially if the practice is new to you. When I began, I could only last a couple of minutes before my mind began to wander. Guided meditations are incredibly helpful in getting you started.

Using a video or script gives your mind a voice and instructions to follow rather than attempting to do it alone.

There are plenty of videos online, but here are some of my favorites that have helped me in the past.

SCAN ME

Guided Mindfulness Meditation on Overcoming Anxiety

Starting with shorter guided meditation videos and working your way up to the longer ones can be beneficial. Even five minutes can have a big impact on your mental well-being.

SCAN ME

LET GO of Anxiety, Fear & Worries Meditation

Journaling to Self-Reflect on Fears

Journaling is rather underrated, considering the numerous proven benefits.

Research has shown that journaling can have a positive effect on anxiety, depression, and recovery from emotional trauma and that there is an even greater improvement when journaling for more than 30 days (Sohal et al., 2022).

The key to effective journaling is consistency rather than length or frequency. You may prefer to write for ten minutes daily, or you may be happier when you spend 30 minutes writing once a week. To be consistent, you should set an alarm on your phone because we all know how hectic life can get.

Journaling doesn't have to involve a traditional notebook and pen. You can use a document on your computer or phone, or you can even use voice notes to record how you process your fears and emotions. You may find that writing comes easily to you, but if you struggle to get started, these journal prompts can help.

- Complete the sentence. I'm afraid of ____________ But my biggest fear is ____________
- When did your fears begin?
- What does facing your fears mean to you?
- What is the worst-case scenario that could realistically happen??
- Personify your fear. If my fear were a person, it would be __________
- Continue to imagine your fear as a person. Ask your fear what it hopes to achieve in your life.
- What do you need to overcome your fear?
- How is your fear limiting your life?
- What healthy steps can you take to overcome your fear?
- How would your future self handle this fear?
- What does your life look like once your fears are behind you?

Lily feared relationships, being judged, rejected, and failing as a partner. Though both parents had been happily remarried for well over 20 years, it wasn't until Lily started journaling that she could trace her fears back to their divorce, which happened almost 30 years ago when she was still a young child. Despite hardly remembering the divorce, Lily traced her own fear of failure back to her parents' failed relationship, and with this realization, she was better able to process her past and present emotions.

Exercise: The Fear Ladder

The fear ladder is a cognitive behavioral technique that supports gradual exposure to fears. Take a piece of paper and draw a ladder on it. Next, think about your fear that is influencing toxic behavior. Take your time to consider all of the situations that trigger your fear. Remember, you are in a safe space, and you can use breathing techniques if you start to feel overwhelmed.

Once you have identified these situations, plot each one on a rung of the ladder. The first rung should be the situation that is least tense, with the top rung being the most tense. As part of gradual exposure, begin by facing the situation on the first rung. If your fear is rejection, your first rung might be asking your closest friend for coffee, while the last rung could be asking someone on a date. After you climb each rung, reflect on your progress and how this step has reduced your toxic responses.

Facing fears can be a little bit like the darkness before the light, the dip of a rollercoaster before the high. You have to courageously work through the hard stuff in order to see brighter results. It's this light at the end of the tunnel that will help you in the next chapter of your life, giving you a fresh start in your relationships and making your communication and connections more positive!

CHAPTER FIVE: A NEW LEAF

> *Effective communication is 20% what you know and 80% how you feel about what you know.*
>
> *—JIM ROHN*

In all my years as a life coach, this is one of the quotes that rings so true to me and many clients. Communication is a tricky thing, and one of the biggest assumptions we make is that communication is complete once the words have been spoken.

Whether it's how you feel about what you know or what you think you know, this 80 percent has a massive impact on the other person's response. The cycle continues when you listen and only hear what you want to hear. Imagine if your first sentence was only 20 percent effective and the second was even less so. As a result, communication quickly breaks down.

The L in the REFLECT framework is all about learning healthy patterns of interactions, but before we begin, it's crucial to put past communications behind us. We will start by looking at what often goes wrong in our communication, but this isn't a chance to revisit the past and beat yourself up about how you may have mishandled situations. These past mistakes are now learning opportunities!

Turning the Tide

Poor communication in a toxic relationship of any kind is a huge stressor for both parties. No relationship is problem-free, but in a toxic one, poor communication means problems aren't resolved quickly or easily; in fact, it's more likely that they escalate. In the next chapter, we will take time to consider how others feel. For now, think about the last time you fell into one of the following negative communication patterns or were on the receiving end and how you felt.

Complaints and Criticism

During the "honeymoon" phase of a relationship, the other person is flawless, but then, like yourself, imperfections become apparent, and the criticism begins. A person can quickly start to feel like nothing they do is good enough when complaints and criticism become the norm.

In fact, criticism is one of the Four Horsemen, which are four behaviors that are a strong sign of a relationship failure. Don't forget that a complaint addresses a behavior, while criticism attacks a person's character.

Imagine a person who spends all morning cleaning their house (on top of their own work) only for their partner to come home and complain right away that the garden is a mess.

It's not a criticism, but it still leaves the other person questioning why they bother.

Contempt

Contempt is a form of mean and nasty behavior that goes beyond criticism. It's another of the Four Horsemen that can be displayed through words of disrespect, mocking, sarcasm, and name-calling. It can also be shown in negative body language, such as eye scrolling, hand gestures, scoffing, or huffing in response.

This behavior is a direct attack on a person's self-esteem and is fueled by deep negative thoughts about the other person.

Contempt can also be displayed as hostile humor, something that Freud called "disguised aggression."

For some, it could look like a person is being funny, but really, their humor is only intended to cause psychological pain.

An example would be someone saying to their coworker, "If you think someone is laughing at you, they probably are." It doesn't sound like much, but it can cause the receivers to doubt themselves in all interactions.

Defensiveness

The third of the Four Horsemen is often a response to criticism. Someone who feels under attack may become defensive as a way of self-protection. However, it's often just a sign of shifting responsibility by blaming others and making excuses. When responsibility isn't taken, it's easy to fall into the victim mentality trap.

Picture a couple discussing their finances, and one mentions how the other spent $100 over the budget. Defensiveness would reply, "Well, last month, you spent $150 over the budget." It doesn't solve anything; it's just an attempt to excuse the mistake.

Stonewalling

If you have teens, you may well have come up against stonewalling, but this is due to their age and developmental stages rather than a sign of toxic behavior. Stonewalling, the last of the Four Horsemen is when a person tries to communicate an issue with you, but instead of responding effectively, you go silent, respond with monosyllabic answers (much like teens), change the subject, or act busy. In some cases, this can be a self-soothing response or a chance to calm down, but it's an evasive tactic that prevents you from dealing with the problem at hand. It can come across as if you don't care about the situation or the person trying to talk to you.

A common example of stonewalling nowadays is picking up and using your phone when someone is trying to have a serious conversation with you. There is nothing on your phone that is more important than the conversation at hand.

Gaslighting

Gaslighting is high up on the list of negative communication patterns and a narcissistic form of manipulation. This is a type of psychological control where misleading and untrue information is fed to a victim in order to have them question their own version of events, their reality, and, in extreme cases, their sanity. While questioning their own self-identity and self-worth, the gaslighter is able to emotionally, physically, or financially control the person. Gaslighting often starts with subtle acts of manipulation, sometimes even in the early stages of a relationship.

If a person tries to explain that they are feeling controlled in a relationship and expresses this, the gaslighter may respond with, "Are you sure I am trying to control you?" sparking the seeds of doubt. They would follow up their question with a justification that comes across as caring, such as "I'm only trying to help you make the best choices."

Steamrolling and Interrupting

In some ways, steamrolling and interrupting can be related to stonewalling and defensive communication, as they are techniques that result in a person not being able to express themselves. Steamrolling involves talking over a person or quickly changing the subject, and of course, interrupting someone means that they don't have a chance to finish what they are saying, whether that's their thoughts or feelings. Both steamrolling and interrupting can be incredibly frustrating and lead to arguments.

A father repeatedly interrupts his young daughter, which frustrates her. Due to her age, she is unable to control her emotions, so the two end up shouting at each other. This pattern of negativity is only made worse when the daughter, who learned from a poor example, interrupts her father, and things escalate.

Negative Interpretations

Negative interpretations go back to making inaccurate assumptions. We hear what a person has said, though perhaps not the correct message. Then, in our minds, we rewrite the message. Sometimes, we will rewrite this narrative to make it fit with our own thoughts or beliefs.

There are two ways this can backfire. It's possible that you hear something and misinterpret it as an insult. Or you hear what is meant to be constructive criticism and catastrophize it so that it becomes more of a big deal than it ever was. With today's digital communication and, in particular, emojis, we have to be careful not to negatively interpret written messages.

Imagine a parent who has asked a favor from their adult child but they can't do it. After half an hour of sending the message but not receiving a response, the parent texts back, "Don't worry, your brother will do it when he comes for lunch on Sunday." This could be a genuine message not to cause stress, but it could also be interpreted negatively as if the brother is the golden child who comes home for lunch every week and fixes all the problems.

Aggressive or Threatening Communication

Unfortunately, the list of potential aggressive or threatening communication is extensive and can be subjective, especially among different cultures. Some cultures naturally speak louder than others, which can be perceived as aggressive by those from different cultures.

Some American cultures (indigenous, Alaskan native, and Latin American) tend to speak with a softer tone than, for example, certain Eastern Asian cultures. Additionally, for some Asian cultures, direct eye contact may be considered aggressive (Think Culture Health, n. d.).

Overall, aggressive and threatening communication is any form of communication in which the other person feels disregarded, disrespected, or victimized. The person will try to dominate a situation, be loud to the point of overbearing, and have low levels of tolerance and plenty of criticism and interruptions.

Passive-Aggressive Messages

Though a person may not feel as threatened as with aggressive communication, that doesn't mean passive-aggressive communication isn't just as upsetting. A passive-aggressive communicator will often agree with what a person says but then "forget" what it was or not do what was asked of them because they "forgot." Procrastination and backhanded compliments can be a form of passive-aggressive. If passive-aggressive communicators have manipulative tendencies, they may also use gaslighting to make the other person question what they really meant.

One woman walks into her friend's house and says, "I wish I could be the type of person who could cope with all this clutter." Although it may come across as a compliment, in reality, they are just insulting the other person's home.

The situation would be even worse if the woman added a follow-up comment along the lines of "Oh, you know I didn't mean it like that, silly."

With these negative communication patterns in mind, there is one particular word I would like you to focus on—patterns! I would be lying if I said that my wife and I never raised our voices, and you would be hard-pressed to find a parent who has never complained about their children!

These patterns become problematic when they are frequent and cause significant damage to your communication and relationships.

Now that you have identified your own negative patterns, the only way to truly turn the tide is by recognizing your mistakes.

5 Quick and Easy Emotional Regulation Hacks

There are several aspects of emotional intelligence, but essentially, you have two parts: recognizing your emotions and managing them. So far, we understand the need to correctly identify emotions. Feeling frustrated or angry is not the same when the underlying emotion is fear.

High-pressure situations can lead to heat-of-the-moment emotions and reactions fueled by impulsivity and speedy reactions that you often don't mean, resulting in toxic behavior. The goal here is to turn our impulsive reactions into thoughtful, constructive, and meaningful replies.

To do this, we are going to follow the **three steps of PIM: Pause, Identify, and Manage.** The first part is often the hardest, mainly because the habit of reacting is ingrained in the body and the brain. So, let's begin here.

1. The 10-second rule...or even 20!

Remember how the brain can process anywhere from 1,000 to 3,000 words in a minute? That's just the words. We aren't considering all the emotions that are racing around too. Perhaps it's asking too much of the brain to produce a logical response that isn't fueled by feelings in the same instant.

Despite its outstanding ability, give your brain a chance to process what you have heard. Count to 10 or 20 if you need it, and during this time, fact-check. Did you hear what you wanted to hear, or were you actively listening? Is it worth asking for clarification? What exactly are you feeling right now? Does it go back to fear? Whether it's 10, 15, or 20 seconds, this is enough to put some space between the cause of your emotions and your response.

2. Deep Breathing: Calming the Nervous System

Stress, anger, and fear can all trigger your fight-or-flight response, which is a response to protect you from danger, but sometimes the body can be a little overprotective. Still, once that fight-or-flight response is activated, your heart rate increases, breathing quickens, your muscles tense, and your body is flooded with adrenaline. To help calm the body down, you need to stimulate the vagus nerve, which activates the rest-and-digest response. Deep breathing might feel like recycled advice, but it activates the vagus nerve, and this sends a signal to the rest of the body, letting it know that the danger or stressor has passed.

While there are many deep breathing techniques, the 4-7-8 method can be highly effective. Inhale for 4 seconds, hold for 7, and exhale for 8. This can be particularly helpful for calming down because you are exhaling for longer than you are inhaling. Deep and intentional breathing can also help you remain in the present, slowing a racing mind and preventing an impulsive reaction.

3. "Name it to Tame It" Technique

Moving on from the pause, it's time to identify. The science behind naming intense emotions is pretty fascinating, and something as simple as saying how you feel out loud can reduce the intensity of emotions.

When we feel a strong emotion, the amygdala kicks the fight-or-flight response into action. However, when we identify and label our emotions, the prefrontal cortex comes into play, and this part of our brain is responsible for emotional regulation and reasoning (Braintastic, n.d). It's as simple as saying, "I feel angry" or "I feel terrified."

Pair this with deep breathing and remind yourself that this is just an emotion and that your emotions can't hurt you. You also have the ability to control how you respond to your emotions, an empowering reminder in itself.

4. Take a Time-Out

When things are too intense, and you can't get a break to accurately identify your emotions, give yourself a time-out. This is often the case when you are with others and the conversation continues. It might not be appropriate to start naming your emotions.

You don't need to go into long explanations. It's enough to say, "Excuse me, I just need a moment to gather my thoughts." During this time, you can use calming techniques or go for a quick walk to separate yourself from the situation. It's not about ignoring the issue, and you do need to go back and address it. Just think of this as a time-out to allow your brain to regroup and your body to calm down. Take a moment to reflect on how this technique could have been beneficial in a previous heated conversation.

5. Visualize Positive Outcomes

Moving on to managing your emotions, it's time to tell both your body and brain that you are in control of your feelings and your response. On that note, don't forget that you can contribute to a positive outcome, but you can still only control your own thoughts and emotions. Visualization works because the subconscious isn't aware of the past or future—it lives in the present. When you regularly imagine a situation, the subconscious believes it to be true.

Begin by closing your eyes and imagining yourself in a difficult situation with someone. Each time they say something hard for you to accept, picture yourself taking that necessary pause while you connect with your feelings. Take deep breaths as you imagine yourself doing the same thing. Next, visualize how you would respond to this person in a calm, controlled manner and how they also start to relax as your conversations flow with respect and understanding. This is like a mental rehearsal that better prepares you by showing your subconscious what it means to respond thoughtfully and not react impulsively.

One of the most significant outcomes of following the PIM steps is that taking a step back makes it easier to see your role in the tension more clearly. It allows for perspective and accountability, and quite often, it's in these moments you realize that an apology might be necessary.

The Power of an Apology

Apologizing is hard at the best of times, but it is a crucial step in mending broken connections. Whether a person chooses to forgive you or not is up to them, but you can greatly increase the possibility with a genuine apology. Apologizing gives you a chance to be humble and honest, as well as taking accountability for your actions. For the other person, it's a way for them to find their dignity after you have hurt them. For both of you, it's a chance to repair a damaged relationship.

A genuine apology has four elements:

- Taking responsibility for the offense and admiting that this behavior isn't acceptable.

- An explanation for what happened without making excuses.
- To express your remorse, to let others know you regret it, or that you are ashamed, even humiliated by your actions.
- To make amends, whether that is rectifying a wrong in the cause of physical damage or committing to being more sensitive to the emotional suffering caused.

Look at the difference between the two apologies:

1. "Sorry for whatever happened; mistakes were made."
2. "I'm sorry for losing my temper. I had a hard day, which I know isn't an excuse because you have had a hard day, too. I promise to try and express myself better next time."

Not only is the second sentence specific, but the use of "I" in the beginning shows how the person is taking responsibility for the mistake. In contrast, the first sentence uses the passive voice, which avoids accountability and does not specify who made the mistake.

This art of a genuine apology takes practice, and it may help to write your thoughts down and read them to the person rather than send a message or email. It's true that a message or email is better than nothing, but face-to-face will deliver a more heartfelt apology.

Owning Your Words and Actions

Previously, we covered the importance of being accountable for your actions as one of the fundamental differences between being a toxic person and having toxic traits. Building on that idea, I want to take a moment to briefly highlight the importance of sincerity and accountability, and to help with this, there is no better example than with children.

Recently, my son picked up a photo frame and accidentally dropped it. Fortunately, the glass only fell out but didn't break. I only discovered what had happened when I found the glass hidden under the sofa. When I asked him what had happened, he replied, "Nothing." Okay, zero accountability—but he's young, and we're working on it. After I explained that it's better to be honest than to lie, as that would upset me more, he confessed.

Logically, the next thing would be an apology, but I made the mistake of saying something along the lines of, "There will be no bedtime story until you apologize." Forcing him to say sorry meant he said it without really meaning it, making it just an empty apology. He didn't think about his actions or how they might have made me feel; he just wanted his bedtime story. Honestly, I was left feeling unsatisfied, even though he's just a young child learning his way.

The point of this example is once again to consider perspectives. Imagine the child who struggles to say sorry is now an adult who feels obliged to say it just to ease the peace. Would you trust them? Would you respect them? Would you feel motivated to show your vulnerabilities to this person? This is exactly how the person who received your toxic behaviors is feeling. Let's begin with a real-life example of a sincere apology that actually takes responsibility for both words and actions.

- **The Insincere Apology:** "I'm sorry I made fun of you in front of our friends, but you left yourself open to it. It won't happen again."

- **The Sincere Apology:** "Last night at dinner, I made fun of you in front of our friends. There was no excuse for it. Looking back at what happened, I'm ashamed of what I did, and I'm sorry. I won't let that happen again because I can see how much it hurt you. I'll talk to our friends and make amends with them too."

Your accountability doesn't end here. You may have heard of the boy who cried wolf, repeating the same words too many times, only for the villagers to not believe him when a wolf really did appear. To sincerely own your words and actions, you have to follow through with what you have said. With the example above, you would have to talk to your friends and not humiliate the person again. If these actions don't occur or the humiliation continues, your words are empty.

It all sounds easy, but like a child who is faced with an ultimatum, what can you do when the apology doesn't feel sincere? Regardless of age, if it's not sincere, the behavior won't change. The other person, regardless of your relationship with them, will respect you more if you ask them for some time to think about the situation than to fake an apology.

An example could be, "I'm trying hard to see your point of view, but I need a little time to get this right. I would appreciate it if we could talk about this again soon."

Once again, the value in this sentence is following up on your words and delivering a sincere apology. Don't worry if you're still finding it difficult to apologize sincerely. Additional tips on how to perfect your apology will be shared later.

Building Bridges, Not Walls

An apology is a good start to breaking down the walls you have built between yourself and others, but in order to build a bridge, it's essential to make changes in the way you communicate. In the 1960s, clinical psychologist Marshall Rosenberg developed nonviolent communication as a solution to address the violence in his hometown. Today, nonviolent communication (NVC) is a strategy to help improve communication in all types of relationships, but it is particularly effective in romantic relationships.

Essentially, NVC is the use of compassionate language and has several benefits. NVC helps build self-awareness as you start to pay more attention to your feelings and needs. Honesty increases as you get better at communicating those needs, which can lead to greater intimacy and compassion for yourself and others. As you get better at responding rather than reacting, relationships experience fewer conflicts.

To turn negative communication patterns into nonviolent communication, it's worth examining how past habits can be transformed into the core elements of NVC:

- Evaluations become observations

- Thoughts become emotions
- Strategies become universal needs
- Demands become requests

Let's explore these concepts in more detail.

Observations

Observations refer to raw information that we directly hear or see. This sounds simple enough, but the brain has a habit of taking an observation and turning it into a story, which then transforms into an evaluation. If somebody arrives late, your observation would be that they arrived late. However, if you say they are always late, it becomes an evaluation because you have mixed the observation with a generalization and an attack on the person.

Observations are wonderful because, as the first stage of communication, they increase the chances of the other person listening to you because your words aren't just another criticism. In return, they will be more willing to respond to you in a compassionate way rather than reacting to your words. These observations also reduce the use of right or wrong thinking, which tends to happen in evaluations, and enable you to use accountable language.

Nevertheless, it's not easy to separate observations from evaluations. You need to practice leaving judgments and interpretations out of the message. To get better at this, treat your observations as snapshots from a video recorder. A video recorder can only capture what you can see and hear!

Emotions

It's scary to open up about our feelings, but considering people aren't mind readers, difficult conversations need an emotional explanation. As soon as you tell someone that you are anxious, hurt, or experiencing any other emotion, the other person can start to understand your needs without making assumptions. Expressing how you feel also allows you to take responsibility for your own emotions rather than coming across as blaming others.

Expressing our emotions can have two potential problems. The first is that emotions can often come across as thoughts. The second is that, if not expressed correctly, it can seem that you are making others responsible for how you feel.

If you say to someone, “I feel that you are making fun of this situation,” although you have the word “feel,” it’s a thought you are having because you aren’t defining exactly how you feel. In the second scenario, notice the difference between saying, “You make me feel angry when you don’t listen” and “I feel angry when you don’t listen,” In the first sentence, even though the word “feel” is used, the other person is the source of your anger, whereas in the second sentence, you are owning your emotion.

Needs

All humans have a basic set of needs, such as food, water, shelter, rest, and connection. When these needs aren’t met, our survival is threatened. NVC doesn’t just take into account the basic needs but also considers our core values and deepest desires. These will look different for each individual, but common needs can include collaboration, support, respect, consistency, and understanding.

The key to expressing needs is to keep the need universal. This way, the other person doesn’t feel like an unmet need is a criticism or a failure of theirs.

If you were to say, “I need support,” you would be expressing a universal need. However, as soon as you say, “I need support from you,” you would be implying they don’t give you support.

From the previous example, you can see that the words “I need” don’t automatically indicate a universal need that increases connections. I could tell you right now that I need a cold drink while lying by a pool. This describes a strategy to achieve the basic human needs (hydration and rest). Again, avoid strategies in your messages.

If you were talking to your teen, instead of saying, “I need you to text me every hour,” which sounds controlling, you can say, “I need reassurance you are safe.”

Requests

For needs to be met and willingly, we need to ensure our requests are clear and reasonable. It's important to remember that other people cannot read our minds. If your request isn't specific enough, it's likely that your needs won't be met, and the other person may become frustrated due to the lack of clarity. For instance, asking someone to be more considerate doesn't provide enough direction, but asking them to consider the feelings of others during a meeting provides precise direction.

To reduce conflict, it's also critical that requests don't come across as complaints. Even if you follow the first steps and say, "I feel like you never have time for me," it still comes across as negative compared with asking, "Could we make plans for the weekend so that we can spend some quality time together?"

Don't forget that everybody has the right to decline a request, even if you have expressed your request in the best way possible. To prevent any conflicts from arising, approach the situation with curiosity. Without being defensive, demanding, or complaining, ask why they said no and if there is anything you can do to help.

To master the skill of nonviolent communication, practice with the following sentence:

When ______________ (your observation), I feel________________ (your emotion) because I need _______________ (universal need). Would you be able to __________ (your request)?

Here are some examples:

When ***I see dirty clothes all over the floor***, I feel ***frustrated because*** I need t***o feel like more than just the maid***. In the future, would you please be able to ***put your laundry in the basket?***

When ***I sent you the messages, and you didn't reply***, I felt ***worried that*** something had happened to you, and I needed ***to know you were safe***. In the future, ***can you reply, even if it's just a short message?***

When ***I sense that you aren't listening to me***, I feel ***ignored,*** and I need ***to know that my opinions are valued too***. Next time we have a serious conversation, ***could you consider leaving your phone somewhere else?***

Ideally, you want to keep your sentences below 45 to 50 words so it doesn't become a long-winded speech. Here are some top tips to implement NVC into your communications:

- Actively listen to what other people are telling you. I know there is a lot of thought and concentration going on, but if you don't listen to the actual message someone gives you, your next observation will be inaccurate.

- Take a breath before you respond, and if that's not enough, kindly ask the person if you can have a minute or two. Calm yourself, and then go back to the conversation. There is no pressure to respond at the moment!

- Make sure the other person is comfortable talking to you about their feelings. If bridges have been burned, it may take time for them to speak openly to you. Pushing them or resorting to manipulation is crossing their boundaries.

- Accept that some people will not care about your feelings. Remember that you are only responsible for your thoughts, feelings, and actions.

- Practice compassion. Recognize the efforts you have taken to implement NVC, knowing that it wasn't easy. Be kind to yourself when you don't get it right the first time. It's a process!

NVC can actually be used by abusers as a form of manipulation. In the final section, we will discover how to rid your words and actions of manipulative traits.

Break Free from Manipulative Words and Actions

Not all manipulation is obvious. If this is something you have been doing for a long time, it has become second nature, and you may not even consider it manipulative behavior. Manipulation is any use of emotional pressure to control another person's decisions or actions. Here are some ways you could be manipulating others, intentionally or unintentionally:

- You use guilt trips to get what you want
- You are determined to get your own way, even taking advantage of the kindness of others
- You are nice to people you don't like because you will gain from it
- You throw around threats and promises like they are going out of style, all to bend others to your will
- You make some empty threats and promises to get your way
- When someone says no, you see this as an opportunity to continue persuading that person
- You disrespect people's refusal and will resort to other tactics to change their mind
- You criticize other people's friends and family in order to create distance between them
- You withhold attention and/or affection until someone does what you want
- You have issues with jealousy
- You tend to create drama for your benefit, so much so you could have your own drama show

Not all manipulation is bad. When you smile at another person, your intention is to encourage them to smile, which is still manipulating their emotions.

But when this turns into coercion, manipulation can have extremely harmful effects on relationships. Other people will be full of negative thoughts about you that can lead to perceived negative emotions.

As awful as it is to hear, some people may dread being around you because of the effect you have on how they feel. Your manipulation can cause others to doubt their reality.

Self-Esteem

As the motivation for manipulation is power and control, it's essential to start by improving your self-esteem to overcome your insecurities. This can be done by journaling your achievements and using positive affirmations.

There is nothing like comparing yourself to others to bring down your self-esteem. Instead, remind yourself that self-worth isn't based on tangible items, status, or wealth.

Even with your flaws, you are good enough as a human being—that's self-worth!

Triggers

While working on your self-esteem, take the time to recognize patterns in your manipulative behavior.

Noticing what triggers your manipulative traits through awareness and reflection will help you identify causes to stop the behavior before it happens. It will help if you ask those closest to you for some feedback, especially if you struggle to spot such behaviors.

Ask them how your manipulative behaviors made them feel in the past.

Asserting Yourself

You want to avoid passive-aggressive and aggressive communication and master the skills of assertive communication. To do this, remember the HONEST acronym:

- **H:** Hold your ground. Maintain your position and beliefs respectfully, but know that you aren't always right
- **O:** Open-mindedness. Actively listen to others and consider their perspectives without judgment
- **N:** Nonverbal cues. Be aware of your tone of voice, especially for

sarcasm. Check that facial expressions, hand movements, and posture are not overbearing or threatening

- **E:** Express yourself clearly. Be honest, direct, and concise when expressing thoughts and emotions. Sometimes, fewer words are more effective!

- **S:** Self-awareness. Constantly be mindful of your emotions, and calm your emotions before responding

- **T:** Take responsibility. Be accountable for your words and actions. When things go wrong, admit your part in it

Respect Boundaries

When someone says "no," you accept and respect it.

There are exceptions.

If that person has said no, it's because they have a boundary in place that protects their emotional, physical, and mental needs.

Not everyone has healthy boundaries in place and will struggle to say no. In this case, you need to read signs of their discomfort.

Do they pause before responding?

Do they take a step back?

Are they fidgeting?

Others will use sentences that mean no without saying the word, for example, "Thanks for the invite, but I can't make it."

Just because you don't hear the word no, it doesn't mean you can attempt to change their mind.

Manipulative people tend to have weak boundaries themselves.

It would be beneficial for you to work on developing healthy boundaries to see how useful they are as a form of self-protection and just what it feels like when someone crosses one of your boundaries!

TOXIC COMMUNICATION	HEALTHY COMMUNICATION
Criticism: "You never listen to me!"	**Feedback:** "I feel unheard when I speak. Can we talk about it?"
Defensiveness: "It's not my fault!"	**Accountability:** "I understand my role in this. Let's work on it."
Stonewalling: Ignoring or shutting down.	**Active Listening:** "I hear you. Let me think about how I can help."
Blame: "This is all your fault."	**Collaboration:** "How can we work through this together?"
Yelling or **Passive Aggression**	**Assertiveness:** Calmly expressing needs with "I" statements.
Manipulation: "If you loved me, you'd do this."	**Respect:** Setting boundaries and valuing the other person's feelings.

Exercise: Conflict Rewind

We can learn a lot from our previous mistakes, and although dredging up past conflicts can be painful, it's a crucial step in identifying where you can improve.

Trace the conversation back to the moment when it started to turn toxic. This could be gaslighting, defensiveness, or an insult you regret.

Brainstorm three or four ways you could have responded after taking a moment to pause, calm down, identify, and manage your emotions.

These responses could include asking for clarification, an apology, or "I" statements to express how you feel.

Consider how the other person may have replied to your response and reflect on how you both feel after this improved and healthy communication.

There is one thing that I have said before, but I want to reiterate it.

You will likely be feeling quite low about yourself after considering how your past behavior has affected the lives of others, more so if you were unaware of the extent of the impact.

There are two paths ahead of you.

One will lead to negative thought patterns and potentially worse symptoms of anxiety and depression if you beat yourself up over the past.

The second path leads to accepting that these mistakes were made and making sure that the techniques in this chapter are implemented and the same mistakes aren't repeated!

A crucial factor we have yet to discuss is **empathy**, which is so important for healthy communication and building meaningful relationships that it warrants a chapter of its own.

TRIGGER	TOXIC REACTION	NON-TOXIC REACTION
Partner critiques you	**Defensive:** *"You're always blaming me!"*	**Seek clarity:** *"Can you explain what you mean?"*
Someone forgets an important date	**Passive-aggressive:** *"I guess I don't matter!"*	**Express feelings:** *"I felt hurt when you forgot; can we talk about it?"*
Conflict arises in a group setting	**Blame:** *"This is all your fault!"*	**Take responsibility:** *"I think I could have approached this differently."*
You make a mistake at work	**Avoidance:** *Ignore it and hope no one notices.*	**Acknowledge:** *"I made a mistake; here's how I'll fix it."*
Friend doesn't reply to a message	**Assumption:** *"You're ignoring me on purpose!"*	**Check in:** *"Is everything okay? I noticed you haven't replied."*
Partner gets upset during a discussion	**Escalate:** *"Why are you always so dramatic?"*	**Validate:** *"I can see you're upset. Let's talk about it."*

CHAPTER SIX: HEART WIDE OPEN

> *I think we all have empathy. We may not have enough courage to display it.*
>
> — *MAYA ANGELOU*

One of the common things we hear about narcissists, or at least those with narcissistic personality disorder, is that they have little to no empathy. But what if we took a different perspective, much like Angelou?

What if empathy was like a seed already within you, but it just needs the right conditions to germinate and thrive? And what if, for the conditions to be achieved, you need to break down your emotional barriers and let other people in? It's only natural that this requires some courage!

What Exactly Is Empathy?

Previously, we discussed the importance of perspective and seeing things from different points of view. Empathy takes this to the next level and enables you to connect on an emotional level and feel the same things they are feeling. There are three types of empathy:

- **Affective empathy:** The ability to appropriately respond to another person's emotions. For example, not reacting to anger with anger.

- **Somatic empathy:** The ability to feel what someone else is feeling. You can feel someone's frustration when they can't do something.

- **Cognitive empathy:** The ability to understand a person's emotional response to a situation. Your child is crying because they are scared of the dark, and you recognize that this must be scary for them.

Some people make the mistake of interchanging the words empathy and sympathy. The meanings are similar, but still with a significant difference.

Sympathy is understanding that someone is going through a particular experience, especially a difficult one, and feeling sorry or compassion for that person. Empathy is sharing the same emotions.

Brené Brown, a research professor whose focus is on vulnerability, shame, and empathy, explains sympathy with one clear example:

"I'm over here, and you're over there. I'm sorry for you, and I'm sad for you. And while I'm sorry that happened to you, let's be clear: I'm over here." (Abram, 2013)

For someone to have empathy, they would be standing "over there" feeling the same sadness.

At this point, it's worth noting that narcissists are often attracted to empaths; it's like the yin to their yang. Narcissists crave validation and attention. Empaths have high levels of compassion and are quick to validate the needs of a narcissist because they feel their pain.

Empathy is one of the five core elements of emotional intelligence, the others being self-awareness, self-regulation, social skills, and motivation. Self-awareness and self-regulation refer to the ability to recognize one's own emotions and manage them. Someone with toxic traits may not have problems with self-awareness and self-regulation, but tapping into another person's emotions can be exceptionally challenging—but not impossible!

The Narcissist and Empathy Debate

After telling his wife she was a hindrance and replaceable at any moment, she left him. Marcos lost everything and hit rock bottom. Throughout his life, Marcos felt that he was different from everyone else. He couldn't understand why he got so angry when he saw other people suffering. Online research informed him that therapy was the only way forward for him, which is when he was diagnosed with NPD.

His lack of empathy has been hard for him, especially raising three children. He genuinely couldn't feel the feelings they had when they were upset or needed comfort. However, thanks to therapy, he has been able to develop more cognitive empathy. Although he can't share their suffering, he has learned how to understand why they are feeling that way.

Marcos is in the minority! It is estimated that between 2 and 16 percent of people with NPD seek professional help (Ambardar & Bienenfeld, 2023). As we have seen, someone with NPD won't notice that they have a problem. Furthermore, they may even feel that their lack of empathy is a benefit for them. Not having to deal with those pesky emotions keeps them on the path to success.

Whether it's NPD or you are dealing with narcissistic traits, empathy is a complex matter. Brain scans have shown that people with NPD have less gray matter in the left anterior insula, the area of the brain related to empathy, compassion, and cognitive function, as well as abnormal levels of white matter in the anterior insula, where compassion is processed and generated (Graham, n.d.). These parts of the brain might be different from someone who doesn't have NPD, but it doesn't mean that these parts are nonexistent. Empathy is generated, just not used.

This explains why some narcissists have the ability to show immense empathy toward their pet or a small child but then appear emotionless with others. Some will have the ability to withhold empathy as a way of controlling another person, while others have the ability to show or even fake empathy, especially when they are going to gain from it.

Because the root cause of narcissistic behaviors is a severe lack of self-esteem, it's also worth considering that a lack of empathy is a form of self-protection. It's possible that some situations allow the narcissist to show their vulnerability, and other situations that make them feel helpless cause them to withhold their empathy, more so if the situation causes them to feel shame.

Further research has shown that narcissists can empathize but only when instructed to put themselves in the position of the other person. When watching a video of domestic abuse, the narcissistic participants showed similar levels of empathy to non-narcissistic participants when told to imagine how the victim felt. Those who weren't given instructions showed no empathy. In the same study, participants' heart rates (an indication of empathy) were also measured while they watched a video about a couple breaking up. Narcissists who were instructed to see the perspective of the couple had an increased heart rate compared with those who weren't given instructions (Mitrokostas, 2018).

All of this confirms that narcissists and those with NPD can develop and show empathy, but there is no guarantee that this is automatic.

When It Doesn't Come Easy

Let's take away the idea that you are unwilling to express empathy but that it's extremely difficult for you. You may have certain barriers that make you come across as uncaring and even, on occasion, hurtful.

Cognitive Biases

Cognitive biases are inaccurate thinking patterns that impact how we see the world. A few in particular can prevent or reduce empathy.

The first is confirmation bias, which involves the habit of looking for, interpreting, and remembering information that supports or confirms our beliefs and opinions. At the same time, we ignore anything that goes against our beliefs and opinions. This could lead to showing less empathy to those who contradict you.

Fundamental attribution error is when we blame a person's behavior on their character rather than considering all contributing factors to the situation.

If your partner is at home on the sofa, you might be tempted to label them as lazy instead of considering that they are ill. Similarly, if a team member can't finish a task, you might assume they are incompetent and not because they didn't have the necessary resources.

In-group bias refers to the tendency to prefer and trust people within our own groups, whether that's friendships, religion, or workplace departments. This is particularly dangerous because there isn't just the risk of showing less or no empathy to those outside your group. There is also the risk of discrimination.

Dehumanization

With an inflated sense of self, dehumanization can be a common barrier for those with narcissistic traits. Dehumanizing a person is when we devalue a person, dismiss them, or deprive them of positive human qualities.

Making someone out to be less than human is almost the polar opposite of empathy! Aside from derogating people, it makes aggression and harming others easier.

There is an argument to be made that dehumanization is a strategy for emotional regulation.

For example, some healthcare workers may dehumanize patients as a form of self-protection from the suffering they witness daily. Nevertheless, it's important not to use this as an excuse for improper behavior or a lack of empathy.

Victim Blaming

An extreme example of this is when someone blames the victim of a crime rather than the criminal. When you hear about someone who has been raped, you question why they didn't fight or run instead of recognizing that it was unquestionably the rapist in the wrong.

You may find yourself using phrases like "If you had just answered your phone, I wouldn't have lost my temper." Although this might be true, there could have been a number of reasons why they didn't answer the phone, and your temper is your responsibility. The angry outburst pulls all the attention to your feelings and not what the other person is going through.

Lack of Self-Awareness

Emotional intelligence is fortunately a part of most school curriculums today, but for us, the closest we got to emotional intelligence was learning adjectives! This means that the majority of adults lack self-awareness. Even if you are aware of your own emotions, there is the obstacle of managing these emotions and the reactions they cause. Considering the variables involved, the bigger obstacle is understanding how your words and actions affect another person.

A simple joke can cause one person to laugh in hysterics, but the next person could find it incredibly offensive. A partner could brush off your harsh words one day, but if they have had a stressful day themselves, they can find your attitude to be frustrating or hurtful.

Fear and Insecurity

This is another barrier that can't be used as an excuse, but understanding how fear and insecurity can impact your ability to empathize with others is a great step forward. You may have many fears, but let's take the fear of abandonment as an example.

A fear of abandonment is also an insecurity. It can lead to overbearing behavior and codependency. You may go out of your way to ensure that someone doesn't leave you, taking away any independence they have. Your fears may push the other person away because it is better that they leave now than later on. Either way, you are taking away their emotions in place of your own. You aren't the only person with fears and insecurities!

Fatigue and Stress

Exhaustion can affect our ability to pay attention and actively listen to those we are communicating with. Actively listening isn't just about listening to words, but it's also about reading a person's body language to understand better how a person is feeling. It's very likely that an empath will give you a verbal message that is not necessarily true; they say what they think they want you to hear. Getting better at reading other people will allow you to see if their nonverbal cues match their verbal message. This is especially true of microexpressions, which are flashes of emotions that are harder to fake.

As for stress, it has a habit of consuming our minds and distracting us. Constant worry about what has happened and what may happen inhibits our attention too. If this is combined with cognitive biases ("They can't possibly have as much stress as I do"), you will find it hard to empathize with the problems of others.

Multitasking

Imagine the number of times you have been in the kitchen doing dishes, preparing dinner, thinking about the messages you haven't sent yet, and all the other things you attempt to juggle at once. At the same time, your loved one is telling you about your day. You don't have to be a narcissist or have toxic traits to miss out on what they are telling you. However, not giving this person the respect they deserve is a lack of respect. Somebody once told me that if your children want to tell you something, it's essential that you put aside everything else and listen because, at that moment, you are the most important person they want to talk to.

This same principle should be applied to anyone who wants or needs your attention.

At first, you may have thought that overcoming your barriers to empathy would require a huge effort. In reality, they are all small changes that only require your motivation and can make unbelievable changes in how people perceive you. Next, we will move on to these changes.

5 Practical Ways to Stepping Into Someone Else's Shoes

If developing empathy requires motivation, the first thing to do is understand why you want to work on this skill. Why do you need to increase your empathy? Is it to strengthen your relationship or to connect better with your children? Do you need empathy to achieve a personal or professional goal?

Your why shouldn't be based on things like wealth, popularity, or other things that narcissism encourages you to chase. Jim Carey made a great point about this:

"I think everybody should get rich and famous and do everything they ever dreamed of so they can see that it's not the answer." (Burns, 2021)

To help you consider your why, ask yourself what makes you happy. Then, ask yourself what makes you feel fulfilled. You might think they are the same, but happiness is a short-term emotion, whereas fulfillment is a long-term state of being. Receiving your paycheck will make you happy, but fulfillment comes when you take some of that paycheck and use it to help others, for example.

Paint a vivid picture of how empathy will help you in life. Imagine what it would feel like for you and your team as you hit your goals together.

At the same time, consider how your low levels of empathy are holding you back from all the things you want to achieve. When this picture is clear, you will have the motivation to start overcoming barriers.

Mastering Self-Awareness

From my perspective, self-awareness is the cornerstone of empathy and a great place to start to overcome several barriers. Self-awareness lets you focus on yourself and your actions, thoughts, and emotions. You may think that having narcissistic traits means you overly focus on yourself and should be focusing more on others, but this teaches you how to pay attention to the reality of what you do rather than an internal story that you tell yourself. It also helps with self-control, confidence, and self-esteem.

If you want to be able to understand the emotions of others, you first have to understand your own, and this requires expanding your vocabulary. In the past, my emotional vocabulary was limited to words like fine, good, stressed, or angry. But I realized that these words are not enough to describe how I am feeling accurately. So, I banned myself from using these words to describe how I was feeling and forced myself to pause throughout the day and choose one of the 27 main emotions we experience:

- Admiration
- Adoration
- Aesthetic appreciation
- Amusement
- Anxiety
- Awe
- Awkwardness
- Boredom
- Calmness
- Confusion
- Craving
- Disgust
- Empathetic pain
- Entrancement
- Envy
- Excitement
- Fear
- Horror
- Interest
- Joy
- Nostalgia
- Romance
- Sadness
- Satisfaction
- Sexual desire
- Sympathy
- Triumph

Self-aware people also take time for self-reflection, whether that's through journaling or taking time to think. They are able to recognize their strengths and areas for improvement. They have a clear idea of their values and beliefs and will make decisions that align with them. Finally, they also understand the reason behind their behaviors. Whether an action is good or bad, ask yourself why you did what you did.

How to Find Common Ground with Others

Aside from increasing empathy, common ground can bring people closer together, especially through reduced conflict. It makes forming new friendships easy and can also help to disrupt echo chambers where everyone's views are the same. Common ground isn't just about interests but also about finding topics and opinions you can agree on. It's okay if you disagree. The important thing is to accept this and try to find something you can agree on, even if it's just agreeing to disagree.

Open-ended and follow-up questions are excellent opportunities for finding common ground. Instead of asking someone, "Did you enjoy your holiday?" which will lead to a yes or no answer, ask, "What did you enjoy about your holiday?" Perhaps they tried a hobby you like or a food that you have never tried. My only advice with open-ended questions is to avoid sensitive topics that could easily lead to conflicting opinions, such as religion and politics.

Taking a genuine interest in other people provides the chance to see aspects of yourself in others, and it's this connection that makes empathy easier. Once you have started opening up more with those who make it easy to empathize, broaden your horizons, and actively seek out people who are different from you to enhance this skill.

Reading The Hidden Messages

Before trying to decode the not-so-obvious messages, life and empathy would be less challenging if you make the effort to listen actively. Actively listening means hearing what a person is saying but also tapping into their thoughts and feelings. The first step toward active listening is to give a person your full attention without tangible distractions like mobile phones or mental noise. Mental noise refers to the continuous stream of thoughts about things like what you need to add to your shopping list or what time you said you would meet your friend.

Mental noise that is particularly damaging is judgment. Instead of listening, your mind might judge what a person is wearing, why they are telling you the things they are telling you, or worse, negative thoughts like how ridiculous they sound. There is no time for judgment when you are listening, and we have already seen that multitasking doesn't work in our favor. To tame the judgments, think about how hard it was for this person to have this conversation with you, especially if you haven't been the kindest person to approach in the past.

Interrupting a person is a surefire way to quickly kill any empathy you have created. It shows a lack of respect, and it throws the other person's thought trail off. If you interrupt a person, you haven't given them a chance to finish what they were going to say, which could be exactly what you interrupt them for. Never assume you know what they are about to say, and don't start forming your response until they have finished speaking.

As for reading emotions, the eyes and mouth often give away the most information. It's best to look at images online of different facial expressions to better distinguish subtle differences. After facial expressions, the tone of voice can tell you more about a person's emotions. A tense voice can indicate anger compared with a softer tone, which may suggest that someone is feeling nervous. Sometimes, gestures are easier to read. Look for people fidgeting as a sign of anxiety or nerves, stepping away from you in order to create distance, or blocking themselves by crossing arms or placing an object between you.

It's necessary to remember that not one verbal or nonverbal cue will give you all the answers to a person's emotions. Focusing on one area won't give you the whole picture.

It's best to practice scanning for all nonverbal cues while listening. It may sound like a lot to do at once, but you will get better at reading emotions with practice.

Be Curious About What's Beyond Your Comfort Zone

Imagine following the same routine every day, from talking to the same people to listening to the same news channel. Without vast exposure to the differences in the world around you, you aren't going to have the opportunity to see different perspectives, and this is a sure way to fuel your biases and stereotypes of others.

In many ways, stepping out of your comfort zone requires the same steps as overcoming fears. It's about understanding what makes you feel uncomfortable and managing the emotions that this discomfort creates. Then, you can break down the steps to what makes you feel uncomfortable into more manageable steps.

Stepping out of your comfort zone forces you to understand what it is like when other people feel confused, embarrassed, nervous, or self-conscious. Previously, you may have mocked someone for their clothing choice, making them feel self-conscious. When you actively choose to wear something that makes you feel self-conscious, you have firsthand experience of the other person's emotions.

Curiosity is a great way to break down your biases toward those who are in different groups than yourself. Take some time to learn about different cultures, traditions, and beliefs. Watch movie genres you wouldn't normally watch or books written by authors from around the world. Just as we practice looking at things from a fictional character's point of view, we can also do the same to get better at understanding and sharing their emotions.

Manage Your Distractions

A little bit of self-care goes a long way to managing exhaustion and stress. Self-care isn't about spoiling yourself or luxury. It's about taking care of your physical and emotional needs.

These simple acts put you in a better position to fulfill your responsibilities, but they also provide you with the energy for self-awareness, managing your stress, and taking care of those who need you.

Self-care is an individual practice, but self-awareness will help you tune into your needs.

There are various areas of self-care. For each of the following, think of a way that you could practice self-care that will help you develop more empathy:

- **Physical self-care:** eating a balanced diet, drinking enough water, getting regular exercise, creating a healthy sleep routine
- **Mental self-care:** setting goals, journaling, learning new skills, working on personal growth
- **Emotional self-care:** setting boundaries, journaling about your feelings, finding healthy outlets for built-up emotions
- **Environmental self-care:** decluttering your home, workspace, organizing documents, making lists, creating a calming area in your home
- **Financial self-care:** taking care of debt, saving, keeping track of your budget, learning about investments
- **Social self-care:** ending relationships with people who encourage toxicity, building a support system
- **Recreational self-care:** traveling, enjoying a good movie/series, spending time in nature, doing puzzles or creative activities
- **Spiritual self-care:** taking regular time for self-reflection, meditation, mindfulness, breathwork

Don't feel the need to start all of these tips to develop empathy at once.

To build strong habits that stick for a lifetime, it's best to commit to a few and then add to them instead of overwhelming yourself with too many at once. Trying to take on too much can cause more stress and distractions!

Pick a few that make more sense to you and that genuinely motivate you.

Exercise: Empathy Challenge

Imagine your partner comes home and makes a comment that doesn't sit right with you, prompting you to snap back at them.

Think about what could have happened if you had considered what they might have been through that caused them to comment the way they did. Just like your own behavior, this is not an excuse but a strategy to stop things from spiraling out of control.

For this exercise, try to spend a whole day thinking about things from a different point of view, about how they are feeling and their needs in certain situations.

Ask yourself, "What must they be thinking and feeling right now?" and "What could I do to improve their situation?" You should aim for a whole day because it reduces your automatic reactions and encourages empathetic observation as a new healthy habit. What did you learn from the experience? What did you learn about the other person's emotional needs? Wake up the next day with the determination to continue this practice.

After dedicating significant time to overcoming negativity, fear, and anxiety, it is time to move on to the next chapter and fill the void with positive thoughts and actions.

CHAPTER SEVEN: BYE BYE BAD VIBES

> *Positive thinking will let you do everything better than negative thinking will.*
>
> — *ZIG ZIGLAR*

Ziglar's words may seem obvious, but people often overlook the power of the concept. Picture any of the things that you need to do today. I will use ironing as an example because it's certainly not something I love. The process of ironing is going to be the same, no matter what. As always, I have options. I can complain about the ironing, get all grumpy, and ruin the mood of my entire family. Or I can put on a good movie, work my way through the pile, and enjoy the sense of achievement once it's done.

Naturally, the best choice is the latter, but with everything that is going on in our minds and the tendency to lean toward the negative, the positive option isn't going to occur without effort. This is where the C in the REFLECT framework applies, the technique of creating genuine positivity.

Why See the Glass Half Full?

The glass half full or half empty is probably the most common metaphor related to positive thinking, and it does actually explain how various people will have different mindsets toward life and experiences. It's not about looking at the world through rose-colored glasses and ignoring the negative aspects of life. It's about being able to think positively about yourself, your abilities, other people, and the challenges you face.

There are several benefits to positive thinking, physical and mental. It's a great way to manage stress levels because positively facing stressful situations can reduce anxiety. Chronic stress and anxiety can increase the risk of diseases such as diabetes, high blood pressure, and heart disease. Positive thinking not only reduces stress levels but also increases immunity to help reduce the risk of illnesses.

In the real world, stress isn't just going to disappear. Those with a pessimistic outlook are going to struggle to handle the ongoing turmoil stress causes. But when you learn how to increase your positivity, you get better at coping with problems, and therefore, your resilience builds as you fix problems instead of giving up hope.

Positive thinking has a wonderful effect on relationships. It's contagious! Being around someone who looks for positive things can bring more fun, happiness, and enjoyment into the relationship. You can inspire each other to achieve more and help each other through the more challenging times. And this isn't just limited to romantic relationships. Positive thinking can improve relationships with family, friends, and coworkers.

There is something essential that you have to bear in mind with positive thinking—it can't be forced. In today's society, there is a lot of what's called toxic positivity. This is when we tell ourselves or hear messages that there is only room for positivity. We may be scrolling through social media with "Positive vibes only" or a friend telling us "It could be worse." You may have even heard yourself using phrases like "Look on the bright side" or "Think happy thoughts."

On the outside, things could be worse, but there might be a bright side. These phrases are only attempts to reassure, but toxic positivity tends to cover or bury the negative instead of accepting it. It can leave people feeling like their problems or perceived negative emotions aren't valid, despite seeing how all emotions are valid, and everyone has the right to express their emotions.

In the case of ironing, toxic positivity would mean ignoring my dread of such a tedious task and forcing myself to smile through the mountain. Suppressing thoughts and feelings often only leads to them resurfacing and becoming more assertive. My negative thoughts would only make them worse. Genuine positivity is accepting that ironing is not a task I enjoy but one that is essential and will make me feel better once it's done.

What many people forget is that whether the glass is half full or half empty, it can always be refilled!

Are You a Negativity Nancy or Negative Ned?

To an extent, we are all negative Nancys or negative Neds. Our brains are hard-wired this way as a survival technique. Cavemen had to err on the side of caution and assume a rustle in the bushes was a sign of danger. If not, they may have found themselves as a predator's next meal. Although humans have evolved and don't face the same dangers as in the past, the basic need to stay safe still encourages us to err on the side of caution.

In Chapter 4, we began to understand cognitive distortions, focusing on catastrophizing. Now, it's time to discover other tendencies to lean toward negative thinking.

- **Filtering:** In a situation where there are positives and negatives, you tend to filter the positives and only focus on the negatives.
- **Discounting the positive:** This is another type of filtering, but in this case, when you think of a positive, you dismiss its value.

- **Polarization:** This all-or-nothing thinking causes you to think in black and white. You may end up with unrealistic standards, lack of motivation, and/or setting yourself up for failure.
- **Overgeneralization:** One isolated event becomes a pattern of defeat, often combined with words like always and never, for example, saying "I always mess up" after one mistake.
- **Jumping to conclusions:** There is a situation, and without evidence to support your thoughts, you assume the worst and then react based on the assumption.
- **Personalization:** Taking everything to heart and taking responsibility for everything, even things that are out of your control.
- **Emotional reasoning:** An emotional reaction you experience proves something is real or true, but there is no evidence to support this.
- **Shoulds:** Should statements are based on rules we set for ourselves about how things "should" go a certain way. When things don't go as expected, even if the rules are unreasonable, it's easy to become disappointed, frustrated, or guilty.
- **Labeling:** Placing negative labels on yourself and/or others, including when there is no reason for them. These labels end up attacking a person's character rather than their one-off actions.
- **Always being right:** Nobody likes being wrong, but the need to always be right becomes a cognitive distortion when you go to great lengths to prove your point.

Chapter 4 also covered cognitive reconstructing and the five steps to reframe negative thoughts for more realistic and positive thoughts. The same steps can be used for any type of cognitive distortion. However, take some extra time to identify which type of cognitive distortion your negative thought is. The better you know your thought patterns, the easier it is to spot triggers and make changes.

These cognitive distortions feed the inner critic, and before you know it, negative self-talk takes over. You need to be accountable for your less than ideal behavior, but at the same time, you are committed to improving and should show yourself some self-compassion. Some of your actions may not have been the best choices, but that doesn't mean you're not intelligent! Be kind to yourself. If self-compassion doesn't come easy, imagine a loved one in the same position as you. What would you say to them? You might say to a friend, "That was stupid," but you would never tell them that they are stupid. Have the same compassion for yourself.

If the distorted thought continues to appear despite attempts at reframing, it's time to delve deeper into why. Ask yourself if this thought is bringing you any benefits and if it will help you become the person you want to be. Or is it just going to continue to cause you pain?

For additional help identifying and modifying cognitive distortions, you can use Socratic questioning. Named after the great thinker himself, Socratic questioning is a series of open-ended questions that pushes you beyond your comfort zone and increases your perspective. Use the following questions to further challenge your cognitive distortions:

- What is the problem?
- Why is this problem significant?
- What assumptions have you made?
- Can a different assumption be made?
- What would an outsider think about this problem?
- How would an outsider respond to this problem?
- How can you rephrase the problem for clarification?
- What has led you to your beliefs?
- What additional information do you need?
- What evidence supports your beliefs?
- What reasons do you have to doubt the evidence?
- What evidence are you ignoring?
- Finally, is this the worst-case scenario or not?

Imagine your Socratic questioning as an interview between yourself and yourself in the third person. Each question should provide you with the opportunity for a follow-up question (one of the above or others that are specific to your situation) so that you can learn more about your thoughts.

Just because negative thoughts can become manageable, it doesn't mean that life is automatically full of joy and positivity. In the final section of this chapter, we will cover ways to embrace a positive lifestyle without making it toxic!

Turning Frowns Upside Down

Chris wasn't a negative person, but he wasn't a positive person either. He felt like he was just floating through life with a solid routine. He worked, paid the bills, and kept fit and healthy. However, nothing he did made him feel enthusiastic, happy, or excited. Looking through an old photo album with his sister, he saw a picture of them horse riding as children. The image reminded him of how much he enjoyed horse riding, and he decided to take up his old hobby again. It was only one hour every couple of weeks, but it was enough to change his outlook on life.

So many things that contribute to positivity are subjective, including love, happiness, hope, and levels of satisfaction. What will bring satisfaction into your life can differ significantly from the next person. What we all have in common is that we deserve some time to ourselves for the things we enjoy in life. This isn't the same as being self-centered because you aren't constantly putting your needs above the needs of others. It's an act of self-care that ensures you are mentally looking after yourself so that you are in a better position to care for others.

If you had one hour a week where you had no responsibilities or obligations, what would you do to bring happiness and positivity into your life? Don't just think about it, make it happen!

Two daily practices that take only a few minutes and have been scientifically proven to increase positivity are gratitude and positive affirmations.

Gratitude

Once a year, many of us take the time to give thanks for what we have; however, this is just a snapshot of gratitude, and we miss out on all the benefits on the other 364 days of the year.

One study on gratitude involved three groups of people. One group was asked to write a few sentences each week about situations that had occurred and made them feel grateful. The next group was asked to write about things that had annoyed or irritated them and the third group was asked to write about things that had happened without any emphasis on how the events made them feel.

After ten weeks, the group that wrote about what made them feel grateful was more optimistic, felt better about their lives, and even had fewer doctor's visits than the group that had focused on the negatives (Harvard Health Publishing, 2021).

There are two sides to gratitude. On the one hand, a state of gratitude is about acknowledging that life is good and there are things worth living for. On the other hand, gratitude is also about recognizing that there are external sources of goodness in life beyond what comes from within.

The source of that goodness can come from other people, nature, actions, or anything else in the world that adds to this goodness of life.

It's not just about people who go out of their way to do something for you.

Recently, I was talking to someone who lives in the UK, and they told me that within the last seven months, there had only been four days without rain. At that moment, I felt grateful for the sun on my face!

Gratitude is often about the simple, everyday pleasures that are all too often overlooked or unnoticed.

Here are some activities you can try to start practicing gratitude:

- **Rapid-fire gratitude:** You have one minute to list ten things you are grateful for. Try to combine this with mindful gratitude and list things that you are grateful for in the present moment.

- **Gratitude journaling:** Spend a few minutes a day writing about what you are grateful for in your life and why.

- **A gratitude jar:** Every day, write what you are grateful for on a small slip of paper and place it inside a jar. When the jar is full, look back and read all the slips.

- **A gratitude board:** Use photos, images, quotes, or anything that reminds you of things you are grateful for. Keep your board in a place where you can see it frequently.

- **A gratitude walk:** Go for a mindful walk and make a mental note of all the things you are grateful for along the way. Use all five of your senses to tune into nature.

- **Sharing your gratitude:** Write letters or simple Post-it notes to let others know how grateful you are to have them in your life.

Positive Affirmations

Positive affirmations are short phrases that are repeated to cultivate a positive mental attitude. Science has shown that these affirmations can improve education, health, and relationships. These phrases can create a positive feedback loop that leads to lasting positive effects (Cohen & Sherman, 2014).

Understanding how positive affirmations work has become simpler, thanks to neuroplasticity. Previously, negative thoughts that were replayed in the mind created strong neuro connections that were easy to retrieve. As soon as these thoughts weren't repeated, the connections started to get weaker during the synapse pruning stage. The first time a positive affirmation is said, a new neuro connection is created, and with repetition, the connection becomes stronger.

For positive affirmations to work, you have to truly believe in the words you are repeating. So, it's important that you choose affirmations that you can relate to and feel comfortable saying. That's not to say that the affirmations have to be true. Phrases such as "I love myself" or "I am confident" may not reflect your current state, but by telling your brain this, you will change your way of thinking, and soon enough, you will love yourself and be confident.

Here are some more examples of positive affirmations:

- I am enough
- I am a good person
- I trust myself
- I am stronger than my fears
- I am capable
- I choose to focus on the positive
- I am open to receiving love
- I am worthy of joy and happiness
- I let go of fear and embrace healing
- I allow myself to make mistakes and learn from them
- I am safe
- I am in the right place and going in the right direction

Feel free to change, combine, or write your own affirmations. Just remember to use the present tense and avoid all negative words (e.g., never) and negative contractions (e.g., don't).

Positive affirmations can be used at any time of the day, but they will be especially useful in times of high stress. If you feel the physical symptoms burning up inside you, take a few deep breaths and use your go-to positive affirmation.

Increasing positivity doesn't mean there won't be difficult moments in the future. It's the tough times in life when self-care should also become more of a priority. Take extra time for self-reflection to understand what your mind and body need and then fulfill those needs.

Finally, when the going gets tough, spend time with those who are filled with positivity. Just like other people's negativity can rub off on you, so can positivity.

While you may think that this is the time you need to hold on to your own positivity as much as possible, sharing it with others can boost your happiness; after all, your glass is refillable!

Exercise: "Positivity Jar"

Much like the gratitude jar, the positivity jar encourages a daily practice whereby you focus on something good in your life. It fosters a positive mindset and is a great way to break yourself out of negative thought patterns. You just need a jar and small pieces of paper. Commit to writing one thing daily on a piece of paper and add it to the jar. To make it part of your routine, you can do it at the end of the day, say after dinner.

However, if you find yourself stuck in a negative moment, take the opportunity to force your brain to think of something that makes you feel happy or excited. Once a week or month, open your jar, read your pieces of paper, and reflect on all these positive things. If you have written things about others, pass that positivity on and give them the note.

Rome wasn't built in a day, and considering you might be tackling toxic behaviors that you have been dealing with for a long time, you are going to need to be patient with yourself. In our final chapter, we will see how that is possible!

CHAPTER EIGHT: SLOW AND STEADY

> *The road to success is always under construction.*
>
> — *LILY TOMLIN*

It's only natural to want to see instant change. You have worked hard to understand your behaviors, and it's been painful to accept how these behaviors have impacted the lives of your loved ones.

It can even be frustrating that you haven't reached the best version of yourself yet.

At this stage, it's crucial not to let frustration undo the progress and revert to old habits. The final stage of the REFLECT framework will show you how to trust the process!

Patience in Transformation

Life is often focused on getting from point A to point B, but then we realize it's not that simple. We break things down and aim to get from A to Z. Right when we are about to reach Z, something happens that throws us off course. This is because the goal is only the destination, and we overlook the journey process.

Personal growth isn't something you achieve after a certain amount of time or a number of steps. You won't wake up one morning and think, "That's it, I've achieved personal growth." It should be something that you wake up and experience every morning.

The transformation you hope to achieve takes time and patience. But it's not all about you. You will have to extend your patience to those you have hurt in the past. You may have promised change before, only to continue with the same toxic traits. Your loved ones have fallen for empty promises in the past and are going to be cautious about trusting you this time.

Just as you can't rush or force your own change, you can't rush or force them into forgiving you and moving forward.

We live in a world where instant gratification is the norm, so patience is increasingly difficult. The root cause of impatience is frustration, especially when you feel like your needs and wishes aren't being met. This often gives stress, anxiety, and anger a chance to surface. However, patience is a skill that can be learned.

The first step to patience is mindfulness and embracing the present moment. The journey you are on will involve continuous change and growth. This means your thoughts and emotions won't remain the same, your values and beliefs may grow with you, and all of these changing circumstances can mean you aren't always in tune with who you are and where you are going.

Get good at sitting and being comfortable with the present moment. Put down the technology, ignore the to-do list for a moment, and just sit with your feelings. Sometimes, these feelings will bring you great joy. Gratitude mindfulness is about tuning into your senses, focusing on your breath, and contemplating all the things you are grateful for.

Other times, mindful moments can bring up feelings of discomfort. Impatience is especially uncomfortable because mindfulness can feel like you are doing nothing, and if you are doing nothing, how can you possibly be making steps toward your goals?

Use mindfulness as a chance to get good at sitting with feelings of discomfort. Even after you mend broken bridges and increase positivity in your life, there will still be challenging times ahead, leading to inevitable uncomfortable feelings. Start with short periods of discomfort and gradually expose yourself to longer amounts.

Mindfulness can also give you a chance to practice acceptance. Just like uncomfortable feelings, there will be unpleasant situations ahead, and some will test your patience. Acceptance isn't about giving up and not attempting to change things. It's about realizing that there are moments when change is not within your control. This can be any situation, from being stuck in traffic to giving your partner space and time to heal. Focus on what is in your control, like using this time in traffic for deep breathing and mindfulness or committing to showing your partner that this time, it's for real.

Great news for those of us who find waiting a challenge! Learning to resist the temptation of instant gratification is definitely possible—no fate or destiny involved. According to fresh looks at the iconic Marshmallow Experiment, there's hope for everyone to master the art of patience.

In the 1960s, Professor Walter Mischel conducted the marshmallow experiment on a group of 4- and 5-year-olds. Each child was offered a choice: one marshmallow now or two marshmallows later. One marshmallow was left on the table, and the adult left the room for 15 minutes. Some children barely waited until the door was closed, but others made it to the full 15 minutes (Clear, n.d.).

Recent studies give us more insights. It turns out, a child's ability to hold off for the extra marshmallow can be shaped by many factors—like their background, how much they trust the marshmallow-promiser, and their past experiences.

This suggests that with the right environment and guidance, anyone can boost their self-control muscles. So, if you ever felt bad about not passing the Marshmallow Test, cheer up! Delaying gratification isn't a fixed trait—it's a skill we can all develop with a little practice (and maybe a few marshmallows along the way).

Delayed gratification may not be related to freeing yourself from toxic traits, but it will help you develop more patience. Try it with a few simple examples first. For example, instead of a reward after completing each task on your to-do list, think of a bigger reward once you have finished two or three items.

Don't forget that right now, you are growing, even if it doesn't feel like it. Each page you read gives you knowledge and chances to practice newly acquired skills. Instead of chasing the dream, enjoy this moment and rest assured that you are exactly where you should be!

Potential Bumps Along the Road

If personal growth and transformation were easy, we would all be doing it! Some people never start, while others start and give up at the first obstacle. Others are more realistic and don't expect instant results but soon give up when they don't see the results as quickly as they had hoped.

> *I trained for 4 years to run 9 seconds, and people give up when they don't see results in 2 months.*
>
> — *USAIN BOLT*

Success requires patience and determination, but certain beliefs can get in the way of both. One of the worst is the assumption that change happens automatically. Reading this book is like following a recipe. Unless you actually follow the recipe steps, you won't get the desired meal outcome. Knowledge will only take you so far and your growth depends on you actively using the skills you have learned on a regular basis. On a similar note, don't wait for the right time! Yes, you have a lot on your plate, but you will still have all the same responsibilities next week and probably next month. The longer you wait to start, the greater the risk of never getting around to it.

Two other beliefs to get past are the perfection belief and the fear of mistakes. You may find yourself asking what the best way to start your personal growth is, more so if your toxic traits have affected multiple people.

There is no perfect way to start because there is no such thing as perfection. Spending time on such a question leads to procrastination, and once again, you may never begin. This takes us to the fact that mistakes will be made.

Accept that personal growth can be messy, and you may have moments when your behavior resembles past toxic traits. That's not to say that you are your old self and haven't made any progress. Those around you will notice you are going in the right direction and understand setbacks, but they may not accept you giving up at the first sign of challenges.

Relapse Isn't Failure: How to Bounce Back

Those bumps along the road can make you feel like you have taken one step forward and two steps back. In these moments, you may feel like a failure, believing that you will never be able to completely break free from your toxic behaviors. Failure is defined as a lack of success, and since you haven't finished your ongoing personal growth journey, you haven't failed.

Relapses are a normal part of any recovery, and like toxic behaviors, it's helpful to be able to recognize the potential triggers that could cause a relapse. One common factor is high levels of stress, especially if this stress lasts for a long period of time. Times of conflict can cause you to slip back into old habits, and it doesn't have to be just with one person. Conflicts at work can lead to toxic behaviors arising in the home and vice versa. Moments of insecurity and vulnerability can stir up all those fears that you had been working on overcoming.

The trick is not to wait until a full-blown argument before taking action. The earlier you spot the signs, the easier it is to rectify your behavior. While these early signs can be quite specific to your own situation, one thing I have noticed is to pay attention to other people's faces. Someone who has been hurt will be working on forgiveness and moving forward, but at the same time, you may notice a distinctive look on their face that cries, "Here we go again," or worse, "I knew the change wouldn't last." This is the sign that urgent action needs to take place, and here are the steps to get yourself back on track after a relapse.

Step 1: Recognize your relapses but without judgment.

It's important not to feed your inner critic with more negativity because you have been working hard to overcome this, and you don't want to take four metaphorical steps back.

Also, I know it hurts to slip back into the habit of hurting the person you care about, but this is another source of fuel for hostility. Instead, take a moment to recognize your growth because, in the past, you wouldn't have been able to spot your toxic behaviors.

Step 2: Reflect on what has triggered your relapse.

It's time to attack the cause of your relapse and head-on. If you are going through an incredibly stressful period, discover stress management techniques that work for you, whether that's exercise, mindfulness, or a combination of both.

Face your conflicts; don't assume they will just disappear, as the chances are, they will only escalate. And if your fears are taking over again, or your self-esteem has taken a knock, take time to work on this.

Step 3: Apologize and make amends

Be careful of assuming that the previous apology will work again. After all, with a little perspective, you can understand that it will be hard for them to believe.

Tweak your apology to fit the relapse. This might include phrases like "I know you have heard this before" and "I'm sorry for my relapse." It may also help to explain the trigger of your relapse, not as an excuse, but as a way of showing your vulnerabilities and perhaps even asking for help.

Step 4: Revisit the REFLECT framework

No new skill is mastered in a day or after one attempt. Ongoing personal growth requires ongoing learning, so it's okay to go back and refresh your steps, strategies, and techniques. Use positive affirmations such as "I am changing and growing every day" to remind yourself that this is a work in progress.

Step 5: Focus on your progress, not perfection

The affirmation above also serves as a reminder that the goal isn't perfection, as this is unrealistic and sets you up for failure. If you are constantly striving to be perfect, you will be permanently disappointed. It doesn't feel like it right now, but when you look back, you will see that each relapse is an opportunity to grow.

Kacey had been working hard at overcoming her insecurities and opening up to her partner. She had been using the fear ladder and gradual exposure, and her calming techniques were beginning to have a positive effect.

One day, her toxic ex posted something on social media that triggered a wave of past memories from their relationship, and she interpreted it as a personal dig at her. Suddenly, she felt like she was back to square one and shut down, unable to explain this to her partner. He was devastated and thought he had done something wrong.

For Kacey, there was a tornado of emotions that kept growing, which resulted in everything from tearful moments to angry comments comparing her partner to her ex.

She decided that she first needed some time and distance to work out what was going on, so she grabbed her journal, jumped in her car, and drove to her favorite calming spot.

After journaling about how she was feeling, what triggers she recognized, and how they connected to her toxic behavior, Kacey felt she was in a better position to effectively communicate with her partner.

She took accountability for her actions, apologized, and then decided to take a leap of faith and open up about her past relationship. Her partner noticed her progress and her genuine remorse, so they looked at ways she could regain her self-esteem and confidence in discussing her flaws and struggles.

If Kacey had allowed herself to sit in self-judgment and negativity, the toxicity would have spiraled and likely ended her relationship. Although this was her first relapse, she learned that it was a step toward growth, not a leap off the failure cliff.

Trusting the Process

Why should you place your trust in such an intangible process? Firstly, it's another part of acceptance. There is no magic pill that is going to enable you to overcome your toxic traits, and although this might sound depressing, it's actually inspiring. Certain things are out of your control, but your personal growth isn't one of them, as long as you persevere in those smaller steps.

Life will throw curveballs and there won't be a magic pill to fix these curveballs either. This is why you need to have faith in your abilities and know that you have what it takes to overcome everything that comes flying your way. You may need some extra information or new skills to do so, but with patience and time, you will get there.

Having trust in the process is good for your health. How many times have you stressed about things not going according to your plan, most likely because you are focusing on the result and not how you are going to get there?

Knowing that you will get there takes away this stress and replaces it with positivity and optimism. Isn't it better to know that you will achieve what you want in a month or in a year than never at all?

Part of trusting the process is to remind yourself to be patient. However, it's also about having the right mindset, and in this case, it will require a growth mindset. A fixed mindset is where you believe your abilities and skills are fixed and there is no room for improvement. A growth mindset embraces challenges, focusing on progress instead of the end result. The growth mindset is supported by neuroplasticity because the fact that we can't learn new things past a certain age is now a myth.

The word "can't" is detrimental to the growth mindset. Imagine if one trait you want to overcome is your temper. For six days of the week, you have controlled your temper, but on the seventh day, you lose it. Cognitive distortions kick in, and you tell yourself that you will never be able to control your temper despite the evidence presented in the last few days.

Rather than saying, "I can't control my temper," change the sentence to "I can't control my temper yet." By simply adding the word "yet" to the end of the sentence, you are telling yourself that you are trusting the process and it will happen.

For those dark times when you lack faith in both yourself and the process, turn to your loved ones for inspiration. Remind yourself why they are so amazing and a crucial part of your life.

> *If you can remember why you started, then you will know why you must continue.*
>
> — *CHRIS BURKMENN*

Now that you are growing and overcoming your toxic flaws, your friends and family deserve the opportunity to see what a wonderful and caring person you really are.

While the road to success may always be under construction, never forget that you are the builder. You have the tools to build that road, and more importantly, you have the ability to choose which direction you build that road!

CONCLUSION

What a journey it has been so far! At the beginning of this book, it's likely you knew something wasn't quite right, but you couldn't exactly put your finger on what that was.

You experienced strain and tension in your relationships, but if you were completely honest with yourself, you may not have fully realized the extent of your role in this.

It's an unpleasant experience reflecting on your own flaws and how this has caused such suffering for those you love. I commend you for doing this, and you should be proud of yourself. Many wouldn't make the effort to do the same and would continue leading a life that ignores the needs of others.

The point of self-reflection and discovering more about yourself wasn't to make you feel bad about who you are. Instead, it was the first step toward identifying the root cause of your toxic behavior. That's not to say you can blame your past and not hold yourself accountable.

It was a chance for you to understand that apparent anger, frustration, and contempt are actually caused by deep-seated fears of inadequacy and low self-esteem. Whether your biggest fear is showing your vulnerable side or being abandoned, you need to overcome these fears if you want to leave your toxic traits in the past.

When you start working on yourself, you are laying the foundations for a clean slate. This is when you can begin to understand how your communication has built a wall between you and meaningful connections with others.

Toxic behaviors aren't just physical and verbal abuse; they can also be not listening to people or constantly interrupting them. You laid the foundations, and now it's time to build bridges through nonviolent communication that doesn't involve any form of manipulation, intentional or not.

Don't forget the importance of a genuine, heartfelt apology when building bridges.

Picture a world where everyone has the ability to take on other people's perspectives and then take that to the next level and actually feel the pain and suffering of others. As we take baby steps, let's work on your ability to empathize with those around you.

A lack of empathy often stems from differences and an inability to respect the fact that we are all entitled to our individual beliefs, values, and thoughts.

Ironically, to close these gaps, you need to accept that people are different and then look for common ground. It's the similarities you share with others that will allow you to share how a person feels, both their joys and sorrows.

It would also be nice to picture a more positive world, but this is out of your control. What you are accountable for is your own positivity.

Cognitive reframing will help prune out those automatic negative thoughts, and then practicing things like gratitude and positive affirmations will create new neuro connections that can strengthen with time and regular practice.

The REFLECT framework is ***a*** process for you to trust, as it will guide you through the beginning of your transformation. Here's a recap:

- **R:** recognize toxic traits
- **E:** explore perspectives
- **F:** face your fears
- **L:** learn healthy patterns of interaction
- **E:** empathize with others
- **C:** cultivate positivity
- **T:** trust the process

Nevertheless, this isn't ***the*** process, as my friend Simon quickly discovered. Simon had pretty much ruined his relationship with his brother. It started in high school with some healthy competition but escalated to ridiculous levels. Simon went out of his way to get one up on his brother. He would purposely wait until his brother bought a car so that he could buy a better one. He also bought a bigger house than his brother despite not needing it and putting himself in financial trouble. Additionally, he would choose girlfriends that give him a reason to show off than women he actually liked. His brother didn't retaliate, but they grew further and further apart. After several failed relationships, Simon soon realized that he needed his older brother in his life and began the REFLECT process.

Unfortunately, Simon focused on the A to B, and after making amends with his brother, he felt that he had achieved his goal. But old patterns started to resurface, and by the time their father passed away, the brothers were once again not speaking. Now more than ever, Simon needed a relationship with his brother, so he began the process again, but this time, he accepted that this wouldn't be achieved overnight. Instead, he knew it was something he would have to continue to work on.

This change in Simon's mindset opened more doors than he could ever imagine. He now rents his brother's annex, and they have weekly game nights where they can put aside the notion that men don't have feelings and talk openly and honestly. Simon's finances are back on track, and he is now in a position to put down a deposit on a house with his girlfriend, a woman he admires and respects. At the same time, he knows that while this is success and a reason to celebrate, there is more to his journey and his unique process.

Change is scary. It's the unknown and the unpredictable. Your mind might be tempted to focus on everything that could go wrong, but you have the wisdom and the tools to embrace this much-needed change. It won't be instant, but it will happen if you start today with small, manageable, and consistent steps.

I have one last thing to ask of you. Considering the misuse of the word narcissist, there are so many people walking around in life, maybe even those you know, who are suffering from toxic traits but want to overcome them.

There is a way you can help them without attempting the impossible and changing the world. By sharing your opinions of this book on Amazon, you can let others know that they can also find their own process to freeing themselves from toxic traits and leading a more positive, connected life. It will only take a 30 seconds, but it can change someone's life who was once in the same situation as you.

Thank you in advance, and rather than wishing you luck, I hope you thrive in the new life that lies ahead of you!

BIBLIOGRAPHY

"A Quote by Brené Brown." n.d. https://www.goodreads.com/quotes/357565-owning-our-story-can-be-hard-but-not-nearly-as.

"A Quote by Chris Burkmenn." n.d. https://www.goodreads.com/quotes/1301857-if-you-can-remember-why-you-started-then-you-will.

Abram, Tracie. 2013. "Barriers to Empathy." MSU Extension. September 27, 2013. https://www.canr.msu.edu/news/barriers_to_empathy.

Ackerman, Sandra. 1992. "The Development and Shaping of the Brain." Discovering the Brain - NCBI Bookshelf. 1992. https://www.ncbi.nlm.nih.gov/books/NBK234146/.

Ambardar, Sheenie, MD. 2023. "Narcissistic Personality Disorder." Medscape. September 27, 2023. https://emedicine.medscape.com/article/1519417-overview?form=fpf.

Bradberry, T., & Greaves, J. (2009). Emotional Intelligence 2.0. TalentSmart.

Brown, B. (2012). Daring Greatly: How the Courage to Be Vulnerable Transforms the Way We Live, Love, Parent, and Lead. Gotham Books.

Burns, Stephanie. 2021. "What 'Finding Your Why' Really Means." *Forbes*, May 24, 2021. https://www.forbes.com/sites/stephanieburns/2021/05/24/what-finding-your-why-really-means/?sh=79c242ee73f4.

Caruso, Catherine. 2023. "A New Field of Neuroscience Aims to Map Connections in the Brain." Harvard Medical School. January 19, 2023. https://hms.harvard.edu/news/new-field-neuroscience-aims-map-connections-brain

Clear, James. 2020. "The Marshmallow Experiment and the Power of Delayed Gratification." James Clear. February 4, 2020. https://jamesclear.com/delayed-gratification

Cohen, Geoffrey L., and David K. Sherman. 2014. "The Psychology of Change: Self-Affirmation and Social Psychological Intervention." *Annual Review of Psychology* 65 (1): 333–71. https://doi.org/10.1146/annurev-psych-010213-115137.

Diary, A Coach's. n.d. "Week 6 | Every Success Story Has Some Patience." https://acoachsdiary.blogspot.com/2022/02/week-6-every-success-story-has-some.html.

"Disney Affirmations." n.d. Disney in Your Day. https://www.disneyinyourday.com/disney-affirmations/.

"Empathy Quotes." n.d. BrainyQuote. https://www.brainyquote.com/topics/empathy-quotes.

Graham, Sarah. n.d. "Narcissistic Personality Disorder and Brain Structure." Children of Narcissisits. https://childrenofnarcissists.org.uk/narcissistic-personality-disorder-and-brain-structure/

Hanson, R., & Hanson, F. (2018). Resilient: How to Grow an Unshakable Core of Calm, Strength, and Happiness. Harmony.

Harvard Health. 2021. "Giving Thanks Can Make You Happier." August 14, 2021. https://www.health.harvard.edu/healthbeat/giving-thanks-can-make-you-happier.

Lee, Royce J., David Gozal, Emil F. Coccaro, and Jennifer R. Fanning. 2020. "Narcissistic and Borderline Personality Disorders: Relationship With Oxidative Stress." *Journal of*

Personality Disorders 34 (Supplement): 6–24. https://doi.org/10.1521/pedi.2020.34.supp.6.
"Lily Tomlin Quotes." n.d. Brainy Quote. https://www.brainyquote.com/quotes/lily_tomlin_379145.
Mcleod, Saul, PhD. 2023. "Perceptual Set in Psychology: Definition & Examples." *Simply Psychology*, June. https://www.simplypsychology.org/perceptual-set.html.
Miller, Joshua D., Donald R. Lynam, Colin Vize, Michael L. Crowe, Chelsea E. Sleep, Jessica L. Maples-Keller, Lauren R. Few, and W. Keith Campbell. 2017. "Vulnerable Narcissism Is (Mostly) a Disorder of Neuroticism." *Journal of Personality* 86 (2): 186–99. https://doi.org/10.1111/jopy.12303.
Mitrokostas, Sophia. 2018. "New Research Suggests That Narcissists Might Be Able to 'learn' Empathy — but There's a Catch." *Business Insider*, August 2, 2018. https://www.businessinsider.com/can-narcissists-learn-empathy-2018-8.
One Planet. n.d. "Rethinking How We Consume." One Planet Network. https://www.one-planetnetwork.org/programmes/sustainable-lifestyles-education/about.
"P!Nk – Try." n.d. Genius. https://genius.com/P-nk-try-lyrics.
"P!Nk (Ft. Khalid) – Hurts 2B Human." n.d. Genius. https://genius.com/P-nk-hurts-2b-human-lyrics.
"Quote About Perspective | Self Help Daily." 2016. Self Help Daily. February 24, 2016. https://www.selfhelpdaily.com/tag/quote-about-perspective/.
Rosenberg, M. B. (2003). Nonviolent Communication: A Language of Life. PuddleDancer Press.
Razzetti, Gustavo. 2018. "How to Conquer Your Blind Spots." Fearless Culture. March 25, 2018. https://www.fearlessculture.design/blog-posts/how-to-conquer-your-blind-spots.
Ronningstam, E. n.d. "Narcissistic Personality Disorder: Guide for Providers." Mass General Brigham McLean. https://www.mcleanhospital.org/npd-provider-guide#:~:text=NPD%20in%20DSM%2D5,meet%20the%20diagnosis%20of%20NPD.
Sandberg, S., & Grant, A. (2017). Option B: Facing Adversity, Building Resilience, and Finding Joy. Knopf.
Sohal, Monika, Pavneet Singh, Bhupinder Singh Dhillon, and Harbir Singh Gill. 2022. "Efficacy of Journaling in the Management of Mental Illness: A Systematic Review and Meta-analysis." NIH. March 18, 2022. https://www.ncbi.nlm.nih.gov/pmc/articles/PMC8935176/.
"Steve Pavlina Quote: 'Fear is not your enemy. It is a compass pointing you to the areas where you need to grow.'" n.d. https://quotefancy.com/quote/1526426/Steve-Pavlina-Fear-is-not-your-enemy-It-is-a-compass-pointing-you-to-the-areas-where-you.
"Truman Capote Quotes." n.d. Goodreads. https://www.goodreads.com/quotes/6767721-i-tell-you-my-dear-narcissus-was-no-egoist-he.
U.S. Department of Health and Human Services Office of Minority Health. n.d. "Communication Styles." *Think Cultural Health*. https://thinkculturalhealth.hhs.-gov/assets/pdfs/resource-library/communication-styles.pdf.
Vater, A., and S. Moritz. 2018. "Does a Narcissism Epidemic Exist in Modern Western Societies? Comparing Narcissism and Self-Esteem in East and West Germany." NIH. January 24, 2018. https://www.ncbi.nlm.nih.gov/pmc/articles/PMC5783345/.
Weiss, M. (2018). Healing from Hidden Abuse: A Journey Through the Stages of Recovery from Psychological Abuse. Morgan James Publishing.

Wilczek, Frank, and Quanta Magazine. 2023. "Einstein's Parable of Quantum Insanity." Scientific American. September 23, 2023. https://www.scientificamerican.com/article/einstein-s-parable-of-quantum-insanity/

Winch, G. (2017). Emotional First Aid: Healing Rejection, Guilt, Failure, and Other Everyday Hurts. Plume.

"Zig Ziglar Quotes." n.d. Brainy Quotes. www.brainyquote.com/quotes/zig_ziglar_125675.

YOUR FREE TOOLKIT FOR BREAKING TOXIC CYCLES

Thank you so much for purchasing this bundle! Your journey toward calm, healthy relationships starts here, and I'm excited to share 7 exclusive tools to help along the way.

Your Free 7-in-1 Toolkit Includes:

🗣 **Shut Down Toxic Talk — Smart Scripts for Sticky Situations**

Exact phrases to neutralize negativity and stay in control.

📕 How to Deal with a Toxic Person: Practical Workbook

Real exercises to manage and reduce toxic influence.

🧭 Healthy Boundaries Cheatsheet

23 ready-to-use scripts to say "no" confidently and protect your peace.

🗓️ 30-Day Workbook: Detox Your Life

Daily steps to clear toxic habits and strengthen self-worth.

🌟 Cheat Sheet: Stop Being Toxic in 10 Easy Steps

Simple mindset shifts to drop negativity and grow positivity.

🎧 Audiobook: How to Master Your Emotions

Audio guide to build calm, resilience, and emotional balance.

✅ Checklist: Say No Without Feeling Guilty

Packed with practical advice and tools, these resources help you take the first step toward a brighter, less toxic life—one where you're finally in control of your emotions and relationships.

Scan the QR code below to access your materials

SCAN ME

If you experience any difficulty downloading these tools, please contact me at **chase@chasehillbooks.com**, and I'll send your copies as soon as possible.

Thanks for being here — I can't wait to see you thrive!

www.ingramcontent.com/pod-product-compliance
Ingram Content Group UK Ltd.
Pitfield, Milton Keynes, MK11 3LW, UK
UKHW011335140426
11870UKWH00023B/263

9 788397 599970